INFORMATION INDIA
1997-98 AND 1998-99

About the Authors

S.P. Agrawal (*b.* 1929) was Director, National Social Science Documentation Centre, ICSSR, Government of India and Member Secretary, Indian Association of Social Science Institutions. He was also the Vice-Chairman of the Asia and Pacific Information Network in Social Science (APINESS). In 1998 he was awarded the degree of Doctor of Philosophy in Education (*Honoris Causa*) by International University Foundation. Presently, he is Member, IFLA Round Table on Research in Reading, International Committee for Social Science, Information and Documentation, Board of Studies of National Archives of India and Hindi Advisory Committee, Ministry of Coal, Government of India. He is also Fellow of the Society of Ethnobotanists. Born and brought up in the cradle of freedom movement, which he joined at the tender age of twelve, he gained an insight into political problems and developed a sense of responsibility which bore fruit as an information scientist. He has written extensively on various aspects of Education, Indian Polity and Library and Information Science.

Mithilesh Gupta (*b.* 1934) did her M.A. (Political Science) from Aligarh Muslim University, and B.Ed from B.R. Ambedkar University, Agra. She was awarded Best Teacher's Award by Indian Council of Child Education, New Delhi. She has been assisting S.P. Agrawal in his writing work, in Political Science and Education in particular since 1957.

CONCEPTS IN COMMUNICATION INFORMATICS & LIBRARIANSHIP—86

General Editor : **S.P. AGRAWAL**

INFORMATION INDIA : 1997-98 AND 1998-99
Global View

S.P. AGRAWAL
former Member Secretary
Indian Association of Social Science Institutions, and
former Director, National Social Science Documentation Centre
ICSSR, Government of India, New Delhi

MITHILESH GUPTA
former Vice-Principal
Government of National Capital Region, Delhi

Assisted by
M.W.K. SHERWANI
former Asstt. Educational Adviser
Ministry of Human Resource Development, New Delhi

CONCEPT PUBLISHING COMPANY, NEW DELHI-110059

ISBN 81-7022-915-4

First Published 2002

Published and Printed by
Ashok Kumar Mittal
Concept Publishing Company
A/15-16, Commercial Block, Mohan Garden,
NEW DELHI - 110059 (India)

Phones : 5648039, 5649024
Fax : 091-11-5648053
Email : publishing@conceptpub.com

GENERAL EDITOR'S INTRODUCTION

Today we stand on the threshold of a new age. Information technology is the third revolution in the history of mankind after agriculture and industrial development which are the first and second revolutions respectively. "Knowledge is power, information is liberating, education is the premise of progress in every society, in every family... Information and freedom is unthinkable without democracy and democracy is unimaginable without freedom of information." These are the sovereign words of wisdom spoken by UN General Secretary Kofi Annan in Global Knowledge 97' Conference held in Toronto (Canada) in June, 1997.

In the modern explosion of knowledge information has assumed a great importance in the progress of present-day society. It is nerve centre of every field of activity, be it economic, political or social. We cannot take proper and judicious decisions on any field of knowledge without having basic facts about it. The newer forms of information technology has revolutionised our life by providing users with rapid access to rest amounts of knowledge.

There are a number of ways in which information is stored or packaged for exchange. These are books, audio tapes and discs, microfilm in the form of microfiche, video tapes, etc. Of these the oldest way for information retrieval is the book. It is so efficient and inexpensive that in the developing countries like India it is still used widely as a form of information storage and exchange. It will continue for long for conveying the information and it will not be easy to be supplanted by electronic communications systems. In the developed countries where information technology has made a tremendous development the information in the form of a book is still relevant.

The focus of the present volume is on India as it was in 1997-98 and 1998-99. In this compilation every effort has been made to give all important facets not only of India but also of the world as a whole. The challenges facing the world global economic and social development and significant international reports have been included. Relating to India it has been attempted to provide almost all embracing facts and figures with regard to various sectors of development. Detailed account has been given about important aspects as well as other social areas which are of significance in any discussion on India

It is observed that the data collected by various national and international organisations from different sources and also used here, do not necessarily relate to the same year in a few cases.

It is of great consolation that previous editions of this publication placed in the hands of the discerning users as also of the reviewers have been received well. It is hoped that like the previous editions the present end volume would also be of equal interest to a large category of readers from different disciplines and professions, administrators, business magnates, economic analysts, journalists, planners, researchers, students and those preparing for various competitive examinations.

S.P. AGRAWAL

CONTENTS

PART ONE

WORLD OVERVIEW

1

OVERVIEW OF WORLD BANK ACTIVITIES IN FISCAL 1997 : World Bank Annual Report, 1997

Fiscal 1997 marked an escalation of the process of renewal at the World Bank, building on the vision of an institution that delivers development results and reflecting the Bank's guiding principles of greater selectivity in activities, strengthened partnerships, emphasis on client needs, increased results orientation, cost-effectiveness, and a strong commitment to financial integrity.

The Bank's regional assistance strategies in fiscal 1997 addressed the specific needs of its clients as they face the challenges of adjusting to a rapidly changing global economy. Examples include :

— Following a request for support by the Bank's African clients in fiscal 1996, capacity building remained high on the agenda. Efforts to mainstream capacity-building activities into all Bank operations were initiated, and development of a partnership framework began.

— In East Asia, where successful economic development has taken a heavy toll on the environment, and "brown environmental issues" such as air and water pollution are threatening health and sustainable development, the Bank increased its support for the sector with loans and related advice for water supply and sanitation for example, which increased more than two-and-one-half times over the fiscal 1996 level.

— As the reforms of the 1990s took root in South Asian countries, the Bank supported its clients as they shifted their focus to a second generation of reform: In India this involved responding to several requests for assistance at the state level to help evaluate fiscal situations and identify policy options to promote fiscal sustainability.

— Strengthening safety nets to protect the most vulnerable people from the adverse effects of reform is a priority for many of the Bank's clients, especially in the Eastern Europe and Central Asia region. In fiscal 1997 the Bank supported innovations to generate income and create assets for the poor through social investment funds in a number of countries and through projects such as support to the Ukrainian authorities to protect people adversely affected by coal sector restructuring.

— In Latin America, where the legacy of recent years has made countries acutely aware of the importance of sound financial markets, the Bank supported a number of programmes to restore confidence in financial systems, such as in Argentina, Mexico, and Venezuela.

— Supporting reform programmes to speed growth by promoting

international competitiveness and opening up to global markets was a focus for clients in the Middle East and North Africa region. Loans to Jordan and Tunisia for example, are helping promote private sector participation in the wider world economy and facilitating important recent initiatives such as the proposed association of MENA countries with the European Union.

One of the year's most significant achievements was the initiative to address the debt of the heavily indebted poor countries (HIPCs), which combines powerful, partnerships to meet new needs, using nonlending and lending services with funding drawn not only from the Bank but from other partners. An other was the Executive Board's unanimous approval of the Strategic Compact in March 1997.

The STrategic Compact is a plan for fundamental reform to make the Bank more effective in delivering its regional program and in achieving its basic mission of reducing poverty. The compact is an expression of the Bank's business strategy and focuses on the external delivery of higher-quality products and services to the Bank's clients. The compact was the outcome of extensive consultation throughout the organization, reflects the input of clients and share-holders, and has the support and partnership of all the Bank's shareholders.

Through the compact, the bank's shareholders and management are investing in and implementing a series of changes over thirty months to transform the way the institution does business : Improving its products, speeding up its processes, lowering its cost, making it more demand driven, and increasing its development impact. The compact will also establish clear performance criteria against which progress will be measured and for which management will be held accountable.

The compact's vision is of a professionally excellent institution that responds quickly to the evolving and varying needs of its clients and provides a wide range of high-quality services; that operates through partnerships and acts as a catalyst for private-pubic collaboration; and that builds capacity and knowledge for the entrire development community.

The compact is rooted in the recognition of the need for change if the Bank is to be effective in the rapidly changing global economy where private capital flows are five times greater than official assistance, where many different actors (from multilateral banks to non-governmental organizations) now play a much greater role in development, and where technological change has revolutionized the way business is done. The Bank has been slow to respond to these changes in the past. But as this *Annual Report* decribes, change was well under way to meet the Strategic Compact's objectives by the end of the fiscal year.

The central objective of the compact is to make the Bank more efficient and to increase the development effectiveness of everything it does. In terms of lending effectiveness, for example, it is expected that the proportion of projects rated satisfactory will increase from 66 per cent to 75 per cent, meaning that an extra $2 billion a year of the Bank's lending will have greater impact.

The compact takes a comprehensive approach to increasing the Bank's development effectiveness in four priority and related areas : refueling current business activities; refocusing the development agenda, retooling the Bank's knowledge base; and revamping institutional priorities. It will:

— Shift resources from overhead and administration to frontline operations, with the goal of frontline resources accounting for 60 per cent of the budget and supporting activities accounting for 40 per cent. The Bank's management has committed to redeploying $170 million internally to support frontline operations because the basic business of the Bank need to be better funded.

— Develop new financial products and advisory services—with the emphasis on increasing flexibiity and timeliness for clients.
— Rebuild technical expertise in key areas of development and expand the Bank's focus in those areas—with the social sectors, institution building, and the private sector being immediate priorities.
— Further decentralize activities to the field to allow Bank staff to work more closely with clients in order to better customize country assistance strategies, design more appropriate conditionality and build local ownership of development programmes.
— Strengthen the Bank's information management system to collect, synthesize, and disseminate the best in development thinking.
— Create new and stronger partnerships with other organizations to enable the Bank to be more selective and to specialize in those areas where it has a comparative advantage.
— Reform the Bank's human resources system to create a more flexible, performance-based, and diverse institution.
— Eliminate cumbersome, inefficient processes to make the Bank quicker, leaner, and more cost-effective.

Client benefits promise to be substantial : higher-quality and more relevant products and services backed by an effective, modern knowledge-management system; and a staff that combines state-of-the-art technical skills and global experience within the context of a flatter, faster, more flexible and more decentralized organization.

The compact's overall costs will be met through a stringent program of savings and redeployment. Net additional investment under the compact is $250 million. This funding will be phased in to ensure that it is in line with the Bank's absorptive capacity: $100 million annually in fiscal 1998 and 1999 and $50 million in fiscal 2000; budgets will return to the fiscal 1997 level, in real terms, by fiscal 2001. Approval to the compact's funding will be contingent on the Executive Board's annual review of the Bank's budget and work programme.

The fundamental retooling of the Bank's operations must be judged by its impact on development effectiveness. Therefore, a broad range of specific measures for gauging effectiveness and accountability are being developed. These include:

— tracking development progress made by the Bank's client countries (using the expanded *World Development Indicators*[1])
— setting targets for responding to clinets. Clearly defined business standards have been set for managing the portfolio and for lending and non-lending services : *for example*, the Bank is aiming to get projects approved within five months of appraisal and economic and sector reports to clients within five months of onset; and

---

1. World Bank, 1997. *World Development Indicators*, Washington, D.C.

— monitoring the main determinants of what makes projects go well or badly, such as ensuring that projects are well prepared, well supervised, and that implementation problems are recognized and dealt with quickly.

In line with the Bank's aim for increasing results, portfolio management programmes to improve the current portfolio accelerated during fiscal 1997 through the quality-at-entry and portfolio improvement programmes. A key innovation was the concept of projects at risk, which is helping to identify the potential as well as actural problem projects. The concept continues to be refined but already is serving as an additional tool for portfolio management as well as enabling more accurate reporting on the status of the portfolio.

Staff were encouraged to recognize problems early and to address them proactively. The portfolio improvement programme, for example, targeted poorly performing segments of the portfolio for speical attention. Coupled with improvements in quality-at-entry for new operations, these intensified portfolio management efforts should lead to higher rates of satisfactory outcomes.

"Stretch targets" for client responsiveness are providing a measure for imporving results and client focus. They included substantial cuts in elapsed time for provision of services during the fiscal year. The average time elapsed between appraisal and board consideration was reduced from 9.3 months in fiscal 1996 to 7.8 months in fiscal 1997, and projects are becoming effective more quickly. The average time between board approval and effectiveness is down from 6.6 months in fiscal 1996 to 6.1 months in fiscal 1997.

By the end of the fiscal year, 96 per cent of the backlog of Implementation Completion Reports (ICRs) was cleared. ICRs lay the foundation for a better furture lending programme based on strategies that are well grounded in experience, evaluation, and lessons learned.

A more cost-effective, results-oriented Bank will lead to a stronger International Development Association (IDA). IDA borrowers will get a better-quality product, and IDA donors will have greater confidence that their contributions are being used even more effectively.

In fiscal 1997, disbursements from IDA continued to increase, reflecting greater emphasis on implementation. Disbursements reached a record $5,979 million, of which $4,815 million was for investment projects.

The temporary decline in new IDA commitments in fiscal 1997 reflects both increased selectivity and the concentration of IDA resources on improving implementation and the quality of the existing portfolio. Selectivity is based on attaching increased importance to the policy prerequisites for IDA lending of all types. Improvements in policy performance in many countries are expected to be reflected in future increases in IDA commitments. While it is not yet possible to measure fully the transitional effect of the reorganization of the Africa regional office, it is estimated to have been small. To the extent that this may have contributed to delays in new commitments during fiscal 1997, the now completed renewal programme should result in fiscal 1998 commitments returning to at least the level of fiscal 1996 (in SDR terms) as delays are overcome and a quicker, more effective regional programme ensues.

Promoting transparency, accountability, and institutional capacity is critical to successful, sound, and equitable development and has been a key aspect of the Bank's development agenda in recent years. Building on these principles, the Bank's president, in his 1996 Annual Meetings speech, emphasized the importance of eliminating corruption. The anti-corruption measures contained in the Bank's procurement guidelines, its standard bidding documents, and its legal technical assistance were strengthened in fiscal 1997. Many governments have strongly committed themselves to fight corruption, and the Bank has worked with them to support their efforts to improve governance and public sector management programs that aid efficient resource allocation and reduce the possibilities for corruption, through lending and non-lending services. The Economic Development Institute's (EDI)[2] Governance Programme, initiated in fiscal 1994 to build national integrity systems to fight corruption, is one example. EDI held more than thirty governance-related activities in more than a dozen countries across five regions in fiscal 1997.

Creating new and stronger partnership with other organizations is enabling the Bank to be more selective and specialize in those areas where it has a comparative advantage. In fiscal 1997, progress was made in developing joint programmes and information sharing with international financial institutions, United Nations Organizations, academia, foundations, business, Non-governmental organizations (NGOs), and others. Some of these partnerships are described throughout this *Annual Report.* A framework for cooperation in financial sector activities was agreed between the World Bank Group and the International Monetary Fund (IMF), and a cooperation agreement was finalized with the World Trade Organization. It will facilitate closer working relations for promoting global trade and helping developing countries adopt open policies to support growth and eliminate poverty.

The Business Partnership Center, launched early in the fiscal year to serve as a focal point of contact for the business community and for developing strategic partnerships with business groups, handled over 1,000 inquiries from members of the business community, had over 90,000 visitors to its World Wide Web site, and featured in more than forty international conferences. It is discussing potential partnership arrangements with more than fifteen groups worldwide.

The high level of NGO involvement in Bank-supported development activities was maintained in fiscal 1997, with 47 per cent of projects involving NGO participation in some capacity and with NGO liaison staff now active in seventy-two of the Bank's resident missions.

The Country Assistance Strategy (CAS) positions the country client at the center of the Bank's operational work. It is the key tool for shaping and driving the Bank's country-level work. Management and the board worked closely together to improve the strategic focus of CASS in fiscal 1997. The CAS has evolved considerably in its seven-year history, mirroring many concomitant changes in the Bank itself—for example, this year, social issues of development began to be integrated into CAS work. Greater efforts were also made to further build the results of poverty assessments into CASS; and to strengthen the private sector focus, a number of CASS were prepared jointly by the Bank and the International Finance Corporation (IFC) in fiscal 1997, including those for Brazil, Indonesia, Mexico, and Poland. As part of a larger strategy to link lending and learning activities, EDI helped prepare the CAS for Russia.

---

2. The Economic Development Institute (EDI) designs and delivers training programmes for Bank clients, providing policy lessons, skills building, and outreach to civil society, EDI issues its own annual report, which is available from : New Products and Outreach, The Economic Development Institute, The World Bank, 1818-H Street, N.W. Washington, D.C. 20433, USA.

The CAS starts with a diagnosis of country challenges and client governments' concerns and priorities. It takes into account what others are doing and the lessons learned about what has worked and what has not worked in the Bank's and others' programmes in the country. CASS are discussed with the authorities of the borrowing country and increasingly with other partners and stakeholders.

Bank operations in countries emerging from conflict are an increasingly significant part of the Bank's work, and the document "A Framework for World Bank Involvement in Post Conflict Reconstruction"[3] provided a conceptual and operational framework for Bank staff working to help countries move from conflict to sustainable economic development.

Much of the Bank's postconflict reconstruction work has been in rebuilding infrastructure, but capacity is also needed to promote economic adjustment and recovery, to address social sector needs, and to build institutional capacity. Some lending operations in fiscal 1997 involve unique postconflict elements, including clearing land mines in Bosnia and Herzegovina and Croatia, demobilization and reintegration of ex-combatants in Bosina, and reintegration of displaced people in Bosnia and Rwanda.

Two overall objectives for Bank intervention are set out in the framework: to facilitate the transition to sustainable peace after hostilities cease and to support economic and social development. The famework outlines a five-stage process for Bank involvement corresponding to various phases of postconflict reconstruction.

Sound financial systems are key to economic development, yet one in five developing countries is at risk of facing banking problems. The Bank has speeded up its response to clients facing financial crisis and supported those vulnerable to such risk. It prepared a series of loans to help the Bulgarian government implement a stabiliztion and reform programme to address its financial crisis, for example. The first loan, in August 1996, helped to restructure enterprises and supported banking sector rehabilitation and the acceleration of privatization. This was followed by a loan in May 1997 to reduce shortages of vital commodities and build public confidence in the reform programme.

To explore how the World Bank Group might better help its clients promote and facilitate private sector involvement in infrastructure, and in response to the proposal made by the Governor for Japan during the 1996 Annual Meetings, an infrastructure working group was established in fiscal 1997. It was report to the 1997 Annual Meetings on how public-private partnerships might be expanded to meet the growing investment gap.

The Bank helped refocus the international community's attention on the needs of the 70 per cent of the poor in developing countries who live in rural areas by calling for a renewed focus on agriculture and rural development in fiscal 1997. The Executive Board endorsed the paper, "Rural Development : From Vision to Action,"[4] which set out a strategy for supporting rural development

---

3. World Bank, 1997. "A Framework for World Bank Involvement in Postconflict Reconstruction." Environment and Social Policy Division, Environment Department, Washington, D.C.
4. World Bank, 1997. "Rural Development : From Vision to Action." Agriculture and Natural Resources Department, Washington, D.C.

by improving rural strategy formulation and consensus building; improving project quality; increasing international awareness; and building staff capacity.

Nonlending activities are an increasingly important service to clients. The Operations Evaluation Department (OED) conducted a review of the Bank's self-evaluation proceses for nonlending services as well as a review of the EDI. Its recommendations for stronger evaluations across all areas of the Bank's work have been incorporated into strengthened self-evaluation programs that will be carried out by management over the coming years.

Building a sound knowledge base to support non-lending (as well as lending) activities is at the heart of the Strategic Compact. The Bank is made up of an unmatched repository of experience and understanding about development issues, which too often has been underused. Too much knowledge has been locked up in reports that do not provide real-time and relevant advice to clients, colleagues, and partners. To meet client needs more effectively and better equip Bank staff, work began on developing a knowledge management system in fiscal 1997 to disseminate and apply lessons of experience among staff and clients. Through this system, complex information is distilled into usable formats for delivery to those who need it : policy-makers, parliamentarians, NGOs, and journalists, in ways that build vital understandings in member countries.

Four networks established in fiscal 1997 are at the center of the new knowledge-based Bank. They are :

- Human Development;
- Environmentally and Socially Sustainable Development;
- Finance, Private Sector and Infrastructure; and
- Poverty Reduction and Economic Management.

The networks link staff who work in related sectors across the Bank so they interact more effectively across the organization and with partners outside the Bank and play a major role in strategic thinking. In fiscal 1997 the Human Development network prepared the first of a new World Bank product—sector strategy papers—for the health, nutrition, and population sector. Sector strategy papers are cross-cutting studies that are the sector equivalent of CASS. They present the World Bank's corporate strategy for the sector.

The regional renewal programmes began in fiscal 1996 moved towards completion during fiscal 1997. They aim to de-layer and simplify decision-making and delegate increased responsibility to the field—twenty-one country directors have been or are being relocated to field offices.

During fiscal 1997, the IBRD's Executive Board approved new policies governing the concentration of its loan portfolio and the size and management of its liquid assets. These changes were designed to enhance the IBRD's flexibility in managing its finances and thereby better meet the changing needs of its clients while preserving a strong, conservative financial standing.

Fiscal Year in Review

Against this background, commitments by the Bank were $19,147 million—$14,525 million from the IBRD and $4,622 million from IDA, 36 percent of those, totaling $1,646 million, were from the Interim Trust Fund. A total of 241 projects were approved, 141 by the IBRD and 100 by IDA. Seven loans on IDA-like terms, totaling $83.5 million from resources provided by the Trust Fund for Gaza

Table 1.1 : Operational and Financial Overview, Fiscal Years, 1993-97

(millions of us dollars unless otherwise noted)

Item	*FY93*	*FY94*	*FY95*	*FY96*	*FY97*
IBRD					
Commitments[a]	16,945	14,244	16,853	14,656[b]	14,525
Disbursements[a]	12,942	10,447	12,672	13,372[b]	13,998
Net disbursements to all borrowers[a]	2,331	(731)	897	1,213	2,094
Net disbursements to current borrowers[a],	2,865	19	1,651	2,100	3,258
excluding prepayments[a]	3,319	983	2,238	2,882	4,301
Net Income	1,130	1,051	1,354	1,187	1,285
Financial return on average investments	6.07%	3.53%	5.69%	4.43%	5.00%
New MLT borrowings in FY after swaps	12,676	8,908	9,026	10,883	15,139
Average cost of new MLT borrowings in FY after swaps	5.97%	4.99%	6.31%	5.28%	5.01%
Subscribed capital	165,589	170,003	176,438	180,630	182,426
Statutory lending limit	179,787	185,865	195,248	197,785	198,705
Loans and callable guarantees outstanding	104,606	109,468	123,676	110,369	105,954
as a % of statutory lending limit	58%	59%	63%	56%	53%
Headroom	75,181	76,397	71,572	87,416	92,751
Interest coverage ratio	1.16%	1.16%	1.19%	1.18%	1.22%
Reserves-to-loans ratio	11.7%	13.9%	14.3%	14.1%	14.0%
IDA					
Commitments	6,752	6,592	5,669	6,861	4,622
Disbursements	4,947	5,532	5,703	5,884	5,979
Net disbursements	4,580	5,110	5,205	5,322	5,364
Development credits outstanding	56,158	62,810	72,032	72,821	76,124
Accumulated surplus	1,194	1,365	1,995	1,790	1,998
IBRD/IDA Joint Activities					
Administrative expenses	1,254	1,389	1,540	1,376	1,188

a. Excludes guarantees and loans to the IFC.

b. Includes the refinanced/rescheduled overdue charges of $168 million for Bosnia and Herzegovina.

and the West Bank, were approved for the West Bank and Gaza. Three partial guarantees, totaling $420 million, were approved. Gross disbursements amounted to $19,977 million—$13,998 million from the IBRD, and $5,979 million from IDA. Table 1 presents a comparative overview of Bank operations and finances for fiscal years 1993-97.

Assistance to the poorest countries—those with a per capita gross national product of $785 or less (in terms of constant 1996 United States dollars)—totaled $7442.9 million—$3,080.9 from the IBRD and $4,362.0 from IDA.

Some 29 per cent of total Bank investment lending during the year directly targeted the poor compared to 32 per cent the year before. These projects supported activities to increase the productivity and economic opportunities of the poor, to develop their human resources, and to provide social safety nets (for a description of each such targeted project, turn to the project summaries after Section Three).

During fiscal 1997, fifty-five out of sixty-two borrowers (89 per cent) took advantage of the new single-currency loans first made available in fiscal 1996. Measured in terms of volume, $12.9 billion out of $14.5 billion (89 per cent) in new loan commitments were in single-currency loans.

The IBRD has 180 members. At the end of the fiscal year, action was pending on membership in the IBRD for the Federal Republic of Yugoslavia (Serbia/Montenegro). IDA has 159 members. At the end of the fiscal year, action was pending on membership in IDA for Barbados, Ukraine, Venezuela, and the Federal Republic of Yugoslavia (Serbia/Montenegro).

2

TRANSNATIONAL CORPORATIONS, MARKET STRUCTURE AND COMPETITION POLICY World Investment Report, 1997

Introduction

The present Report provides a comprehensive analysis and policy discussion of international investment issues. The Report examines the interrelationship between transnational corporations, market structure and competition policy. This issue is particularly relevant because the liberalization of foreign direct regimes allows a greater presence of transnational corporations in host countries with important implication for market structures and competition.

Overview

Foreign Direct Investment (FDI) continues to be a driving force of the globalization process that characterizes the modern world economy. The current boom in FDI flows, which has been accompanied by increasing flows of foreign portfolio equity investments, underscroes the increasingly important role played by transnational corporations (TNCs) in both developed and developing countries. This role has been facilitated by the liberalization of FDI policies that has taken place in many countries in recent years, as part of an overall movement towards more open and market-friendly policies. However, reaping the benefits of FDI liberalization requires not only that barriers to FDI are reduced and standards of treatment established — the focus of most FDI liberalization to date — but also that competition in markets is maintained. This third component of FDI liberalization—maintaining the proper functioning of markets in which TNCs invest — is the special topic of this year's *World Investment Report*, which examines the interaction between FDI, market structure and competition, and looks at policy implications.

GLOBAL AND REGIONAL TRENDS

The growing size and importance of international production

With an estimated $7 trillion in global sales in 1995 — the value of goods and services produced by some 280,000 foreign affiliates — international production outweighs exports as the dominant mode of servicing foreign markets. The growth of global sales has exceeded that of exports of goods and services by a factor of 1.2 to 1.3 since 1987. But as far as developing countries are concerned, despite their growing involvement in international production — of the world's 45,000 parent firms, 7,900 firms were based in developing countries in the mid-1990s, compared to 3,800 in the late 1980s — exports continue to be the principal mode of delivering goods and services to foreign markets.

The gross product of foreign affiliates, a measure of their output, almost tripled between 1982 and 1994, and its share of world output rose slightly, from 5 per cent in 1982 to 6 per cent in 1994. In developing countries, the output of foreign affiliates has contributed (in 1994) more to gross domestic product than it has in developed countries: 9 per cent compared to 5 per cent.

The global FDI stock, a measure of the investment underlying international production, increased fourfold between 1982 and 1994; over the same period, it doubled as a percentage of world gross domestic product to 9 per cent. In 1996, the global FDI stock was valued at $3.2 trillion. Its rate of growth over the past decade (1986-1995) was more than twice that of gross fixed capital formation, indicating an increasing internationalization of national production systems. The worldwide assets of foreign affiliates, valued at $8.4 trillion in 1994, also increased more rapidly than world gross fixed capital formation.

The upward trend manifested in all of the indicators of international production, in absolute terms as well as in relation to various macro-economic indicators, suggests that international production is becoming a more significant element in the world economy. Its importance is apparent in the activities in which TNCs are involved. On the technology side, for example, an estimated 70 per cent of the global payments of royalties and fees constitute transactions between parent firms and their foreign affiliates.

... was manifested in 1996 in the $1.4 trillion worth of investment in foreign affiliates

Transnational corporations raise capital from a variety of sources at home and abroad: commercial banks, local and international equity markets, public organizations and their own corporate systems in the form of internally generated profits for reinvestment. Taking all these sources of finance into account, investment in foreign affiliates — the investment component of international production — was an estimated $1.4 trillion on 1996. Of this, only $350 billion, i.e., a quarter, were financed by FDI flows. This means, therefore, that the weight of international production is also considerably larger: expressed as a ratio of world gross fixed capital formation, about one-fifth was undertaken by foreign affiliates. (This measure does not capture additional investment controlled by TNCs via various non-equity measures, including corporate alliances.)

Foreign-direct-investment flows set a new record level of $350 billion, in the midst of a new FDI boom, ...

Returning to FDI flows themselves, the boom that began in 1995 continues, with inflows setting a new record of around $350 billion in 1996, a 10 per cent increase. Fifty-four countries on the inflow side and twenty countries on the outflow side set new records in 1996. Unlike the two previous investment booms in 1979-1981 and 1987-1990 (the first one being led by petroleum investments in oil producing countries, and the second one being concentrated in the developed world), the current boom is characterized by considerable developing-country participation on the inflow side, although it is driven primarily by investments originating in just two countries — the United States and the United Kingdom. There are signs that an even greater number of countries will take part in the present boom as it unfolds on the inward side (e.g., developing countries in Latin America), as well as on the outward side (e.g., France, Germany and Asian developing countries).

During 1995-1996, the share of developing countries in global inflows was 34 per cent. Although this is not much higher than the developing-country share during the investment boom at the beginning of the 1980s, qualitatively it reflects a wide variety of location-specific advantages enjoyed by developing countries over and above natural resources. The composition of the top developing-country recipients has also changed dramatically between these two investment booms, with oil producing countries now featuring far less prominently among the top recipients. Interestingly, the developing-country share of global inflows has been on the rise during the current boom, while during the 1987-1990 boom it declined. That decline went hand in hand with a boom in intradeveloped country mergers and acquisitions (M&As), at that time in response to heightened protectionist pressures in key develooped countries. As in earlier FDI booms, the bulk of FDI flows goes to a limited number of developing countries.

... with cross-border mergers and acquisitions and inter-firm agreements as the driving force behind TNC activity ...

Even in the current boom, cross-border M&As, especially in the United States and Western Europe, are playing as important role in boosting FDI, although this time there is no ensuing decline in the developing country share of inflows. The value of such M&As increased by 16 per cent in 1996, to $275 billion. If majority held transactions only are taken into account, the value of cross-border M&As in 1996 would be $163 billion, or 47 per cent of global FDI inflows (though the measured values are not strictly comparable).

Complementing the increases in M&As and FDI flows, the number of cross-border inter-firm agreements [equity and non-equity, other than strategic research-and-development (R&D) partnerships] has also increased. In 1995, nearly 4,600 such agreements were concluded, compared with about 1,760 in 1990. These agreements take place primarily between firms based in developed countries: United States firms participated in 80 per cent of them, European Union firms in 40 per cent and Japanese firms in 38 per cent. Recently, firms based in developing countries have also begun to conclude such agreements actively. The number of cross-border inter-firm agreements (other than strategic R&D partnerships) with developing-country firm participation has increased in absolute numbers, as well as a share of the world total (from 27 per cent during 1990-1992 to 35 per cent during 1993-1995). Although there was a decline in 1995, the number of strategic R&D partnerships (in core technologies, such as information technologies and biotechnology), has also been rising steadily since 1990. Again, developing-country firms assumed a bigger role in strategic partnerships (3 per cent in 1989 to 13 per cent in 1995), suggesting that these firms may have attained sufficient technological sophistication and capacity to make them worth having as partners.

... and with an increasing transnationalization of the largest TNCs based in both developed and developing countries

Despite the growing number of small and medium-sized enterprises with investments abroad, a good part of FDI continues to be concentrated in the hands of a small number of companies. The largest 100 TNCs, ranked on the basis of the size of foreign assets, own $1.7 trillion assets in their foreign affiliates, controlling an estimated one-fifth of global foreing assets. In the United States, 25 TNCs are responsible for half of that country's outward stock, a share that has remained almost unchanged during the past four decades. For six out of nine developed countries for which such data are available, 25 TNCs account for more than a half of their respective countries' outward stocks.

For the first time, two developing-country TNCs, Daewoo Corporation (Republic of Korea) and Petroleos de Venezuela S.A. (Venezuela), have entered the list of the top 100 TNCs. Daewoo Corporation also tops the list of the 50 largest TNCs based in developing countries for the second year running, while Royal Dutch Shell (United Kingdom/Netherlands) continues to top the list of the largest 100 TNCs for the fifth consecutive year. With foreign sales amounting to $2 trillion and foreign employment close to 6 million persons in 1995, the largest 100 TNCs are prominent actors in international production. The top 50 TNCs based in developing countries, however, are catching up. While their foreign assets totalled only $79 billion in 1995, the increase in these assets between 1993 and 1995 was 280 per cent — compared with 30 per cent for the top 100 firms.

Both the top 100 TNCs worldwide and the top 50 developing-country TNCs are becoming more transnationalized, at a faster rate in the latter case. The food firms in the list of the top 50 developing-country TNCs exhibited the biggest increase in transnationality (measured on the basis of a combined index of the ratios of foreign assets, foreign sales and foreign employment in their respective totals) — from 16 per cent in 1993 to 36 per cent in 1995. On the whole, smaller firms tend to be more transnationalized than larger ones; for example, Solvay SA (Belgium) ranked seventy-fourth on the basis of the size of foreign assets, but ranked fifth on the basis of the transnationality index in the list of the top 100 TNCs. And Panamerican Beverages Inc. (Mexico) took the first place in the list of the top 50 developing-country firms on the basis of the transnationality index, as opposed to twenty-first on the basis of the value of foreign assets.

The Triad (European Union, United States and Japan) is home to 87 per cent of the top 100 TNCs and accounts for 88 per cent of their foreign assets. Likewise, China, the Republic of Korea, the Hong Kong Special Administrative Region of the People's Republic of China (hereinafter: Hong Kong, China) and Mexico are home to 56 per cent of the top 50 firms based in developing economies, and account for two-thirds of their foreign assets. Electronics is the most important industry as far as the largest TNCs are concerned, accounting for some 16 per cent of all firms' foreign assets in each of the two lists of top TNCs. Automotive and chemical firms also feature prominently in both lists, but more so in the list of the top 100 firms. Petroleum and mining firms, although few in number, tend to rank high in both lists.

The growth of international production has been facilitated by ongoing liberalization ...

The expansion of international production would not have been possible if it were not for the ongoing liberalization of FDI regimes. The trend towards greater liberalization was sustained again in 1996, with 98 changes in the direction of investment liberalization and promotion of a total number of 114 changes in investment regimes introduced during that year in 65 countries. Over the period

1991-1996, indeed, some 95 per cent of a total of 599 changes in the regulatory FDI regimes of countries were in the direction of liberalization. They mostly involved the opening of industries previously closed to FDI, the streamlining or abolition of approval procedures and the provision of incentives.

The desire of governments to facilitate FDI is also reflected in the dramatic increase in the number of bilateral investment treaties (BITs) for the protection and promotion of investment throughout the 1990s. As of January 1997, there were 1330 such treaties in the world, involving 162 countries, a threefold increase in half, a decade. Around 180 such treaties were concluded in 1996 alone — one every second day.

The pattern of these treaties has changed considerably in recent years. While virtually all BITs used to have one developoed country as a partner, and such countries took part in 83 per cent of all such treaties as of the end of the 1980s, by 1996 only 62 per cent of the world total involved developed countries. Indeed, countries in Central and Eastern Europe and developing countries have begun to conclude BITs among themselves. At the beginning of 1997, 16 per cent of all BITs were among developing countries, rising from 11 per cent at the end of the 1980s. In 1996 alone, nearly a third of all BITs were concluded between developing countries, led by China, Chile, Algeria and the Republic of Korea.

New ground is being broken at the regional and multilateral levels. Negotiations on an investment framework are taking place in the Organisation for Economic Co-operation and Development, with the conclusion of a free-standing Multilateral Agreement on Investment rescheduled for May 1998. In the framework of the discussions on a possible Free Trade Area of the Americas, a Working Group on Investment has been established, as well as a Working Group on Competition Policy. In the meantime, the Ministerial Meeting of the World Trade Organization in Singapore in December 1996 established two working groups to examine the relationship between trade and investment and between trade and competition policy. Independently of these developments, the ASEAN members are preparing to launch the ASEAN Investment Area. Cooperation among ASEAN members in the area of investment has already progressed with the signing of a protocol (in September 1996) updating the 1987 ASEAN Agreement for the Promotion and Protection of Investment.

... and holds good prospects for being sustained into the next century

The ongoing globalization of production begs the question of whether the upward trend in FDI flows witnessed to date will continue into the next century. A survey of foreign investors suggests that this may, indeed, be the case. More specifically, foreign sales are expected to increase as a proportion of total sales, especially for Japanese and United States firms. Production by foreign affiliates is also expected to increase as a proportion of total production by TNCs, while home-country exports are expected to remain constant. Mergers and acquisitions, joint ventures and other equity and non-equity types of inter-firm agreemetns are expected to go hand in hand with the growth in FDI. Although smaller firms will be stepping up investments abroad, large firms will continue to account for the lion's share of outward investments. Corporate restructuring in developed countries, aimed at improving efficiency and modernization, is expected to continue, giving rise to efficiency-seeking investment. However, accessing markets will remain the principal motive for investing abroad: survey respondents placed twice as much weight on production for local markets than on labour-cost factors. Countries in developing Asia and, to a lesser extent, in Latin America and Central and Eastern Europe, are likely to be the main beneficiaries of the corporate restructuring. Investment at home generally will be given a lower priority than it has received until now. In contrast, investment in the same region will continue to be significant, while investment in more distant countries is likely to increase, thus broadening the geographical scope of international production. Foreign investors foresee dramatic increases in investments in infrastructure, distribution, non-financial services and automobiles, but slower growth in financial services and real estate. All in all, the growth of FDI is expected to remain brisk over the next five years, both in terms of absolute levels and as a proportion of corporate investment.

The United States is by far the largest FDI recipient and investor abroad,...

Developed countries investments abroad reached an all time high of $295 billion in 1996. The investment picture for developed countries is dominated by the United States, which, with $85 billion is by far the largest home country (by a margin of $31 billion over the United Kingdom, the second largest home country), as well as, with $85 billion, the largest recipient country (by a margin of $42 billion over China, the second largest recipient) in 1996. Around two-fifths of United States outflows go to the European Union and around 30 per cent to developing countries. Growing consumer markets have encouraged United States investments in the latter, while sluggish growth in the former has led to a decrease in its share of United States outflows. Investment flows into the United States — mostly in the form of M&As — were stimulated by its strong and sustained growth performance and potential for high profits.

Western Europe received $105 billion in inflows and invested $176 billion abroad in 1996. More European Union investment is now directed to non-European Union countries than in 1992, when the internal market was completed. These countries are investing increasingly outside Western Europe, mostly in North America, developing Asia and, to a lesser extent, Central and Eastern Europe. Nearly a half of the European Union's investment outflows take the form of M&As. The share of European Union inflows accounted for by M&As, however, is considerably smaller because of regulatory and other barriers in existence in some countries (such as Italy and Germany) on this mode of investment. Japanese investment in the European Union is declining — to almost $2 billion in 1994, compared with nearly $7 billion at its peak in 1990.

Overall, however, the recovery of Japan's outward investment continues, with outflows reaching $23 billion in 1996, slightly over half their peak level of $41 billion during 1989-1991. (It should be noted that reinvested earnings, estimated at $14 billion in the manufacturing sector alone in 1994, are not included in these figures.) Japanese outflows are geared overwhelmingly towards developing Asia and the United States. But in Asia, China is no longer the favourite location and in fact, its share of Janapese outflows declined in 1996. Brazil is beginning to receive Japanese investment, with Japanese outflows there (on the basis of notifications) tripling in 1996 over 1995. On the inward side, Japan remains a small FDI recipient, with inflows declining to $220 million in 1996.

... but developed countries are becoming, on the whole, less important hosts

Although developed countries received a record $208 billion in FDI flows in 1996, there has been a steady decline in their share of global inflows since 1989. That decline can be attributed partly to the increasing attractiveness of developing countries, especially those that are gowing rapidly and have large domestic markets. Furthermore, some developed countries that are large outward investors are small investment recipients, especially in relation to the size of their economies; notable examples are Germany, Italy and Japan. And as the rationalization of production through FDI in response to regional integration arrangements among developed countries (notably, the European Union) has reached a high level, firms are turning increasingly towards untapped markets found mostly in the developing world.

Developing countries — even some of the least developed ones — enjoy rapidly growing investments, ...

In light of the above, it is not surprising that developing countries received $129 billion of FDI inflows in 1996 and invested $51 billion abroad — both amounts are all-time highs. There share of world inflows rose to 37 per cent in 1996 (from 30 per cent in 1995), while their share of outflows was 15 per cent in that year. With $42 billion, China was the largest developing-country recipient; the country's success can be attributed mostly to its large and growing domestic market, "soft landing" and macro-economic reforms, as well as to measures to promote investment in provinces other than those in the coastal areas.

Every developing region saw an increase in inflows. Even the 48 least developed countries experienced an increase in inflows of 56 per cent in 1996, to $1.6 billion. Cambodia was the largest recipient in this group of countries. In addition, and despite the small size of inflows (both in absolute values and as a share of all developoing-country inflows), FDI is very important for many of these economies; inflows in as many as eight countries reached 10 per cent as a share of gross fixed capital formation in 1995.

Within the group of the least developed countries, there are significant disparities in performance as regards FDI. The Asian least developed countries are benefiting from the Asian industrializing economies' process of industrial restructuring in the framework of the "flying-geese" model, not only because they offer complementary locational advantages in the form of low-cost labour, but also because of their geographical proximity to them. More than four-fifths and nearly two-fifths, respectively, of cumulative investments received by Bangladesh and Myanmar over the period 1990-1994, for example, came from developing Asia. Since a similar "in-tandem" restructuring process is not taking place in Africa, the least developed countries in that continent do not have the same opportunity to benefit from the type of intra-regional FDI inflows that is the outcome of this process in Asia.

... with new record levels in South, East and South-East Asia, ...

With $81 billion in inflows in 1996, South, East and South-East Asia received about two-thirds of the developing-country total in that year. The 25 per cent increase in these inflows over 1995 was also in sharp contrast with the large decline in the rate of growth of exports and, to a lesser extent, of the gross domestic product, in that year. China accounted for over two-fifths of the $16 billion increase in investment inflows in the region.

Next to China, Singapore was the second largest investment recipient, with inflows worth $9 billion, exceeding the combined inflows of the other newly industrializing economies (Hong Kong, China, Republic of Korea and Taiwan Province of China). Flows into Hong Kong, China, were $2.5 billion in 1996. Foreign-investor confidence in Hong Kong, China, after its reversion to China on 1 July, 1997 is strong, as indicated by a number of surveys of foreign (and local) companies. Indonesia, Malaysia, Philippines and Thailand together received some $17 billion in 1996, an increase of 43 per cent over 1995. Together, ASEAN members have, however, seen their share of the region's investment inflows decline, from 61 per cent during 1990-1991 to below 30 per cent during 1994-1996, attributed to domestic capacity constraints, infrastructure bottlenecks and, in particular, stiff competition from other economies. A 34 per cent increase in investment flows to India (to $2.5 billion) pushed total inflows to South Asia to $3.5 billion. Investment from other Asian economies in India, especially from the Republic of Korea, are outstripping those of some developed countries, such as the United States and the United Kingdom.

South, East and South-East Asia are emerging as important outward sources of FDI. Indeed, the region is the largest source of FDI in the developing world, with outflows increasing by 10 per cent in 1996, to $46 billion. Hong Kong, China is the single largest outward investor ($27 billion in 1996). Recently, the geographical scope of developing Asia's outward FDI has expanded to include non-traditional destinations, such as the European Union, Central and Eastern Europe and Africa. The extent to which Asian developing economies are transnationalized is reflected in the increasing ratios of investment outflows to gross fixed capital formation for the region as a whole, as well as for individual economies. That ratio, for example, is higher for Singapore (14 per cent) and Malaysia (11 per cent) than for Western Europe (10 per cent) and the United States (9 per cent).

... as well as Latin America and the Caribbean, ...

Investment flows into Latin America and the Caribbean increased by 52 per cent in 1996, the highest increase of any developing region, to a record level of nearly $39 billion. Far-reaching changes in the regin's FDI regimes — both at the national level and through the conclusion of bilateral investment treaties — have certainly contributed to this performance. Even during the turbulence in portfolio investment flows into that region in 1994 and 1995, FDI flows registered small but steady increases. Latin America and the Caribbean now account for 30 per cent of all developing country inflows. Investment inflows into Argentina tripled in 1996 to $4.3 billion, propelled by the country's membership in MERCOSUR (which contributed particularly to automobile investments), the liberalization of mining legislation and privatization schemes. But the most not worthy performance has been that of Brazil. With nearly $10 billion, Brazil has surpassed Mexico (with around $8 billion) as the star performer in Latin America in 1996. (In the first four months of 1997, inflows were over $4 billion — two and a half times higher than inflows in the same period in 1996). This represents a dramatic reversal: in 1992, with $2 billion, Brazil ranked third in the region (after both Mexico and Argentina). The upswing in Brazil's inflows is the outcome of large investments in automobiles (in the context of intra-regional production rationalization triggered by MERCOSUR) and the reactivation of its privatization programme. Foreign-investor confidence in Brazil (and in the region as a whole) is high: in a recent survey, company executives expressed more confidence in Latin America's prospects now than five years ago, placing Brazil, Mexico and Chile in top places.

The United States remains the foremost foreign investor in the region, with firms investing now more heavily in Brazil than in any other country there. Canada's investment in Latin America and the Caribbean is also sizeable, but concentrated mostly in mining and exploration. Western Europe's investment in Latin America and the Caribbean (largely from Germany and Spain) is on the rise, and is mostly directed towards Brazil, Argentina and Mexico (in natural resources and services). Almost a half of Western Europe's investment into the region has come through privatization schemes, but in 1995 and 1996 greenfield investment has also been prevalent in automobile manufacturing. Japanese investment in Latin America remains small and highly concertrated in tax havens in the Caribbean. Intra-regional investment has increased substantially, with Chile, Brazil and Argentina being the principal source countries, and Argentina, Peru and Venezuela the principal destinations. Developing Asian countries continue to invest in export-related industries, although market-seeking investments spurred by the region's recent integration efforts are also on the rise.

... with signs of revival of FDI flows to Africa ...

Africa continues to receive small levels of investment flows (nearly $5 billion in 1996), an increase of only 5 per cent the smallest of any developing region. On average, Africa's share of developing-country inflows has more than halved between 1986-1990 and 1991-1996—to 5 per cent in the latter period. Political unrest, armed conflict, low domestic investment levels and frequent changes in economic policies that affect business calculations of expected risks and returns have contributed to this relative decline.

However, Africa's investment performance looks less gloomy when put into perspective. In relation to the size of a number of economies, those investments can be fairly significant. For the region as a whole, the ratio of investment inflows to gross fixed capital formation was 5.4 per cent, compared with 5.5 per cent for Asia and 5.9 per cent for Western Europe during the first half of the 1990s. Putting the size of Africa's FDI stock in relation to the size of Africa's domestic market (GDP) yields a share of 10 per cent — compared with 14 per cent for Asia, 18 per cent for Latin America and the Caribbean and 13 per cent for Western Europe in 1995. While these figures suggest that the significance of the investment that Africa receives (without the benefit of large intra-regional investment) is certainly not negligible, they do not say anything about Africa's need for investment nor, for that matter, the continent's potential.

Prospects for increased flows to some parts of Africa are encouraging. Favourable growth performances, further investment and trade liberalization and privatization, regional cooperation agreements and the establishment of links with other regions are all likely to increase the region's attractiveness. In addition, South Africa could begin to play a significant role as a "growth pole", contributing to the region's economic development through FDI and trade. As regards the former, South Africa's contribution could be through the provision of investment capital, adding to capital formation in the recipient economies; the transfer of technology; the development of local human resources; and the opening up of its own market to the exports of foreign affiliates that have invested in neighbouring economies. Indeed, the question has arisen whether South African firms can induce the development of new industries, especially in manufacturing, in its neighbours by establishing an intra-regional division of labour in the framework of which production at home is upgraded to capital-and technology-intensive activities. In this "flying geese" process of industrial restructuring and upgrading, Sourth Africa would play the lead role, similar to the role played by Japan in the context of Asia's development. At this point in time, however, it appears that the necessary conditions for this type of intra-regional restructuring to occur are still far from being met, including — to stay within the metaphor — because many of South Africa's neighbours are still in the "nest-building" stage.

... and of growing non-oil investments in West Asia, ...

After large disinvestments in West Asia in 1995 that resulted in negative inflows, particularly in Saudi Arabia and Yemen, inflows attained a level of nearly $2 billion in 1996. Excluding these two countries, investment flows into West Asia show a much more stable trend. In fact, the volatility of inflows to these two countries — albeit important ones — masks considerable improvements in the investment performance of other countries in the region in response to successful efforts to create business-friendly environments.

Over time, the share of West Asia in total developing country investment inflows has been declining — from 30 per cent during the first half of the 1980s to only 2 per cent during the first half of the 1990s. That shift reflects largely decreasing investment flows to oil producing economies (Saudi Arabia, Oman, Qatar and United Arab Emirates). While petroleum naturally remains the most popular industry in these economies, in the non-oil producing countries (Jordan, Lebanon and Turkey) investments go mainly to manufacturing and services.

... while a slow-down in privatization contributed to a decline in FDI flows to Central and Eastern Europe.

In 1996, FDI flows to Central and Eastern Europe experienced a decline — to $12 billion from $14 billion in 1995, partly reflecting declines in privatization-related investments in Hungary and the Czech Republic. As long as investment flows to that region depend to a large extent on the participation of foreign investors in privatization programmes, a certain degree of "lumpiness" — year-to-year volatility — is to be expected. The decline might also stem from other problems related to the transition to a market economy. Foreign investors, for example, might have overestimated the region's ability to absorb investments and might have temporarily shelved their plans for expansion. However, despite the decline, flows in 1996 were still more than twice as high as the annual average during 1992-1994. The estimated FDI stock in Central and Eastern Europe was $46 billion in 1996 — almost comparable to the 1996 investment flows to China ($42 billion).

Investment flows to Central and Eastern Europe remain concentrated in the Czech Republic, Hungary and Poland, together accounting for some two-thirds of the region's inflows. Transnational corporations from Western Europe dominate the investment picture, followed by corporations from the United States and, more recently, the Asian newly industrializing economies. A small but growing share of inflows is attributed to corporations based in Central and Eastern Europe itself. This is also reflected in the fact that 16 per cent of the BITs concluded by

Central and Eastern European countries has been with other countries in the same region.

Accompaning the FDI boom, foreign portfolio equity investment in developing countries has also accelerated, ...

Substantial flows of foreign portfolio equity investment to emerging markets is a recent phenomenon dating only from the early 1990s. The year 1993 was the watershed for such flows when their level trebled, to $45 billion, from the previous year. However, the level of these flows fell in the two subsequent years in response to the Mexican peso crisis —by 27 per cent and 2 per cent in 1994 and 1995, respectively—but recovered in 1996. The volume of new equity raised on international capital markets by emerging markets in that year increased by 34 per cent, reaching some $15 billion.

In principle, foreign portfolio equity investment and direct investment are quite distinct. By definition, foreign portfolio equity investment is distinguished from FDI by the degree of management control that foreign investors exercise in a company. Portfolio equity investors usually provide only financial capital without any involvement in a company's management, and typically have a shorter-term investment horizon than direct investors. The latter have a significant and long-lasting management interest in the company in which an investment is made. In general, the dividing line between the two types of investment is the threshold of a 10 per cent equity stake. In practice, however, the distinction between the two categories of investment is often less clear-cut and is subject to a number of qualifications.

The overriding motivation for investment by portfolio equity investors is their participation in earnings of local enterprises through capital gains and dividends. Transnational corporations tend to be more interested in accessing markets and resources and, more generally, in the contribution that an investment can make to the competitiveness of the transnational corporate system as a whole. The contrast in motives between TNCs and portfolio equity investors is not, however, always so stark. In the notable case of venture capital investment, the investment horizone tends to be somewhat longer than for foreign portfolio equity investment, and the existence of significant (and perhaps also long-term) management control is not unusual, although the foremost motivation is to share in the capital gains of the equity of a local enterprise when it is listed eventually on the stock exchange.

... encouraged by the liberalization and globalization of financial markets and the growth of funds in the hands of institutional investors.

Two major factors lie behind the rise in foreign portfolio equity investment flows into emerging markets: the liberalization and globalization of financial markets and the concentration of substantial financial resources in the hands of institutional investors. Investments into emerging markets have been facilitated by the rapid provision of market information made possible by improvements in communications technology and the willingness of portfolio euqity investors to bear greater risks in the expectation of reaping higher returns in these new and fast-growing markets. The higher returns have been made possible by the sustained superior growth performance of emerging markets in comparison to that of developed economies during the 1990s. Stock market capitalization in emerging markets has also grown much faster than that in developed countries. However, as in the case of FDI flows, portfolio equity investment flows have remained skewed towards a small group of mostly upper middle-income emerging markets, along with two large low-income countries with impressive growth performances and prospects. (Asia alone accounted for 53 per cent of net foreign portfolio equity investment flows to emerging markets in 1995). This is not surprising. For many large institutional investors, it is more attractive to invest in more mature emerging markets that tend to have a relatively large market capitalization and provide high liquidity levels, relatively fast and reliable settlement systems and a generally more developed market infrastructure.

There is also a certain level of concentration when it comes to the origin of foreign portfolio equity investment flows. Over the period 1992-1994, it is estimated that more than 35 per cent of flows to emerging markets originated in the United States, 15 per cent of Japan and 11 per cent in the United Kingdom. In recent years, investors from Hong Kong and Singapore have also invested in emerging markets. For the United States, the most important source country, investment flows to emerging markets have followed the global trend, increasing substantially in 1993, decreasing in 1994 and 1995, and rising again in 1996, despite a clear upturn in stock-market returns in the United States.

In light of the vastly increased volume of foreign portfolio equity investment flows to emerging markets, the impact of these flows on host-country economies is likely to be significant. Although such investments can make an important contribution to the financing of equity capital of local companies, concerns have been expressed by host countries particularly as regards the volatility of these flows and their effect on exchange rates. In order to address this issue, its necessary to investigate the causes of that volatility and the availability of measures or mechanisms to reduce or withstand it.

FOREIGN DIRECT INVESTMENT, MARKET STRUCTURE AND COMPETITION POLICY

As countries liberalize their FDI policies, it becomes important to ensure the efficient functioning of markets ...

As countries liberalize their FDI regimes and firms increase their investment activities across national borders, maintaining the proper functioning of markets assumes increasing importance. Freer flows of FDI mean a greater reliance on market forces to determine the volume and distribution of FDI and its economic impact. Countries, especialy developing countries that are liberalizing rapidly, are, therefore, intereted in ensuring that the reduction of regulatory barriers to FDI and the institution of standards of treatment are not accompanied by the emergence of private barriers to entry and anti-competitive behaviour of firms. Competition and competition policy in relation to FDI need, therefore, to be better understood. Part Two of *WIR 97* focuses on the relationships between FDI, market structure and competition, and considers policy implications arising from these relationship, especially as they concern developing countries. The discussion of these issues rounds out, therefore, discussions in previous Reports, of FDI liberalization and related regulatory frameworks, including those relating to international investment arrangements.

The ultimate objective of FDI liberalization is to enhance economic growth and welfare in countries. Success in this respect depends not only on increasing FDI flows — and the capital, technology, managerial know-how and market access associated with them — but also on ensuring that the industries and markets in which TNCs participate operate efficiently. In market-based economies, the efficient functioning of markets depends on the contestability of markets — or the ease with which firms can enter and exit them — and the extent and nature of competition in markets. Foreign-direct-investment liberalization, by removing formal barriers to the entry of FDI, can increase the contestability of national markets and inject greater competition into them. However, because of the ownership-specific assets of TNCs, their transnational organizational structures and the relatively greater competitive strengths that they often have vis-a-vis domestic firms, FDI could also increase concentration, and TNC, could indulge, like dominant firms generally, in restrictive or anti-copetitive practices. Government policy and practices aimed at attracting investments that grant exclusivity or allow firms, dometic or foreign to erect informal impediments to the entry of other firms could contribute to the potential for such practices.

... through the adoption and implementation of competition policies.

Governments rely on several policy tools to ensure that their markets remain contestable and that competition in markets is maintained as far as possible, so that economic growth and welfare are not adversely affected by the inefficient allocation or use of resources. The tools of such policy include trade policy, FDI policy, regulatory policy with respect to domestic economic activity, and competition policy. While the first three comprise rules and regulations that serve several purposes and not only that of maintaining competition with a view to fostering efficiency, the last relates specifically to the rules and regulations — implemented by competition authorities — with respect to arrangements among firms/suppliers and the conduct of individual firms/suppliers, generally but not exclusively, in national markets. It is increasingly recognized that consistency and coherence between the diffeent policies — some of which, as mentioned above, could serve competing objectives — are important. This is reflected in the fact that, in many developing countries, trade liberalization, FDI liberalization and domestic deregulation are currently taking place simultaneously. This ensures that the contestability and competition introduced by one set of policies are not undermined by another; but it also makes the pain of adjustment to competition, especially for hitherto protected domestic firms, a problem requiring attention and action by governments.

While the relevant markets for many products remain national in scope even in a globalizing world economy, ...

Even as barriers between national markets are reduced and producers can locate anywhere in the world (or in a region) to transact with buyers also located anywhere, the markets for many products remain national in scope. These include markets for products that can only be delivered through the presence of the producer at the location of the buyer — notably, services — and markets in countries that have significant restrictions on trade. The interaction of TNCs with the structure of these national markets, the process of competition and the performance of firms and industries within host countries all therefore, continue to be of interest, especially for developing countries.

...opening up to inward FDI can contribute towards the contestability of host country markets ...

The opening up of economies to inward FDI can contribute directly towards increasing the contestability of — or potential competition in—host country markets. Sellers participating in these markets can now include not only domestic producers and (in the case of goods and tradable services) exporters from other countries, but also TNCs from other countries that establish affiliates (as well as contractual arrangements with other firms) to produce in and for local markets. Furthermore, TNCs, with their ownership-specific or competitive advantages, are often better able than domestic firms to overcome some of the cost-related barriers to entry that limit the number of firms in an industry and the market for its products. This potential for increasing competition by allowing FDI entry is particularly important for many service markets, in which competition through arm's length international trade is not possible or is limited.

... even though TNC activity may decrease or increase market concentration in host country markets, ...

Transnational corporations typically participate to a greater extent in industries that are more concentrated, at the national as well as the international level. This is largely due to the fact that industry concentration and the competitive advantages that enable firms to become transnational share common causes. However, inward FDI, when it takes place, can itself affect the concentration of producers in a host-country industry and, hence, of sellers in the market for its products. The nature of this effect depends, initially, upon whether or not the mode of entry is such as to add to the number of suppliers (and the quantity supplied) in a market and, subsequently, upon several factors related to the relative size, competitive strength and mode of competition of foreign affiliates and domestic and other firms competing in a market. In developed host countries, on balance, these factors are likely to be conducive towards reducing market concentration — or, at least, not to increase concentration.

In developing economies, the picture is more complex. Although the mode of entry of FDI into developing economies — generally, greenfield investment — is conducive to reducing concentration, market concentration has often been found to increase. Several factors may be involved: the disparity in size between foreign affiliates and domestic firms; the greater production efficiency or sales capability of foreign affiliates (which can lead to the exit of domestic enterprises that have yet to build up the necessary capabilities to withstand international competition, or to their merger with foreign firms); the use of modes of competition that are new to host country markets; the introduction of new products for which no other local producers or substitutes are available; and, most importantly in the case of tradable goods and services, restrictions on international trade that give local producers protected markets. If there is a sizeable number of domestic firms that have accumulated some competitive strengths and/or the capabilities to learn from foreign firms, increased concentration is less likey. Similarly, the presence of imports can curb the possible dominance of foreign affiliates in a market. The increasing role of small and medium-sized TNCs and TNCs from developing countries, with sometimes smaller competitive advantages compared with those of large TNCs from developed countries, is also likely to contribute towards lessening the tendency towards greater concentration of host country markets in industries with substantial inward FDI.

... and influence the performance of firms and industries — and, ultimately, consumer welfare — accordingly.

The production efficiency of foreign affiliates is often higher than that of domestic firms in host developing countries. The implications of this for welfare in the host economy depend upon whether competition is maintained when FDI takes place, and markets work efficiently. If competition — between foreign affiliates themselves, between foreign affiliates and importers, and between foreign affiliates and domestic firms — is lacking, and foreign affiliates operate in highly concentrated markets with low contestability, the benefits to consumers from the entry of more efficient TNCs, in the form of lower prices, improved quality, increased variety, as well as innovation and the introduction of new products, may be limited. In addition, there may be scope for TNCs to engage in anti-competitive business practices that serve to keep new entrants out or result in inefficiencies and reduced consumer welfare.

In particular, if a host country market remains, or becomes, concentrated after the entry of TNCs, there may be a potential for TNCs to engage in business practices, including restrictive business practices, that could have anti-competitive consequences, especially in markets that are characterized by low contestability. The main types of anti-competitive behaviour include, as in the case of purely domestic firms, collusion among producers/sellers of the same product; monopolizing mergers and acquisitions; exclusionary vertical practices; and predatory behaviour. In the case of TNCs, these practices may sometimes be specifically related to, or facilitated by, the cross-border relationships and contacts that are specific to operating in more than one country.

Consumer welfare in host country markets may also be affected adversely it market-power inducements are granted by host country governments to TNCs in order to attract investments by the latter. These inducements include guaranteed exclusive rights of production and/or exclusive rights of sale of a product in the host country market, often supported by protection in the form of prohibitive tariff or non-tariff restrictions on trade. The granting of these inducements has direct anti-competitive effects, with adverse implications for efficiency and the benefits from FDI. Such inducements, like other incentives, are based on the objective of maximizing the long-term benefits (in the form of capital, technology, management know-how, and market access) that FDI is expected to bring; but, given the potential for adverse effects on the efficient functioning of markets, a careful assessment of costs and benefits is necessary if the granting of these inducements is to be justified.

In regional and global markets, competition and efficiency can go hand in hand with greater concentration ...

In a liberalizing and globalizing world economy, TNCs operate increasingly in markets that are no longer national but regional or global in scope, with transactions between sellers and buyers of a given product from several different countries taking place across national boundaries. In various industries, TNCs take advantage of the widening scope of markets to restructure their operations and/or integrate their value-added activities internationally, either within their corporate systems or through inter-firm alliances and agreements, achieving efficiencies in production through functional specialization and economies of scale and scope.

The efficiency gains that some TNCs are able to reap through integrated international production enables them to lower prices, to introduce better quality products, or to introduce new products to capture a greater market share. This leads some industries (and markets) to become more concentrated at the regional or global level, a trend that affects all countries.

However, concentrated market at the regional or global levels need not necessarily affect competition, industry performance or consumer welfare adversely. For one thing, such markets are, by definition, more contestable or open as regards entry (and exit) than segmented national markets, simply because sellers (and buyers) from a number of locations can participate in them. Furthermore, when integraged international production (including at the R&D stage of the value chain) for regional or global markets enables firms to overcome the high costs of, and reap the economies of scale and scope associated with innovation in industries with rapidly changing technology, it could actually enhance competition (through innovation), although the number of independent firms that perform a particualr function may diminish. Consumers located in different national economies benefit when buying in those regional or global markets.

Particularly high degrees of concentration in regional and global markets would, of course, raise competition concerns. Business practices by regionally or globally dominant firms, including TNCs, could affect the continued contestability of the relevant markets and the sustainability of the benefits that the greater openness to FDI and trade is expected to bring.

... and can be further enhanced in a quick supply response through FDI.

In today's world economy, a number of factors facilitate the ease and speed with which TNCs can provide a supply response to a change in market conditions — signalled, for example, by a non-transitory price increase — through the establishment of new production facilities to enter a market. These factors are based on the reality that nearly all countries seek to attract FDI, many firms already have foreign affiliates in place, technological developments make the establishment of new affiliates relatively easy and competitive pressures often make the exploitation of new opportunities irresistible. More specifically, the supply response of many TNCs could be rapid, rivalling that of domestic producers and importers in a country because of the scanning capabilities of TNCs, their experience in trade and FDI; their access to resources within and outside their corporate systems, and access to markets; their ability to spread risks and enter into alliances to overcome entry barriers such as those of R&D; and their ability to draw upon existing affiliates for assistance. If supply response through FDI and non-equity arrangements by TNCs is relatively fast — with, say, not more than one to two years elapsing between the identification of an opportunity and the servicing of a market — it would be deserving of attention when considering the degree of competition in a given market. This is particularly important with respect to competition in markets for services, many of which cannot be traded across borders. All this suggests that the speed of the supply response through FDI must therefore, be considered routinely — by competition authorities in developed and developing countries alike — when defining the relevant market for a product, or assessing the implications for competiton of certain changes occurring in a market.

The possibility that new FDI will provide a viable supply response underlines the growing importance of FDI as a factor influencing contestability. Markets may not, however, always continue to remain contestable and competitive. This has several policy implications.

3

HUMAN DEVELOPMENT REPORT, 1998

Introduction

The *Human Development Report*, since its launch in 1990, has defined human development as the process of enlarging people's choices. This year's Report examines consumption from the perspective of human development. It concludes that despite a dramatic surge in consumption in many countries, all is not well: more than a billion people lack the opportunity to consume in ways that would allow them to meet their most basic needs. Other consumers—including me and most likely you and the societies in which we live—are consuming in ways that cannot be long sustained environmentally or socially and that are quite often inimical to our own well-being.

It is a truism that bears repeating: more is not invariable better. Consumption has grown at an unprecedented pace in this century, reaching some $24 trillion in 1998, but that growth has not yielded only benefits. Yet we appear to be on a runaway consumption train. For the more than one billion people living at or near the margin, increased consumption is essential. For those at the top, increased consumption has become a way of life. Yet we know, and this year's Report shows, that some aspects of consumption are undermining the prospects of sustainable human development for all.

When consumption erodes renewable resources, pollutes the local and global environment, panders to manufactured needs for conspicuous display and detracts from the legitimate needs of life in modern society, there is justifiable cause for concern.

Those who call for changes in consumption, for environmental or other reasons, are often seen as hair-shirt ascetics wishing to impose an austere way of life on billions who must pay for the waste of generations of big consumers. Advocates of strict consumption limits also are confronted with the dilemma that for more than one billion of the world's poor people increased consumption is a vital necessity and a basic right—a right to freedom from poverty and want. And thre is the ethical issue of choice: how can consumption choices be made on behalf of others and not be seen as a restriction on their freedom to choose?

The Report poses these hard questions and concludes that the need is not so much for more consumption or for less, but for a different pattern of consumption—consumption for human development. It marshals environmental, developmental, technological and moral arguments to present a critique of consumption patterns that are inimical to human development, and an agenda for action to create an enabling environment for sustainable consumption for human development.

Poor people and poor countries need to accelerate the growth of their consumption, but they need not follow the path trodden by the rich and high-growth economies. Production techniques can be made more environmentally friendly. Environmental damage can be reversed. The global burden of reducing environmental damage and underdevelopment can be shared more equitably. And patterns of consumption that harm society and reinforce inequalities and poverty can be changed. Above all, we must make a determined effort to eradicate poverty and expand the consumption of more than one billion desperately poor people who have been left out of the global growth in consumption.

OVERVIEW

Changing today's consumption patterns—for tomorrow's human development

World consumption has expanded at an unprecedented pace over the 20th century, with private and public consumption expenditures reaching $24 trillion in 1998, twice the level of 1975 and six times that of 1950. In 1900 real consumption expenditure was barely $1.5 trillion.

The benefits of this consumption have spread far and wide. More people are better fed and housed than ever before. Living standards have risen to enable hundreds of millions to enjoy housing with hot water and cold, warmth and electricity, transport to and from work—with time for leisure and sports, vacations and other activities beyond anything imagined at the start of this century.

How do these achievements relate to human development? Consumption is clearly an essential means, but the links are not automatic. Consumption clearly contributes to human development when it enlarges the capabilities and enriches the lives of people without adversely affecting the well-being of others. It clearly contributes when it is as fair to future generations as it is to the present ones. And it clearly contributes when it encourages lively, creative individuals and communities.

But the links are often broken, and when they are, consumption patterns and trends are inimical to human development. Today's consumption is undermining the environmental resource base. It is exacerbating inequalities. And the dynamics of the consumption-poverty-inequality-environment nexus are accelerating. If the trends continue without change—not redistributing from high-income to low-income consumers, not shifting from polluting to cleaner goods and production technologies, not promoting goods that empower poor producers, not shifting priority from consumption for conspicuous display to meeting basic needs—today's problems of consumption and human development will worsen.

But trend is not destiny, and none of these outcomes is inevitable. Change is needed—and change is possible.

In short, consumption must be shared, strengthening, socially responsible and sustainable.

- *Shared.* Ensuring basis needs for all.
- *Strengthening.* Building human capabilities.
- *Socially responsible.* So the consumption of some does not compromise the well-being of others.
- *Sustainable.* Without mortgaging the choices of future generations.

Human life is ultimately nourished and sustained by consumption. Abundance of consumption is no crime. It has, in fact, been the life blood of much human advance. The real issue is not consumption itself but its patterns and effects. Consumption patterns today must be changed to advance human development tomorrow. Consumer choices must be turned into a reality for all. Human development paradigms, which aim at enlarging all human choices, must aim at extending and improving consumer choices too, but in ways that promote human life. This is the theme of this report.

The 20th century's growth in consumption, unprecedented in its scale and diversity, has been badly distributed, leaving a backlog of shortfalls and gaping inequalities.

Consumption per capita has increased steadily in industrial countries (about 2.3% annually) over the past 25 years, spectacularly in East Asia (6.1%) and at a rising rate in South Asia (2.0%). Yet these developing regions are far from catching up to levels of industrial countries, and consumption growth has been slow or stagnant in others. The average African household today consumes 20% less than it did 25 years ago.

The poorest 20 per cent of the world's people and more have been left out of the consumption explosion. Well over a billion people are deprived of basic consumption needs. Of the 4.4 billion peoople in developing countries, nearly three-fifths lack basic sanitation. Almost a third have no access to clean water. A quarter do not have adequate housing. A fifth have no access to modern health services. A fifth of children do not attend school to grade 5. About a fifth do not have enough dietary energy and protein. Micronutrient deficiencies are even more widespread. Worldwide, 2 billion people are anaemic, including 55 million in industrial countries. In developing countries only a privileged minority has motorized transport, telecommunications and modern energy.

Inequalities in consumption are stark. Globally, the 20 per cent of the world's people in the highest-income countries account for 86 per cent of total private consumption expenditures—the poorest 20 per cent a minuscule 1.3 per cent. More specifically, the richest fifth:

- Consume 45 per cent of all meat and fish, the poorest fifth 5 per cent.
- Consume 58 per cent of total energy, the poorest fifth less than 4 per cent.
- Have 74 per cent of all telephone lines, the poorest fifth 1.5 per cent.
- Consume 84 per cent of all paper, the poorest fifth 1.1 per cent.
- Own 87 per cent of the world's vehicle fleet, the poorest fifth less than 1 per cent.

How rewarding is today's pattern of consumption in terms of human satisfaction? The percentage of Americans calling themselves happy peaked in 1957—even though consumption has more than doubled in the meantime.

Despite high consumption, poverty and deprivation are found in all industrial countries and in some they are growing. This year's Report presents a new index of poverty in industrial countries—a multi-dimensional measure of human deprivation, on the same lines as the human poverty index presented in *Human Development Report 1997* for developing countries but more appropriate to the social and economic conditions of the industrial countries.

The new Human Poverty Index (HPI-2) shows that some 7 to 17 per cent of the population in industrial countries is poor. These levels of deprivation have little to do with the average income of the country. Sweden has the least poverty (7%), though ranked only thirteenth in average income. The United States, with the highest average income of the countries ranked, has the highest population share experiencing human poverty. And countries with similar per capita incomes have very different levels of human poverty. The Netherlands and the United Kingdom, for example, have HPI-2 values of 8 per cent and 15 per cent, despite similar income levels.

HPI-2 shows conclusively that under-consumption and human deprivation are not just the lot of poor people in the developing world. More than 100 million people in rich nations suffer a similar fate. Nearly 200 million people are not expected to survive to age 60. More than 100 million are homeless. And at least 37 million are without jobs, often experiencing a state of social exclusion. Many conclusions about deprivation apply to them with equal force.

> *Ever expanding consumption puts strains on the environment—emissions and wastes that pollute the earth and destroy ecosystems, and growing depletion and degradation of renewable resources that undermines livelihoods.*

Runaway growth in consumption in the past 50 years in putting strains on the environment never before seen.

— The burning of fossil fuels has almost quintupled since 1950.
— The consumption of fresh water has almost doubled since 1960.
— The marine catch has increased fourfold.
— Wood consumption, both for industry and for household fuel, is now 40 per cent higher than it was 25 years ago.

Yet growth in the use of material resources has slowed considerably in recent years, and much-publicized fears that the world would run out of such non-renewable resources as oil and minerals have proved false. New reserves have been discovered. The growth of demand has slowed. Consumption has shifted in favour of less material-intensive products and services. Energy efficiency has improved. And technological advance and recycling of raw materials have boosted efficiency in material use, now growing more slowly than economies. Call this dematerialization. The per capita use of basic materials such as steel, timber and copper has stabilized in most OECD countries—and even declined in some countries for some products.

So, non-renewables are not the urgent problem. It is two other crises that are nudging humanity towards the "outer limits" of what earth can stand.

First are the pollution and waste that exceed the planet's sink capacities to absorb and convert them. Reserves of fossil fuels are not running out, but use of these fuels is emitting gases that change the ecosystem—annual carbon dioxide (CO_2) emissions quadrupled over the past 50 years. Global warming is a serious problem, threatening to play havoc with harvests, permanently flood large areas, increase the frequency of storms and droughts, accelerate the extinction of some species, spread infectious diseases—and possibly cause sudden and savage flips in the world's climates. And althouth material resources may not be running out, waste is mounting, both toxic and non-toxic. In industrial countries per capita waste generation has increased almost threefold in the past 20 years.

Second is the growing deterioration of renewables—water, soil, forests, fish, bio-diversity.

- — Twenty countries already suffer from water stress, having less than 1,000 cubic metres per capita a year, and water's global availability has dropped from 17,000 cubic metres per capita in 1950 to 7,000 today.
- — A sixth of the world's land area—nearly 2 billion hectares—is now degraded as a result of overgrazing and poor farming practices.
- — The world's forests—which bind soil and prevent erosion, regulate water supplies and help govern the climate—are shrinking. Since 1970 the wooded area per 1,000 inhabitants has fallen from 11.4 square kilometres to 7.3.
- — Fish stocks are declining, with about a quarter currently depleted or in danger of depletion and another 44 per cent being fished at their biological limit.
- — Wild species are becoming extinct 50-100 times faster than they would naturally, threatening to tear great holes in the web of life.

The world's dominant consumers are overwhelmngly concentrated among the well-off—but the environmental damage from the world's consumption falls most severely on the poor.

The better-off benefit from the cornucopia of consumption. But poor people and poor countries bear many of its costs. The severest human deprivations arising from environmental damage are concentrated in the poorest regions and affect the poorest people, unable to protect themselves.

- — A child born in the industrial world adds more to consumption and pollution over his or her lifetime than do 30 to 50 children born in developing countries.
- — Since 1950 industrial countries, because of their high incomes and consumption levels, have accounted for well over half the increase in resource use.
- — The fifth of the world's people in the highest-income countries account for 53 per cent of carbon dioxide emissions, the poorest fifth for 3 per cent. Brazil, China, India, Indonesia and Mexico are among the developing countries with the highest emissions. But with huge populations, their per capita emissions are still tiny—3.9 metric tonnes a year in Mexico and 2.7 in China, compared with 20.5 metric tonnes in the United States and 10.2 in Germany. The human consequences of the global warming from carbon dioxide will be devastating for many poor countries—with a rise in sea levels, Bangladesh could see its land area shrink by 17 per cent.

Almost a billion people in 40 developing countries risk losing access to their primary source of protein, as overfishing driven by export demand for animal feed and oils put pressure on fish stocks.

— The 132 million people in water-stressed areas are predominantly in Africa and parts of the Arab states—and if present trends continue, their numbers could rise to 1-2.5 billion by 2050.

— Deforestation is concentrated in developing countries. Over the last two decades, Latin America and the Caribbean lost 7 million hectares of tropical forest, Asia and Sub-Saharan Africa 4 million hectares each. Most of it has taken place to meet the demand for wood and paper, which has doubled and quintupled respectively since 1950. But over half the wood and nearly three-quarters of the pàper is used in industrial countries.

The poor are most exposed to fumes and polluted rivers and least able to protect themselves. Of the estimated 2.7 million deaths each year from air pollution, 2.2 million are from indoor pollution, and 80 per cent of the victims are rural poor in developing countries. Smoke from fuelwood and dung is more dangerous to health than tobacco smoke, but every day women have to spend hours cooking over smoky fires.

Leaded petrol, used more in developing and transition economies than in industrial countries, is crippling human health, permanently impairing the development of children's brains. In Bangkok upto 70,000 children are reported to be at risk of losing four or more IQ points because of high lead emissions. In Latin America around 15 million children under two years of age are at similar risk.

These environmental challenges stem not only from affluence but also from growing poverty. As a result of increasing impoverishment and the absence of other alternatives, a swelling number of poor and landless people are putting unprecedented pressures on the natural resource base as they struggle to survive.

Poverty and the environment are caught in a downward spiral. Past resource degradation deepens today's poverty, while today's poverty makes it very hard to care for or restore the agricultural resource base, to find alternatives to deforestation, to prevent desertification, to control erosion and to replenish soil nutrients. Poor people are forced to deplete resources to survive; this degradation of the environment further impoverishes them.

When this reinforcing downward spiral becomes extreme, poor peole are either forced to move in increasing numbers to ecologically fragile lands. Almost half the world's poorest people—more than 500 million—live on marginal lands.

The poverty-environmental damage nexus in developing countries must be seen in the context of population growth. In the developing world pressures on the environment intensify every day as the population grows. The global population is projected to be 9.5 billion in 2050, with more than 8 billion in developing countries. To feed this population adequately will require three times the basic calories consumed today, the equivalent of about 10 billion tonnes of grain a year. Population growth will also contribute to overgrazing, overcutting and overfarming.

How people interact with their environment is complex. It is by no means simply a matter of whether they are poor or rich. Ownership of natural resources, access to common properties, the strength of communities and local institutions, the issue of entitlements and rights, risk and uncertainty are important determinants of people's environmental behviour. Gender inequalities, government policies and incentive systems are also crucial factors.

In recent times environmental awareness has been increasing in both rich and poor countries. The rich countries, with greater resources, have been spending more on envrionmental protection and clean-up. The developing countries, though they have fewer resources, have also been adopting cleaner technologies and reducing pollution, as in China.

The world community has also been active on environmental problems that directly affect poor people. Such areas include desertification, biodiversity loss and exports of hazardous waste. For example, the Convention on Biological Diversity has near-universal signature, with over 170 parties. The Convention to Combat Desertification has been ratified by more than 100 countries. But the deterioration of arid lands, a major threat to the livelihoods of poor people continues unabated.

And there are other immediate environmental concerns for poor people, such as water contamination and indoor pollution, that have yet to receive serious international attention. Global forums discuss global warming. But the 2.2 million deaths yearly from indoor air pollution are scarcely mentioned.

Rising pressures for conspicuous consumption can turn destructive, reinforcing exclusion, poverty and inequality.

Pressures of competitive spending and conspicuous consumption turn the affluence of some into the social exclusion of many. When there is heavy social pressure to maintain high consumption standards and society encourages competitive spending for conspicuous displays of weatlh, inequalities in consumption deepen poverty and social exclusion.

Some disturbing trends:

— Studies of US households found that the income needed to fulfil consumption aspirations doubled between 1986 and 1994.

— The definition of what constitutes a "necessity" is changing, and the distinctions between luxuries and necessities are blurring. In the 1980s Brazil, Chile, Malaysia, Mexico and South Africa had two to three times as many cars as Austria, France and Germany did when they were at the same income level 30 years earlier.

— Household debt, especially consumer credit, is growing and household savings are falling in many industrial and developing countries. In the United States households save only 3.5 per cent of their incomes, half as much as 15 years ago. In Brazil consumer debt, concentrated among lower-income households, now exceeds $6 billion.

Many voice concerns about the impact of these trends on society's values—and on human lives. Do they further deepen poverty as households compete to meet rising consumption standards—crowding out spending on food, education and health? Do these patterns motivate people to spend more hours working—leaving less time for family, friends and community?

And is globalization accelerating these trends in competitive spending and rising standards?

Globalization is integrating consumer markets around the world and opening opportunities. But it is also creating new inequalities and new challenges for protecting consumer rights.

Globalization is integrating not just trade, investment and financial markets. It is also integrating consumer markets. This has two effect—economic and social. Economic integration has accelerated the opening of consumer markets with a constant flow of new products. There is fierce competition to sell to consumers worldwide, with increasingly aggressive advertising.

On the social side local and national boundaries are breaking down in the setting of social standards and aspirations in consumption. Market research identifies "global elites" and "global middle classes" who follow the same consumption styles, showing preferences for "global brands". There are the "global teens"—some 270 million 15 to 18 year olds in 40 countries—inhabiting a "global space", a single pop-culture world, soaking up the same videos and music and providing a huge market for designer running shoes, t-shirts and jeans.

What are the consequences? First, a host of consumption options have been opened for many consumers—but many are left out in the cold through lack of income. And pressures for competitive spending mount. "Keeping up with the Joneses" has shifted from striving to match the consumption of a next-door neighbour to pursuing the life styles of the rich and famous depicted in movies and television shows.

Second, protecting consumer rights to product safety and product information has become complex. Increasingly, new products with higher chemical content, such as foods and medicines, are coming on the market. When information is not adequate, or safety standards are not strictly enforced, consumers can suffer—from pesticides that are poisonous, from milk powder that is contaminated.

At the same time the consumer receives a flood of information through commercial advertising. An average American, it is estimated, sees 150,000 advertisements on television in his or her lifetime. And advertising is increasing worldwide, faster than population or incomes. Global advertising spending, by the most conservative reckoning, is now $435 billion. Its growth has been particularly rapid in developing countries—in the Republic of Korea it increased nearly threefold in 1986-96, in the Philippines by 39 per cent a year in 1987-92. In 1986 there were only three developing countries among the 20 biggest spenders in advertising. A decade later there were nine. And in spending relative to income, Colombia ranks first with $1.4 billion, 2.6 per cent of its GDP.

Poor countries need to accelerate their consumption growth—but they eed not follow the path taken by the rich and high-growth economies over the past half century.

Not only have consumption levels been too low to meet basic needs for more than a billion people, their growth has often been slow and interrupted by setbacks. In 70 countries with nearly a billion people consumption today is lower than it was 25 years ago. It cannot be raised without accelerating economic growth—but growth has been failing many poor people and poor countries. Despite the spectacular growth of incomes for many people in Asia, only 21 developing countries worldwide achieved growth in GDP per capita of at least 3 per cent each year between 1995 and 1997—the rate needed to set a frame for reducing poverty.

Some suggest that developing countries should restrain their consumption in order to limit environmental damage. But this would mean prolonging the already scandalously deep and extensive deprivation for future generations.

Developing countries today face a strategic choice. They can repeat the industrialization and growth processes of the past half century, and go through a development phase that is inequitable, and creates an enormous legacy of environmental pollution. Or they can leapfrog to growth patterns that are:

— Pro-environment, preserving natural resources and creating less pollution and waste.
— Pro-poor, creating jobs for poor people and househodls and expanding their access to basic social services.

If poor countries can leapfrog in both consumption patterns and production technologies, they can accelerate consumption growth and human development without the huge costs of environmental damage. They can incorporate many of the available technologies that are not only less environmentally damaging but clean—solar energy, less energy-intensive crop production, cleaner paper production technologies.

Leapfrogging technologies will enhance the prospects for development by saving the huge costs of environmental clean-up that many countries are now incurring. The cost savings will go beyond the dirct costs of cleaning up old toxic sites, scrubbing coal power plants and so on. Health care costs linked to environmental damage can also be saved. And leapfrogging will bypass the lock-in that can result from inappropriate infrastructure development.

Some argue that the scope for cheap, effective and politically less contentious anti-pollution policies is very limited in poor countries. This is a myth. Many actions have already been taken. And further options exist:

— Higher yields can be achieved through more intensive agricultural methods rather than more fertilizers and pesticides.
— Phasing out lead in petrol costs only 1-2 cents per litre for the refinery, as Mexico and Thailand have shown.
— Solar power and compact fluorescent lightbulbs can increase efficiency fourfold and reduce the need for rural electricity grids.
— Clean four-stroke engines can be made compulsory for motorcycles and three-wheelers, as Thailand has done.

These show what is possible. But to realize the potential, more needs to be done to develop and apply innovations

Affluent societies in industrial countries also face strategic choices. They can continue the trends in consumption of the past decade. Or they can shift to consumption that is pro-people and pro-environment.

Continuing past trends would increase industrial countries' consumption by four to five fold over the next half century. Some argue that growth must be slowed and consumption downsized. But the real issue is not growth of consumption but its impacts on people, the environment and society. If societies adopt technologies that diminish the environmental impact of consumpton, if patterns shift from consumiing material goods to consuming services, growth can help, not hinder, moves to sustainability. The strategic choices of rich countries as the world's dominant consumers, will be critical in determining the future.

4

ASIAN FINANCIAL CRISIS AND WORLD ECONOMY International Monetary Fund Annual Report, 1998

1. ASIAN FINANCIAL CRISIS PROPELS IMF ACTIVITY TO NEW LEVELS IN 1997-98

The Asian financial crisis that broke out in July 1997 in Thailand, and its subsequent global reverberations, dominated the IMF's work in 1997-98, absorbing an unprecedented amount of time of the Executive Board, management, and staff. The crisis—whose global consequences continued after the end of the financial year—also prompted a record level of IMF lending in 1997-98, adding immediacy to the need to strengthen the financial resources of the institution to enable it to continue playing a fully effective role in the globalized world economy. The crisis also led to the creation of a new lending facility (the Supplemental Reserve FAcility); stepped-up work on strengthening the conduct of IMF surveillance; and, more generally, led to the elaboration of a framework for strengthening the architecture of the international monetary system. Separately, the Executive Board undertook an extensive review—drawing on both internal and external assessments—of the IMF's concessional lending facility for low-income countries (the Enhanced Structural Adjustment Facility) and continued its work aimed at ensuring the uninterrupted availability of financial resources for the ESAF. Together with the World Bank and other creditors, the IMF made important headway in implementing the initiative to reduce the external debt burden of a number of heavily indebted poor countries (the HIPC Initiative).

The Asian financial crisis had a major impact on the scale of *IMF financial assistance* in 1997-98. During the year, member countries draw SDR 19.0 billion ($25.6 billion)[1] from the IMF's General Resources Account in the credit tranches—nearly four times the level of the previous year. The IMF approved nine new Stand-By Arrangement's, with total commitments of SDR 27.3 billion, and four new Extended Arrangement,s with total commitments of SDR 2.8 billion. The largest Stand-By Arrangements were for Korea (which also made use of the new Supplemental Reserve Facility), Indonesia, and Thailand; the largest Extended Arrangment was for Argentina. In addition, the IMF approved eight new ESAF Arrangements with commitments totaling SDR 1.7 billion. As of April 30, 1998,

[1]As of April 30, 1998, SDR 1 = $1.34666.

14 Stand-By Arrangements, 13 Extended Arrangements, and 33 ESAF Arrangements were in effect with member countries. Net of repayments of previous drawings, total IMF credit outstanding rose to a record SDR 56 billion ($75.4 billion) as of April 30, 1998, compared with SDR 40.5 billion ($55.3 billion)[2] a year earlier.

In December 1997, the Executive Board established the Supplemental Reserve Facility to provide additional financial assistance to members facing exceptional balance of payments difficulties attributable to a large short-term financing need resulting from a sudden and disruptive loss of market confidence.

As a result of the large new demands on the IMF's resources in 1997-98, its net uncommitted usable resources (adjusted to meet the requirement to maintain adequate working balances of currencies) declined to SDR 22.6 billion at the end of April 1998 from SDR 43.5 billion a year earlier. Over the same period, the IMF's liquid liabilities rose sharply—reflecting an increase in members' reserve tranche positions—and its liquidity ratio fell to 44.8 per cent as of April 30, 1998, from 120.5 per cent a year earlier.

In January 1998, the IMF's Board of Governors adopted the Executive Board's recommendation that total IMF quotas be increased by 45 per cent (to SDR 212 billion from SDR 146 billion) under the Eleventh General Review of Quotas. The increase will take effect after members having not less than 85 per cent of total quotas as of December 28, 1997, have consented to their quota increases.

The IMF's work on *surveillance issues* intensified following the outbreak and spread of the financial crisis to other Asian economies and the subsequent pressures on other emerging market economies. Surveillance was also intensified in recognition that promoting good governance, making budgets more transparent, improving data collection and disclosure, and strengthening financial sectors are increasingly important if countries are to establish and maintain private sector confidence and lay the groundwork for sustained growth.

In a preliminary review in March 1998 of the *implications for IMF surveillance of the Asian Financial crisis*, the Executive Board drew five lessons:

— effective surveillance depends critically on the timely availability of accurate information;
— the focus of surveillance has to extend even further beyond short-term macro-economic issues, yet remain appropriately selective;
— surveillance at the country level should pay more explicit attention to policy interdependence and the risks of contagion;
— the crucial role of credibility in restoring market confidence underscores the importance of transparency; and
— effective surveillance depends fundamentally on the willingness of members to take the IMF's advice.

In July 1997, the Executive Board adopted *guidelines clarifying the IMF's role in governance issues*. The guidelines call for a more comprehensive treatment, in the context of both bilateral consultations with members under Article IV and IMF-supported programmes, of governance issues within the IMF's purview and expertise; for evenhanded treatment of member countries; and for enhanced

[2]As of April 30, 1997, SDR 1 = $1.36553.

collaboration with other institutions—notably the World Bank—to make better use of complemantary areas of expertise The guidelines identify two areas in which the IMF can make a particular contribution: improving the management of public resources and supporting the development and maintenance of a transparent and stable regulatory environment conducive to efficient private sector activities.

Similarly, in an effort to enhance the accountability and credibility of members' fiscal policies, the Interim Committee, at its April 1998 meeting, adopted a *Code of Good Practices on Fiscal Transparency: Declaration on Principles.*

In December 1997, the Executive Board reviewed members' progress in *providing data to the IMF for surveillance* and saw scope for improvement. Recent experience also suggested the need to complement traditional "core" indicators with data on reserve-related liabilities, central bank derivative transactions, private sector external debt, and prudential banking system indicators.

To guide members in *disseminating data to the public*, the Executive Board endorsed a two-tier approach: the Special Data Dissemination Standard, established in March 1996 for countries that have or might seek access to international financial markets, and a less ambitious General Data Dissemination System, approved in December 1997, for all member countries.

The importance of *strengthening members' financial sectors* was a recurring theme of Board discussions in 1997-98—including the importance of enhancing IMF and World Bank collaboration so that emerging financial sector problems are promptly identified, each institution takes the lead in its own areas of responsibility, and the IMF's macro-economic analysis and the Bank's sectoral policy recommendations are fully coordinated.

To enhance the transparency of its surveillance, the IMF in May 1997 introduced Press/Public Inforamation Notices—following the conclusion of Article IV consultations. PINs summarize the Executive Board's assessment of member countries' economic policies and prospects. Of the 136 Article IV consultations in 1997-98, 77 resulted in the issuance of PINs. PINs appear on the IMF's website, http://www.imf.org, and are published three times a year as *IMF Economic Reviews.*

At the Annual Meetings in Hong Kong SAR in September 1997, the Interim Committee issued a *Statement on the Liberalization of Capital Movements Under an Amendment of the IMF's Articles of Agreement.* The statement invited the Executive Board to complete its work on a proposed amendment to make the liberalization of capital movements one of the purposes of the IMF and extend, as needed, the IMF's jurisdiction in this area. In 1997-98, the Board considered various aspects of such an amendment and, to help inform its work, sponsored a high-level seminar in March 1998 to elicit views from a wide range of private and official observers outside the IMF. At its April 1998 meeting, the Interim Committee noted the progress made thus far and the provisional agreement reached by the Executive Board on that part of the amendment dealing with the IMF's purposes. The Committee asked the Board to pursue with determination its work on other aspects, including policy issues, with the aim of submitting an appropriate amendment of the Articles for the Committee's consideration as soon as possible.

Since the Mexican financial crisis of 1994-95, the IMF has taken a number of steps to enhance the functioning of the international monetary system. The heightened challenges posed by the ongoing globalization of financial markets—as exemplified by the Asian financial crisis—highlighted the need for further efforts in this direction. In its continuing discussions of additional initiatives to *strengthen the architecture of the international monetary system*, the Executive Board in 1997-98 identified the following imperatives:

— improving international and domestic financial systems;
— strengthening IMF surveillance further;
— promoting the wider availability and greater transparency of information regarding economic data and policies;
— reinforcing the central role of the IMF in crisis management; and
— introducing more effective procedures for involving the private sector in forestalling or resolving financial crises.

2. MAIN DEVELOPMENT IN THE WORLD ECONOMY IN 1997-98

The dominant developments in the world economy and for the IMF in 1997/98 were the Asian financial crisis and its repercussions. The crisis broke out in July 1997 in Thailand when, following several episodes of exchange market pressure and reserve lossses, the authorities abandoned the peg of the baht to the U.S. dollar. The forced exit from the U.S. dollar peg, in turn, raised doubts about the viability of exchange rate arrangements elsewhere. Spillover effects were soon felt in other countries in the region, especially Indonesia, Malaysia, and the Philippines, exposing underlying structural weaknesses in these economies. Measures to tighten liquidity conditions in Indonesia failed to stem the growing exchange market pressures, and the Indonesian authorities allowed the rupiah to float in mid-August. The situation worsened markedly over the next two months and spillover effects spread to other countries. In Hong Kong SAR, strong pressures on the Hong Kong dollar in October led to a surge in interest rates, followed by a substantial equity market decline. In Korea, downward pressures on the won intensified in late October, following the attack on the Hong Kong dollar, and equity prices fell sharply, reflecting diminished confidence about economic prospects and the growing difficulties encountered by the financial sector in rolling over external loans. After making efforts to defend the won, the Korean authorities widened the daily fluctuation band from 4½ per cent to 20 per cent in late November, and subsequently requested financial support from the IMF.

The unfolding crisis, which saw exchange rates and equity prices plunge dramatically, was one of the worst in the postwar period. It was centered in countries that had long pursued prudent fiscal policies and enjoyed high saving rates. What went wrong? The key elements, especially in Thailand, were a buildup of inflationary pressures, manifested in large external deficits and inflated property and stock markets; main tenance for too long of pegged exchange rate regimes, which came to be viewed as implicit guarantees of exchange value, encouraging unhedged external borrowing—often at short maturities; lack of timely and relevant data and information; lax enforcement of prudential rules, as well as weaknesses in the institutional structures of supervision in financial systems; government-directed lendng practices that led to a sharp deterioration in the quality of banks' loan portfolios, in turn reducing the scope for raising interest rates; and problems of governance that, together with political uncertainties, worsened the crisis of confidence. External elements also played a role: foreign investors under-estimated the risks associated with their search for higher yields during a period of sluggish economic growth in Japan and Europe and low international interest rates, and contagion effects of the crisis led to an excessive devaluation of the affected currencies.

Global Overview

The financial turmoil that erupted in southeast Asia in mid-1997 quickly began to take its toll on demand and activity in the affected countries. It also began to have a dampening impact on global growth late in the year and in early 1998. In 1997 as a whole, however, world output growth continued at about 4 per cent, with slower growth in Africa, Asia, and the Middle East offset by faster expansion in the industrial countries, the developing countries of the Western Hemisphere, and the countries in transition (Table 4.1) Growth in the volume of world trade rebounded in 1997 to 9½ per cent, matching the expansion of 1995—the most rapid rate for two decades. The acceleration was widely shared between the advanced and developing country groups, but the growth in trade of the transition economies slowed somewhat.

Associated with the Asian crisis was a dramatic drop in net private capital flows to emerging market economies (Table 4.2). Such flows had reached a record $240 billion in 1996, with Asia attracting more than 40 per cent of the total. After rising further in the firt half of 1997, net flows fell steeply, as the crisis in Asia deepened, and for the year as a whole were about $70 billion less than in 1996. Net flows to the developing countries of Asia fell by more than $60 billion to about $40 billion—the lowest inflow since 1992. The developing countries of the Middle East and Europe saw a smaller decline in inflows, while flows to the Western Hemisphere, Africa, and the countries in transition actually increased. In the first quarter of 1998, net capital inflows to emerging market countries remained close to their already reduced levels of late 1997.

The sharp declines in private capital flows to emerging market economies in Asia, although cushioned to some extent by an increase in official financing flows, required substantial adjustments in these countries' external positions. For the Asian developing countries, taken together, the current account deficit narrowed by almost $30 billion in 1997. And by early 1998, the countries most affected by the crisis—Indonesia, Korea and Thailand—were each running current account surpluses. In 1997 as a whole, a widening of current account deficits among a number of Latin American countries, relfecting the increase in foreign direct investment in the region, was the main counterpart to the narrowing of deficits in the Asian emerging markets (Table 4.3). In late 1997 nd early 1998, however, a number of advanced economies—most notably the United States—and the oil-exporting countries began to show signs of deteriorating current account balances.

Consumer price inflation declined further in each of the main country groups in 1997. The decline was helped by the weakness of primary commodity prices, including those for oil. In early 1998, oil prices fell further; indeed, by April 1998, in SDR terms, oil prices were about 31 per cent lower than a year earlier, while non-oil commodity prices had fallen by 20 per cent over the same period. To some extent, the declines reflected the reduced demand for commodities in the countries embroiled in the Asian crisis; the sharp depreciation of these countries' currencies may also have led to reductions in the foreign currency prices of their commodity exports.

The redirection of financial flows towards the mature markets following the onset of the crisis, together with prospects for lower inflation, contributed to significant declines in medium and long-term interest rates in the industrial countries in late 1997 and early 1998—in some cases to 50-year lows. This easing of financial conditions, particularly in North America and in western Europe, contributed, in turn, to further gains in equity markets, with many indices reaching new peaks. These developments helped support the growth of domestic demand in industrial countries at the same time that net exports began to be adversely affected by the Asian crisis.

In foreign exchange markets, after considerable initial strengthening during 1997-98, the yen experienced strong selling pressures for most of the period, reflecting market concerns about progress in Japan's economic recovery. After falling to ¥ 127 per dollar at the end of April 1997, the yen rebounded sharply in May and early June to reach a high of ¥110. With the recovery losing momentum by midyear and with concerns about the domestic financial sector, the yen subsequently weakened anew; by the end of April 1998, it had depreciated to ¥132 per dollar. Although the deutsche mark depreciated further against the dollar during 1997 and in early 1998, the depreciation in nominal effective terms was moderate. The pound sterling rose steeply in 1997 and in early 1998, owing mainly to short-term cyclical factors.

Advanced Economies

Cyclical divergences remained sizable among the advanced economies in 1997. Economic activity was strong in the United States and the United Kingdom, with both economies operating close to capacity and unemployment rates at their lowest in many years. The major economies of continental Europe saw a strengthening of growth in the second half of 1997 and in early 1998, but significant margins of slack remained in most of these countries. The Japanese economy faltered after the firt quarter of 1997, then slipped into recession in the fourth quarter of the year, with output contracting in the first quarter of 1998 by 5.3 per cent at an annual rate. The impact of the Asian crisis on the advanced economies varied depending on two main factors. The first was the importance of trade and financial links with the crisis economies; these links were generally closest in the Asia-Pacific region.[3] The second was the economy's starting position. The dampening effects of the crisis had a relatively large adverse impact on Japan, where activity and confidence were already weak; by contrast, these effects most likely helped contain inflationary pressures in countries facing the risk of overheating.

After a strengthening of growth in 1996 following four years of weak recovery, self-sustaining growth seemed to be taking hold in Japan in the early part of 1997. But activity declined sharply in the second quarter and picked up only weakly during the remainder of the year. The loss of growth before the middle of the year was attributable primarily to domestic factors, including an increase in the consumption tax in April 1997, cuts in public spending, and financial sector fragility. In the latter part of the year, concerns about the Asian crisis and about the domestic financial sector, together with a renewed softening of equity prices,

---

[3]For example, in 1996, trade with the Asian newly industrialized and developing economics represented 5 per cent of GDP in Japan, compared with 1½ per cent to 3 per cent in the major industrial economies of Europe and North America.

contributed to continued weakness in domestic spending. For the year as a whole, GDP grew by 3/4 of 1 per cent. The Japanese authorities responded to these developments by announcing a large fiscal stimulus package in April 1998 and by taking steps to address banking problems, including making public money available to strengthen deposit insurance and boost bank capital. Nevertheless, uncertainties remained about how the banking sector measureswould be implemented. In July 1998, the Japanese authorities announced a series of further banking sector initiatives in a Comprehensive Plan for Financial Revitalization, including a "bridge bank" facility intended to facilitate the resolution of failed institutions and measures to strengthen bank supervision and increase transparency.

Table 4.1 : Overview of the World Economy
(Annual per cent change unless otherwise noted)

	1994	1995	1996	1997
World output	3.9	3.6	4.1	4.1
Advanced economies	3.1	2.5	2.7	3.0
Major industrial countries	2.8	2.0	2.5	2.8
United States	3.5	2.0	2.8	3.8
Japan	0.6	1.5	3.9	0.9
Germany	2.7	1.8	1.4	2.2
France	2.8	2.1	1.5	2.4
Italy	2.2	2.9	0.7	1.5
United Kingdom	4.3	2.7	2.2	3.3
Canada	3.9	2.2	1.2	3.8
Other advanced economies	4.5	4.3	3.8	4.0
Memorandum				
Industrial countries	2.9	2.1	2.5	2.9
European Union	2.9	2.5	1.7	2.6
Newly industrialized Asian economies	7.6	7.3	6.4	6.1
Developing countries	6.8	6.0	6.6	5.8
Africa	2.5	3.0	5.5	3.2
Asia	9.6	9.0	8.3	6.7
ASEAN-4[1]	7.7	8.1	7.1	3.9
Middle East and Europe	0.7	3.6	4.9	4.4
Western Hemisphere	5.1	1.2	3.5	5.0
Countries in transition	-7.6	-1.3	-0.1	1.7
Central and eastern Europe	-3.0	1.4	1.5	2.7
Excluding Belarus and Ukraine	3.0	5.3	3.6	3.1
Russia	-12.6	-4.0	-2.8	0.4
Transcauscasus and central Asia	-10.2	-4.3	1.5	2.2
World trade volume (goods and services)	9.3	9.5	6.6	9.4
Imports				
Advanced economies	9.7	8.9	6.4	8.6
Developing countries	7.1	11.9	9.3	12.1

(Contd.)

Table 4.1 : (Contd.)

	1994	1995	1996	1997
Countries in transition	7.8	18.3	7.6	5.4
Exports				
Advanced economies	8.8	8.8	5.9	9.8
Developing countries	13.2	10.6	8.7	10.8
Countries in transition	8.3	12.3	4.9	3.5
Commodity prices				
Oil[2]				
In SDRs	-7.8	1.9	24.3	-0.9
In U.S. dollars	-5.5	8.0	18.9	-6.0
Non-fuel[3]				
In SDRs	10.8	2.1	3.1	1.6
In U.S. dollars	13.6	8.2	-1.3	-3.7
Consumer prices				
Advanced economies	2.6	2.5	2.4	2.1
Developing countries	50.7	21.7	13.7	8.5
Countries in transition	268.4	124.1	41.4	27.8
Six-month LIBOR (in per cent)[4]				
On U.S. dollar deposits	5.1	6.1	5.6	5.9
On Japanese yen deposits	2.4	1.3	0.7	0.7
On deutsche mark deposits	5.3	4.6	3.3	3.4

1. Indonesia, Malaysia, the Philippines and Thailand.
2. Simple average of spot prices of U.K. Brent, Dubai and West Texas Intermediate crude oil. The average price of oil in U.S. dollars a barrel was $19.18 in 1997; the assumed price is $14.59 in 1998 and $15.94 in 1999.
3. Average, based on world commodity export weights.
4. London interbank offered rate.

In the other advanced economies in the Asia-Pacific region, cyclical positions were generally stronger than in Japan when the Asian crisis erupted. In Australia, growth strengthened during 1997 against a background of subdued inflation, a budget near blanace, and a reduced current account deficit. Partly as a result of the Asian crisis, however, the Australian dollar depreciated substantially against the currencies of other industrial countries late in the year. In Hong Kong SAR, by contrast, competitiveness deteriorated as a result of regional currency depreciations, and interest rates rose sporadically to relatively high levels in the face of intermittent pressures on the currency. These developments, together with the effusion of the regional crisis on trade and confidence, rapidly reduced the over-heating pressure that had emerged in early 1997 and led to a sharp contraction of activity in early 1998. As in Hong Kong SAR, a strong financial sector helped limit the contagion of the regional crisis in Singapore and Taiwan Province of China, although in both significant currency depreciation and marked increases in domestic interest rates occurred.

The advanced economies of North America and Europe were less adversely affected by the Asian crisis. U.S. economic performance in 1997 was exceptionally strong, with GDP growing at 3¾ per cent, the fastest growth in nine years. Furthermore, inflation in terms of the GDP deflator was the lowest in 32 years, unemployment fell to its lowest level in 24 years, and the federal budget was virtually in balance for the first time since the early 1970s. The strength of the U.S. economy provided essential support for global growth in the face of the Asian crisis. The weakening of external demand associated with the Asian crisis, and the strength of the U.S. dollar, dampened potential inflationary pressures in the U.S. economy and shifted the balance of arguments against monetary tightening in late 1997 and early 1998. Canada also experienced strong growth in 1997, but with significant slack remaining, inflation eased further. A considerable widening of the current account deficit, inpart owing to weak global commodity markets, contributed to downward pressures on the Canadian dollar. Official interest rates were raised in late 1997 and in January 1998, mainly to offset the consequences of the currency depreciation for monetary conditions.

Table 4.2 : Net Capital Flows to Developing Countries, Countries in Transition, and Newly Industrialized Economies[1]

(Billions of U.S dollars)

	1984-89[2]	1990-96[2]	1994	1995	1996	1997
Total						
Net private capital flows[3]	15.2	148.1	160.5	192.0	240.8	173.7
Net direct Investment	12.9	63.1	84.3	96.0	114.9	138.2
Net portfolio investment	4.7	54.1	87.8	23.5	49.7	42.9
Other net investment	-2.5	30.9	-11.7	72.5	76.2	-7.3
Net official flows	23.9	15.3	-2.5	34.9	-9.7	27.3
Change in reserves[4]	-13.8	-81.2	-77.2	-120.5	-115.9	-54.7
Developing countries						
Net private capital flows[3]	18.2	131.2	136.6	156.1	207.9	154.7
Net direct investment	12.1	56.8	75.4	84.3	105.0	119.4
Net Portfolio investment	4.2	49.3	85.0	20.6	42.9	40.6
Other net investment	1.9	25.1	-23.8	51.2	60.0	-5.3
Net official flows	25.8	15.6	9.1	27.4	-3.4	15.8
Change in reserves[4]	5.4	-55.7	-42.4	-65.6	-103.4	-55.2
Africa						
Net private capital flows[3]	3.6	4.4	10.6	13.8	4.5	8.9
Net direct investment	1.1	2.9	3.6	4.2	5.3	7.7
Net Portfolio investment	-0.8	-0.2	0.5	1.4	-0.3	2.6
Other net investment	3.3	1.6	6.5	8.1	-0.6	-1.3
Net official flows	5.1	7.1	8.1	5.2	6.5	6.7
Change in reserves[4]	0.2	-1.9	-4.4	-1.4	-6.4	-11.3
Asia						
Net private capital flows[3]	13.0	55.9	63.1	91.8	102.2	38.5
Net direct investment	4.5	32.2	43.4	49.7	58.5	55.4
Net Portfolio investment	1.5	6.8	11.3	10.8	10.2	-2.2

Table 4.2 : (Contd.)

	1984-89[2]	1990-96[2]	1994	1995	1996	1997
Other net investment	7.0	16.9	8.3	31.3	33.5	-14.7
Net official flows	7.7	8.4	6.2	5.1	9.3	17.7
Change in reserves[4]	-2.1	-29.0	-39.7	-29.0	-48.9	-17.2
Middle East and Europe						
Net private capital flows[3]	1.7	25.2	15.5	14.8	20.7	16.1
Net direct investment	1.1	3.0	4.2	5.1	4.3	5.1
Net portfolio investment	4.4	12.8	12.5	8.4	7.9	6.8
Other net investment	-3.8	9.4	-1.2	1.3	8.6	4.2
Net official flows	4.8	-1.8	-1.2	-4.8	-5.8	-1.3
Change in reserves[4]	7.2	-6.4	-3.1	-9.4	-21.2	-14.3
Western Hemisphere						
Net private capital flows[3]	-0.2	45.7	47.4	35.7	80.5	91.1
Net direct investment	5.3	18.7	24.3	25.3	36.9	51.2
Net Portfolio investment	-0.9	29.9	60.6	-0.1	25.2	33.5
Other net investment	-4.6	-2.8	-37.5	10.5	18.5	6.5
Net official flows	8.2	1.8	-4.0	22.0	-13.4	-7.3
Change in reserves[4]	0.5	-18.4	4.7	-25.9	-27.0	-12.3
Countries in transition						
Net private capital flows[3]	-1.0	12.8	18.4	29.8	21.3	34.5
Net direct investment	-0.2	6.3	5.4	13.2	13.1	18.2
Net Portfolio investment	-	2.0	4.1	2.9	2.2	7.3
Other net investment	-0.8	4.6	8.9	13.6	5.9	9.0
Net official flows	0.2	0.5	-11.0	8.4	-5.5	0.8
Change in reserves[4]	-3.6	-7.8	-8.5	-35.9	0.4	-6.2
Newly industrialized economies[5]						
Net private capital flows[3]	-2.0	4.1	5.5	6.1	11.7	-15.4
Net direct investment	1.0	0.1	3.5	-1.5	-3.2	0.6
Net portfolio investment	0.5	2.8	-1.2	0.0	4.6	-5.0
Other net investment	-3.6	1.2	3.2	7.6	10.3	-11.1
Net official flows	-2.0	-0.8	-0.6	-0.9	-0.8	10.7
Change in reserves[4]	-16.0	-17.7	-26.3	-19.0	-12.9	6.7

1. Net capital flows comprise net direct investment, net portfolio investment and other long and short-term net investment flows, including official and private borrowing.
2. Annual averages.
3. Because of data limitations, "other net investment" may include some official flows.
4. A minus sign indicates an increase.
5. Hong Kong SAR, Korea, Singapore, Taiwan Province of China, and Israel.

European countries' cyclical positions continued to diverge notably in 1997 and early 1998. In the United Kingdom, output grew by 3¼ percent in 1997, and unemployment fell by year-end to 5 per cent—a 17-year low. In Germany, France, and Italy, growth strengthened moderately in 1997 after faltering in the two preceding years. Unemployment rates remained high in all three countries but dclined somewhat in France beginning in mid-1997 and in Germany in early 1998. In Germany, growth was driven mainly by continued buoyancy in exports; however, machinery and equipment investment and, subsequently, demand for consumer products picked up. The recovery in France, which also relied heavily on exports, became better balanced, with a pickup in domestic demand emerging in the second half of 1997. Despite a large fiscal correction, growth in Italy also firmed in 1997, with the pickup sustained by a recovery of private consumption, a strengthening of export growth, and a replenishment of inventories. Inflation was less than 2 per cent in Germany, France, and Italy in 1997.

Table 4.3 : Selected Economies: Current Account Positions

(Percent of GDP)

	1995	1996	1997
Advanced economies			
Major industrial countries			
United States	-1.8	-1.9	-2.1
Japan	2.2	1.4	2.2
Germany	-1.0	-0.6	-0.3
France	0.7	1.3	2.7
Italy	2.3	3.2	2.9
United Kingdom	-0.5	-0.1	0.3
Canada	-1.0	0.4	-2.0
Other advanced economies			
Australia	-5.6	-4.0	-3.4
Austria	2.4	-1.8	-1.8
Finland	4.1	3.8	5.3
Greece	-2.1	-2.6	-2.9
Hong Kong SAR[1]	-3.9	-1.3	-1.5
Ireland	2.8	2.0	1.8
Israel	-5.6	-5.6	-3.4
Korea	-2.0	-4.9	-2.0
New Zealand	-3.7	-4.0	-7.0
Norway	3.3	7.1	5.5
Singapore	16.8	15.7	15.2
Spain	0.2	0.3	0.5
Sweden	2.1	2.5	3.1
Switzerland	6.9	7.3	8.3
Taiwan Province of China	2.1	4.0	2.6
Memorandum			
European Union	0.6	1.1	1.4
Developing coutnries			
Algeria	-5.3	2.7	6.7
Argentina	-1.5	-1.9	-3.8
Brazil	-2.5	-3.1	-4.1

Table 4.3 : (Contd.)

	1995	1996	1997
Cameroon	-0.4	-2.4	-1.3
Chile	-2.1	-5.4	-5.3
China	0.2	0.9	2.4
Cote d'Ivoire	-6.0	-4.8	-4.5
Egypt	2.3	-0.3	0.3
India	-1.6	-1.2	-1.5
Indonesia	-3.3	-3.3	-2.6
Malaysia	-10.0	-4.9	-4.8
Mexico	-0.5	-0.2	-1.8
Nigeria	-3.7	2.4	0.4
Pakistan	-3.4	-6.5	-6.0
Philippines	-4.4	-4.7	-5.2
Saudi Arabia	-4.2	0.2	0.2
South Africa	-2.0	-1.3	-1.5
Thailand	-8.0	-7.9	-2.0
Turkey	-0.6	-1.5	-1.7
Uganda	-2.5	-1.8	-0.9
Countries in transition			
Czech Republic	-2.7	-7.6	-6.3
Hungary	-5.7	-3.8	-2.2
Poland[2]	3.3	-1.0	-3.2
Russia	1.3	0.5	-0.3

1. Includes only goods and non-factor services.
2. Based on data for the current balance, including a surplus on unrecorded trade transactions, as estimated by IMF staff.

Elsewhere in continental Europe—Denmark, Finland, Ireland, Luxembourg, the Netherlands, Norway, Portugal, and Spain—economic growth continued strong in 1997 after periods of sluggishness; more convincing expansions emerged in Austria, Belgium and Sweden. In some of these cases, important structural reforms adopted in earlier years underpinned growth, especially with respect to promoting greater flexibility of labour markets. Subdued growth in Switzerland continued a period of stagnation that has spanned almost five years, but activity picked up in the first quarter of 1998. Inflation in these countries remained fairly uniformly low.

In March, 1998, the European Commission determined that 11 of the 15 EU member states had qualified to participate in European Economic and Monetary Union (EMU) in 1999. The Commission based its recommendation (which included as input the European Monetary Institute's convergence report) on its assessment of the countries having met the convergence criteria for 1997 as outlined in the Mastricht Treaty for inflation, public finances, interest rates and exchange rates. Of the other four EU countries, Denmark, Sweden and the United Kingdom had indicated that they did not wish to participate immediately in EMU; the Greek Government aimed to join EMU in 2001. In March 1998, the Drachma joined the exchange rate mechanism (ERM) of the EU, with an announced central parity against the European Currancy Unit (ECU) that implied a depreciation of 12½ per cent; at the same time, the Irish pound was revalued by 3 per cent in terms of its central parity.

Developing Countries

A number of developing countries experienced contagion in their financial markets from the Asian crisis during 1997, and many others began to feel other economic effects from the crisis around the turn of the year, including generally higher risk premiums on foreign credits. These influences aggravated a number of other problems limiting growth, such as loss of competitiveness, lower commodity prices, and domestic and external imbalances. In the developing countries as a group, economic growth slowed to 5 ¾ per cent in 1997 from about 6½ per cent in 1996. The slowdown was significant in Asia, but most marked in Africa. In the developing countries of the Western Hemisphere, in contrast, growth in 1997 was actually stronger than in the previous two years but weakened in the first quarter of 1998. The slower growth was the result of spillovers from the Asian crisis and policy measures to reduce vulnerability to adverse shifts in investor sentiment and to widening current account deficits.

In the Asian region, financial markets in China remained relatively immune to the contagion effects of the crisis, reflecting the country's appropriate macro-economic policies undertaken since 1993, the fact that its capital inflows consisted mainly of direct investment with limited vehicles for financial speculation, and its large foreign exchange reserves. While China's real exchange rate appreciated somewhat as a result of the currency depreciations of its Asian trading partners, its trade position remained strong and the current account continued in surplus. The authorities remained committed to not devaluing the renminbi, a policy critical to restoring stability in the region. Also, inflation remained low following the sharp drop in 1997. In India, output growth declined to about 6 percent in 1997 from about 7½ per cent in 1996. The rupee weakened against the dollar in late 1997, partly because of spillovers from the regional crisis, but its exchange value was little changed on a real multilateral basis. In Pakistan, the government adopted a programme to strengthen macro-economic policies and implemented structural reforms following the widening of macro-economic imbalnces and the threat of a foreign exchange crisis in late 1996 and early 1997.

In Latin America, consumer price inflation declined in Brazil to 4¼ per cent in 1997, while output growth at 3 percent remained much the same as in the previous year. In response to spillovers from Asia, the authorities tightened monetary and fiscal policies significantly in October and November 1997 and thereby restored confidence and halted the drain of foreign exchange reserves. In Argentina, output grew by a robust 8½ per cent, while prices remained broadly stable; as in Brazil, financial market pressures emerged in October, with a significant stock market correction and widening spreads on sovereign debt. In Mexico, the Asian crisis led to a marked increase in exchange market and interest rate volatility. A substantial temporary increase in interest rate helped stabilize the exchange rate, but the peso fell against the dollar in February 1998. In Chile, the peso came under pressure in December but stabilized by late January after moderate foreign exchange market intervention and a sizable increase in interest rates.

For the Middle East and Europe region, the direct spillovers from the Asian crisis were limited, with temporary declines in equity prices in some countries and a widening of interest spreads on internationally traded debt. In the Islamic Republic of Iran, real GDP growth slowed to 3¼ per cent in 1997 from 4¾ per cent in 1996, reflecting stagnant non-oil exports, cutbacks in government capital expenditure associated with a decline in oil revenue, and delays in structural reforms. In Turkey, growth continued close to 7 per cent in 1997, while in Egypt successful efforts at macro-economic stabilization and structural reform in recent years helped growth pick up to 5 per cent. Jordan continued to reap the benefits of successful implementation of stabilization and reform policies, with continued robust growth in output, further declines in inflation, and a narrowing current account deficit.

Economic growth in Africa in 1997 was just 3¼ per cent. The disappointing outcome mainly reflected the impact on a number of countries of poor weather, declines in commodity prices, and, in a few cases, armed conflicts. Among the largest countries in the region, growth in South Africa slowed to 1¾ per cent in 1997, owing to weaknesses in domestic and external demand. Nigeria was also affected by weak domestic demand, worsened by a lack of foreign investor confidence. In Algeria, growth slowed significantly, owing mainly to the impact of drought on agriculture and further delays in the recovery of industrial activity. In Kenya, growth weakened partly as a result of financial market pressures related to political uncertainties. Inflation remained under control in most of the region.

Transition Economies

In 1997, both Russia and the transition countries recorded positive growth for the first time in eight years. For the countries as a group, output grew by 1¾ per cent and inflation was reduced to about 27 per cent—testimony to the progress since early in the decade with stabilization and reform policies in most countries.

Spillovers from the Asian crisis were most apparent in Russia, Ukraine, and, among the Baltic countries, in Estonia. In Russia, where the ruble came under attack in late October and November, and again in late January 1998, the authorities defended the exchange rate by raising interest rates sharply. There were associated steep declines in the stock market. The pressures arose despite an external current account close to balance; they reflected a persistently weak fiscal position characterized by poor revenue collection, concerns about how the external position might evolve if the fiscal imbalance were not dealt with, and the decline in oil prices. In Ukraine, although 1997 appeared to have brought single-digit inflation and positive growth within reach, inadequate fiscal adjustment led to increased reliance on official short-term forein borrowing. Coupled with slow progress on structural reforms, this heightened Ukraine's vulnerability to adverse developments; thus, when the Asian crisis intensified in late 1997, exchange market pressures forced the authorities to tighten monetary conditions sharply. In Estonia, domestic pressures on financial markets, associated with a burgeoning current account deficit, were ggravated by contagion from the Asian crisis. Interest rates rose substantially in October and November 1997, and equity prices, which had earlier risen steeply, dropped sharply.

A numbr of other transition countries experienced little impact from the Asian crisis in their financial markets or in their access to external finance, despite their openness to international capital markets. While the Czech Republic suffered a currency crisis in May 1997, in part triggered by the events in Thailand, it responded by tightening fiscal and monetary policies. The result was a significant narrowing of the Czech current account deficit, albeit at the expense of slower growth, and the subsequent deepening of the Asian crisis brought only limited further turbulence. Hungary also experienced little exchange market pressure from the Asian crisis, owing in no small measure to the country's markedly improved fiscal, growth, and trade performance following the implementation of strong adjustment measures since 1995. In Poland, output grew by about 7 percent in 1997, maintaining the solid expansion of almost six years.

The critical importance of adjustment and reform was highlighted particularly sharply in Albania and Bulgaria. The financial crisis in Bulgaria that had begun in 1996 extended into 1997, and output declined for a second consecutive year. In Albania, the crisis that flared up in March 1997 with the collapse of financial pyramid schemes also led to a drop in output during the year. But in both cases, following significant policy improvements, macro-economic imbalances narrowed and growth resumed toward the end of 1997 and in early 1998. Bulgaria also recorded a dramatic decline in inflation in 1997, with the currency board arrangement introduced as part of the IMF-supported program playing a central role.

3. WORLD ECONOMIC OUTLOOK

The Executive Board regularly reviews global economic developments and policies, based on World Economic Outlook reports prepared by the staff. The reports, which are usually published twice a year, contain comprehensive analyses both of prospects for the world economy and for individual countries and regions, and of topical issues.

In 1997-98, the Board held three discussions on the World Economic Outlook: in August 1997, December 1997 (on the basis of an "Interim Assessment" by the staff), and March 1998.[4] The central focus was the Asian financial crisis.[5] In August 1997, a number of Directors had already cautioned that, while there were many reasons to believe the world expansion could be sustained, there was no room for complacency about the risks and fragilities confronting individual countries that could affect regional and global economic and financial conditions. Especially in the developing world, large external imbalances and fragile banking systems, several Directors noted, had adversely affected investor confidence and heightened the risks assoicated with volatile capital movements. These difficulties were not expected to affect the generally positive long-term prospects of those countries, provided that disciplined macroeconomic policies and the necessary structural reforms were implemented on a timely basis to ensure the elimination of unsustainable economic imbalances. Directors stressed, however, that those policy efforts would have to be supported by a broader range of institutional reforms aimed at increasing the efficiency of public administration, developing human capital, strengthening financial sector management, setting up transparent regulatory and legal systems, and improving governance. Such reforms would help establish and maintain private sector and investor confidence, which are critical for sustained, high-quality growth.

In their March 1998 discussion, Executive Directors agreed that, while the

---

4. The three reports were published as IMF, *World Economic Outlook*, issues dated October and December 1997 (the latter subtitled Interim Assesement) and May 1998.
5. Chapter V reviews the Board's discussion of the causes and appropriate policy responses to the crisis.

financial market turmoil in Asia would have a significant negative impact on short-term growth prospects for the world economy, the slow-down was likely to be less pronounced than in earlier episodes of global economic weakness (in 1974-75, 1980-83 and 1990-91). Corrective actions by most countries at or near the center of the turmoil, the robust economic performance of most industrial countries, and policy reforms in many developing and transition economies over the past decade were seen as critical in containing the crisis and its global repercussions. Although growth projections for countries at the center of the crisis had been lowered considerably since the August 1997 discussion of the World Economic Outlook, Directors in March 1998 felt that prospects for other developing and transition economies remained generally encouraging.

This said, Directors noted that uncertainty still remained regarding the resolution of the crisis; resolute implementation of reforms by the crisis countries was therefore essential. Recent declines in oil and other commodity prices, moreover, could lengthen the adjustment process in some crisis countries and pose considerable challenges for commodity and oil-exporting countries in all regions. Also in re-evaluation of risks by international lenders as a result of the crisis, while welcomed, could limit financial flows to developing and transition economies to levels below those justified by the fundamentals. More generally, Dirctors were concerned that some emerging market economies had relied too heavily on foreign borrowing and short-term instruments to finance public deficits, thus increasing their risk of future financing difficulties.

Advanced Economies

In their March 1998 review of the outlook for the advanced economies, Directors observed that the spillovers from the Asian crisis for Japan were particularly unwelcome, given that its nascent recovery had already stalled in the first half of 1997; this stalling was due both to a fiscal policy that, in hindsight, was overly tight and to continuing fragilities in the financial system. Directors stresed that boosting confidence and fostering stronger sustainable growth in Japan—through a combination of macro-economic, financial sector, and structural policies—was critical, given the economy's importance for the region and for the world. Economic recovery should be supported by a more expansionary fiscal stance in the near term, while maintaining the objective of medium-term consolidation. Some Directors noted that a permanent tax cut would boost the prospects for an increase in private consumption but cautioned against overreliance on increased public works spending since it would have only a temporary impact and had not proven very effective in the past. In contrast, some other Directors expressed reservations about the effectiveness of tax cuts, fearing that the increase in disposable income might be added to household saving with little or no effect on consumption and growth. Pointing to the government debt accumulated in recent years and the prospective fiscal pressures associated with an aging population, some Directors argued that any backsliding with fiscal consolidation would pose risks while having little positive effect on activity.

Directors noted indications from the Japanese authorities that a substantial fiscal stimulus package would soon be announceed. They emphasized that, to have significant and durable effects, the measures needed to be accompanied by serious regulatory and financial sector reforms. Most Directors welcomed recently announced measures committing public funds to protect depositors of failed institutions and to recapitalize viable ones. These measures promised to restore public confidence and strengthen banks' willingness to lend. Directors cautioned, however, against indiscriminate support to banks where closures or consolidation were more appropriate. They suggested that any further allocation of public funds be accompanied by clear measures to facilitate the write-off of bad bank loans to ensure a fair sharing of the burden of restructuring costs and to limit moral hazard. At its April 1998 meeting, the Interim Committee welcomed the Japanese economic policy package, as well as Japan's steps to strengthen its financial system.

Directors agreed that the U.S. economy, in contrast to the Japanese economy, was likely to suffer relatively little from adverse developments in Asia, owing largely to the strength of its cyclical position prior to the crisis and to the positive developments in bond markets, which, in the view of many Directors, reflected a "flight to quality" of international investment flows. They judged the current stance of monetary policy as appropriate, noting that the moderating effects of the Asian crisis—together with the appreciation of the U.S. dollar and the decline in world commodity prices—had alleviated the need for an increase in official interest rates. In view of the tightening labor market conditions, however, the authorities would need to monitor the situation closely, looking for signs that would tip the balance of monetary policy assessment in either direction.

The risks posed by the Asian crisis for the advanced economies in Europe were also likely to be relatively small, Directors agreed. Among the economies operating near full capacity, Directors believed that the previous year's monetary tightening and continued fiscal consolidation in the United Kingdom were likely to keep demand close to productive capacity limits and hold inflation near to target. But further action would be warrantd if inflation prospects worsened. In the same vein, the Interim Committee in its April 1998 meeting emphasised the need for the U.K. authorities to remain vigilant as always to inflation risks. In Germany, France and Italy, where output—while remaining below potential—had recovered quite well since the beginning of 1997, Directors expected the overall impact of the Asian crisis also to be small. Some Directors, however, cautioned against overoptimism, noting that exports had been the main source of demand growth in some of these countries. A weakening of export markets could slow, and possibly stall, the recovery if domestic demand did not pick up. In continental Europe generally, with monetary union among a large number of countries scheduled to begin in nine months, attention had to be given to labor and product market reforms, to continuing fiscal consolidation, and to monetary policy in the transition period.

Developing and Transition Countries

Directors noted that the Asian crisis was affecting most developing and transition economies, albeit to varying degrees. The effects were being felt through, for example, increases in risk premiums in borrowing costs, lower commodity prices, losses in competitiveness to countries at or near the center of the turmoil, or the slowdown in demand in those countries. Several countries—including Brazil, Chile, the Czech Republic and Mexico—that had suffered exchange market pressures in connection with the Asian crisis had been able to avoid full contagion through appropriate policy adjustments. Although these countries had generally weathered the crisis well, Directors felt it prudent for them to continue strengthening policies to avoid further challenges down the road. In this connection, it was particularly important to contain external imbalances, avoid overheating, and enhance the quality and timeliness of economic and financial information generally. Also critical was a strong financial sector infrastructure, including prudential regulation, internationally accepted accounting standards, and, for some, pre-established exit rules regarding shifting from a fixed exchange regime to a flexible one (see Chapter VI). Several Directors welcomed China's commitment not to devalue its currency and its efforts to strengthen its banking system.

Many Directors expressed concern about recent trends in commodity prices and the potentially adverse implications for commodity-exporting developing countries of both a deterioration in the terms of trade and increased price volatility. For Africa, the impact of these forces, combined with poor weather and the continuing heavy debt burden, was of particular concern. Nevertheless, Directors remained cautiously optimistic about Africa's growth prospects, based on the expectation of continued implementation of macroeconomic adjustment and structural reforms and of an appropriate flow of foreign assistance. Directors underscored the need to promote a favourable environment for foreign direct investment, including through a further opening up of their economies.

Regarding the economies in transition, Directors expressed satisfaction that both Russia and the transition countries as a group had recorded positive growth in 1997 for the first time since the transition began. They noted, however, that although considerable progress was being made in macro-economic stabilization in virtually all countries, differences in the pace of reform and progress in transformation appeared to have grown larger. Most countries had made substantial progress toward reasonable fiscal balance, but sizable deficits continued to be registered in a number of countries, including Russia and Ukraine. Financing these deficits through foreign currency and short-term borrowing, Directors observed, put the sustainability of fiscal policies in question, indirectly threatened to undermine the soundness of banking sectors, and endangered hard-earned economic stabilization achievements. Severe revenue collection problems in a number of transition countries, moreover, were preventing governments from carrying out their proper functions. Further tax policy reform and improvements in tax administration were unlikely to show their full effect, Directors recognized, unless the political will to collect taxes was also strengthened. Directors also advised central and eastern European transition countries to improve the cost-effectiveness of their social security and welfare systems, and thereby reduce the overall level of government spending.

5

UNITED NATIONS TRADE AND DEVELOPMENT REPORT, 1998

Introduction

The present Report examines current performance and prospects in the world economy with special reference to the financial crisis that has rocked the world and has challenged policy-makers everywhere over the past year. It assesses the causes of the current crisis and its consequences, particularly for developing countries, and puts forward recommendations on how future crisis might be prevented.

Overview

As financial markets expand and integration deepens, each episode of crisis comes with greater force inflicting greater damage the real economy. The cost of crisis in East Asia is about 1 per cent of global output this year alone or some $260 billion, equivalent to the annual income of sub-Saharan Africa. Prospects for the years ahead are extremely uncertain, but the risks are on the downside. Further, policy errors might well drive the world economy into a deep recession.

International financial instability and the world economy

For some time the UNCTAD secretariat has maintained that the world economy needs to grow by at least 3 per cent, year in, year out, if a dent is to be made in unemployment in industrialized countries and poverty in developing countries. Most countries in the South need to grow at twice this rate if they are to overcome their social and technological handicaps and close the income gap with the small club of rich industrial economies. During the 1990s this 3 per cent target has been reached only in 1996-97, thanks to recovery in Latin America and Africa and continued strong growth in East Asia and the United States.

Last year's *Trade and Development Report* argued that international financial instability censtituted the single most important impediment to attaining steady and rapid growth. Modern financial markets are organized less to create wealth and employment than to extract rent by buying and selling second-hand assets, and the "discipline" these markets exert on policymakers reinforces the advantages of existing wealth holders. The *Report* came out once more against "big-bang" financial liberalization in developing countries, pointing out that successful examples of modern industrialization and development distinguished themselves by the way they managed integration into the global economy.

The dramatic turnaround in the economic fortunes of the East Asian economies leaves this conclusion unshaken. Contrary to the tenets of financial orthodoxy, the problems of those countries do not stem from resistance to a globalizing world and the discipline of global market forces. Rather, the crisis occurred because governments failed to manage integration into global capital markets with the same prudence and skill they had earlier shown in managing trade liberalization. Throwing caution to the wind, the voices of orthodoxy ordained even larger doses of financial liberalization.

The speed at which some of the most successful developing countries in East Asia have been derailed by volatile financial flows has taken the international community by surprise. During the annual meeting of the Bretton Woods institutions in Hong Kong, China, in September 1997, it was generally held that the ongoing disturbances were no more than a blip and would cause only a temporary slowdown of growth in the region. The IMF indicated that it expected growth to accelerate in 1998 in Thailand, and to remain broadly unchanged in other countries of the region. Even in its *Interim Assessment* of December 1997, the Republic of Korea and the countries of ASEAN, with the exception of Thailand, were expected to register positive growth in 1998. Since then, estimates have been constantly lowered, both for the region and for the world economy as a whole, as the promises of the policies adopted in response to the crisis failed to be fulfilled.

Countries that year after year enjoyed growth rates of 8 to 10 per cent annum, maintained full employment and went a long way towards eradicating poverty are now suffering a severe economic contraction. Output is projected to decline for 1998 as a whole by at least 12 per cent in Indonesia and by 6 to 8 per cent in the Republic of Korea and Thailand. With the exception of China and its Taiwan Province, no country in the region can expect to register satisfactory growth this year. Expectations of a quick recovery have had to be pushed back several years into the future.

Clearly, and although there are no simple remedies, the international community has yet to learn how to manage such turmoil, let alone prevent it. Indeed, the international policy response has contributed to the severity of the crisis by failing to appreciate the full gravity of the situation, and by placing too much faith in conventional policy prescriptions. While the rash of bank closures undermined confidence throughout East Asia, the hike in interest rates failed to restore it. Rather, while unsuccessful in stopping the downward spiral in exchange rates, high interest rates added to the woes of debtors, forcing them to cut down on their activity and liquidate assets, while economies were driven into deep recession. Nor was confidence helped by official pronouncements on the alleged structural weaknesses of the economies in crisis. External financing was used not to support the domestic currency and stop the exchange rate losses of unhedged debtors, but to maintain convertibility and free capital flows. The credit crunch has bitten so deep that, despite favourable exchange rates, exports have stagnated or fallen as access to trade credit was drastically curtailed.

A strategy of introducing a standstill and bringing borrowers and lenders together with a view to rescheduling debt before committing external funds did not find favour, apparently for fear that the crisis would spread. But the course chosen did not prevent contagion. Rather, it precipitated the translation of what was intitially a liquidity crisis into a solvency crisis, leaving behind a large stock of debt, part of which now appears to be unpayable.

A few lessons are now evident. First, the worst time to "reform" a financial system is in the middle of a crisis. Second, when currency turmoil is associated with financial difficulties, raising interest rates over an extended period may simply worsen the situation by bringing about widespread corporate and bank insolvencies. Finally, currencies should not be left to sink while funds are used to bail out the international creditors.

The events of the past year should serve to underline the warning in last year's *Trade and Development Report* of a potential backlash against the contradictions of a globalizing world. When a colossal global market failure and measures taken to bail out creditors are paid for at the expense of the living standards of ordinary people, and of stability and development in the debtor developing countries concerned, who is to say that justice has been served?

In East Asia the trend of decades of rising incomes has been reversed, and unemployment, under-employment and poverty are reaching alarming levels. Many of the lost jobs have been in sectors that had helped to reduce poverty by absorbing low-skilled workers from the countryside. Rising food prices and falling social expenditures have further aggravated social conditions and contributed to growing poverty. Even on conservative estimates, the proportion of the Indonesian population living on incomes below the poverty line in 1998 is expected to be at least 50 per cent greater than in 1996. Similarly, poverty in Thailand can be expected to increase by at least one third.

As the crisis drags on, it will be increasingly difficult for the new poor to recover from deprivation and return to their previous occupations and living standards. Moreover, the social harm could persist long after economic recovery is achieved. Judging from the mounting evidence of growing child malnutrition and declining primary school enrolments, the impact of the crisis on human resources will spill over into future generations.

Safety net measures can act as palliatives to cushion the impact of the crisis on poor and vulnerable groups, but they are in no way a lasting solution. Only the resumptin of rapid and sustained growth can bring unemployment and poverty levels back down to pre-crisis levels. Policy should turn from deflation to reflation, supporting the unemployed by lowering interest rates, expanding liquidity and raising public expenditure, thus breaking out of a vicious circle that could do incalculable harm.

Global Remifications

The consequences of the East Asian crisis for global growth and development will depend on the course taken by international trade and capital flows. A precise assessment is difficult, not only because of the complexities of global interdependence, but also because of the fickle nature of financial market sentiments, and uncertainties regarding policy response in other countries. However, the deflationary impact of the crisis is proving deeper than initially expected. Current projections for 1998 suggest a drop of at least one percentage point (at market exchange rates) in world output growth from the rate reached in 1997.

The revisions to estimated GDP growth have been more substantial for developing than for developed countries. Growth in developing countries in 1998 is expected to be half that of 1997, falling to less than 2.5 per cent. In view of the bleak prospects for recovery in East Asia, the tendency noted in *TDR 1997* for the income gap between North and South to widen can be expected to continue. For the first time for many years, growth in the developing world, excluding China, will fall below that of the developed world. Even in China it is unlikely to exceed 6 per cent, which would be only about one half of the average rate achieved since the beginning of the decade.

Developing countries are trapped in a corner. To lessen the risk of contagion, many emerging markets have introduced pre-emptive monetary and fiscal restrictions in an attempt to maintain market confidence and to reduce their vulnerability to a reversal of capital flows. In so doing they have choked domestic demand and lowered growth prospects still further.

According to current projections by some financial institutions no significant declines are expected in capital flows to emerging markets in Latin America and Eastern Europe. Nevertheless, it is notable that the spreads on bonds of such emerging markets that went up sharply last autumn have not come down significantly. Many emerging-market currencies are now trading at all-time lows against the dollar, despite hikes in domestic interest rates. The fruits of the hard work of the developing world, both assets and goods, are now going for a song. But they may decline even further in value before the appetite for risk of global investors returns. Flight to safety appears to underline much of the recent boom in bond prices and the continued stock market rally in the United States.

Since East Asia accounts for a quarter of world trade, much of the global impact of the crisis will be transmitted through changes in trade flows. The impact will depend primarily on what happens to exports to the region, shifts in relative competitive positions in third markets and, more importantly, the effect of the crisis on commodity prices.

By the spring of 1998, the East Asian countries most directly affected by the crisis had undergone an import compression in the order of 30 to 40 per cent, while their exports had stagnated or fallen. Other Asian developing countries have exhibited similar trends, though to a lesser extent. In consequence, world trade, which grew in volume by 9.5 per cent in 1997, the second highest rate in two decades, can be expected to grow much more slowly in the current year.

There is considerable variation among developing countries in their dependence on Asian markets for exports. Those markets absorb, on average, about 10 per cent of Latin America's total merchandise exports; the proportion is as high as 25 per cent for Peru and over 38 per cent for Chile. Also, almost 60 per cent of total Latin American exports to OECD countries are potentially vulnerable to Asian competition. While competition in third markets is less important for African countries, a number of them depend directly on East Asia for 25-35 per cent of their total export earnings.

East Asian economies provide important markets for metals, agricultural raw materials and energy products, both for domestic consumption and as inputs into their export industries. Thus, reduced or sluggish exports and cut-backs in domestic absorption are expected to exert a major influence on the prices of such commodities. By contrast, increases in East Asian exports of a small number of commodities may have only a limited impact on world commodity markets.

While other influences have certainly been at work, the crisis in East Asia is the single most important factor in the recent downturn in commodity prices. Non-oil prices, which had begun to decline in 1996 after two years of sustained increase, started to level off in 1997. However, with the outbreak of the crisis, further downward pressures were evident. Between June 1997 and April 1998, non-oil commodity prices declined by some 10 per cent At one point in late spring 1998, the price of oil was down by over 40 per cent from its peak in 1997.

From Chile, Jamaica, Paraguay and Peru in Latin America to Gabon, Sudan,

United Republic of Tanzania and Zambia in Africa, and to Kazakhstan, Mongolia and Myanmar in Asia, developing countries in all regions are dependent, to varying degrees, on metals and agricultural raw materials for much of their export earnings. The loss of export earnings may be as much as one quarter for some of these countries, corresponding to as much as 12 per cent of GDP in some cases. For oil exporters, expected shortfalls are equally or even more dramatic.

Declines in export earnings are already forcing cuts in government spending in countries where they are an important source of fiscal revenue, such as Chile and Mexico. They are also hurting major developed-country commodity exporters such as Australia, Canada and New Zealand, exerting pressure on their currencies. By contrast, in major industrial countries, partcularly in the United States and Western Europe, the benefits of declining commodity prices and improving terms of trade appear, so far, to have outweighed the loss of earnings due to lower exports to East Asia. However, the longer-term impact of adjustment of the external balances of the Asian economies is expected to be quite different.

Latin America is perhaps the region most susceptible to adverse influences from East Asia. Growth is expected to slow to around 3 per cent on average, following the highest rate attained for a quarter of a century in 1997. Even so, current account deficits are expected to continue to rise. Latin America thus remains particularly vulnerable to an interruption of capital inflows.

In Africa, growth had already slowed down in 1997 due to declining commodity prices and adverse weather conditions. The impact of the crisis can be expected to vary considerably among countries, oil and food importers will benefit from lower prices, while exporters of metals and oil and other fuels are particularly vulnerable. For sub-Saharan Africa growth in 1998 is not expected to be much higher than in 1997, and even this forecast may be over-optimistic.

The impact of the crisis on transition economies will occur in large part through declines in prices of energy products. However, in view of the structural weaknesses in its financial system and of fiscal imbalances, the Russian Federation is particularly vulnerable to shifts in market sentiment, and its currency and stock markets have already suffered large declines. Many Central and Eastern European economies are not directly affected by the crisis because of weak trade linkages, and the region as a whole is expected to register a positive, though moderate, growth rate for the second successive year since the beginning of the transition, although there is considerable uncertainty surrounding prospects for the Federation.

Coming on top of a possible cyclical slowdown, the impact of the East Asian crisis on the United States economy may be quite important. The economy continued to grow vigorously in 1997, driven by private spending in excess of incomes. Inflation continued to fall even though growth exceeded by a wide margin the rate officially considered to be compatible with stable inflation. The process of adjustment in East Asia, the appreciation of the dollar, and lower commodity prices all contribute to lower inflation, but by the same token they lower incomes and purchasing power in United States export markets, with the result that there is likely to be a substantial increase in the United States trade deficit. Private spending cannot be expected to continue at the recent pace, while the fiscal surplus will be a drag on economic activity. All in all, it is probable that growth of the economy will slow down significantly in the second half of the year.

This prognosis of a benign slowing of the United States economy could be upset by financial factors. Since the extended period of recovery has been associated with an expansion of bank lending, the slowing down of growth may create repayment difficulties for many borrowers. Furthermore, declining company earnings and margins may lead to a reassessment of the level of equity prices. Difficulty in servicing bank loans or a sharp correction in stock prices would reinforce the existing deflationary impulses and lead to a rougher landing than currently foreseen.

Should domestic demand slow down sharply, the contribution of the United States to the growth of global demand would fall even as the trade deficit widened. There would consequently be an enlargement of the global demand gap brought about by the crisis in East Asia and the sharp swing in trade balances of the region. Any such gap is unlikely to be filled by strong demand in Europe or Japan. In the European Union, with the exception of the United Kingdom, growth has so far depended on exports, and the Asian crisis is expected to reduce both output and export growth by over 0.5 percentage points. The situation in the United Kingdom is similar to that of the United States, although inflation is faster. In the other major European Union countries exports to Asia have started to decline rapidly. Thus, any recovery in domestic demand would only replace the decline in net exports without creating any additional stimulus. Moreover, the uniform monetary policy of the newly operative European Central Bank cannot be expected to provide any stimulus to demand in the earlier stages of monetary union, but to err on the side of deflation rather than inflation.

Recovery of the Japanese economy will be crucial to recovery in the rest of Asia. The current recession in Japan has prevented it from playing the same role as that of the United States during the Mexican recovery. Despite the recently introduced package of public expenditures and tax cuts, growth is expected to remain negative for the year. A policy of relying on yen devaluation to boost external demand would create a risk of further currency instability in the region, and in international financial markets more generally. Without a strong recovery in domestic demand Japan will not be able to provide an expanding export market for other Asian economies.

However, there is no reason why Japan could not provide considerable external financing to those countries in the form of long-term lending. The impact of such lending would most likely be greater on growth in Japan itself, as well as in the newly industrializing economies (NIEs), than a domestic fiscal package of an equal magnitude, since the money would largely be recycled to Japan in the form of increased imports. Indeed, a regional approach could prove a more effective way of dealing with the crisis than has so far been the case under standard multilateral initiatives.

Because of the nature of the crisis, recovery in East Asia is likely to be much slower than it was in Mexico after 1995. A crisis of over-investment and financial fragility is more difficult to resolve than one of over-consumption. Restructuring balance sheets and adjusting the stock of debt and assets takes much longer than a realignment of consumer spending.

Perhaps the worst possible outcome of the crisis is further bouts of financial instability in emerging markets, a large correction of equity prices in the major industrial countries, together with a sharp slowdown in the United States economy, prolonged recession in East Asian NIEs and Japan and increased trade imbalances in the major industrial countries. Any such outcome would put increased pressure on banking systems in the developed world. The result might not only be a world economy in deep recession, but also a re-emergence of trade conflicts that could wreak havoc. If that is to be avoided, countries in surplus, namely Japan and the members of the European Union, must increase their contribution to world demand, and deflationary policies in East Asia must be reversed.

Management of Financial Crises

The East Asian experience has laid bare certain weaknesses in the international approach to the management of crises involving sudden withdrawal of foreign capital and massive and sustained attacks on the currency. As a result of this approach, what appeared to be a liquidity crisis has been translated into a solvency crisis, through a collapse of currencies and asset prices. This process hurts not only those with external liabilities but also the economy as a whole, owing to its effects on output and employment.

There are four possible lines of defence against an attack on the currency:

(i) Domestic policies, primarily monetary policy;
(ii) Maintaining a sufficiently high level of precautionary foreign reserves and credit lines;
(iii) Recourse to an international lender of last resort; and
(iv) Imposition of a debt standstill and exchange restrictions, accompanied by initiation of negotiations for a rapid debt workout.

Under normal conditions, interest rate differentials are important determinants of international capital movements, and monetary policy can alter the incentives for capital flows. However, as events in East Asia have shown, under conditions of panic, the effects of monetary tightening can be quite different, since interest rate hikes may simply point to declining creditworthiness and greater default risk. Intensified difficulties among debtors can eventually lead to exchange-rate stabilization owing to the resulting squeeze on sales of domestic currency, but at the expense of depressing the economy rather than through bringing back foreign capital.

Maintenance of precautionary reserves or credit lines in amounts adequate to meet outflows during a currency attack poses problems of cost and feasibility. One way of accumulating reserves for this purpose would be to sterilize some of the capital inflow, i.e. to purchase it with the proceeds of domestically issued debt. But such a strategy is likely to entail two sorts of costs: firstly, there is a cost to the economy as a whole, since the rate of interest on foreign loans usually exceeds the return on foreign reserves; and, secondly, there is a cost to the public sector, since the real interest on government debt typically also exceeds the return on reserves.

Alternative approaches might be to cover the short-term external liabilities of the private sector by long-term public borrowing matched by short-term investment abroad, or to arrange a private lender of last resort. But the borrowing or credit lines could be very large, especially if allowance is made also for withdrawals by non-residents from stocks and bonds. Moreover, a country may not have access to such borrowing or credit lines, and there is no assurance that monies under credit lines would be available as needed. Besides, net costs in both cases could be substantial.

Financial assistance coordinated by the IMF in recent years has usually come only after the collapse of the currency, and has taken the form of bailouts designed to meet the demands of creditors and to prevent defaults. Such operations have a number of drawbacks: they protect creditors from bearing the costs of their decisions, thus shifting the entire burden to debtors and creating moral hazard for creditors; and by securing *ex-post* public guarantees for private debt they reduce perceived default risks. More importantly, the sums required have been increasing and are reaching the limits of political acceptability in countries providing them. This is also one of the main impediments to the establishment of a genuine lender-of-resort facility which would stabilize currency markets and thus avoid the transformation of currency attacks into solvency crises.

In the absence of timely provision of adequate liquidity to counter attacks on a currency, a liquidity crisis will eventually lead to widespread defaults and bankruptcies. The most effective way to prevent such an outcome would be through extension and application of insolvency principles such as those in chapter 11 of the United States Bankruptcy Code. Based on the premise that the value of a firm as a going concern exceeds that of its assets in the event of liquidation, those principles are designed to address financial restructuring rather than liquidation. The procedures allow for a stand-still on debt servicing in order to provide the debtor (who is left in possession) with a breathing space from its creditors, and so prevent a "grab race" for assets that is likely to be detrimental not only to the debtor but also to unprotected creditors. The debtor thus has an oppottunity to formulate a debt reorganization plan, and equal treatment for creditors is also guaranteed. During the reorganization the debtor is provided with access to the working capital needed for its operations, by granting a seniority status to the new debt contracted. Reorganization is followed by resolution, and insolvency procedures may accelerate the process by discouraging holding-out by particular classes of creditors.

The application of such principles to international debtors was raised in *TDR 1986* during the sovereign debt crisis. It was there noted that under such conditions, the debtors "experience the financial and economic stigma of being judged *de facto* bankrupt, with all the consequences that this entails as regards creditworthiness and future access to credits. At the same time, they are largely without the benefits of receiving the financial relief and financial reorganization that would accompany a *de jure* bankruptcy handled in a manner similar to chapter 11 of the United States Bankruptcy Code".

The increasingly private character of external debt in developing countries has not only increased the likelihood of harmful debt runs and asset-grab races by creditors and investors, but also has given greater pertinence to these bankruptcy principles in the management and resolution of international debt crises. However, a ful-fledged international chapter 11 is neither practical nor necessary. Article VIII of the Articles of Agreement of IMF may provide a statutory basis for the application of debt standstills through the imposition of exchange controls if a currency comes under attack, and it can be combined with the existing practices for restructuring debt through negotiations.

While standstills could be sanctioned by IMF, a conflict of interest might arise since countries affected by its decisions are also its shareholders and the Fund itself is often a creditor. It may be desirable to place standstill authority with an independent panel whose rulings would have legal force in national courts. A standstill could be decided unilaterally by the debtor country facing an attack on its currency, once its reserves or currency fall below a certain threshold, and then be submitted for approval to the panel within a specified period. Such a procedure would halp to avoid a panic, and be similar to GATT safeguard provisions allowing countries to take emergency actions. During the standstill and the subsequent negotiation of a debt reorganization debtor-in-possession financing could be provided by IMF "lending into arrears", which would require much smaller sums than bailout operations.

Procedures of this kind would meet the need once again evident in the East Asian crisis to safeguard debtor countries from the over-reaction of financial markets. In the words of the New York Court of Appeals, which had once ruled in favour of a debtor government that had imposed a unilateral standstill, this would be "in entire harmony with the spirit of bankruptcy laws, the binding force of which ... is recognized by all civilized nations."

Prevention of Financial Crises

The crisis in East Asia has once again focused the attention of the international community on ways and means of preventing such crises. A number of proposals have been made for measures to be taken at global, national and regional levels. However, global initiatives regarding the international financial system have not gone to the root cause of the problem. On the contrary, some such initiatives could reduce the autonomy and flexibility of national policy-makers in introducing measures needed to protect their economies from volatile and speculative capital flows.

With greater integration of financial markets and increased scope for contagion, the international surveillance of national policies has gained added importance in ensuring the stability of the international monetary and financial system. However, it has so far been unsuccessful in preventing international financial crises and currency turmoil; not is it clear that recently proposed improvements will lead to more effective implementation:

- Major financial crises are typically connected to large shifts in macroeconomic conditions external to countries where the crisis originated. External factors are as important as domestic ones in triggering both capital inflows and capital outflows. However, existing modalities do not address the problems of policy surveillance due to unidirectional impulses from changes in the monetary policies of the United States and a few other OECD countries which exert a strong influence on capital movements and exchange rates. There are no mechanisms under the existing system of global economic governance for dispute settlement or redress regarding these impulses;
- The focus of attention of the proposed improvements in surveillance continues to be the role of domestic policies in generating financial fragility and crisis. However, even in this more limited area, the record has been mixed, in large part because of the tendency to ignore that markets can go wrong;
- While improvements in the timeliness and quality of information concerning key macroeconomic and financial variables is essential for effective surveillance, emphasis on the inadequacy of information as the major reason for the failure to forecast the East Asian crisis appears

> misplaced or exaggerated. Although the crisis has pointed to certain weaknesses in available information, these did not play an essential role. Rather, there was inadequate evaluation of the implications of the available data, including those in the periodic reports of BIS, for countries' ability to continue to obtain funding from international financial markets.

Similarly, the contribution to the East Asian crisis of weaknesses in domestic financial regulation and supervision has led to increased attention to reform in this area. However, while such reform can reduce the likelihood of financial crises, experience indicates that, owing to the vulnerability of the financial sector to changes in economic conditions and to unavoidable imperfections in the regulatory process itself, even a state-of-the-art system of financial regulation does not provide fail-safe crisis prevention.

There are serious weaknesses in the regulatory framework for cross-border lending and investment at the source of such flows. They have been an important cause of the shifting of a disproportionate share of the cost of resulting crises onto debtors. A number of proposals have been made for new rules and institutions directed at exerting tighter control over international lenders and investors. While some could be adopted without major changes in existing institutions and policy regimes, other would require, to varying degrees, new and far-reaching international agreements, which might be difficult to achieve owing to uncertainties with regard to their effectiveness or to the concentration of power which they would entail.

Collaboration and consultation at the regional level are capable of contributing to the prevention of financial crises. Their potential role is particularly important with respect to the prevention of currency disorders and contagion effects. Initiatives in this area, which may involve monitoring mechanisms or more ambitious arrangements linked to the provision of mutual external financial support, can benefit from the long and wide-ranging experience of the European Union.

However, none of these proposals for crisis prevention is capable of eliminating the need for active national policies in respect of the balance of payments and external liabilities. In this respect exchange rate policies and controls over capital movements merit particular attention.

There is no reason to condemn managed-exchange-rate regimes and sacrifice currency stability in the interest of free capital mobility. The alternative of freely floating rates, combined with capital mobility, would undermine currency stability with attendant consequences for trade, investment and growth. A currency board system can eliminate problems for debt management due to currency mismatches, and has proved a useful vehicle in certain countries for halting hyperinflation. But such systems do not insulate economies from instability of external origin, since the effects of capital inflows and outflows are transmitted to levels of economic activity and to goods and assets prices, and may include threats to banking stability.

However, managed-exchange-rate regimes are vulnerable to large accumulations of short-term external debt and to other potentially volatile capital inflows. Even if used flexibly, such regimes are likely to be sustainable only if accompanied by active management of external liabilities, which may often entail recourse to capital controls.

Capital controls are a tried technique for dealing with unstable capital movements. The measures traditionally focused mainly on cross-border transactions of residents and non-residents. However, owing to deregulation and recent developments in banking technique, accounts and transactions denominated in foreign currencies are now often available to residents. Since they can affect macroeconomic variables such as the exchange rate in much the same way as cross-border transactions, they are also a legitimate target for controls. Postwar experience has been marked by frequent use of such controls in industrial countries, and they have also played an important role in policies adopted by several developing countries during recent years in response to large capital inflows.

The extent of successful recourse to capital controls suggests that current initiatives aiming to restrict national freedom of action in this area are inappropriate. The probability of financial crises can be reduced by better macroeconomic fundamentals, effective prudential regulation and supervision of the financial system, and improved corporate governance. But these entail structural reforms with an unavoidably long time-scale: in industrial countries decades were typically required to complete such reforms and to build the institutions needed. Moreover, such actions at national level will not provide fail-safe insulation against currency attacks, which also respond to conditions in international financial markets and in the countries of international lenders and investors. The harm inflicted by currency attacks could be contained by new arrangements for crisis management such as a proper international lender of last resort or a framework for debt standstills and work-outs, but these too are powerless to prevent them from starting and causing damage. Thus, in the absence of global mechanisms for stabilizing capital flows, controls will remain an indispensable part of developing countries' armoury of measures for the purpose of protection against international financial instability, so that for the foreseeable future flexibility regarding governments' options rather the imposition of new constraints is required.

THE WORLD ECONOMY : PERFORMANCE AND PROSPECTS : GLOBAL TRENDS

1. World Output

The East Asian crisis has come at a time when certain weaknesses and imbalances in the global economy were also prevalent. Before the crisis, global growth depended on expansion in the United States and East Asia. With the notable exceptions of China and its Taiwan Province, the fast-growing economies of East Asia, together with the United States, were the major contributors to global demand, running large external deficits financed by private capital inflows. In virtually all industrial countries except the United States and the United Kingdom exports were the engine of faster growth, especially so in Japan and continental Europe, where domestic demand was sluggish owing to restrictive fiscal policies. These disparities were reflected in increased exchange rate instability and trade imbalances, with Western Europe and Japan running large surpluses.

In East Asia the attempt to adjust exchange rates and reduce external deficits to sustain rapid growth has had the opposite effect: it has eliminated or reduced the deficits but only by disrupting growth. The East Asian crisis has thus increased the magnitude of the global demand gap and produced even greater trade imbalances and currency volatility. The policy response, in turn, has done nothing to alleviate the risks to global trade and growth posed by these imbalances;

rather, it has tended to accentuate them.

The direct impact of the Asian crisis on global economic developments was not significant in 1997, although growth in the East Asian countries dropped sharply in the last quarter of the year. Slower growth in Asia and Africa was more than offset by accelerated growth in other countries and regions. Growth in world output increased slightly in 1997, to reach 3.2 per cent (Table 5.1), while inflation remained low in most countries at levels not experienced since the 1950s —in large part owing to a continued decline in commodity prices, notably the price of oil.

Growth in developed market economies registered only a slight improvement in 1997, reaching 2.7 per cent, and was largely due to an acceleration of growth in the United States Improvements in economic conditions in the European Union, where the larger members had been struggling to initiate a sustained recovery, was also a contributory factor. Exports remained the major source of demand growth in the European Union, although investment demand had started to recover in a number of countries. By contrast, growth continued to be erratic in Japan, falling from 3.9 per cent in 1996 to less than 1 per cent in 1997.

Table 5.1 : World Ouput, 1990-1998

(Percentage chagnes over previous year)

Region/country	1990-1995	1996	1997[a]	1998[b]
World	1.9	3.0	3.2	2.0
Developed market-economy countries *of which:*	1.7	2.5	2.7	1.8
United States	2.3	2.8	3.8	2.3
Japan	1.4	3.9	0.9	-1.3
European Union	1.3	1.7	2.5	2.6
of which:				
Germany	1.7	1.4	2.2	2.3
France	1.1	1.5	2.4	2.5
Italy	1.1	0.7	1.5	2.2
United Kingdom	1.2	2.2	3.3	2.1
Transition economies	-8.2	-1.6	1.4	2.2
Developing countries	4.9	5.9	5.4	2.3
of which:				
Latin America	3.3	3.6	5.2	3.1
Africa	1.1	4.6	3.3	3.7
Asia	6.4	7.1	5.9	1.8
of which:				
China	12.4	9.6	8.8	6.0
Other countries	5.1	6.4	5.0	0.5
Memo item:				
Developing countries, excluding China	4.0	5.3	4.9	1.7

Source: UNCTAD secretariat calculations, based on data in 1990 dollars.
a Estimate.
b Forecast.

For the transition economies of Central and Eastern Europe, 1997 marked the very first year of positive growth for the region as a whole since 1989, though performance continued to diverge widely among countries. In the Russian Federation the contraction of the economy appeared to be coming to an end, although contagion from the Asian crisis will probably prevent any significant expansion. In 1997 growth averaged only a little over 1 per cent, nevertheless constituting a significant improvement on the nearly 2 per cent decline in 1996.

In contrast to both the developed and the transition economies, growth in developing countries as a whole declined in 1997, in part as a consequence of the financial turmoil in East Asia. Nevertheless, at 5.4 per cent, it was still far above the rates attained in those economies. Growth slowed down in China, but the decline was even more pronounced in the Asian countries hit by the financial crisis. Growth in Africa also fell sharply, to a level barely adequate to keep pace with population, because of declining commodity prices and adverse weather conditions, as well as continued civil strife in some countries. Unlike in the other developing regions, economic performance in Latin America in 1997 was the best for a quarter of a century. Continued expansion of exports and a strong recovery in investment resulted in an acceleration of growth, which reached 5.2 per cent in 1997, while price stability was consolidated with a decline in the rate of inflation.

2. World Trade

The volume of world exports rebounded to an impressive increase of 9.5 per cent in 1997, after slowing down from 9.0 per cent in 1995 to 5.0 per cent in 1996 (Table 5.2); in value terms the expansion was only one thrid as high. As a consequence, the divergence which has been evident between the growth trend of world trade and that of world output in recent years widened further. The stronger than expected volume growth of world exports in 1997 is the second highest in more than two decades and comes close to the record rate of 10 per cent in 1994. With the exception of African exports and Chinese imports, there was a widespread acceleration, at varying rates, in the volume growth of individual countries' and regions' exports and imports. Latin American imports in particular grew by over 21 per cent because of strong GDP growth, compared with 12.5 per cent for exports. For the same reason, the growth rates of both export and import volume in the United States reached double digits (12 per cent). Also notable is the performance of the European Union, where exports grew faster than imports, and that of the transition economies, where imports grew faster than exports.

Of particular significance in 1997 is the recovery of growth in export volume in Japan and other Asian countries, and more so in China, where exports rose by over 20 per cent, compared with a reduction of 1 per cent the previous year. Japan, China, and South and East Asia all had rates of growth of exports exceeding that of imports. And despite the slump in GDP growth in Japan and the countries affected by the financial crisis, there was a slight increase in the rate of import growth in all these developing countries of Asia, except China.

For 1998, expectations are for a reduced expansion of world trade. The outcome, however, is clouded by uncertainties, especially those relating to an export-led recovery in Asia. For the most affected Asian economies, the sharp fall in their real effective exchange rates and the existence of spare production capacity, together with sound economic fundamentals and past performance records, argue in favour of a reasonably strong export-led recovery. On the other hand, there are offsetting factors such as higher import costs and a severe liquidity crisis and credit crunch. Currently discernible in these countries

Table 5.2 : Exports and Imports by Major Regions and Economic Groupings, 1995-1997

(Percentage changes in volume over previous year)

	1995	1996	1997
Exports			
World	9.0	5.0	9.5
Developed market-economy countries	7.6	4.2	8.8
of which:			
Japan	4.0	-0.5	9.5
United States	8.7	6.3	11.9
European Union	8.5	4.0	8.0
Transition economies	17.5	7.5	11.0
Developing countries	11.5	6.0	11.5
of which:			
Africa	5.0	7.0	5.5
Latin America	12.0	11.0	12.5
South and East Asia	13.0	6.5	10.5
China	17.5	-1.0	20.5
Memo item:			
Six major East Asian economies[a]	14.5	6.5	10.0
Imports			
World	9.0	5.0	9.0
Developed market-economy countries	8.2	3.8	7.9
of which:			
Japan	12.5	2.0	2.5
United States	7.0	5.7	12.0
European Union	7.5	2.5	6.5
Transition economies	17.0	14.5	16.0
Developing countries	11.0	6.5	10.0
of which:			
Africa	6.5	0.5	11.5
Latin America	3.0	11.5	21.5
South and East Asia	15.5	5.5	6.5
China	9.0	7.0	5.0
Memo item:			
Six major East Asian economies[a]	15.5	4.5	5.5

Source: WTO Press Release, 19 March, 1998, Table 2; UNCTAD secretariat estimates.

a Hong Kong, China; Republic of Korea; Malaysia; Singapore; Taiwan Province of China; Thailand.

are a greater contraction of imports and a lack of any significant expansion of exports. The behaviour of imports is perhaps to be expected in view of the experience of previous episodes of large devaluations, when imports first contracted before expanding. The behaviour of exports, however, appears to be a departure from the previous experiences of rapid recovery, which tended to continue for about three years after devaluation.

The effects of the crisis differ considerably among the most severly affected countries, and there is the potential for spillover in various ways into other countries and the world economy in general. As a group, the five most affected countries (Indonesia, Malaysia, the Philippines, the Republic of Korea and Thailand — hereafter referred to as Asia-5) account for only a relatively modest share of global economic activity. In 1996, for instance, they accounted for 3.6 per cent of output, around 7 per cent of both exports and imports, 6 per cent of FDI inflows, 4 per cent of FDI stocks and less than 4 per cent of gross international bank lending. In terms of trade flows, these five countries accounted for less than 10 per cent of the exports or imports of countries outside Asia. Their share in both imports and exports was 2.5 per cent in the EU, but around 8.5 per cent in the United States. Hence a substantial change in the economic performance of these countries is unlikely to have a major impact on the trade and growth of countries outside Asia.

However, the Asia-5 countries constitute a key part of the trade-investment network in the Asian region. Their shares in the exports of Japan, China and Singapore, for instance, are considerably higher than those of the United States, and they also trade intensively with one other. The crisis is affecting seriously all the countries in the region which, taken together, have provided an important impetus to the expansion of global output and trade in recent years. Therefore, as discussed in greater detail in chapter II, the implications of the crisis for global trade can go well beyond what might be expected on the basis of the relative importance in the world economy of the countries suffering from the financial crisis.

3. Commodity Markets

In 1997, while non-oil primary commodity prices remained at the same level as in the previous year, prices of both oil and manufactured products fell by some 6 per cent (Table 5.3). Underlying the apparently stable price for non-oil commodities was a sharp increase in the prices of tropical beverages, in contrast to falling prices for agricultural raw materials. While there was an increase in the prices of commodities that had suffered significant damage from unfavourable climatic conditions caused by El Nino, commodity prices in general were on a declining trend. During 1985-1997, the rise in non-oil primary commodities as a group was a mere 2.2 per cent per annum in current dollar terms, giving a yearly decline of 0.5 per cent in real terms. The decline in real terms was particularly pronounced for all the major tropical beverages (coffee, cocoa and tea) and some metals (particularly tin and tungsten). Despite recovery in both nominal and real terms during the 1990s, prices of non-oil commodities remained relatively depressed.

Worth noting is the apparent lack of correspondence between commodity prices and industrial demand during the current cycle. Prices of agricultural raw materials, for instance, declined by around 10 per cent in 1997 even though GDP in developed market-economy countries grew by 2.7 per cent. In contrast, when GDP in those economies grew by 3 per cent in 1994, there was an increase of 14.6 per cent in the prices of agricultural raw materials. While it is evident that some commodities were in ample supply (sugar, for instance), the relatively low rate of inflation in developed economies was a disincentive to speculative buying of commodities, as was the sharp appreciation of the dollar in both 1996 and 1997 after relative stability during the first half of the 1990s.

Table 5.3 : World Primary Commodity Price, 1995-1998

(Percentage changes over previous year)

Commodity group	1995	1996	1997	April 1998[a]
All commodities[b]	9.9.	-4.2	0.0	-4.5
Food and tropical beverages	4.5	2.1	2.1	-6.9
Tropical beverages	1.1	-15.2	33.3	-11.5
Coffee	0.7	-19.1	54.7	-15.3
Cocoa	2.7	1.2	11.2	-0.6
Tea	-10.3	8.8	25.8	15.5
Food	5.9	6.8	-4.0	-6.1
Sugar	10.8	-9.9	-4.9	-25.1
Beef	-31.2	-6.4	4.0	-3.1
Maize	15.5	25.0	-25.3	-9.5
Wheat	18.5	16.2	-22.6	-8.9
Rice	-10.1	5.0	-10.7	17.8
Bananas	0.1	7.5	4.3	49.3
Vegetable oilseeds and oils	10.3	-4.2	-0.9	9.7
Agricultural raw materials	15.0	-9.9	-10.3	-2.5
Hides and skins	4.3	-23.7	-19.8	-10.5
Cotton	22.3	-17.4	-1.5	-13.3
Tobacco	-11.2	15.6	15.5	-1.3
Rubber	38.6	-11.9	-28.3	1.0
Tropical logs	5.4	-20.1	-5.5	-2.0
Minerals, ores and metals	*20.2*	*-12.1*	*0.0*	*-1.7*
Aluminium	22.3	-16.6	6.2	-7.3
Phosphate rock	6.1	8.6	7.9	0.0
Iron ore	5.8	6.0	1.1	2.8
Tin	13.7	-0.8	-8.4	3.6
Copper	27.2	-21.8	-0.8	2.2
Nickel	29.8	-8.8	-7.6	-9.3
Tungsten ore	49.6	-17.9	-9.3	0.0
Crude petroleum	9.3	20.8	-6.0	-21.4
Memo item:				
Manufactures[c]	11.1	-3.6	-5.7	—

Source: UNCTAD, *Monthly Commodity Price Bulletin*, various issues; United Nations, Monthly Bulletin of Statistics, various issues.

a Change from December 1997.

b Excluding crude petroleum.

c Unit value index of exports of manufactures from developed market-economy countries.

Oil prices in 1997 started to decline later than prices of most other primary commodities. There were various contributory factors in addition to a slowing of demand growth in a number of countries affected by the Asian crisis. An unseasonably warm winter in the Northern Hemisphere reduced the demand for heating oil, while there was a marked expansion in supplies, particularly in OPEC member countries where a 10 per cent increase in quotas was approved in November 1997, and a considerable build-up of inventories—from the previous year — of crude and oil products at all stages of the marketing chain.

While the prices of agricultural commodities appeared to have more or less stabilized most metal prices and the price of petroleum continued to decline until April 1998. The problems faced by commodity markets have been compounded by the adverse effects of the Asian crisis. From June 1997 to April 1998, non-oil commodity prices declined on average by 10.6 per cent, with larger falls in agricultural raw materials (12.0 per cent) and metals (17.3 per cent) than in food and beverages (10.1 per cent).The corresponding decline in the price of oil was 24.6 per cent. To a large extent, these price falls were associated with the Asian crisis, notably in the case of copper, nickel and natural rubber. Many of the fast-growing economies in Asia have become major markets for a wide range of commodities, including high-value foodstuffs, agricultural raw materials, metals and fuel, which are supplied by other developing countries. Many of them are also major commodity suppliers. The ASIA-5 are in fact themselves major exporters of a wide range of food items and agricultural raw materials, such as vegetable oilseeds and oils, coffee, bananas, tea, cocoa beans, natural rubber, tin and copper.

While lower oil prices will benefit oil-importing developing countries, some 25 developing countries are dependent on petroleum for 20 per cent or more of their foreign exchange earnings. Again, the decline in commodity prices in general will help to keep inflation down in developed countries, but as discussed in greater detail in chapter II, it will adversely affect a large number of developing countries highly dependent on commodity export earnings.

6

WORLD DEVELOPMENT REPORT, 1998-99

Introduction

This Year's *World Development Report*, the twenty-first in this annual series, examines the role of knowledge in advancing economic and social well-being. It begins with the realization that economies are built not merely through the accumulation of physical capital and human sill, but on a foundation of information, learning, and adaptation. Because knowledge matters, understanding how people and societies acquire and use knowledge and why they sometimes fail to do so is essential to improving peopl's lives, especially the lives of the poorest.

The information revolution makes understanding knowledge and development more urgent than ever before. New communications technologies and plummeting computing costs are shrinking distance and eroding borders and time. The remotest village has the possibility of tapping a global store of knowledge beyond the dreams of anyone living a century ago, and more quickly and cheaply than anyone imagined possible only a few decades ago. And distance education offers the potential to extend learning opportunities to millions who would otherwise be denied a good education.

But with these opportunities come tremendous risks. The globalization of trade, finance and information flows is intensifying competition, raising the danger that the poorest countries and communities will fall behind more rapidly than ever before. In our enthusiasm for the information superhighway, we must not forget the villages and slums without telephones, electricity, or safe water, or the primary schools without pencils, paper, or books. For the poor, the promise of the new information age—knowledge for all—can seem as remote as a distant star. To bring that promise closer to reality, the implications of the information revolution must be thought through with care and made part of the development agenda.

As part of its contribution to such a daunting task, this *World Development Report* considers two sorts of knowledge: technical knowledge (for example, about farming, health, or accounting) and knowledge about attributes (the quality of a product, the credibility of a borrower, or the diligence of a worker). The Report calls the unequal distribution of technical know-how *knowledge gaps* and the uneven knowledge about attributes *information problems*. It argues that both types of problems are worse in developing than in more technologically advanced countries, and that they especially hurt the poor. This analysis suggests three lessons of particular importance to the welfare of the more than 4 billion people in developing countries:

First, developing countries must institute policies that will enable them to narrow the knowledge gaps that separate them from rich countries. Examples of such policies include making efficient public investments in lifelong education opportunities, maintaining openness to the world, and dismantling barriers to competition in the telecommunications sector.

Second, developing country governments, bilateral donors, multilateral institutions, non-governmental organizations, and the private sector must work together to strengthen the institutions needed to address information problems. As societies become more complex, mechanisms for reducing information problems, such as accounting standards, disclosure requirements, and credit rating agencies, and for enforcing contract performance, through effective laws and courts, become increasingly important.

Third, no matter how effective we are in these endeavours, problems with knowledge will persist. We cannot eliminate knowledge gaps and information failures, but by recognizing that knowledge is at the core of all our development efforts, we will sometimes discover unexpected solutions to seemingly intractable problems.

Overview

Knowledge is Like Light. Weightless and intangible, it can easily travel the world, enlightening the lives of people everywhere. Yet billions of people still live in the darkness of poverty—unnecessarily. Knowledge about how to treat such a simple ailment as diarrhea has existed for centuries—but millions of children continue to die from it because their parents do not know how to save them.

Poor countries—and poor people—differ from rich ones not only because they have less capital but because they have less knowledge. Knowledge is often costly to create, and that is why much of it is created in industrial countries. But developing countries can acquire knowledge overseas as well as create their own at home. Forty years ago, Ghana and the Republic of Korea had virtually the same income per capita. By the early 1990s Korea's income per capita was six times higher than Ghana's. Some reckon that half of the difference is due to Korea's greater success in acquiring and using knowledge.

Knowledge also illuminates every economic transaction, revealing preferences, giving clarity to exchanges, informing markets. And it is lack of knowledge that causes markets to collapse, or never to come into being. When some producers began diluting milk in India, consumers could not determine its quality before buying it. Without that knowledge, the overall quality of milk fell. Producers who did not dilute their milk were put at a disadvantage, and consumers suffered.

Poor countries differ from rich in having fewer institutions to certify quality, enforce standards and performance, and gather and diseminate information needed for business transactions. Often this hurts the poor. For example, village moneylenders often charge interest rates as high as 80 per cent, because of the difficulty in assessing the creditworthiness of poor borrowers.

This *World Development Report* proposes that we look at the problems of development in a new way—from the perspective of knowledge. There are many types of knowledge. In this Report we focus on two sorts of knowledge and two types of problems that are critical for developing countries:

- *Knowldge about technology*, which we also call technical knowledge or simply know-how. Examples are nutrition, birth control, software engineering, and accountancy. Typically, developing countries have less of this know-how than industrial countries, and the poor have less than the non-poor. We call these unequal distributions across and within countries *knowledge gaps.*

- *Knowledge about attributes*, such as the quality of a product, the diligence of a worker, or the creditworthiness of a firm—all crucial to effective markets. We call the difficulties posed by incomplete knowledge of attributes *information problems.* Mechanisms to alleviate information problems, such as product standards, training certificates, and credit reports, are fewer and weaker in developing countries. Information problems and the resulting market failures especially hurt the poor.

The relationship between knowledge gaps and information problems, their impact on development, and the ways that international institutions and developing-country governments can better address them are the central themes of this Report.

As we shall see, considering development from a knowledge perspective reinforces some well-known lessons, such as the value of an open trade regime and of universal basic education. It also focuses our attention on needs that have sometimes been overlooked: scientific and technical training, local research and development, and the critical importance of institutions to facilitate the flow of information essential for effective markets.

Approaching development from a knowledge perspective—that is, adopting policies to increase both types of knowledge, know-how and knowledge about attributes—can improve people's lives in myriad ways besides higher incomes. Better knowledge about nutrition can mean better health, even for those with little to spend on food. Knowledge about how to prevent the transmission of AIDS can save millions from debilitating illness and premature death. Pubic disclosure of information about industrial pollution can lead to a cleaner and more healthful environment. And microcredit programmes can make it possible for poor peopole to invest in a better future for themselves and their children. In short, knowledge gives people greater control over their destinies.

The twin issues of knowledge gaps and information problems cannot be untangled in real life: to unleash the power of knowledge, governments must recognize and respond to both types of problems, often simultaneously. For the sake of clarity, however, we analyze these issues separately, beginning with knowledge gaps.

Narrowing Knowledge Gaps

Closing knowledge gaps will not be easy. Developing countries are pursuing a moving target, as the high-income industrial countries constantly push the knowledge frontier outward. Indeed, even greater than the knowledge gap is the gap in the capacity to create knowledge. Differences in some important measures of knowledge creation are far greater between rich and poor countries than the difference in income.

But developing countries need not reinvent the wheel—or the computer, or the treatment for malaria. Rather than re-create existing knowledge, poorer countries have the option of acquiring and adapting much knowledge already available in the richer countries. With communications costs plummeting, transferring knowledge is cheaper than ever. Given these advances, the stage appears to be set for a rapid narrowing of knowledge gaps and a surge in economic growth and human well-being. Why, then, isn't this transfer occurring as fast as we might expect? What conditions are necessary for developing countries to make fuller use of the global stock of knowledge?

Part One of the Report starts with a discussion of the importance of knowledge for development and of the risks and opportunities that the information revolution poses for developing countries. It then examines three critical steps that developing countries must take to narrow knowledge gaps:

- *Acquiring knowledge* involves tapping and adapting knowledge available elsewhere in the world—for example, through an open trading regime, foreign investment, and licensing agreements—as well as creating knowledge locally through research and development, and building on indigenous knowledge.
- *Absorbing knowledge* involves, for example, ensuring universal basic education, with special emphasis on extending education to girls and other traditionally disadvantaged groups; creating opportunities for lifelong learning; and supporting tertiary education, especially in science and engineering.
- *Communicating knowledge* involves taking advantage of new information and communications technology—through increased competition, private sector provision, and appropriate regulation—and ensuring that the poor have access.

Just as knowledge gaps exist between developing and industrial countries, so too are there large gaps within countries. Strategies for closing these gaps often include the same elements, and applying them effectively will go a long way toward reducing inequality and eliminating poverty.

But even if knowledge gaps could be closed entirely, with everyone in developing countries enjoing access to the same know-how as well-educated people in the industrial countries, developing countries would still be at a disadvantage in another respect: knowledge about attributes. Because knowledge about attributes is required for every transaction, it must be generated on the spot and constantly refreshed. This requires a variety of market and non-market mechanisms to collect and disseminate information, many of which are weak or lacking in developing countries.

Addressing Information Problems

Without knowledge about attributes, markets cannot function properly. When the government steps in and addresses the problem, for example by establishing standards and certification (as it did for milk quality in India), the market functions better and everybody benefits.

Institutions, broadly defined to include governments, private organizations, laws, and social norms, contribute to establishing recognized standards and enforcing contracts, thus making possible transactions that would otherwise not occur. Rich countries have more-diverse and more-effective institutions to address information problems than do poor countries. These institutions make it possible for people to engage in economic transactions that improve their lives—from buying milk, to finding a job, to getting an education, to obtaining a loan. Information problems are often at the core of the difficulties that poor people in developing countries encounter in their daily struggle to survive and to improve their lives.

Part Two of tne Report begins by discussing the nature and extent of these problems, noting that they are a major impediment to development—and especially severe for the poor. The uneuqal distribution of information can never be entirely eliminated, but it can be ameliorated, in part through institutional innovations designed specifically for developing-country settings and the special problems confronting poor people. The rest of Part Two considers some specific problems involving information. It also describes some promising solutions in three areas where these problems are most severe, and where addressing them can make a major contribution to achieving sustainable growth that benefits the poor:

- *Processing the economy's financial information*, particularly by ensuring transparency through effective accounting and disclosure, and by designing regulatory approaches that work in information-scarce settings.
- *Increasing our knowledge of the environment*, by conducting research to provide the underpinnings for effective environmental policies, and by disseminating information to create incentives for pollution reduction and responsible stewardship.
- *Addressing information problems that hurt the poor*, and taking the time to learn about their needs and concerns, so that society can then offer them useful information and assist them in devising ways to reduce their isolation from markets and to improve their access to formal institutions.

Most of the difficulties that developing countries face involve both knowledge gaps and information problems. To be effective, the solutions must address both issues—sometimes sequentially, often simultaneously. Because, the possibilities for improving human well-being are so immense, we return to these twin themes throughout the Report, beginning with the story of the green revolution, which shows dramatically how knowledge gaps and information problems—and their solutions—play out in the real world.

The Green Revolution: A Paradigm of Knowledge for Development

Few stories better illustrate the potential of knowledge for development—or the obstacles to diffusing that knowledge—than that of the green revolution, the decades-long, worldwide movement dedicated to the creation and dissemination of new agricultural knowledge. This quest, breeding new seeds for enhanced agricultural productivity, was undertaken in the early postwar years by a vast array of agents—non-profit organizations governments, multilateral institutions, private firms, banks, village moneylenders, land-rich farmers, and landless labourers—all working, deliberately or not, to improve the daily bread (or rice, or maize) of people everywhere. The English economist Thomas Malthus had predicted in the 18th century that the population of any country would eventually outstrip its food supply. What the green revolution showed instead was that Malthus had underestimted how quickly knowledge in agriculture, in transportation, in mechanization—would transform food production. By the second half of the 20th century, world food supply was more than keeping up with population growth.

Since the early 1950s, Asia and South America have more than doubled yields of staple crops. Africa, which also lags in other measures of development and knowledge, has seen only modest yield increases). Global gains in output per hectare have been dramatic, particularly for wheat, maize and rice. And although the impact of the green revolution on the poor was initially a matter of controversy, time has made it clear that poor people have benefited significantly, through higher incomes, cheaper food, and increased demand for their labor.

The early steps in the green revolution mostly involved narrowing knowledge gaps. The first step was to narrow the gap between what scientists already knew about plant genetics and the widespread ignorance on this score in developing countries, reflected in the unavailability there of new crop strains based on this knowledge. This gap was narrowed largely through the research and development efforts of governments and non-profit organizations. But why was their action necessary? Why didn't private, for profit firms make a greater effort to address for security? Why didn't they, for example, try to commercialize existing scientific knowledge about genetics by developing more productive plant varieties themselves?

The answer is that the knowledge embodied in the seed of a new plant variety is not easily appropriated by any breeder, seed company, farmer, or even country. The varieties most suitable for transfer to developing countries, once transferred, could be easily reproduced. Farmers had only to collect the seeds from the plants grown from the original seeds and replant them. That meant no repeat business for seed developers, and not enough profit to make their effort worthwhile.

Put another way, improved seeds, like many other research outputs, have many of the characteristics of a public good. A public good is one whose full benefits in the form of profits cannot be captured by its creator but instead leak out to society at large, without the creator receiving compensation. Because private entrepreneurs have diminished incentives to provide such goods, the tradition of entrusting public entities with providing them is long. (A good example is the agricultural research the U.S. government funded in the 19th century.) Indeed, it is widely recognized in many fields that, without some collective action, there will be far too little research into developing new knowledge.

After the first modern seed varieties proved successful in the early 1960s, many developing countries established national agriculture research organizations, as some had already done, mainly with public funding, to develop second-generation varieties better suited to local conditions. As a result, the number of new varieties of rice and maize released by national research organizations doubled between 1966 and 1985.

To disseminate this knowledge, developing-country governments established agricultural extension services. At first the main job of the extension agents was to inform farmers about the new seeds and techniques. But the best extension agents—and the most effective extension services—quickly learned that listening was also an important part of the job. By listening to farmers and learning from them, extension agents not only gained a better understanding of the farmers' needs and concerns. They also sometimes stumbled upon seed varieties and cultivation techniques that the researchers had missed. This two-way flow of information furthered the local adoption and adaptation of green revolution technology.

At this point in the story, the focus shifts to information problems. The driving force in the early stages of the green revolution had been the creation, dissemination, and adaptation of agricultural know-how. But the potential of these innovations could not be unleashed until millions of small farmers planted the new seeds. For this to happen, a variety of information problems had to be addressed. In particular, what assurance did farmers have that the seeds would work? Why should a farmer risk his livelihood on the say—so of an extension agent? This uncertainty, coupled with the inability of the poor to obtain credit—another classic market failure closely related to information problems—had significant implications for the rate of adoption of the new seeds.

Large landholders and farmers with more education were among the first to try the new seeds, for a variety of reasons. Farmers with extensive landholding could limit their risk by trying new seeds in test sowings on only a part of their land. They could also more quickly recover the fixed cost of their early adoption by applying what they learned across their larger farms. Educated farmers were better equipped to find out about the new varieties in the first place, and to learn the changes in cultivation practices needed to make the most of them. Perhaps most important, however, more-prosperous farmers had ready access to credit and the ability to absorb risk. Poor farmers, unable to borrow and lacking insurance or the savings to fall back on in the event of failure, could only watch and wait until their wealthier neighbours proved the value of the new seeds.

Why didn't banks or village moneylenders lend small farmers the money to buy the new seeds and fertilizer? Many poor people would repay small loans at reasonable interest, if such loans were available. But the costs of identifying the good credit risks among the poor are high relative to the size of the loans they would take out. Unsure which prospective borrowers will repay, lenders charge high interest and require collateral, which the poor often lack. Even when the poor have assets (small landholdings) that could be pledged as collateral, weak legal infrastructure, including lack of land title and ineffective courts, means that enforcement of collateral pledges may be weak. Without enforcement, incentives to repay are limited, and this weakens incentives to lend. The result is that the poor often cannot borrow.

In recent years microcredit schemes have arisen to address these problems. But at the time of the green revolution, poor farmers' lack of credit, combined with their scant education (also partly attributable to lack of credit) and other factors, meant that they were often the last to adopt the new crop strains. The resulting lag between the introduction of new seeds and their widespread use can be seen in the slow expansion of areas sown with new varieties.

The costs of these delays were significant. If all the information problems could have been addressed—that is, if farmers could have been immediately persuaded of the potential of the new seeds, and if mechanisms had existed to provide credit to poor farmers—the productivity gains from the green revolution would have been even greater. One study found that, for a farm family with 3.7 hectares, the average loss of potential income over five years from slow adoption and inefficient use of high-yielding varieties was nearly *four times* its annual farm income before the introduction of the new seeds.

Eventually, the green revolution did boost the incomes of poor farmers and the landless. A survey in southern India concluded that, between 1973 and 1994, the average real income of small farmers increased by 90 per cent, and that of the landless—among the poorest in the farm community—by 125 per cent. The poor benefited greatly from increased demand for their labour, because the high-yielding varieties demanded labour-intensive cultivating techniques. Calorie intakes for small farmers and the landless rose 58 to 81 per cent, and protein intakes rose 103 to 115 per cent.

What Knowledge Gaps and Information Problems mean for Development

The story of the green revolution shows how creating, disseminating, and using knowledge can narrow knowledge gaps. It also shows that know-how is only one part of what determines society's well-being. Information problems lead to market failures and impede efficiency and growth. Development thus entails the need for an institutional transformation that improves information and creates incentives for effort, innovation, saving and investment and enables progressively complex exchanges that span increased distances and time.

The relationship between knowledge gaps and information problems is clear from the history of the green revolution, because with time it became obvious that improved varieties of plants were necessary but not sufficient to improve the lives of the rural poor. The twin challenges of knowledge for development—knowledge gaps and information problems—are also illustrated in many other examples in this Report. How they will be manifested in the next green revolution, perhaps involving gene splicing and cloning, we can only guess. We can be sure, however, that whether or not new technologies are used in ways that help the poor will depend on how well society addresses knowledge gaps and information problems.

Part Three of the Report considers the policy options for responding to these challenges from two perspectives:

- *What can international institutions do?* Chapter 9 discusses how—by creating new knowledge, transferring and adapting knowledge to the needs of developing countries, and managing knowledge so that it is kept accessible and constantly refreshed—international institutions can help developing countries bridge knowledge gaps and resolve information problems.
- *What should governments do?* Drawing on the first two parts of the Report, Chapter 10 describes how the governments of developing countries can narrow knowledge gaps, address information problems, and design policies that take into account the reality that information and markets are always imperfect.

The rest of this Overview sketches the main conclusions from these two chapters.

What can International Institutions Do?

Development institutions have three roles in reducing knowledge gaps: to provide international public goods, to act as intermediaries in the transfer of knowledge, and to manage the rapidly growing body of knowledge about development.

Just as there are national public goods, so there are internatinal ones, and many types of knowledge fall into this category. No single country will invest enough in the creation of such goods, because the benefits would accrue to all countries without the creating country receiving full compensation. But international institutions, acting on behalf of everyone, can fill this gap.

One of the best-known examples, the Consultative Group for International Agricultural Research, funded the green revolution through its worldwide sponsorship of agricultural research. It illustrates the standard response of public funding for research when there are large social returns (which exceed the private returns). Another response is to provide financial incentives for private researchers to focus on the needs of developing countries, such as the need for an affordable vaccine for AIDS.

Perhaps even more important is the role of development institutions as intermediaries. International research may produce knowledge useful for development, but the most important knowledge for development comes from developing countries themselves. Each change in policy in one country produces knowledge that may help another. Every project, successful or not, yields information about what works and what does not. Amassing this knowledge, assessing it, and making it available to others is a task beyond the capacity (and self-interest) of any single country. So the task falls to international institutions.

How well these institutions perform depends on their ability to manage vast amounts of information. For example, every World Bank staffer who works in a developing country accumulates knowledge about a particular sector or region or activity. Often this knowledge is used for the specific task requiring it, then shelved. Think how much more valuable it would be if that knowledge were made available to every other staff member working on similar issues and projects. Then add the much greater benefit to be had from sharing that knowledge with the rest of the world.

The information revolution is making it easier to manage this wealth of knowledge. By 2000, the World Bank intends that relevant parts of its knowledge base will be made available to clients, partners and stakeholders around the world. The objective is to develop a dynamic knowledge management system capable of distilling knowledge and making it available for further adaptation and use in new settings. To do that effectively, however, also requires building the capability in developing countries to assess and adapt relevant policy and technical knowledge to local situations, and when necessary to crearte new knowledge, which in turn may be relevant for other countries.

International institutions can thus make important contributions. But it is what developing countries do themselves that will determine how effectively they make use of knowledge and deal with information failures. Different countries start from different positions and face different problems. But some generalizations can be made, and some are offered in the following sections:

What Should Governments Do?

When development is considered from the perspective of knowledge three key insights emerge:

- Because the market for knowledge often fails, there is a strong rationale for public action. The state is in a unique position to narrow knowledge gaps—for example, by adopting an open trade regime, supporting life-long learning, or establishing a sound regulatory environment for a competitive telecommunications industry.
- Information is the lifeblood of markets, yet markets on their own do not always provide enough of it, because those who generate information cannot always appropriate the returns. Public action is thus required to provide information to verify quality, monitor performance, and regulate transactions to provide the foundation for successful market-based development.
- No matter how successful a government may be in this endeavor, knowledge gaps and information failures will remain. Every policy reform and every development programme or project will be implemented in an environment that suffers from these problems to varying degrees. Even actions that on the surface have little to do with knowledge gaps or information failures are almost certain to be affected by them.

How should developing-country governments proceed, given the magnitude of knowledge gaps and the universality of information failures? Chapter 10 draws some policy conclusions from the discussions in the rest of the Report.

National Strategies to Narrow Knowledge Gaps

The Report considers a number of steps that governments can take to facilitate the acquisition, absorption, and communication of knowledge. Although it is useful for expository purposes to discuss each of them separately, in the real world they are intertwined. Policies adopted in one area have important repercussions on—and possible synergies with—each of the others. The acquisition of knowledge, whether imported from abroad or created at home, requires the absorption of knowledge, abetted by universal basic education and opportunities for lifelong learning. The exploding capacity and plummeting costs of communications technology greatly expand the potential for both the acquisition and the absorption of knowledge, creating new opportunities for two-way information flows. Government strategies to narrow knowledge gaps are most effective when they make the most of these synergies. But they also need to address information failures in their design and implementation.

Policies for Acquiring Knowledge

For developing countries, acquiring knowledge involves two complementary steps: obtaining knowledge by opening up to knowledge from abroad, and creating knowledge not readily available elsewhere. Three key means of facilitating the acquisition of knowledge from abroad are an open trading regime, foreign investment, and technology licensing.

Improving the policy and business environments to create conditions favourable to trade, especially exports, is one of the most important ways for countries to obtain knowledge from abroad. To compete in the global market place, exporting firms must meet international benchmarks for efficiency and design. As a result, exporters tend to invest more in knowledge than firms that do not export.

Openness to foreign direct investment goes hand in hand with an open trading regime, and it provides benefits for the acquisition of knowledge in its own right. Because multinational investors are global leaders in innovation, their activities in developing countries can be important in transmitting knowledge. Valuable knowledge spillovers can occur through their training of local staff and through contracts with domestic suppliers and subcontractors. Both are evident in Malaysia, where the local plant of the U.S. firm Intel Corporation now subcontracts a growing part of its production to new firms set up by former Intel engineers. Such spillovers are not limited to manufacturing; they also occur in relatively low-technology service industries, such as food services and hotels.

Technology licensing plays a growing role in developing countries' efforts to acquire knowledge. International licensing and royalties payments worldwide increased from $7 billion in 1976 to more than $60 billion in 1995. Technology licensing is an effective way to get access to some of the new proprietary technologies. Domestic firms can also use licensing to leverage technological development by negotiating access to the underlying design principles of the licensed technologies, as many Korean firms have done.

As the world moves toward a knowledge-based economy, there has been a trend toward stronger protection of intellectual property rights. This trend is reflected in the recently completed agreements in the World Trade Organization (WTO) on the trade-related aspects of intellectural property rights. Intellectual property rights try to balance the incentives for the generation of new knowledge with those for its dissemination. That balance is difficult to achieve. The balance is also evolving, as new technologies bring new issues for negotiation, such as the protection of biotechnology, biodiversity, and computer and information technologies.

Developing countries should participate actively in continuing international negotiations on these issues, to express their concerns that tighter intellectual property rights shift bargaining power toward the producers of knowledge and increase the knowledge gap by slowing the rate of adaptation. These concerns about intellectual property rights have to be balanced against their advantages: they stimulate the creation of new knowledge in the world, including in developing countries. Many developing countries have found that by establishing and enforcing intellectual property rights standards that comply with international practice, they gain access to foreign markets and to foreign technology through direct investment and technology transfer.

Developing countries can take advantage of the large global stock of knowledge only if they develop the technological competence to search for appropriate technologies and to select, absorb, and adapt imported technology. The green revolution showed how new seed strains had to be further developed to suit local conditions. Even in manufacturing, knowledge produced in other countries often has to be adapted to local conditions, such as weather, consumer tastes, and the availability of complementary inputs. Similarly, progress in education, health care, and agricultural extension all require local knowledge that cannot be obtained from abroad.

In fostering the domestic creation of knowledge, governments have a special role in supporting potentially productive research, while establishing the necessary conditions for the private sector, in response to market forces, to apply the new knowledge created. Many developing countries are reforming their public research and development to make it more responsive to the market. Brazil, China, India, Korea, and Mexico have launched vast programmes to help focus public laboratories on the needs of the productive sector. Their measures include corporatizing research institutes, improving the pay and recognition of researchers, and offering firms incentives to contract directly with the public labs.

Policies for Absorbing Knowledge

The explosion of new knowledge, accelerating technological progress, and ever-increasing competitoin make life-long learning more important than ever. To narrow knowledge gaps, soceities must ensure basic education for all and provide opportunities for people to continue to learn throughout their lives. Basic education is the foundation of a healthy, skilled, and agile labour force. Lifelong education beyond the basics enables countries to centrifically assess, adapt, and apply new knowledge.

In the past 30 years, developing countries have made enourmous strides in expanding enrollments at all levels, particularly in primary school. These achievements have been invaluable and should be maintained and expanded. We have seen, for example, the importance of basic education in furthering the adoption of improved agricultural techniques. A growing economy, even a low-income one, needs people with up-to-date technical skills to participate in the global economy. Countries should consider supporting expanded adult education and training. In many cases the most cost-effective way of doing so is to support the private sector's activities in this area, for instance by establishing standards and accreditation procedures, and in some cases by providing subsidies, especially for the poor.

Improving the education of girls is particularly important in countries with large knowledge gaps. The benefits of female education, today widely recognized, include better child nutrition and health and reduced fertility. The recent success of a programme in Bangladesh demonstrates that well-planned government actions can have farreaching impacts, even in societies where girls' education has long been neglected. Nationwide, only about 20 per cent of Bangladeshi women were literate in 1990, and only a third of students in secondary schools were girls. Since then a programme to provide stipends and tuition grants to girls enrolled in secondary school has rapidly increased female enrollments. By 1996, half a million girls were receiving stipends, and as many girls as boys were enrolled in participating schools.

But to sustain economic growth and to compete in the global economy, countries must go beyond basic education, as Korea has done. By 1960 Korea had achieved universal primary education—the basis for a well-educated labour force—which fueled the economy's needs as it industrialized. Incentives were also put in place for extensive private investment in tertiary education, so that by 1995 more than half of college-age adults were enrolled in a college or university. Of these, more than 80 per cent were enrolled in private institutions, and private spending on tertiary education exceeded public spending.

Tapping the private sector is one way to stretch limited government resources: a complementary measure is to improve the quality of public education. To do this, and to address some of the information failures afflicting education, many countries are experimenting with new approaches to providing it. These changes take several forms: decentralizing administration, increasing school autonomy, switching to demand-side financing, increasing information about individual educational institutions, and fostering competition among private, non-governmental, and public providers. In El Salvador, after its civil war, the government improved and expanded the community-managed schools that had sprung up when the public system broke down. Even the poorest communities set up and managed such schools, actually improving quality. One reason is that parents monitor the teachers vigorously. As a result, students lose only about half as many days to teacher absenteeism as in conventional schools.

Policies for Communicating Knowledge in the Information Age

Advances in communications have transformed society before: movable type, photography and telegraphy, the telephone, television, and the fax machine all pushed outward the limits of our ability to store and transmit knowledge. Now the convergence of computing and telecommunications appears ready to shatter those limits, making it possible to send vast amounts of information anywhere in the world in seconds—at an ever-decreasing cost. This new technology greatly facilitates the acquisition and absorption of knowledge, offering developing countries unprecedented opportunities to enhance educational systems, improve policy formation and execution, and widen the range of opportunities for business and the poor. One of the great hardships edured by the poor, and by many others who live in the poorest countries, is their sense of isolation. The new communications technologies promise to reduce that sense of isolation, and to open access to knowledge in ways unimaginable not long ago.

A growing number of developing countries are taking advantage of these opportunities to leapfrog to the new technologies, largely skipping such intermediate stages as copper wires and analog telephones. Already Djibouti, Maldives, Mauritius, and Qatar all have fully digitized telephone networks. In this they have stolen a march on some industrial countries where half or more of the telephone network continues to rely on older technology, more expensive and lower in quality.

Throughout much of the developing world, however, access to even basic communications technology is available only to the fortunate few. South Asia and Sub-Saharan Africa have only about 1.5 telephone lines for every 100 prople, compared with 64 lines per 100 in the United States. Lower incomes account for part of the difference, but many people in developing countries who are ready and willing to pay for a telephone are unable to obtain one. Standing in their way are inefficient state monopolies and regulatory regimes that unintentionally restrict supply. Worldwide, an estimated 28 million people, nearly all of them in developing countries, are on waiting lists for telephone installation. Given the long and uncertain delay, many others who want a telephone and could afford one simply have not bothered to apply.

Fortunately, countries can eliminate these bottlenecks—and lower the costs of telecommunications so that many more people benefit. This can be done by adopting a regulatory system that promotes and ensures competition, to prevent firms with monopoly power in some areas of service provision from using it to gain a stranglehold over others. In most cases, expanded competition should come before privatization to avoid turning a state monopoly into a private one.

Developing countries are discovering that private involvement can rapidly extend telecommunications services, even when incomes are low. Before its reform, Ghana's telecommunications system was dominated by a money-losing state monopoly, only one in 400 people had a telephone, and there was a 10-year wait. The government sold 30 per cent of the state firm to a consortium of domestic and Malaysian investors, approved a competing national franchise that also included foreign investors, licensed five new cellular providers, and approved several Internet service providers, one of which now has an aggressive programme to provide rural access through collaboration with the post office. In 1997, the first year after the reforms, the number of fixed lines increased by 30 per cent, to 120,000, and the pace of installation is expected to accelerate.

One problem that often remains with privatization is that some isolate rural communities are not served, because they have too few people stretched out across too much territory to attract private service providers. The problem for government is knowing how much subsidy is needed to encourage private service to these communities. Chile has had encouraging success with subsidy auctions, a market-like innovation that induces firms to reveal information about their costs, to the benefit of the poor. The government awarded subsidies on a competitive basis to firms providing telephone service to small and remote locales: firms bid against each other for the right to service these areas. Unexpectedly, for half the locales and nearly 60 per cent of the target population, firms proved willing to provide pay phones at no subsidy at all. With additional rounds of bidding going forward, it is expected that 98 per cent of Chileans will have access to pay phones by 2000.

Expanding telecommunications holds the promise to improve every developing country's capacity to absorb knowledge, for example by providing opportunities for high-quality, low-cost adult learning. The Virtual University of the Monterey Institute of Technology in Mexico is a consortium of collaborating universities, including 13 outside the country. It enrolls 9,000 degree and 35,000 non-degree students each year in Mexico and other Latin American countries. It delivers courses through printed texts and live and prerecorded television broadcasts, with communication between students and faculty aided by computers and the Internet.

The African Virtual University, headquartered in Nairobi, seeks to increase university enrollments and improve the quality and relevance of instruction in business, science, and engineering throughout Africa. In each participating country, a local institution is competitively selected to oversee operations. This institution provides hardware and software for interactive courses, registers students, supervises study programs, offers a structured study environment, and awards local course credit. The university has installed 27 satellite receiver terminals throughout Africa and developed a digital library, to compensate for the death of scientific journals in African universities. Although it is too early to assess results, such initiatives are reason to hope that new technology can make a big contribution to narrowing knowledge gaps.

7

GLOBAL FINANCIAL CRISIS TO HIKE WORLD UNEMPLOYMENT
World Employment Report, 1998-99

Introduction

According to *World Employment Report* the number of unemployed workers around the world has never been higher, and will grow by millions more before the end of the year as a result of financial crisis in Asia and other parts of the world. The Report maintains that worker training will be able to resolve this problem among unemployed women, youths, worker trapped in the informal sector and other vulnerable groups.

Signs of renewed economic growth in many parts of the world during the first half of 1997 had sparked hopes for an economic revival that would spur higher jobs growth in all parts of the world. Instead, says the new *World Employment Report*, released recently by the ILO, only the United States, and to a lesser degree, the European Union; have seen reduced unemployment and underemployment.

> "The global employment situation is grim, and getting grimmer" says Director-General Michel Hansenne. "Stubbornly persisting high levels of unemployment and underemployment lead to social exclusion of the young and the old, the less skilled, the disabled and ethnic minority groups — with a strong bias against women in all categories."

Among the Report's Highlights

- Some one billion workers - one third of the world's labour force — remain *unemployed* or *underemployed*, a figure that is largely unchanged from ILO estimates contained in its *World Employment Report 1996-97*.
- Of the one billion total, some 150 million workers are actually *unemployed*, or are seeking or available for work. Of these 150 million, 10 million unemployed have been generated this year due to the financial crisis in Asia alone.
- In addition, 25 to 30 per cent of the world's workers — or between 750 million and 900 million people - are *underemployed*, i.e., either working substantially less than full-time but wanting to work longer, or earning less than a living wage.
- The ILO estimates some 60 million young people, between the ages of 15 and 24, are in search of work but cannot find it.
- The global unemployment and underemployment picture contained in the

1998-99 report contrasts sharply with developments expected since the last *World Employment Report* was issued in 1996, when the ILO said that a number of encouraging signs heralded a global economic revival and would cut unemployment and underemployment worldwide.

Noting that beyond the current financial turmoil, many countries are suffering from long-term employment problems which can be solved only through the combined action of governments, trade unions and employer organization. Mr. Hansenne said, "Among measures to increase competitiveness, growth and employment in a globalizing world economy, the critical role of a high-quality, educated and skilled workforce must gain more prominence."

The ILO says that worker training provides an effective means to resolve this problem among unemployed women, youths, workers trapped in the informal sector, and other "vulnerable groups" such as older workers, the long-term unemployed and workers with disabilities.

"Nations facing rapid globalization and competitive pressure need to invest in skills development and training in their workforce," the report says. "Training and education were at the heart of southeast Asia's economic miracle and could well provide a way out of under-development and poverty for millions of workers in other parts of the world".

Employment Around the World

Here is a global overview of the *World Employment Report* :

Asia

The report says that the three decades of sustained growth, averaging almost 8 per cent per year (or 5.5% per capita) in many countries of east and south-east Asia has had no parallel in recorded economic history, but the situation in the region has deteriorated dramatically in the past year.

In *Indonesia*, steep increases in unemployment and underemployment are being accompanied by food shortages caused by an early drought. The ILO warns that "real wages in 1998 could well fall further than the 15 per cent or so expected drop in per capita GDP. Unemployment in 1998 could reach between 9 and 12 per cent of the labour force, compared to about 4 per cent in 1996, though much of this increase will be reflected in rising underemployment rather than open unemployment".

In *Thailand*, unemployment could rise to about 6 per cent in the labour force in 1998, or almost 2 million jobless, compared to 1-2 per cent or 400.000 to 700.000 unemployed just two years ago. The reliance of many Thais on the traditional safety net of the extended family could trigger a four to five-fold increase in underemployment. The ILO says that the ripple effect of such trends will impact far from the urban centres, because "many people in the rural areas, especially the elderly...rely on remittances from working family members in Bangkok".

In the *Repulic of Korea* job losses have accelerated in the past year, nearly doubling between November 1997 and February 1998 to 5 per cent, and reaching 7 per cent in June of this year.

In *Hong Kong*, the unemployment rate rose sharply to 4.5 per cent at the end of the second quarter of 1998, from 2.9 per cent in 1997.

In *China*, it is estimated that 3.5 million workers will be laid off in 1998 and unemployment will increase to 5-6 per cent. Hopes for increasing productive employment lie in the expanding role of private industry, especially small and medium-sized enterprises.

Furthermore, the ILO fears that labour market conditions in India, Pakistan and Bangladesh, which have so far been spared significant impact from the crisis, could worsen, if the external economic environment turns hostile.

Central and Eastern Europe and the CIS

Despite the benefits enjoyed by a tiny minority, in the 1990s most people in this region continue to suffer dramatic and painful declines in living standards. The ILO notes that "this has been accompanied by a rapid rise (from about zero to over 9 per cent) in unemployment, lower real wages and an increase in income inequality as a result of immense economic and enterprise restructuring".

The collapse of output has led to drastic reduction in demand for labour, lower employment and lower real wages in some countries.

In the Russian Federation, rising economic turmoil has been accompanied by negative growth in real wages, now at less than 60 per cent of their 1989 level. In a growing number of cases, enterprises cannot pay any wages at all to their employees for months at a time. The report notes that althouth GDP in Russia grew at a rate of 0.4 per cent in 1997 after eight years of recession and inflation fell to 15 per cent from 48 per cent in 1996, the current economic crisis, combined with growing political instability, is worsening the situation further. The exchange rate has fallen considerably and accelerated inflation is occurring, nearly daily. Poverty is unfortunately likely to rise.

Poland, by contrast, has begun to see a slow upswing in real wages, to just below 80 per cent of pre-1989 levels. Unemployment is still high at 10.4 per cent in 1998.

In other Eastern European countries, unemployment is 5.4 per cent in the Czech Republic, 8.4 per cent in Hungary, 9.2 per cent in Romania, 13 per cent in Bulgaria and 17.6 per cent in Croatia.

Latin America

In Latin America, a recent improvement in genral output indicators has not been matched by improved employment. Althoughoverall growth reached 5 per cent in 1997, accompanied by a decline in inflation from very high levels and improved real wages in several countries, the ILO says unemployment in the region, increased between 1991 and 1996, reaching 7.4 per cent in 1997.

Latin America faces the danger in 1998 of being caught in a global pull-back by investors in emerging markets, which could push unemployment and underemployment up sharply.

Argentina provides an example: a stabilization and structural adjustment programme was followed by an average annual economic growth rate of 5.8% between 1991 and 1997. However, the employment situation deteriorated, and unemployment *increased* between those years, rising from 6.3 per cent in 1991 to a maximum of 17.5 per cent in 1995, before dropping to around 15 per cent in 1997.

"Unable to work in formal markets, where productivity is high and wages relatively good, many workers have to engage in a number of activities that sometimes just allow them to survive," the report says, citing self-employment, domestic service and employment in micro-enterprises.

In other Latin American countries, the ILO estimates that unemployment in 1998 was 7.9 per cent in Brazil, 11.3 per cent in Venezuela, 3.4 per cent in Mexico, and 15.2 per cent in Colombia.

Africa

In Sub-Saharan Africa, a prolonged period of poor growth and deteriorating labour market conditions has given way to a slight improvement in the employment situation in many countries during 1998. Rising growth rates have been spurred by improvements in the weather and declining drought, an increase in the prices of export products, devaluation of the CFA frane (*Communaute financiere africaine*) to increase competitiveness, and structural reform and political change which made foreign direct investment more attractive.

Nevertheless, the ILO says that Africa's recovery though encouragling, "should not be cause for undue optimism. With a labour force growth of almost 3 per cent and little job creation in the formal sector, most jobs are necessarily created in the informal sector, and in low-productivity agriculture". In addition, with a predicted annual growth rate of 2.9 per cent in the economically active population between 1997 and 2010 (compared with 1.9 per cent for southeast Asia and 1.8 per cent for Latin America), an estimated 8.7 million new job-seekers will enter the labour market every year.

Developed countries

Growth in the developed countries has been encouraging but uneven. The report says that "while between 1993 and 1997 Canada, the Unitd Kingdom, the United States and a few other countries showed good performance, levels of activity in France, Germany and Italy were less robust. Japan is still unable to recover from several years of lack lustre growth".

In the European Union, more than 18 million workers are unemployed this year, the ILO says, noting that "the picture does not take into account the considerable number of `discouraged' workers who have given up hope of finding work, and involuntary part-time workers." However, output and employment showed signs of picking up in Europe by mid-1998, prompting a decline in the average unemployment rate in the European Union to 10.2 per cent in May, compared with 10.70 per cent a year earlier. Although Japan still experiences unemployment rates which are low by the standards of most developed countries, joblessness has begun rising sharply as economic growth has stalled since the mid-1990s.

Social Dimensions of the Problem

"The low-skilled unemployed have poet prospects to find a job even if the overall macroeconomic environment improves," the report says. "The social dimensions of this problem are enormous and have to be tackled with policy measures and programmes aimed at reintegrating the long-term unemployed into the labour market."

• *Young Workers*: The ILO estimates that about 60 million young people around the world between the ages of 15 and 24 are in search of work, with youth unemployment running 20 per cent in many OECD countries. "Low growth has worsened the situation in Western Europe and economic contraction and restructuring have severely limited access to new jobs in Eastern Europe," the report says.

In developing countries of Africa, Asia and Latin America, "urban unemployment rates for young people often reach over 30 per cent," the report notes. The new global turmoil makes young workers even more vulnerable to layoffs-employers react to economic recession by cutting back on hiring new workers. The report also points out the wider dangers of youth unemployment, stressing that youth joblessness can often lead to vandalism, crime, drug abuse, alienation, social unrest and conflict.

The ILO had found examples of programmes that work for young people, however. In many countries of Latin America and Asia, "schemes that provide young people with a foothold in the labour market through short-term in-firm work experience can effectively improve employment outcomes where a demand exists for low or semi-skilled workers, and where economic growth is relatively high".

A key policy approach in many of the European Union countries is to provide financial incentives to firms to hire and provide some training for young workers. In the mid-1990s, these "youth contracts" accounted for almost 25 per cent of youth employment in Italy, 20 per cent in Greece and 12 per cent in France and Spain.

• *The long-term unemployed*: "Long-term unemployment in the labour market is one of the most persistent and serious social issues," the report says. The longer the workers have been unemployed, the smaller their chances of findings a job. Their skill level runs the risk of deteriorating, and employers are increasingly hesitant to employ them.

Long-term unemployment has been particularly severe in the European Union member countries, where more than 60 per cent of the 9 million long-term unemployed in 1996 had been of work longer than two years.

Older workers and women becoming unemployed are more at risk of remaining unemployed for a long period of time. Similarly, workers displaced from declining industries and workers with disabilities are similarly more likely to be among the long-term unemployed than workers in general.

A combination of mutually supportive measures is much more effective in improving employability for the long-term unemployed than "stand-alone" programmes, the report says. Combined measures include subsidized jobs, job search assistance, remedial education, training, and family— or social-problem counselling. Training or placement in actual workplaces allows workers to overcome employers' hesitance to hire the long-term unemployed. Small-scale, community-based reintegration enterprises have been most effective in countering long-term unemployment by providing a range of services to the unemployed while contributing to wider community needs and local economic regeneration.

• *Women and training in the global economy*: Over the past 20 years, women have provided the bulk of new labour supply in developed and developing countries alike. In every region except Africa, the proportion of women in the labour force has grown substantially. Women, for example, have accounted for nearly 80 per cent of all labour force growth in the European Union since 1980. In some countries — Ireland, Italy, Sweden and the United Kingdom — the figure reaches almost 100 per cent.

Two opposing trends have emerged in recent years: one is the expansion and feminization of lower-level jobs in the service sector; the other is the growing number of high-level jobs obtained by women as a result of educational achievement. In many advanced industrial countries, for example, women have been enrolling in large numbers "for degrees in medicine, law, accountancy and business studies, all areas which have previously been dominated by male students," the report says.

There are, by contrast, "fewer examples of women making significant inroads into traditionally male-dominated jobs at intermediate and lower skill levels by pursuing training in these areas," notes the report. The reasons include ingrained discrimination and the declining demand for these types of jobs in many economies.

Confronted with so many barriers in the labour market, increasing numbers of women are launching their own enterprises. "National estimates indicate that 10 per cent of the new enterprises in North Africa, 33 per cent in North America and 40 per cent in the former East Germany were created by women," the report says. The figure for the United States alone surpasses 60 per cent.

• *Informal sector*: The ILO report says the majority of new jobs in developing countries are being created in the informal sector which, according to ILO estimates, employs about 500 million workers. Lack of sufficient job growth in the formal sector of the economy as well as lack of skills of a large section of the labour force have resulted in the growth of the informal sector, where most workers are in low-paid employment in unregulated and poor working conditions.

Concerted action is required to improve the incomes, productivity and working conditions of the large and growing number of workers involved. With institutional support and access to affordable credit, training can make a difference to incomes and working conditions in the informal sector. Training policies, argues the report, would do better to address the needs of those already established in informal production and who require upgrading of specific skills through an introduction to new technologies and new products.

• *Training system reforms*: The ILO report surveys different approaches to training around the world with an eye to highlighting some of the strengths and shortcomings of each system. It also sets out an agenda for improving the efficiency and governance of training systems worldwide to achieve the quality standards required in today's highly competitive world.

While the ILO authors insist that there is no ideal training system, they argue that any successful system needs to take account of three factors: a solid educational base: an appropriate incentive structure in which training priorities are fuelled by real economic demand, and institutional arrangements in which the social partners — employers, workers and government —contribute to improving performance and efficiency.

Most training systems in developing or restructuring economies are in rapid evolution. In East Asia, governments in recent decades massively supported primary and secondary education and carefully monitored international demand in setting vocational training priorities; on the back of the success of this highly structured approach, a more decentralized system is being developed, with less government involvement and more choice from increasingly affluent populations with stronger social institutions.

In Eastern Europe, the governments of centrally planned economies worked to match workforce skills to the demands of state-owned industries which provided additional training. In general, the training needs of workers in this region have suffered as a result of the economic transition.

The direction of reform of training systems worldwide is toward more "demand-led" systems, which respond to the real and immediate requirements of enterprises at the expense of "supply-led" systems, which tend to be driven by the priorities of public officials and established providers of training.

"Demand-led orientation of training systems has various components. Firstly, governments help private agents, both employers and individuals, to sponsor training which is in their own immediate interests. Secondly, in the training which governments sponsor in their own right, more effort is made to incorporate information about market demand for skills, and to replace government provision by private provision, using market-like mechanisms to increase efficiency," the ILO report says. Public sector training providers are forced to compete with others for training contracts.

Public policy increasingly concentrates on encouraging enterprises and individuals to shoulder the major part of training costs, by demonstrating the utility of training and encouraging greater competition in the provision of training. But once again, a number of possible models can coexist.

Training levies, which involve an annual amount being assessed by the government (usually 1 or 2% of the wage bill paid by employers) are in operation in a number of Latin American countries. Other systems, involving a levy plus grant, operate in countries as diverse as France. Singapore and Zimbabwe, where in firms are exempted from taxes on training to the extent that they provide the training themselves. In other words, firms which provide no training to their employees pay the full levy (which goes to fund national training efforts) and firms which do provide training can deduct the expenses from their levy.

8

GLOBAL DIVERSE ISSUES

EDUCATION UNICEF STATE OF THE WORLD'S CHILDREN 1999 REPORT : MAIN FINDINGS AND RECOMMENDATIONS IN BRIEF

An estimated 855 million people—nearly one-sixth of humanity-will be functionally illiterate on the eve of the millennium, according to the report. At the same time, over 130 million children of school age in the developing world are growing up without access to basic eductaion, while millions of others longuish in sub-standard learning situations where little education takes place.

"Girls crowd these ranks disproportionately," says the report, "representing nearly two of every three children who do not receive a primary education (approximatey 73 million of the 130 million out-of-school children)."

Education For All

Over the last decade a consensus has grown concerning why the objectives of Education For All have been so hard to achieve, along with the kinds of changes that will be necessary to improve education quality. "Education planning, whether for an entire society or a single school," says the report, "must start with child rights and be based on the best interests of the child. It must strive to ensure an environment that is free from violence, that fosters democracy and acceptance and that teaches skills which equip students for lives as responsible citizens."

According to a chapter on Education For All, education is an essential human right, a force for social change, and the single most vital element in combating poverty. It also helps empower women, safeguard children from exploitative and hazardous labour and sexual exploitation, promote human rights and democracy, protect the environment, and control population growth.

"Education", stresses the report, "is a path towards international peace and security." The chapter includes examples of initiatives that meet the child's right to education at the international, regional, national and local levels.

The Right to Education

A section in the report on the right to education explores the historical context in which children's right to education has been repeatedly affirmed, including in documents such as the 1948 Universal Declaration of Human Rights, the 1989 Convention on the Rights for the Child, and the 1990 World Summit for Children.

A mid-decade review in June 1996 revealed that the generalized decline and disrepair of education in the 1980s, labelled by many as the "lost decade" for the developing world, has been largely reversed. "Regionally, the rates of progress varied," according to the report. "Both the East Asia and Pacific and Latin America and Caribbean regions neared the goal of universal primary enrolment, and remarkable gains were recorded in the Middle East and North

Africa in recent years."

However in South Asia 50 million children are not in school, and sub-Saharan Africa still cannot provide sufficent classroom space for its rapidly growing population. In Central and Eastern Europe and many of the newly independent countries of the former Soviet Union, once relatively solid and universal access to education is shrinking in the new era of market economies.

The Education Revolution

A section on the "education revolution", whose elements are access to quality learning and child rights, focuses on elements that have emerged as necessary for the success of the principle of education for all. It says schooling:

— should provide the foundation for learning for life;
— needs to be accessible, of high quality and flexible;
— must be gender sensitive and emphasize girls' education;
— needs to involve the state as a key partner; and
— should begin with care for the young child.

"The education revolution is reshaping the edifice of education", says the report. "Under its aegis, schools must become zones of creativity, safety and stimulation for children, with safe water and decent sanitation, with motivated teachers and relevant curricula, where children are respected and learn to respect others." Schools also need to offer young children in the early primary grades a nurturing experience that eases their transition into systems all too often not designed to do this.

Investing in Human Rights

In a section on investing in human rights, the report warns that despite progress of the last decade, the education revolution is in danger of being cut short by a dearth of resources and growing indebtedness in the developing world. This section argues that, despite these obstacle, education is one of the best investments a country can make in order to prosper.

"The commitment to education", says the report, "which foundered on the rocks of debt and structural adjustment during the 1980s, has been renewed in the 1990s by the awareness that human rights are key to human development. As never before, humanity recognizes that human rights are indivisible and that the fulfilment of one right reinforces and promotes another."

The concept of a human right to education, like the rights to freedom of speech and thought and freedom from torture, may still strike many as a novel concept, notes the report. "It is an especially far-reaching and transforming concept in the developing world, where 130 million children who should be in school are not. Even more revolutionary is the insistence of the Convention on the Rights of the Child that this education must consist of a high-quality learning experience in a child-centred, gender-sensitive environment."

Source : *Go Between 73*, February-March 1999.

ENVIRONMENT : UNEP BIENNIUM REPORT, 1996-1997

UNEP has much to celebrate during its 25th anniversary year. It embarks on its next quarter of a century revitalized by a renewed mandate and strengthened by a biennium of significant achievement.

UNEP has learned much from 25 years at the forefront of the global environmental debate, and has changed as it has learned. Over the five years since world leaders met in Rio de Janeiro for the 1992 United National Conference on Environment and Development (UNCED), the Earth Summit, UNEP has placed greater emphasis on concrete results and on delivering its programmes in the regions. It has decentralized where appropriate, forged new partnership with organizations with shared core concerns and strengthened its traditional alliances. In a harsh economic elimate, which places consideration for the health of the planet second to immediate economic reward, UNEP has learned to stretch fewer resources to address increasing problems of environmental degradation. During the 1996-1997 biennium, UNEP has begun to reap the rewards of its reform efforts.

New Mandate

First and foremost among these rewards is UNEP's renewed and strengthened mandate. The Secretary-General, Kofi Annan, said in his report on the reform of the United National to the fifty-first General Assembly of the United Nations that 'High priority must be given to according to (UNEP) the status, strength and access to resources it requires to function effectively . . .

The Road From Rio

The Earth Summit's far-ranging Agenda 21 was a comprehensive action plan that has since provided the framework for UNEP's programme of work. World leaders attending Rio pledged a new way forward to ensure the survival of life on Earth: the Rio Declaration acknowledged the need to change consumption patterns and address global poverty.

Yet despite the promises and commitments of UNCED, despite energetic institutional reform in international agencies, governments and voluntary organizations, and an increasingly sound body of voluntary agreements, codes of conduct and guidelines, progress has been slow, unable to keep pace with new challenges. The sense of urgency generated by Rio has evaporated. Significant environmental problems remain deeply embedded in the socio-economic fabric of all nations, and the funds and political will have not been sufficient to make the necessary impact.

UNEP faced this biennium with fewer resources than ever to take on increasingly intractable global issues. Nonetheless it has notched up important concrete achievements towards the implementation of Agenda 21.

— A major success was publication of the first, *Global Environment Outlook* (GEO-1) at the beginning of 1997. This authoritative report on the state of the environment attracted acclaim and positive publicity worldwide. Though its message is harsh, 'the pace at which the world is moving toward a sustainable future is simply too slow', GEO-1 ushers in a new era in environmental assessment and international scientific collaboration on data collection.

— UNEP has advanced a broad-based chemicals agenda to greatly enhance the protection of the world's peoples and environment from potentially dangerous chemicals. As part of the chemicals agenda, UNEP has developed the voluntary prior informed consent procedure on the trade of hazardous chemicals and pesticides and, jointly with the Food and Agriculture Organization of the United Nations, is convening negotiations for a convention on the issue. UNEP has also laid the scientific and policy groundwork necessary to begin negotiations, convened by UNEP for the beginning of 1998, for a new global chemicals safety convention on persistent organic pollutants.

— As the organization hosting the secretariats of the Vienna Convention for the Protection of the Ozone Layer and the Montreal Protocol on Substances that Deplete the Ozone Layer, UNEP has been at the forefront in the extension and implementation of these agreements. Under them, industrialized countries ceased production and consumption of the most important ozonedepleting substances by the end of 1996. The 1999 deadline for beginning to implement the controls of such substances by the developing world now looks likely to be met. with some developing country governments 'jumping the gun' and reducing their consumption in advance.

— Recognizing UNEP's mandate and achievements in dealing with the aquatic environment, governments designated the organization as the secretariat of the Global Programme of Action for the Protection of the Marine Environment from Land-based Activities.

— UNEP has supported the launch of 188 national, sub-regional and regional cleaner production initiatives in 61 countries as part of its programme of sustainable production in industry including ten national cleaner production centres.

— UNEP has encouraged financial services institutions to incorporate environmental considerations into their business. Two statements of environmental commitment for the banking and insurance industries were successfully launched by UNEP and have since been signed by 103 banks and 70 insurance companies.

— Facing the challenges of new technologies, UNEP has prepared *International Technical Guidelines for Safety in Biotechnology* which were finalized and adopted in Buenos Aires at the 1996 Conference of the Parties to the Convention on Biological Diversity.

— UNEP has greatly increased its activities targeted towards civil society. The number of its national committees, the multi-stakeholder support organizations, rose over the biennium to 14; the UNEP policy on non-governmental organizations (NGOs) and other major groups was adopted specifically to facilitate support for groups active in such issues as desertification control, water and climate change; and UNEP launched its Global Environmental Citizenship programme aimed at improving environmental education, understanding and, consequentially, action by informed citizens.

These and other achievements are outlined in greater detail in the following chapters.

Reform

This impressive list has been achieved despite financial uncertainty. It would not have been possible if, over the biennium, the secretariat had not cooperated in a number of important reforms, both structural and managerial. Following the instructions of the eighteenth session of the Governing Council in 1995, UNEP recast the focus and content of its programme of work. An integrated programme was reoriented around just four environmental issues:

— Sustainable management and use of natural resources.
— Sustainable production and consumption.
— A better environment for human health and well-being.
— Globalization and the environment.

At the same time, UNEP adopted a more decentralized and participatory approach to programme development with accentuated roles for its regional offices. The strategy has been to concentrate on key priorities yet be ready to deal with emerging issues, and ensure that the benefits of the programmes are successfully delivered.

This latter marks an important shift of emphasis, laid out in the 1996-1997 programme of work and now very much in accord with the thinking of the United Nations: that global policy must, in practice, be seen to be implemented at a regional level.

Along with this reorientation, smaller but significant changes in the way in which UNEP opertes have been undertaken, for example the use of more effective communications at lower cost. Tele-conferencing and remote translation facilities for meetings have been highly effective. Greater use has been made of the Internet for the dissemination of information and discussion documents, while internal communications have been imroved by greater reliance on electronic mail. Implementation of the Mercure communications satellite and its integration with UNEP net will lead to further savings and efficiency, and easier contact with a wider range of information suppliers and users. Reforms such as these, including. UNEP's emphasis on results management and its use of performance indicators and other means of verification in the cost-effective delivery of its programme of work, have drawn praise from the United Nations Efficiency Board. This points to UNEP as an example for other agencies to emulate in the drive for 'better service, better value, better management' in the 21st century.

Strengthened Governance

A major change in UNEP's governance was made at the nineteenth session of the Governing Council in response to concerns expressed by some government representatives that the two-year gap between sessions hindered their ability to participate in policy-making between meetings. Following lengthy debate and consultation, the Governing Council agreed to create a High-level Committee of Ministers and Officials and also agreed to maintain a strong role for the Committee of Permanent Representatives.

The High-level Committee meets as an intersessional body and has the mandate to consider the international environmental agenda and make reform and policy recommendations to the Governing Council. It is hoped that the High-level Committee will contribute to the revitalization of UNEP and the fulfilment of its role as the lead environment agency of the United Nations. The inaugural meeting of the High-level Committee was held in New York in June, 1997 immediately following the special session of the General Assembly, and was attended by ministers and senior officials from more than 70 countries.

Resources

The Nairobi Declaration stresses the importance of adequate, stable and predictable resources and member governments have acknowledged that UNEP will need a firm funding base to fulfil its new mandate. The 1996-1997 biennium was, unfortunately, characterized by deep financial difficulties and uncertainties. With contributions falling short of expectations at the end of 1996, UNEP was forced to confront donor governments with an urgent plea: to pay more, to pay earlier, and to make commitments far enough in advance to allow rational long-term planning. Against this trend of late or non-payment, some countries did, however, prepay their 1997 contributions in 1996.

Unlike many agencies UNEP depends almost entirely on voluntary contributions from member governments. In 1996, for example, only 37 per cent of member states contributed to the Environment Fund. With an increasing number of governments facing their own budgetary constraints, the system of voluntary contributions is proving unpredictable and inadequate. The proliferation of organizations operating in the environmental arena has meant that some member nations have had to divert portions of their environmental budgets to other ecological concerns.

In 1996-1997, the shortfall in expected contributions to the Environment Fund under this voluntary system left UNEP with inadequate resources to carry out the programme of work endorsed by its Governing Council. Therefore, at the beginning of 1997, Governing Council was warned that the approved programme could not be carried out in full.

The Environment Fund's budget for the 1996-1997 programme of work had been agreed at a level of $90 million at the eighteenth session of the Governing Council. At the nineteenth session, and for the first time in the 25-year history of UNEP, the Executive Director proposed that the Governing Council revise its budget downwards to $63.5 million.

Readjustment of such an order necessarily had a severe impact on the programme of work. The cuts fell on every element of UNEP's activities.

Fundraising

The impact would have been greater still had not UNEP energetically pursued additional resources through various fundraising efforts and, in 1996-1997, raised an extra $80.1 million through joint projects, trust funds, counterpart contributions from governments, the Global Environment Facility, and private sources. In other words, and to the credit of the UNEP secretariat, for every dollar deposited in the Environment Fund, more than one dollar has been additionally generated.

The successful mobilization of such resources has enabled UNEP to salvage important elements of its programme of work, but it is no substitute for a reliable flow of contributions into the Environment Fund. Many of the additional contributions are tied to specific, highly focused projects, and there is a risk that UNEP's agreed priorities may become distorted if the balance between these two types of funding is not kept in check. For the future, too great a reliance on 'earmarked' funds could endanger UNEP's flexibility, and thus its ability to respond to rapid change, as well as increasing its administrative burden. It is worth reflecting that an entire year's budget for UNEP represents just 20 minutes of global arms spending.

There are reasons to be optimistic, however, even on the financial front. The nineteenth session of the Governing Council agreed that financing would be addressed comprehensively at the next session, and at the inaugural meeting of the new High-level Committee of Ministers and Officials an overwhelming consensus emerged on the need to prioritize the issue of stable financing for UNEP. At the same meeting, some donors who had withheld funds while awaiting the outcome of the debate on governance reinstated pledges or made new commitments.

The Future

Sound institutional reforms, improved governance and the hope of a firmer financial base leave UNEP well placed to face the future. But they will not, of themselves, be enough to reverse worsening environmental trends. The future of the Earth ultimately depends upon the billions of daily choices and decisions made by individuals around the globe, which is why UNEP places a high priority on its Global Environmental Citizenship initiatives. UNEP has in this biennium, as ever, made a priority of finding innovative ways to change attitudes and behaviour, to inform, educate, encourage and learn from NGOs, concerned individuals and groups.

UNEP's programme of work for the next biennium provides the strategic framework to take it into the 21st century. The United Nations has decided that UNEP is to be the voice of environmental authority within the United Nations system, but if UNEP's is to be a voice loud enough to be heard above the clamour of unfettered economic growth and globalization, it will need, as outlined in the Nairobi Declaration, adequate, stable and predictable funding.

Source : UNEP Biennial Report, 1996-97.

FOOD : FAO STATE OF FOOD AND AGRICULTURE REPORT, 1998

The report provides an extensive and in-depth analysis of issues that will have a major impact on global food and agriculture policies in the coming years and decades.

It notes a rise in the number of hungry people despite significant reductions in hunger and malnutrition in several developing regions. The total number of chronically undernourished people in developing countries is now estimated to be 828 million for the 1994-1996 period, up from 822 million for 1990-1992.

Compounded Problem

In addition to weather-related crop damage leading to less domestic food availability in many countries, the problem was compounded by foreign exchange constraints that prevented the import of food to make up the domestic shortfall.

Other factors involved in the growing numbers of hungry people include the growth in the total population and changing demographics that result in a larger proportion of that population being young, which leads to changes in minimum dietary requirements.

The largest absolute numbers of undernourished people are in Asia, while the largest proportion of the population that is undernourished is in sub-Saharan Africa. More striking, says the report, is the fact that contrary to the overall tendency in the developing countries as a whole, the poorest group of countries has not been able to reduce the number or percentage of undernourished since 1969-1971.

In East Asia and Southeast Asia, there are 258 million malnourished people. In South Asia in 1994-1996 there were 254 million undernourished people, up from 237 million in 1990-1992.

The number of hungry is also increasing in sub-Saharan Africa. "Our most recent data on Africa south of the Sahara," said Jacques Vercueil, Director of FAO's Agriculture and Economic Development Analysis Division, "show an increase in malnourished people from 196 million in 1990-1992 to 210 million in 1994-1996. The report also shows that the widening gap in income distribution in many parts of the world is also an important factor in undernourishment."

The overall percentage of malnourished as a part of the world population has declined over the same period, from 20 to 19 per cent. However, the report says, this has not been sufficient to compensate for population growth.

Economic Gains Threatened

Global financial turmoil now threatens earlier economic gains made by many Asian and Latin American countries, including improved food security. Its negative effects on household incomes, employment and prospects for agricultural production and trade could lead to greater food insecurity for millions of people.

> "Efforts to meet the World Food Summit goal of reducing, by at least half, the 1996 number of hungry people in the world by the year 2015 are all the more urgent," said Mr. Vercueil.

Globally, the number of countries facing food emergencies rose from 29 in mid-1997 to 36 in mid-1998, mainly due to the effects of the El Nino weather phenomenon. Since the FAO report went to press, that number has risen to 40, according to the organization's Global Information and Early Warning System.

Feeding the World's Cities

In a special featur on Feeding the World's Cities the report said, "Over the next 20 years, 93 per cent of urban growth will occur in the cities of the developing world. Some of these cities are already huge: the world now has more than 20 megacities with a population of more than 10 million each, while 50 years ago only New York City could claim that distinction." For example, Dhaka in Bangladesh has a population of nine million and is growing at an annual rate of 5 per cent, adding 1,300 city residents every day.

It is a huge task to feed a city of several million people, said the report. A city of ten million people—for example Manila, Cairo or Rio de Janeiro—may need to import at least 6,000 tonnes of food per day. This requires much coordination among producers, transporters, market managers and retailers in stores, on the street and in open-air markets.

By 2005 more than 50 per cent of the world's population will be urban, and food insecurity will become an increasingly urban problem. Consumer needs and the responsibilities of both government and private operatiors as well as marketing facilities are just some of the issues examined in the report.

Rural Non-Farm Income

The State of Food and Agriculture 1998 also contains a special chapter on rural non-farm income, which is income derived from wage activities and self-employment in commerce, manufacturing and other services in rural areas. This kind of income "is an important resource for farm and other rural households, including the landless poor as well as rural town residents", says the report.

The chapter looks at what can be done within rural areas themselves to increse overall economic activity and employment, and to strengthen the links between agriculture and the rural non-farm sector. It says that rural non—farm income activity too often falls into an institutional vacuum with ministries of industry focusing on urban industry and ministries of agriculture on farming. The chapter stresses the importance of greater ministerial coordination.

Source :*Go Between 73*, February-March, 1999.

POPULATION : FIVE-YEAR REVIEW OF POPULATION AND DEVELOPMENT CONFERENCE

Introduction

Progress and challenges in implementing strategies on population and development will be the focus of the international community at a special session of the United Nations General Assembly, to be held in New York from 30 June—2 July, 1999.

The special session, which will take place some five years after the 1994 International Conference on Population and Development in Cairo (Egypt), will provide a forum to review and appraise implementation of the Programme of Action that emerged from the Cairo conference (see *NGLS Roundup,* October 1994). The review and appraisal will be undertaken on the basis of, and with full respect for, the Programme of Action. There will be no renegotiation of the existing agreements, as decided by the General Assembly in a December 1997 resolution.

From now through June 1999, the United Nations Population Fund (UNFPA) is sponsoring a series of review-related activities that will involve governments, donors, the United Nations system, and representatives of civil society including NGOs and the private sector. The review will culminate in an international forum to be held in The Hauge (Netherlands) from 8-12 February 1999; an NGO Forum will be held prior to the Hauge Forum.

Background

The International Conference on Population and Development (ICPD), held from 5-13 September 1994, was convened under the auspices of the United Nations and organized by a secretariat composed of UNEPA and the Population Division of the United Nations Department for Economic and Social Information and Policy Analysis (now integrated into the United Nations Department of Economic and Soical Affairs).

ICPD was the largest intergovernmental conference on population and development ever held with 11,000 registered participants from governments, UN specialized agencies and organizations, intergovernmental organizations and NGOs. More than 180 states took part in negotiations to finalize a Programme of Action in the area of population and development for the next 20 years (see *NGLS Roundup*, January 1997).

ICPD Programme of Action

The Programme of Action, adopted by acclamation, endorses a new strategy emphasizing the integral linkages between population and development, and it focuses on meeting the needs of individual women and men rather than achieving demographic targets. The key to this new approach is empowering women and providing them with more choices through expanded access to education and health services, skill development and employment, and through their full involvement in policy and decision-making processes at all levels. According to UNFPA, one of the greatest achievements of the Cairo conference was recognition of the need to empower women, both as a highly important end in itself and as a key to improving the quality of life for everyone.

One of the primary goals of the Programme of Action is to make family planning universally available by the year 2015 as part of the broadened approach to reproductive health and rights. It includes goals in regard to education, especially for girls, as well as further reducing levels of infant, child and maternal mortality. The Programme of Action also addresses issues relating to population, the environment and consumption patterns; the family; internal and international migration; prevention and control of HIV/AIDS; technology, research and development; and partnership with the non-governmental sector.

The Programme of Action builds upon the World Population Plan of Action, adopted at the World Population Conference held in Bucharest (Hungary) in 1974, and recommendations adopted at the International Conference on Population, held in Mexico City (Mexico) in 1984. It also builds on outcomes of the 1990 World Summit for children, the 1992 UN Conference on Environment and Development, and the 1993 World Conference on Human Rights. The ICPD's major emphases were reaffirmed at the World Summit for Social Development and the Fourth World Conference on Women, both held in 1995.

Coming Up Short

The Programme of Action also provides estimates of the levels of national resources and international assistance required, and it calls on governments to make those resources available. Governments at the Cairo conference agreed that developing countries should cover two-thirds of the costs of a package of basic reproductive health and family palnning services, prevention of sexually transmitted diseases and HIV/AIDS, and related research, data and policy analysis. According to UNFPA, funds needed for these will rise to US$17 billion per year in the year 2000 and to US$21.7 billion in 2015. In 1995, the latest year for which data are available, developing countries spent around US$7.5 billion on such programmes. International assistance, in the form of grants and loans, contributed another US$2 billion. However, while developing countries continue to increase allocations for reproductive health, international assistance has stagnated, heightening concern that donors may not meet their one-third share of the US$17 billion required in the year 2000. Donor spending, including World

Bank loans, increased by 40 per cent in 1994 and by the same percentage in 1995. But this momentum appears to have stagnated with little or no increases since, according to UNFPA.

Aims of the ICPD+5 Review

The ICPD+5 review will:

- Assess progress achieved and constraints faced in implementation of the Programme of Action, as well as provide key future actions for the realization of ICPD goals,
- Highlight special issues such as mobilization of resources made available—bilateral, multilateral and domestic—for population and development;
- Identify priorities for the future; and
- Call on governments and all partners to recommit themselves at the highest political level to achieving the goals and objectives contained in the Programme of Action.

The main document for discussion at ICPD+5 will be a draft report prepared by UN Secretary-General Kofi Annan on further implementation of the Programme of Action Governments were asked to provide their comments by mid-August 1998 for submission to the 53rd UN General Assembly, which will take up the topic in its Second Committee. Issues to be addressed include: population levels and trends; population growth, structure and distribution; reproductive rights and reproductive health; health and mortality; international migration and development; and population and programmes and resources in national action, international cooperation and the non-governmental sector.

Preparations for the ICPD+5 Review

The 31st session of the Commission on Population and Development (CPD), held from 23-27 February, 1998 adopted a draft resolution that calls on UNFPA and the Population Division of the UN Department of Economic and Social Affairs to collaborate and coordinate the ICPD review process (see *NGLS Roundup*, April 1998). The commission also agreed that its 32nd session in March 1999 be extended to seven working days, and that part of the session serve as an open-ended preparatory meeting for the special session.

The Commission on Population and Development decided that the report and outcome of the Hague Forum will be submitted to the commission at its March 1999 session. At that time, the commission will also consider a comprehensive report of the Secretary-General on the quinquennial review and appraisal of the implementation of the Programme of Action, to be coordinated by the Population Division of the UN Department of Economic and Social Affairs.

The draft report of the Secretary-General on further implementation of the Programme of Action will also serve as the text to be discussed at the open-ended preparatory meeting of the CPD. The report will reflect outcomes of the Hague Forum, the quinquennial review, and the preparatory meeting discussion.

NGO Participation in the ICPD+5 Process

The UN General Assembly has stressed the need for effective participation of actors of civil society, particularly NGOs, in preparation for the special session and for their substantive contribution to and active involvement in preparatory meetings and the special session.

Actions taken by UNFPA to ensure that the voices and views of civil society are heard in the process include:

— Encouraging NGO and parliamentary participation on country delegations invited to the Hague Forum and attending the special session;
— Inviting NGOs at all levels with expertise, capacity and dedication to ICPD implementation to the Hague Forum;
— Inviting and includig representatives of civil society as expert participants to UNFPA round table and technical meetings; and
— Inviting NGOs to suggest resource materials to be considered as part of background documentation for UNFPA round table and technical meetings.

NGO Forum

An NGO Forum on ICPD+5 implementation, to be held in the Netherlands at the same site as the Hague Forum, will take place on 6-7 February, 1999. The NGO Forum is expected to examine issues of concern to the NGO community in appraising implementation of the ICPD Programme of Action. The forum will also provide NGOs with an opportunity to articulate the issues they intend to present and discuss at the intergovernmental Hague Forum, which follows.

The World Population Foundation (WPF), based in Hilversum (Netherlands), is serving as the local facilitator and focal point for NGO participation in the NGO Forum. WPF is a non-governmental organization specializing in population and the promotion of reproductive health and rights.

WPF hosted the first meeting on 17-19 July of an NGO advisory group on arrangements for the NGO Forum. Information on NGO Forum preparatios and how to participate can be obtained from WPF.

Source : *NGLS Roundup*, September, 1998.

POVERTY : UNDP REPORT 1998 ON OVERCOMING HUMAN POVERTY : MAIN FINDINGS

According to the report, developing countries have made little progress to eradicate absolute poverty since the 1995 World Summit for Social Development. At the same time rich countries, which have seen their own poverty increase in recent years, are spending fewer resources on social programmes and have progressively reduced their development assistance.

Beating Poverty Most Urgent Issue

Overcoming poverty has become the most urgent issue facing all countries and societies today. Around the world more than two billion people have little or no access to food, basic services or adequate shelter, and 12 million children die each year of curable diseases or malnutrition before their fifth birthday. Nine-hundred million people globally are either unemployed or underemployed, 40 million of them in countries of the Organisation for Economic Co-operation and Development (OECD). "This is not a fitting legacy for the next generation", said UNDP Administrator James Gustave Speth, "particularly at a time when the worst aspects of poverty can be eliminated for the price of 1 per cent of the world's income of US$25 trillion."

At the 1995 Copenhagen World Summit for Social Development, 186 governments committed to making poverty eradication a central goal of their national policies and to pool forces to end global poverty. The UNDP report notes that out of the 130 countries surveyed, only 38 have so far set targets for the eradication of extreme poverty.

Slow Progress in Poor Countries

In some regions of the world, the gap between rich and poor has actually worsened since the summit. In sub-Saharan Africa, between the late 1980s and now, the share of national income going to the poorest fifth of the population dropped from 5.7 to 5.2 per cent. In Latin America and the Caribbean, the poorest fifth receive only 4.5 per cent.

Debt and un-attractive conditions to foreign investors are given as two of the main reasons for poor countries' slow progress. In sub-Saharan Africa, 14 per cent of export revenue goes to debt servicing; in South Asia it is 22 per cent. Foreign Direct Investment (FDI), often hailed as a panacea for poor countries' slow growth, tends to flow toward middle-income rather than low-income economies. Out of about US$120 billion in FDI going to developing countries in 1997, sub-Saharan Africa received only US$3 billion and South Asia US$4 billion. By contrast, China alone accounted for US$31 billion.

Using Aid Creatively

Aid used creatively, stresses the report, remains a vital tool for development and poverty eradication. However in this area the international community has not done enough. Official development assistance is at an all-time low—a more 0.2 per cent of industrialized countries' gross domestic product. Additional resources must be mobilized, but equally important, the delivery of aid will have to be reformed to better meet the needs and aspirations of the poor.

Aid should be directed at building capacities and know-how to allow poor countries to improve their infrastructures, decentralize their governments to bring public administration closer to the people, and manage natural resources in a sustainable way.

> "None of the development goals we are committed to today will be achieved without serious global and national efforts to rid the world of poverty", siad Mr. Speth. "We know that extreme poverty can be eliminated in a generation. We have no ethical alternative but to take on this challenge with all the seriousness it deserves."

Recent Activities Focused on Poverty Eradication

Information, solidarity and the participation of all sectors of society are also essential ingredients for an effective poverty eradication recipe. For this reason, UNDP held activities on all continents during the week of the UN Day for the Eradication of Poverty. The message of the events was that poverty eradication must be a central goal for all social and economic players—from decision-makers to associations, private businesses to NGOs, and municipalities to individuals.

Some of the activities organized to inform and mobilize support included the following:

- *The First Global Forum of the World Alliance of Cities Against Poverty*—At this event on 12-14 October held in Lyon (France), 100 municipalities met to exchange and map out novel strategies to fight urban poverty and expand the opportunities of their citizens.
- *Races Against Poverty*—In Paris on 17 October UNDP joined the 20th edition of the Paris 20-Kilometre Race for the first time to make the theme of this traditional event a race against the clock to end poverty. In Almeria (Spain) UNDP, the municipality, the National Olympic Committee and local associations organized a race to collect funds for social projects directed at the poor in the city and nationwide; another race against poverty was planned in Switzerland in conjunction with the Swiss Olympic Association.
- In New York, five women were awarded prizes for their personal triumphs over poverty and their contribution in their home countries to helping others do the same. The women come from the Dominican Republic, France, India, Jordan and Uganda.
- In Zambia a national workshop on poverty eradication was held.
- In Lebanon the government released its first poverty mapping study.
- In Georgia the National Ballet gave a benefit performance to raise money for social causes.
- Cambodia released its *National Human Development Report*.
- Guatemala launched a book on *Poverty Situation of Mayan Peoples of Guatemala*.

Source : *Go Between 72*, December 1998 - January 1999.

PART TWO

INDIA

9

LAND AND ITS PEOPLE

India that is Bharat covering a land area 32,87,263 sq.km is the seventh largest and the second most populous country of the world. It stretches 3,214 km. from North to South between the extreme latitudes and 2,933 km from East to West between the extreme longitudes. On this 2.4 per cent of earth's surface live 15 per cent (88 crore people) of world's population.

Population

Over 160 million people are added annually to our population (President's Republic day Speech, 25th January 1989). Since 1881, the Census in India has been taken regularly after ten years. According to 1991 Census, the total population of India (including the projected population of Jammu and Kashmir is 846,302,688. As compared 1981 census, it showed an increase of 23.85 per cent. According to 1991 Census, the growth of urban population in the country during the decade 1981-1991, slowed down by about ten per cent as compared to the earlier decade of 1971-1981. However, the number of cities and towns has been consistently increasing. The urban population at present in 25.72 per cent.

Density

The average population of density of per km^2 in 1991 was 267. It varies considerably from State to State.

Sex Ratio

According to 1991 Census (provisional) there are 43.7 crore males and 40.6 crore females; thus for every 1,000 males India has 929 females. Only Kerala has more women than men, i.e., 1,040 per 1,000 men. The lowest female ratio among the State is in Haryana i.e. 874 for 1,000 men and the lowest female ratio among the Union Territories is in Chandigarh where it is 733 per thousand.

Literacy

According to 1991 Census, the literacy percentage is 52.21. Out of this 64.13 per cent of males and 39.29 per cent of females are literate.

Major Religions and Persuasions

Table 9.1 : Major religions and Persuasions, 1991 and 1981 (excluding Assam)

Religion Community	Population		Percentage of Total Population	
	1991	1981	1991	1981
Hindus	67,20,00,000	54,97,24,517	82.41	82.63
Muslims	54,74,00,000	7,55,71,514	11.67	11.36
Christians	1,88,00,000	1,61,74,498	2.32	2.43
Sikhs	1,62,00.000	1,30,78,146	1.99	1.96
Buddhists	63,00.000	47,19.900	0.77	0.71
Jains	33.00.000	31,92,572	0.41	0.48
Other Persuasions	31,00,000	27,56,285	0.38	0.42
Religion not stated	4,00,000	60,217	0.05	0.01

Languages

The detailed data from the 1981 Census which were made available only in 1988, enumerate the main languages spoken in the household and not the mother tongue and groups related languages under a dominant language. By this count, 106 languages are separately recognised. Of these 94 are spoken by 10.000 or more people.

There were 1562 mother tongues, 10 writing system, and 76 languages as used in the school system out of 2000 codified languages.

Eighteen languages have been specified in the Eighth Schedule of the Constitution. These are: Assamesse, Bengali, Gujarati, Hindi, Kannada, Kashmiri, Konkani, Malayalam, Manipuri, Marathi, Nepali, Oriya, Punjabi, Sanskrit, Sindhi, Tamil, Telugu and Urdu.

National Flag

The National Flag is horizontally tricolour with deep saffron (*Kesari*) at the top, white in the middle and dark green at the bottom in equal proportion. The ratio of the width of the flag to its length is two to three. In the centre of the white band is a wheel, in navy blue, which represents the *Charkha*. Its design is that of the wheel (*Chakra*) which appears on the abacus of the Sarnath Lion Capital of Ashoka. Its diameter approximates to the width of the white band and it has 24 spokes.

The design of the National flag was adopted by the Constituent Assembly of India on July 22, 1947. Its use and display are regulated by a code.

State Emblem

The State Emblem of India is an adaptation from the Sarnath Lion Capital of Ashoka as preserved in the Sarnath Museum. In the original, there are four lions, standing back to back, mounted on an abacus with a frieze carrying sculptures in high relief of an elephant, a galloping horse, a bull and a lion separated by intervening wheels (Chakras) over a bell-shaped lotus. Carved out of a single block of polished sandstone, the capital is crowned by the Wheel of the Law (Dharma Chakra).

In the State emblem adopted by the Government of India on January 26, 1950, only three lions are visible, the fourth being hidden from view. The wheel appears in relief in the centre of the abacus with a bull on the right and a horse on the left and the outlines of the other wheels in the extreme right and left. The bell-shaped lotus has been omitted. The words *Satyameva Jayate* from the *Mundaka Upanishad*, meaning *Truth Alone Triumphs* are inscribed below the abacus in Devanagri script.

National Anthem

The song *Jana-gana-mana*, composed by Rabindranath Tagore (1861-1941) was adopted by the Constituent Assembly as the National Anthem of India on January 24, 1950. It was first sung on December 27, 1911 at the Calcutta Session of the Indian National Congress. The complete song consists of five stanzas. The first stanza constitutes the full version of the National Anthem. It reads:

Jana-gana-mana adhinayaka, jaya he
Bharata-bhagya-vidhata
Punjab-Sindhu-Gujarata-Maratha-Dravida-Utkala-Banga
Vindhya-Himachala-Yamuna-Ganga
Uchchala-jaladhi-taranga
Tava shubha name jage,
tava shubha asisa mange,
gahe tava jaya-gatha,
Jana-gana-mana-adhinayaka jaya he
Bharata-bhagya-vidhata.
Jaya he, jaya he, jaya he,
Jaya Jaya Jaya, Jaya he!

Playing time of the full version of the National Anthem is approximately 25 seconds. A short version consisting of the first and last lines of the stanza (playing time approximately 20 seconds) is also played on certain occasions.

The following is Tagore's English rendering of this stanza:

Thou art the ruler of the minds of all people,
dispenser of India's destiny.
Thy name rouses the hearts of Punjab, Sind, Gujarat and Maratha
Of the Dravida and Orissa and Bengal;
It echoes in the hills of the Vindhyas and Himalayas,
mingles in the music of Jamuna and Ganges
and is chanted by the waves of the Indian Sea.
They pray for thy blessings and sing thy praise.
The saving of all people waits in thy hand,
thou dispenser of India's destiny.
Voctory, victory, victory of thee.

National Song

The song *Vande Mataram*, composed by Bankimchandra Chatterji (1838-1894), was a source of inspiration to the people in their struggle for freedom. It has an equal status with *Jana-gana-mana*. The first political occasion on which it was sung was the 1896 session of the Indian National Congress. The following is the text of its stanza:

Vande Mataram!
Sujalam, suphalam malayaja shitalam,
Shasyashyamalam, Mataram!
Shubhrajyotsna pulakitayaminim,
Phullakusumita drumadala shobhinim,
Suhasinim sumadhura bhashinim,
Sukhadam, Varadam, Mataram!

The English translation of the stanza rendered by Sri Aurobindo (1972-1950) in prose[2] is:

I bow to thee, Mother,
richly-watered, richly-fruited,
Cool with the winds of the south,
dark wit the crops of the harvests,
the Mother!
Her nights rejoicing in the glory of the moonlight,
her lands clothed beautifully with her trees in flowering bloom,
sweet of laughter, sweet of speech,
the Mother, giver of boons, giver of bliss.

National Calendar

A uniform National Calendar based on the *Saka Era* with *Chaitra* as its first month and a normal year of 365 day was adopted from March 22, 1957 (along with the Gregorian calendar) for the followig official purposes in particular:

(i) Gazetter of India
(ii) News broadcast by All India Radio and T.V.
(iii) Calendars issued by the Government of India, and
(iv) Government communications addressed to members of the public.

The dates of the National Calendar have a permanent correspondence with the dates of the Gregorian calendar: *Chaitra* 1 falling on March 22 normally and on March 21 in a leap year.

Chitra 1 of *Saka Era* is the New Year Day. *Saka Era* was established in A.D. 78 by Emperor Kanishka of the Saka dynasty, who ruled in the North and North-Western India in the first century of the Christian era. The day, which has been chosen to become the first day of the New Year, is vemal equinox when the day and the night are of equal duration throughout the world. Saka calendar is based on *Solar Chaitra* and not on *Lunar Chaitra. Chaitra Shukla Partipada*

1. As published in *Sri Aurobindo Birth Centenary Library*, Popular edition, 1912, vol. 8 which is celebrated as New Year Day in many parts of the country, is

called differently. It is *Gudi Padwa* in Maharashtra and *Yugadi* in Karnataka based on lunar calendar, etc. April 13, *Baisakhi* in Punjab, *Pongal* on April 14 in Tamil Nadu and *Palia Baisakhi* in West Bengal are based on solar calendar. In solar calendar this discrepancy of 22 or 23 days (between March 22 and April 13/14) has been caused by an astronomical phenomenon called the precession of the equinoxes.

National Animal

The majestic tiger [*Panthera tigris* (Linnaeus)], the national animal of India for its rich colour, illusive design and formidable power, has always been held in high esteem in India. Among the carnivores, the tiger is very georgeous and attractive with roaring voice as symbol of power. Out of eight races of the species known the world over, the Indian race is the Royal Bengal Tiger. The Royal Bengal Tiger is found throughout the country expect the North-Western region and also in Nepal, Bhutan and Bangladesh. As shrinkage of habitat in India dwindled its population to only 1,827 in 1972, the Project Tiger was launched on April 1st 1973. Since then there is a gradual increase in its population. The tiger population 4,430 of the country according to 1989 censes was 4,339. So far 19 tiger reserve have been established covering over 29.716 sq km forest area.

National Bird

The Indian peacock [*Pavo cristatus* (Linnaeus)], the national bird of India, is one of the most beautiful birds, particularly the males having the glistering blue neck and breast, fanshape crest and long magnificent tail. The courtship dance of the male by fanning out the tail before the female is most spectacular. From time immemorial, this bird has found a profound place in Indian literature, folkore and legends.

The Indian peafowl, as the peacock is called, is widely found in the country in south and east of Indus river, Jammu and Kashmir, east Assam, south of Mizoram and the whole of Indian peninsula. It is fully protected under the Indian Wild Life (Protection) Act, 1972.
(*Source: India 1993*).

Presidents of India

January 26, 1950 — May 13, 1962	Rajendra Prasad
May 13, 1962 — May 13, 1967	S. Radhakrishnan
May 13, 1967 — May 3, 1969	Zakir Husain
May 3, 1969 — July 20, 1969	V.V. Giri (Acting)
July 20, 1969 — August 21, 1969	M. Hidayatullah (Acting)
August 24, 1969 — August 24, 1974	V.V. Giri
August 24, 1974 — Febuary 11, 1977	Fakhruddin Ali Ahmed
February 11, 1977 — July 25, 1977	B.D. Jatti (Acting)
July 25, 1977 — July 25, 1982	N. Sanjeeva Reddy
July 25, 1982 — July 25, 1987	Zail Singh
July 25, 1987 — July 25, 1992	R. Venkataraman
July 25, 1997 —	S.D. Sharma
	K.R. Narayanan

Vice Presidents of India

1952-1962	S. Radhakrishnan
1962-1967	Zakir Husain
1967-1969	V.V. Giri
1969-1974	G.S. Pathak
1974-1979	B.D. Jatti
1979-1984	M. Hidayatullah
1984-1987	R. Venkataraman
1987-1992	S.D. Sharma
1993-1997	K.R. Narayanan
1997-	Krishan Kant

Prime Ministers of India

August 15, 1947 — May 27, 1964	Jawaharlal Nehru
May 27, 1964 — June 9, 1964	Guljari Lal Nanda (Acting)
June 9, 1964 — January 11, 1966	Lal Bahadur Shastri
January 11, 1966 — January 24, 1966	Guljari Lal Nanda (Acting)
January 24, 1966 — March 24, 1977	Indira Gandhi
March 24, 1977 — July 28, 1979	Morarji Desai
July 28, 1979 — January 14, 1980	Charan Singh
January 14, 1980 — October 31, 1984	Indira Gandhi
October 31, 1984 — December 1, 1989	Rajiv Gandhi
December 2, 1989 — November 10, 1990	V.P. Singh
November 10, 1990 — June 21, 1991	Chandra Shekhar
June 21, 1991 —	P.V. Narasimha Rao
May 16, 1996 — June 1, 1996	Atal Bihari Vajpayee
June 1, 1996 — April 21, 1997	H.D. Deve Gowda
April 21, 1998 — March 18, 1998	I.K. Gujral
March 19, 1998 —	Atal Bihari Vajpayee

Speakers of the Lok Sabha

1952-1956	G.V. Mavlankar
1956-1962	Ananthasayanam Ayyangar
1962-1967	S. Hukam Singh
1967-1969	N. Sanjieeva Reddy
1969-1975	G.S. Dhillon
1975-1977	B.R. Bhagat
March 1977 — July 1977	N. Sanjieeva Reddy
1977-1979	K.S. Hegde
1980-1989	Balram Jakhar
November 19, 1989 — June 1991	Rabi Ray
Jul 10, 1991 —	Shivraj Patil

Important Days

National Youth Day	January 12
Army Day	January 15
Republic Day	January 26
International Customs Day	January 26

Martyrs' Day	January 30
National Science Day	February 28
International Women's Day*	March 8
World Consumers Rights Day	March 15
World Disabled Day	March (Third Sunday of March)
International Day for the Elimination of Racial Discrimination	March 21
World Forestry Day	March 21
World Meteorological Day	March 23
National Maritime Day	April 5
World Health Day*	April 7
May Day (Worker's Day International Labour Day)	May 1
World Red Cross Day	May 8
World Telecommunication Day*	May 17
World Day for Cultural Development*	May 21
Commonwealth Day	May 24
World No-Tobacco Day*	May 31
World Environment Day*	June 5
International Day of Solidarity with the Struggling People of South Africa*	June 16
World Population Day*	July 11
Hiroshima Day	August 6
Quit India Day	August 9
Nagasaki Day	August 9
International Day of Solidarity with the Struggle of Women in South Africa*	August 9
Independence Day	August 15
Teacher's Day	September 5
International Literacy Day*	September 8
International Day of Peace	September (Third Tuesday of September)
World Tourism Day	September 27
International Day for the Elderly*	October 1
University Children's Day*	October (First Monday of October)
Mahatma Gandhi Birthday	October 2
World Habitat Day	October 5
Air Force Day	October 8
Universal Postal Union Day*	October 9
Day of Solidarity with South African Political Prisoners	October 11
Post Office Day	October 19
World Standard Day	October 14
World Food Day*	October 16
United Nations Day	October 24
World Development Information Day*	October 24
National Re-Dedication Day	October 31
Children's Day	November 14
National Integration Day	November 19

International Day of Solidarity with the Palestinian People*	November 29
World AIDS Day*	December 1
International Day of Disabled Persons*	December 3
Navy Day	December 4
International Volunteer Day for Economic and Social Development	December 5
Flag Day	December 7
Human Rights Day*	December 10
Kisan Day	December 23

---

* Proclaimed by UN System/UNESCO Associated Schools

10

INDIA SINCE INDEPENDENCE

ACHIEVEMENTS

Going back, India that is Bharat was the richest and the most prosperous country in the world. It was then known as the '*Golden Sparrow* '. The standard of living of the common man was reasonably high. Articles of everyday needs were available in plenty. A common man could get easily things like milk, butter, ghee and foodgrains. Literally speaking 'Rivers of milk flowed'. Indian handicrafts and industrial products were known for their excellence of design and quality all over the world. From the richness of this land and from the labour and wisdom of its people had sprung great wealth, great ideas, great skills and arts. Naturally, therefore, foreigners were tempted to come to India for learning as well as loot and plunder.

The well-knit economic organization of the country received a serious setback with the advent of invaders and especially with the British rulers who were primarily concerned wih the governance of the country, not its growth. They were greatly interested in draining out wealth from India. Industrial crafts, industries and agriculture, all suffered heavily. As a result, India became a poor country. People remained underfed ill-housed and scantity dressed.

The statement 'A rich country innabited by the poor people' seems paradoxical and strange. But it is still true to a considerable extent though since independence we have made a spectacular progress in different fields. The giant irrigation dams at Bhakra, Hirakud and Nagarjunasagar, the huge steel mills at Bihilai, Bokaro, Rourkela and Durgapur, the fertiliser factories at Sindri and Nangal; the 1000-tonne per day ammonia plant (said to be the largest in the world) at Tuticorin; the aircraft factories at Bangalore, Hyderabad and Nasik; the locomotive factory at Chittarajan; the atomic reactor at Trombay; the rocket launching station at Sriharikota; the ISRO's establishment like Vikram Sarabhai Space Centre, Trivandrum and Space Application Centre, Ahmedabad; launching of Indian Satellite Bhaskara and Rohini; three axistabilished Geostationary Communication Satelite; APPLE (Ariahe Passenger Payload Experiment), establishment of Indian National Satellite System (INSAT); participation of an Indian Cosmonaut in a joint Indo-Soviet Flight; nuclear explosion of Pokaran, etc., are the prized possessions of the Indian Nation.

November 21, 1988 marked the 25th anniversary of India Space Programme. The Silver Jubilee Year saw the launching of three major programmes; IRS-1A, ASLV-02 and INSAT-1A. Militarily we are among the first five countries in the world.

India is the sixth country to successfully detonate a nuclear device as part of its successful experiment for peace purposes.

We have the third largest reservoir of highly skilled scientific and technical manpower in the world.

India is the fifth nation to have its remote sensing satellite.

We have achieved self-sufficiency in foodgrains.

India is the third largest producer of books in English, next to the U.S.A. and U.K.

The eradication of poverty problem of the masses became the first consideration of the government soon after we achieved independence. We decided to adopt the system of planned development for tackling our problem of poverty which was linked with rising prices, low production, unemployment and inequalities of income.

To frame a development plan for independent India, the *Planning Commission* was set up in March 1950, by a resolution of the Government of India. The aims of planning as defined by the resolution were, 'to promote a rapid rise in the standard of living of the people by efficient exploitation of the resources of the country, increasing production and offering opportunities to all for employment in the service of the community'.

The First Five-Year Plan which was initiated in April 1951 covered the period of 1951-56. So far we have had eight Five-Year Plans and Three Yearly Plans. 1998-99 is the second year of the Ninth Plan (1997-2002). Planning in India was intended, in the words of a resolution of March, 1950, 'to promote a rapid rise in the standard of living of the people by efficient exploitation of the resources of the country, increasing production and offering opportunities to all for employment in the service of the community.'

The most important achievement of planning in the post-independence period is our self-sufficiency in foodgrains. Now we need not import foodgrains for domestic requirements as we did till a few year ago. The highest ever production of 199.32 million tonnes of foodgrains was achieved during 1996-97 as against 51 million tonnes in 1950-51. However, the production declined by 1.0 per cent in 1997-98. Now it is likely to rebound by an estimated 5.3 per cent in 1998-99. Indications are that growth rate in production of agriculture would be about 3.9 per cent in 1998-99.

Our industry has many strengths: a wide range of products, a demonstrable ability to absorb and operate high technology, a large entrepreneural capability and ample managerial and technical skills.

During the Plans industrial production has made rapid strides, both in terms of quality and quantity. As per the index of industrial production, the growth rates achieved in the industrial sector as a whole were 8.6 per cent in 1984-85, 8.7 per cent in 1985-86, 9.1 per cent in 1986-87, 7.3 per cent in 1987-88, 8.7 in 1988-89, 8.6 in 1989 and 8.1 in 1990-91. However, there was setback in 1991-92. But a substantial upsurge was witnessed during 1995-96.

The industrial growth revived slightly to 6.6 per cent in 1997-98 from 5.6 per cent in 1996-97. This revival, however, faltered in 1998-99. The growth rate for April-December 1998 was only 3.5 per cent, down from 5.5 per cent for April-December 1997.

In the year 1950-51, there were only two major units producing iron and steel. Now we have eleven relevant major steel plants. Steel production was about one million tonnes in 1950-51. The production of finished steel is likely to exceed 23.5 million tonnes during 1996-97.

Cotton textile industry holds the second place in the production of cloth in the world. At present there are about 700 textile mills in the country.

In 1951, we had 138 sugar mills in the country. This number increased to 351 in 1987. About half the mills are in the public sector.

The production of cement was 2.69 million tonnes in 1951. The production capacity is likely to reach 140 million tonnes by 2002 AD.

There has been a tremendous increase in power generation and in number of public undertakings. We had only 5 public enterprises in 1951.

The road network in the country has become very elaborate system of national highways, state and district roads and rural roads totalling about 23 lakh kms. This is five and a half times the figure of 4 lakh km of roads in 1950-51. The volume of road transport has been gorwing at an averge rate of 10 per cent. The share of road transport for trade traffic has increased from 11 per cent in 1951 to 60 per cent in 1995.

Prior to Independence, average life span of an Indian was 32 years. Today it has lengthened to 58 years.

Our Constitution can be described as a charter of freedom. It enshrines the supremacy of the will of the people and their resolve to secure for all citizens: justice, social, economic and political; Equity of status and opportunity, and to promote among them all Fraternity assuring the dignity of the inidividual and the unity of the nation. The will of the people is exercised through universal adult franchise and a parliamentary democracy. Election to Parliament and State legislature are open contests for all political parties, and independent candidates also enjoy full scope to express themsleves.

Notwithstanding various problems and the magnitude of the task of conducting elections, we have all general elections with significant success. Barring the period, March 1977 to July 15, 1979 and December 1989 to May 1991 when the Janata Party and National Front were in power at the Centre, the Congress had held the reigns of the Government since the first General Election in 1951-52.

Many political changes accompanied by government changes, especially in States have taken place in the country since Independence, through peaceful and constitutional means. Transfer of power from one party to another has taken place as a natural course and in an orderly manner.

Another historic step in the development of democracy in the country was the inauguration of *Panchayati Raj* in October 1950. The Panchayati Raj aims at giving full authority and responsibility to the village people and helping them play an active role in local development through the Panchayats. There are over 228,500 Village Panchayats in the country covering partially the entire population of India.

With the Panchayati Raj, we now have parliamentary democracy in operation from the Gram Sabha to the Lok Sabha.

We have got an estalished judicial system.

PROGRESS MADE AND TASKS AHEAD

Government continued to follow a multi-pronged strategy on Human Rights matters—strict enforcement of constitutional and legal safeguards, stern action against officials found guilty of human rights violations, providing necessary financial and administrative support to the National Human Rights Commission to enable it to discharge its functions effectively and promotion of human rights awareness both amongst the law enforcing agencies as well as common masses.

In order to strenghten the accountability of the executive of Parliament, 17 department-related standing committees of Parliament were constituted in April 1993 to make detailed examination of Bills, demands for grants, annual reports of the ministries and national basic long-term policy documents presented to the House. This will greatly facilitate the working of Parliament.

The country had its share of national calamities. However, the unprecedented scale of damage in the Maharashtra earthquake stands out among these. In all these instances, Government responded with commendable alertness and provided prompt relief. Governments of several other countries, the World Bank and other institutions promptly offered assistance. A massive reconstruction programme in the earthquake affected areas of Maharashtra was taken up at an outlay of Rs. 1,000 crore. Non-governmental organisations were appropriately associated with the reconstruction programme.

The economic reforms, introduced in 1991 gained momentum and have been pursued consistently. The initial spurt of reforms from 1991-92 to 1993-94 was very successful by all accounts. Economic growth jumped to 7.8 per cent in 1994-95. However, there was a slight slowdown in the pace of reforms in 1995-96. The GDP grew by 7.6 per cent in that year. In 1996-97 there was a little improvement and GDP rose to 7.8 per cent. But it nose-dived in 1997-98 to only five per cent mainly due to volatility in agricultural growth which collapsed to 1.0 per cent in that year. However, based on advance estimates of national income put out by the Central Statistical Organisation on February 9, 1999 the Union Government claimed that things were looking up on the economic front with GDP expected to grow by 5.8 per cent during 1998-99. Still much more needs to be done. Government is aware that the reform is an irreversible and continuous process and needs to be implemented with determination and foresight, keeping the responses and circumstances in the country constantly in view. As a result of this approach, the progress of implementation has been steady and firm and based on a general consensus.

In drawing up the reform package, stress has been laid by the Government on reforms in the financial sector. The financial institutions have necessarily to be restructured and strengthened to enable them to take on the new responsibility imposed by the expanded activity in the private sector. An important policy change was the unification of the exchange rate and the floating of the rupee in March 1993. As a result of this market based exchange rate the Rupee remained remarkably stable during 1993-94 and 1994-95. However, it came under stress in 1995-96. In February 1996 Rupee touched a low of about Rs. 38 per US dollar. However, due to several measures taken by RBI it staged a recovery and in the range of 35-36. After an 18-month period of stability, the exchange rate of the Rupee against the US dollar came under downward pressure in August 1997, arising mainly from the East Asian Crisis. At the end of January 1999, the exchange rate of the Rupee vis-a-vis the US dollar was Rs. 42.50.

Global investors have shown growing confidence in the India market. A number of changes have been made so far in 1996-97 in the areas of foreign investment. The Foreign Investment Council has been set up. The significant point of foreign investment is that the bulk of this, is proposed in sectors like power oil refining, food processing, metallurgical industry, electrical equipment chemicals, electronics and other priority areas. Total foreign investment (direct plus portfolio) during April-December 1996 surged to over US$4 billion.

Government continues to lay a great deal of emphasis on export promotion. The results of changes in the trade policy coupled with the floating of the exchange rate and the general liberalisation of the economy have yielded results and exports have shown good growth during the period of 1993 to 1995. but declaration in the export growth started from 1996-97 and its slowdown has been continuing. In 1997-98 it slowed from 5.6 per cent in US dollar terms to 2.1 per cent. No improvement is perceptible in near future. Performance continues to be a source of major concer in 1998-99 with exports having declined by 2.9 per cent during April-December 1998, compared to a 3.3 per cent growth in the corresponding period of 1997.

Government attaches the highest priority to development of agriculture. The timely provision of adequate and reasonably priced inputs and the creation of a structure that provides for the timely announcement of prices which in turn promotes higher production so as to meet fully the domestic needs of the country as well as exports, are the major objectives of the Government. While agricultural production in 1994-95 was 5.4 per cent, in 1995-96 the production slumped to 0.2 per cent. But it made a grand recovery of 9.4 per cent in 1996-97. However, it again collapsed to 1.0 per cent in 1997-98. It is expected to be 5.3 per cent in 1998-99. As part of the agriculture policy states have been advised to remove all intra and inter-state restrictions on the movement of foodgrains.

It is the Union Government's determination that no vulnerable section of the population—be a women, children, minorities, Scheduled Casts, Scheduled Tribes or Backward Classes — should remain outside the main stream of development. In all areas of development of the poor, resource allocations were considerably enhanced.

The government has relied mainly on three approaches for reduction of poverty and unemployment viz. higher economic growth, anti-poverty and employment programmes and priority to government expenditure on social sectors The poverty ratio declined from 56.4 per cent in 1973-74 to 37.3 in 1993-94 in rural areas and from 49.0 per cent in 1973-74 to 32.4 per cent in 1993-94 in urban areas. For the country as a whole, the poverty ratio declined from 54.9 per cent in 1973-74 to 36 per cent in 1993-94.

The Planning Commission has estimated that additional employment opportunities of the order of 29.74 million were generated during January 1, 1994 to March 31, 1997. This implies an average growth rate of employment of 2.47 per cent per annum compared with 2.31 per cent during July 1, 1983 to December 31, 1993 and 2.32 per cent during January 1, 1978 to June 30, 1983.

The government has decided to set up the Second National Commission on Labour with a view to providing protection to millions of workers. The main focus of the Commission would be to suggest rationalisation of the existing labour laws in the organised sector and an umbrella legislation for ensuring a minimum level of protection to the workers in the unorganised sector.

Increased availability of health care and family welfare services has resulted in reduction of all-India death rate, birth rate and infant mortality rate. The crude death rate declined from 14.9 per thousand in 1971 to 9.8 in 1991 and further to 8.9 in 1997. Similarly the infant mortality per thousand and declined from 129 in 1971 to 80 in 1991 and further to 71 in 1997. The birth rate per thousand also declined from 36.9 in 1971 to 29.5 in 1991 and further to 27.2 in 1997.

Average real wages for unskilled agricultural labour, which reflect the economic conditions of agricultural labourers, have increased by 0.72 per cent in 1995-96, 4.67 per cent in 1996-97 and 4.88 per cent in 1997-98. These trends are consistent with to view that more rapid economic growth has brought about an improvement in living standards of people in general.

Several anti-poverty measures have been in operation for decades focussing on the poor as the target group viz. welfare of weaker sections women and children, and a number of special employment programmes for self and wage employment in rural and urban areas. The Central Plan and non-Plan expenditure on social sectors comprise education, health, water supply, sanitation, housing, slum development, social welfare and nutrition, rural employment and minimum basic services. As a ratio to GDP at market prices these expenditures increased to a record high of 1.91 per cent in 1998-99 (BE) as compared to 1.33 per cent in 1991-92 and 1.75 per cent in 1997-98 (RE). The Central Plan allocation for social sectors and programmes show highest growth of about 36 per cent for family welfare and women and child development in 1998-99 (BE) over 1997-98 (BE). The outlay for health has gone up by about 25 per cent in 1998-99 (BE) over 1997-98 (BE).

In regard to anti-poverty schemes launched by the Union Government it may be pointed out that the Parliamentary Standing Committee on Urban Development has criticised the Government for the manner in which it hand-led the task of poverty alleviation in urban areas. In a report submitted to Parliament, the panel regretted that not only the allocation for poverty eradication programmes was paltry — a mere 0.08 per cent of GDP, the manner in which they were run also left much to be desired. The panel was particularly upset that schemes were being launched, only to be discontinued later, indicating a lack of proper planning. In this context the Committee cited the case of Nehru Rozgar Yojana (NRY), Urban Basic Services, for the Poor (UBSP) and the Prime Minister Integrated Urban Poverty Eradication Programme (PMIUPE), which were discontinued in 1997.

Our relations with our neighbours continued to be cordial, and our interaction in various fields with Bangladesh, Bhutan, Maldives, Nepal and Sri Lanka recorded good progress during the year. In the case of Pakistan, however, its continuing support for terrorism and subversion in Jummu and Kashmir and anti-Indian activities world-wide seriously hampered our efforts at normalising relations. The Prime Minister offered Pakistan a dialogue aimed at establishing good-neighbourly relations as enshrined in the Shimla Agreement. Bilateral talks have since taken place, but the stridency of Pakistan's anti-Indian statement has grown, adversely affecting efforts at improving bilateral ties. There are no quarrels between us and the people of Pakistan. We feel that for good relations between our countries the Government of Pakistan should give up its negative approach and reciprocate our desire to normalise India-Pakistan relations in accordance with the Shimla Agreement.

Our relations with China have improved markedly. The Prime Minister's visit to China in September 1993, and the signing of the agreement on the maintenance of peace and tranquility along the line of actual control have brought them to a new stage of development. The expert group set up under this agreement held its first meeting recently, reflecting the desire of both sides to maintain and continue the interaction on this complex issue.

India values SAARC as an instrument of regional cooperation consistent with the objectives of its charter. The Prime Minister attended the SAARC summit in Dhaka last year. SAARC has recorded progress in dealing with certain important issues of common interest such as poverty, terrorism, population growth, problems relating to the status of women, children, youth and drugs and psychotropic sustenances. We continue to pay an active role in SAARC with a view to promoting its socio-economic and other objectives in accordance with the SAARC charter.

Our interaction with the United States has traditionally ranged over a number of areas from education and science and technology to culture and sports. We have also cooperated in the UN on issues relating to disarmament such as the comprehensive test ban treaty. The response from the United States to our economic liberalisation policies has been very positive and the US investments in India in the last two years were very substantial. We look forward to working with the United States towards mutual understanding, including on those issues on which such understanding needs enhancement. This will reflect the vibrant democratic and secular ideals of our two countries.

Relations with the Russian Federation, drawing upon rich traditions of our friendship of the past, continued with mutual understanding ad cooperation. Despite certain difficulties the two countries face, cooperation in the political, economic, commercial and other areas was sought to be promoted by both sides. The goodwill and understanding that underpins our relations reinforce our joint efforts at identifying possibilities of further cooperation in various areas in today's changed context.

We welcome the signing of the declaration of principles on interim self-government arrangements between Israel and the PLO in September 1993 as a notable step towards peace and stability in West Asia and the restoration of the legitimate rights of the Palestinian people.

India continues to play an active role in shaping the global agenda on issue pertaining to political and security matters, economic and social development, human rights, environment and population.

Concluding Observations

A large part of our population still remains backward. There is a wide gulf between the rich and the poor. *Unemployment* is on the increase. National integration is our urgent need. Erosion in the standard of values, in fact is the topmost blockade, which requires to be checked and a crusade for 'Clean Life, Clean Politics and Clean Administration' is to be given first priority.

India is on the move. The tasks before us are very challenging and tremendous. But there is no causes for despair. By harnessing all our resources and working unitedly and sincerely, we can usher in an era of peace, progress and prosperity.

The 21st century beckons up holding fourth new hopes. We, the people of India, must march ahead as an integrated resurgent.

As *Gurudev Rabindranath Tagore* would advise, we must "hold the faith firm", surely "the day will dawn".

11

ECONOMY AND THE PLAN
An Overview

Introduction

The year 1997 witnessed the culmination of the Eighth Five Year Plan and the beginning of the Ninth Plan period. It is in the light of this that stock can now be taken of the achievements during the Eighth Plan period in relation to the targets set.

The Eighth Five Year Plan (1992-97), was launched keeping in mind the necessity of implementing measures for stabilization and structural adjustment subsequent to the Balance of Payments (BOP) crisis of 1991. The Plan took into account the changes that were to be expected in the economy on account of the adoption of these reform measures, while keeping in mind the poor performance of the economy in the base year, 1991-92. In the base year the rate of inflation was in double digits, while the overall growth rate of GDP for that year was negligible. The BOP situation improved somewhat with a mild improvement in the foreign exchange reserves, while exports continued to be sluggish. It is in the light of these circumstances that the Eighth Five Year Plan set down macroeconomic targets which were somewhat cautious in comparison to the feasible. The targets fixed for the Plan included a rate of growth in GDP of 5.6 per cent, an average industrial growth rate of 7.5 per cent, a savings rate of 21.6 per cent, an investment rate of 23.2 per cent, a Current Account Deficit (CAD) of 1.6 per cent as a percentage of GDP among others.

The Approach Paper to the Ninth Five Year Plan was prepared and presented to the National Development Council (NDC) in December 1996. It envisaged a base-line growth scenario of 6.2 per cent per annum on the average for the Ninth Plan period. It was also indicated that an accelerated growth scenario of 7 per cent per annum was feasible provided certain policy decisions were adopted by the Centre and the States. In its meeting held on January 16, 1997, the NDC approved the Approach Paper and directed the Planning Commission to formulate the Ninth Five Year Plan on the basis of the accelerated growth scenario of 7 per cent. The Draft Ninth Five Year Plan was prepared by the Planning Commission on the basis of the approved Approach Paper, but it could not be put up to the NDC for approval due to the imminent change in government.

The Draft Ninth Five Year Plan seeks to further continue ad consolidate the process of reforms. The targets set therein include a GDP growth rate of 7 per cent, an investment rate of 28.3 per cent, a savings rate of 26.2 per cent and a CAD to GDP ratio of 2.1.

Growth and Sectoral Output

The first year of the economic reforms and also the base year of the Eighth Plan, 1991-92, had a GDP growth rate of less than one per cent as compared to an average annual growth rate of 6 per cent during the Seventh Plan period. As the economy gradually absorbed the initial shock of the stabilisation measures, the GDP growth rates recovered over the years from 5.3 per cent in 1992-93 to 6 per cent in 1993-94, 7.2 per cent in 1994-95 as well as in 1995-96, and in 1996-97 stood at 7.5 per cent as per the latest estimates from CSO. Thus the average GDP growth rate during the Eighth Plan period was 6.64 per cent which is well above the targeted rate of 5.6 per cent, indicating a satisfactory performance in this front. The Advance Estimates indicate that the rate of growth in GDP in 1997-98 is likely to be about 5 per cent.

The good performance of the economy reflects in large measure the successive good performance of the Agricultural sector. After recording a decline of 2.3 per cent in 1991-92, agricultural GDP increased at an average growth rate of 3.96 per cent during the Eighth Plan period as per latest data available. Although there was a decline of 3.4 per cent in 1995-96, agricultural GDP recovered to a growth rate of 8.2 per cent in 1996-97 (at 1980-81 prices). Foodgrains production increased steadily from 168 million tonnes in 1991-92 to about 191.5 million tonnes in 1994-95, 185 million tonnes in 1995-96 and 198.2 million tonnes is expected in 1996-97. Overall the growth of Agricultural GDP during the Eighth Plan was 3.96 per cent which is well above the targetted growth rate of 3.1 per cent.

On the industrial front, all the major industry segments witnessed severe recession during 1991-92. The index of industrial production grew by less than 1 per cent in 1991-92, but picked-up momentum from 1993-94 with a growth rate of 5.98 per cent, increasing to 9.35 per cent in 1994-95, and furhter to 12.14 per cent in 1995-96 but then fell to 7.28 per cent in 1996-97. The average industrial growth during the Eighth Plan period was 7.4 per cent, which is only marginally less than the target rate of 7.5 per cent. The index of manufacturing production grew consistently from 3.5 per cent in 1992-93 to 16.1 per cent in 1995-96 but declined to 6.8 per cent in 1996-97, to give an average growth rate of 9.1 per cent for the Eighth Plan period. The Advance Estimates indicate that the manufacturing sector is likely to grow by 6.4 per cent in 1997-98.

The performance of the Service sector during the Eighth Plan period was quite good, showing an average growth rate of 8.9 per cent during the Eighth Plan period, which exceeds the target rate of 6.2 per cent. The Service sector consits of trade, transport, communication, finance, insurance and community and social services. The sectors which mainly contributed to the good performance are trade, hotels and restaurants, with average growth rate of 10 per cent during the Plan period followed by Financing, insurance, real estate and business services with an average growth rate of 9 per cent during the Plan period.

Savings and Investment

Gross Domestic Saving as a proportion of GDP, average 24.32 per cent during the Eighth Plan period against a target level of 21.6 per cent. The improvement in the savings rate was made possible by a steady increase in the private corporate and the household savings rate during the Plan period. The average corporate savings rate and the average household savings rate was 3.7 per cent and 19 per cent respectively in the Plan period.

Gross Domestic Investment as a proportion of GDP, averaged 25.6 per cent as against a targetted rate of 23.2 per cent. The investment rate got a boost in 1994-95 to 26 per cent due to a higher savings rate of 24.9 per cent in 1994-95 and a CAD of about 1 per cent of GDP. The savings rate in 1996-97 is expected to be 26.1 per cent of GDP, with the CAD expected to be about 1 per cent of GDP. Thus the investment rate is likely to improve further in 1997-98.

Fiscal Developments

The Eighth Plan Document stated that a major aim of fiscal policy should be to roll back the fiscal deficit of the Centre and States, taken together as a percentage of GDP, from an average of 10.6 per cent during the Seventh Plan, and from about 11 per cent in 1990-91, to an average of about 7 per cent during the Eighth Plan period. This implicitly meant that the Centre's fiscal deficit would be required to be brought down to an average of 5 per cent and that of the States to an average of about 2 per cent during the Eighth Plan period. However, despite concious efforts, the fiscal deficit to GDP rate of the Centre was about 6 per cent and that of the States was about 3 per cent during the Eighth Plan period. Although the Centre's fiscal deficit of 6 per cent seems high, over the years it has actually decreased from around 8.3 per cent in 1990-91 to 5 per cent in 1996-97 and is expected to be about 4.5 per cent in 1997-98 (BE) (according to the RBI Annual Report 1996-97). The Primary deficit of the Centre as a percentage of GDP has come down from 4.3 per cent in 1990-91 to 0.37 per cent in 1996-97 (RE) and is expected to be -0.18 per cent in 1997-98 (BE). Unfortunately interest payments as a percentage of GDP has increased continuously from 4 per cent in 1990-91 to 4.6 per cent in 1996-97, and on an average was 4.5 per cent for the Eighth Plan period. This has partly offset the efforts to further reduce the revenue deficit. Revenue deficit of the Central Government which was 3.5 per cent of GDP in 1990-91 has come down to about 2 per cent in 1996-97 (RE) and is likely to be about 2.08 per cent in 1997-98 (BE).

Inflation

The Eighth Plan envisaged that there will be a reasonable degree of price stability. It was surmised that the planned fiscal adjustment would bring down the borrowing requirements of the Government, including the borrowings from the RBI, which would ensure that the annual growth rate of money supply is brought down from about 17 per cent in the recent past to about 11 to 12 per cent in the Eighth Plan period. With income elasticity of demand for money estimated at about 1.5, and the economy planned to grow at about 5 to 6 per cent per year, it was anticipated that the projected monetary growth wouid enable the Government to contain the trend rate of inflation to about 5 per cent per year. The average inflation rate as measured by the Wholesale Price Index (WPI) during the 8th Five Year Plan was about 8.7 per cent. In the terminal year of the plan, the inflation rate is expected to be about 6.4 per cent. Thus, the average inflation rate during the Eighth Plan period was about 8.7 per cent, significantly higher than the projected 5 per cent

Initially, following the stabilisation measures, the overall inflation rate on a point-to-point basis fell from 13.6 per cent in 1991-92 to 7 per cent in 1992-93. However, it accelerated to 10.8 per cent in 1993-94 and to 10.4 per cent in 1994-

95. The annual rate of inflation during 1995-96 has shown a downward trend recording a low of about 5 per cent since January, 1996 and is 6.9 per cent in 1996-97. Price rise continued to be subdued at about 5 per cent during the first half of 1996-97, but showed signs of acceleration during the second half, due to a hike in administered prices of petroleum products and coal.

Balance of Payments

The current account deficit which was about $10 billion in 1990-91 has come down to about $5.9 billion in 1995-96 and $3.7 billion in 1996-97. As percentage of GDP, the current account deficit has declined from about 3.2 per cent in 1990-91 to 1.8 in 1995-96 and 1 per cent in 1996-97. On an average, in the Eight Plan, the current account to GDP ratio has been about 1.2 per cent as against a targetted rate of 1.6 per cent. Trade deficit (RBI data) as a percentage of GDP, which was 3.2 per cent in 1990-91, had fallen to about 1.6 in 1993-94 but increased significantly to about 3.4 per cent in 1995-96 and to 3.45 per cent in 1996-97.

Exports as a percentage of GDP has successively increased from 6.2 in 1990-91 to about 10 per cent in 1995-96 and 9.5 per cent in 1996-97. Net invisibles balance which was negative in 1990-91, improved significantly over the years to touch 1.65 per cent of GDP in 1995-96 and 2.41 per cent in 1996-97.

Despite widening of the current account deficit over the last three years, the foreign exchange reserves position has remained comfortable. India's foreign exchange reserves comprising of foreign currency assets, gold reserves and SDR balances, which stood at $9.2 billion in March 1992 and increased steadily to over $25 billion in March 1995. Although the foreign exchange reserves declined in 1995-96 to $21.7 billion, it stood at $26.4 billion in 1996-97. The movement in the reserves closely reflected the developments in the current account balance and the net capital inflows. The surge in capital inflows specially in the form of foreign portfolio investment helped build up substantial foreign exchange reserves since 1993-94.

The exchange rate of the rupee remained remarkably stable during 1993-94 and 1994-95 following the introduction of the market based exchange rate regime in March 1993. The Rupee however came under stress in the second half of 1995-96. An indication of the widening of the current account deficit and an ebbing of capital flows and the pronounced appreciation of the US dollar against major currencies triggered off market expectations and resulted in depreciation of the Rupee from about Rs. 31.50 in April, 1995 to about Rs. 35.60 per dollar in October, 1995. Following intervention by the R.B.I. the Rupee stabilised in the range of Rupees 34 to 36 until January, 1996. In February, 1996, the Rupee again suffered about of depreciation and touched a low of about Rs. 38 per U.S. dollar. Following a number of measures by the R.B.I. in early February, 1996, the Rupee staged a strong recovery. In March-April, 1996 and has since remained in the range of Rs. 35-36 per U.S. dollar. It stood at Rs. 35.96 in 1996-97 as per the R.B.I. Annual Report 1996-97.

PLAN PROGRESS

Five Year Plans

Planning in India was intended, in the words of the resolution of March, 1950 "to promote a rapid rise in the standard of living of the people by efficient exploitation of the resources of the country, increasing production and offering opportunities to all for employment in the service of the community". Since 1950, Eighth Five Year Plan have been implemented in India. The Approach Paper to the Ninth Five Year Plan was unanimously approved by the National Development Council in its meeting held on 16-01-1997.

The preparation of Five Year Plans involves simultaneously: (a) appraisal of the past trends and performance; (b) assessment of resources; (c) identification of major problems; and (d) determination of measures and policies for future growth. The National Plan comprises of the Central and State Governments' Plans as well as Plans for the private sector more especially for the corporate sector.

The preliminary exercises for preparation of a Five Year Plan start with the consideration of the general approach to the Plan. Evaluation studies are undertaken with the help of Programme Evaluation Organisation, Central Statistical Organisation and various other institutions. The Working Groups and Steering Committees constituted by the Planning Commission for various sectors carry out exercises to provide input for formulation of the Plan.

Discussions are held by the Planning Commission, at both expert-level and political level. The dimensions of the States' Plan are designed in consultation with individual State Chief Ministers. Simultaneously, discussions are also held with Central Ministries, to arrive at a pubic investment programme which is consistent with Plan priorities, known and anticipated constraints, and resources available.

Meetings of the Internal and Full Planning Commission, from time to time, assess the progress of formulation of the Plan and also deliberate in detail on its content and scope. The Five Year Plan Document also is considered by the Union Cabinet, thereafter, final approval is given by the National Development Council (NDC), comprising members of Union Council of Ministers and State Chief Ministers and chaired by the Prime Minister.

Formulation of Annual Plans

The Five Year Plan gets operationalised through the mechanism of Annual Plans. The formulation of the Annual Plan provide the Planning Commission with an opportunity to assess previous year's Plan performance in the various sectors and to suggest a reorientation of policies and modifications of strategies consistent with the changing requirements so as to ensure achievement of the long-term objectives.

In the third quarter of each financial year, the Planning Commission indicates to the State Governments and the Central Ministries the important objectives that should be kept in view while formulating the Annual Plan for the following year and to furnish their Plan proposals, including physical targets and the corresponding financial outlays required, conforming to the guidelines referred to above and within the overall framework of their respective Five Year Plans. The State Governments are advised to furnish their forecasts of financial resources, including proposals for mobilising additional resources, for their Annual Plans, keeping in view the resources and outlay targets fixed for the Five Year Plan, etc. The resource estimates of the State Governments thus furnished are discussed in-depth in a series of meetings during November-December with senior officers of the State Governments. Similarly, in-depth discussions are held with senior officials of the Central Ministries/Departments on their Annual Plan proposals, during October-December of each year.

The Plan outlays arrived at in the meetings between the Deputy Chairman and State Chief Ministers/Lt. Governors in respect of State Plans and at meetings taken by Member Secretary, Planning Commission with the Secretaries of Central Ministries/Departments, regarding the Central Plan forms the basis for budgetary provisions for the Plan for the ensuring year.

Eighth Five Year Plan (1992-97)

The Eighth Plan commenced in April, 1992 against the backdrop of overall changes taking place in the world. These changes had profound impact on both the structure of international relations and the world economy.

Recognising the relevance of developmental planning in the changed scenario of globalisation of the economy, it was resolved that the Planning Commission would work on building a long-term strategic vision of the future with concentration on anticipating future trends and evolving integrated strategies for the achievement of higher possible level of development of the country in keeping with competitive international standards. The Eighth Plan document was endorsed by the National Development Council (NDC) in its forty-foruth meeting, held in May, 1992.

An attempt was made in the Eighth Plan to correct the fiscal imbalances from which the Sixth and Seventh Plan suffered. The non-inflationary manner to be adopted for funding of the Plan in order to avoid debt trap both internally and externally, called for a series of austerity measures which involved a reduction in Government's dissavings, higher resource mobilization both by the Centre and the States and improvement in the performance of public sector units.

The Eighth Plan recognised the essential need to involve people in the process of development. The Plan envisaged substantial devolution of power to the people's organisations at the district, block and village levels. Special attention was paid to employment in the rural areas with the objective of eradicating poverty.

An average growth rate of 5.6 per cent per annum was proposed during the Plan period. The level of national investment was proposed at Rs. 7,98,000 crore.

Eighth Plan (1992-97) Performance

The overall public sector plan outlay during the Eighth Five Year Plan (1992-97) amounts to Rs. 4,34,100 crore at 1991-92 prices. The share of the Central Plan in this amount is Rs. 2,47,865 crore, or 57.1 per cent, whereas the share of State Plans accounts for Rs. 1,79,985 crore, or 41.5 per cent. The Plans of the Union Territories account for the remaining share of Rs. 6,250 crore, or 1.4 per cent of the overall Eighth Plan Public Sector outlay. The Plan outlays by broad heads of development for the Eighth Plan 1992-97 for Centre, States and Union Territories are given in Annexure-1.

A review in real terms (i.e., after allowing for inflation and assuming that the revised estimates for 1995-96 and 1996-97 would materialise), has shown that the Plan performance in financial terms during the Eighth Plan (1992-97) accounts for about 95 per cent of the approved Eighth Plan outlay in the Central Sector. The corresponding proportion works out to about 80 per cent and 109 per cent for State Plan and UT Plans, respectively. Thus, in the case of Centre, the short fall in anticipated Plan expenditure during the Eighth Plan period has been marginal vis-a-vis the approved Eighth Plan outlay. Whereas, there is no shortfall in the case of UT Plans, major shortfalls were likely to occur in the Plan provision as well as expenditure of States vis-a-vis their Eighth Plan approved outlays. The reason for shortfall was lack of mobilising adequate resources due to deterioration in the balance of current revenues, erosion in the contribution of State Electricity Boards (SEBs) and State Road Transport Corporations (SRTCs), negative opening balances, mounting non-Plan expenditure and shortfalls in the collection of small savings, etc. A statement showing the Eighth Plan outlays and progress of expenditure during the Eighth Plan (1992-97) for Centre, States and UTs is given in Annexure-2.

Annual Plan (1997-98)

The total public sector outlay for the Annual Plan 1997-98 has been fixed at Rs. 155750.89 crore. This represents an increase of 7.68 per cent over the approved outlay of Rs. 144635.87 crore for the Annual Plan 1996-97. The Plan aims at strengthening and providing support to the important programmes/projects/ schemes in the States' Sector as well as in the Central Sector. The details of the Plan outlays by broad heads of development for Centre, States and Union Territories for the Annual Plan, 1997-98 are given in Annexure-3.

Annual Plan (1998-99)

For the purpose of Vote on Account the Central Ministries/Departments were requested to formulate plan proposal keeping the level of Gross Budget Support (GBS) at the same level as in 1997-98. Before this, Special Secretary had written to Finance Secretary enclosing the estimates or resources for the Annual Plan 1998-99 on November, 1997.

Annual Plan Document

During the year under report, the Annual Plan 1996-97 document was released and was subsequently placed in the Parliament Library.

The Eighth Five Year Plan had set the target of 5.6 per cent per annum during the Five Year period (1992-97). The gorwth recorded in the Gross Domestic Product was of the order of 5.3 per cent in 1992-93, 6.0 per cent in 1993-94 and 7.2 per cent during 1994-95, as well as in 1995-96 and 7.5 per cent in 1996-97 as per the latest estimates from CSO.

Preparation of the Ninth Five Year Plan (1997-2002)

As a first step for the formulation of Ninth Five Year Plan (1997-2002), Planning Commission had set up a number of Steering Committees and Working Groups dealing with various sectors. These Steering Committees and Working Groups comprised of experts in the respective areas and undertook detailed exercises and submitted reports which formed the major input in the formulation of the draft Ninth Five Year Plan. In all, 23 Steering Committees and 116 Working Groups were set up for the Ninth Five Year Plan.

The Approach Paper to the Ninth Five Year Plan, approved unanimously by the National Development Council (NDC) in its meeting held on 16-01-1997 *inter-alia* includes the following salient features:

(i) The target growth rate of GDP for the Ninth Plan period will be 7 per cent per annum, with agriculture targetted to grow at 4.5 per cent per annum.
(ii) Emphasis to be placed on the Basic Minimum Services as decided in the Chief Ministers' Conference on Basic Minimum Services.
(iii) Revenue deficit of the Government, including Centre, States and PSUs to be sharply reduced through a combination of higher tax collections, control of inessential expenditures particularly non-transparent subsidies, and better recovery of user charges.
(iv) Decentralisation of planning and implementation through greater reliance being placed on States and Panchayati Raj Institutions.
(v) Sharp reduction in Centrally Sponsored Schemes, with the necessary funds being transferred to the States and the Panchayati Raj bodies.

The objectives of the Ninth Plan arising from the Common Minimum Programme of the Government, the Chief Ministers' Conference on Basic Minimum Services and the suggestions put forward by the Chief Ministers of various States during extensive consultation have been spelt out in the Approach to the Ninth Five Year Plan document. "Growth with Equity" is proposed to be achieved with the objectives outlined in the Approach Paper. These are to be viewed in the context of the four important dimensions of State policy viz., (a) quality of life of the citizens; (b) generation of poroductive employment; (c) regional balance; and (d) self-reliance.

The Approach Paper projected a 7 per cent annual GDP growth scenario, with necessary targets of Domestic Savings Rate, Current Account Deficit, Incremental Capital Output Ratio, Investment Rate and total Public Sector Plan size of Rs. 8,75,000 crore.

Ninth Plan Approved

The 48th meeting of the National Development Council (NDC) has approved the Ninth Five Year Plan envisaging a growth rate of 6.5 per cent per annum. Though delayed by two years, the Plan will run its period through to 2001-2002. Also, in view of the differing perceptions among the States on the criteria for allocation of Central funds for major rural poverty alleviation programmes, the Prime Minister, Mr. Atal Behari Vajpayee, announced the Constitution of another expert committee to look into this aspect. Another expert committee would also look into the matter of transfer of Cenrally-sponsored schemes to the States. There was, however, no response from the Central Government to the protests against the recent price increase in case of essential items.

Decentralisation in Plan Formulation

In order to operationalise the concept of decentralised planning, assistance is provided to the States under the scheme of strengthening of planning machinery at State and district levels. For the Ninth Plan, new guidelines have been issued for the scheme. In keeping with the changed scenario consequent on the enactment of 73rd and 74th Amendment Act, States have been asked to set up/

strengthen a cell for Panchayati Raj Institutions in the apex of planning bodies of the State Government. At the district level the existing scheme will continue. The guidelines allow the hiring of consultants for preparation of specific studies relating to Panchayati Raj Institutions and the planning process for preparation of district level plans.

Keeping the NDC's decisions in view, during the Ninth Plan and the Annual Plan (1997-98) discussions, the State Governments were impressed upon the need to allocate more united funds to the PRIs & ULBs so as to enable them to formulate and implement developmental programmes as per the local requirements. As an effort to achieve the objective of improving the quality of life of the people, enhanced level of Additional Central Assistance was provided to the States for providing seven identified Basic Minimum Services and for Slum Development during the Annual Plan 1997-98. States have full flexibility to take up schemes within these services according to their requirements and needs.

ANNEXURE-1

Plan Outlay by Broad Heads of Development for Eighth Plan (1992-97)

(*Rs. crore*)

Sl. No.	Heads of Development	Centre		States & UTs		Total	
		Outlay	%age to total	Outlay	%age to total	Outlay	%age to total
1.	Agriculture & Allied Services ($)	12618.00	5.09	42374.50	22.75	54992.50	12.67
2.	Rural Development	24170.00	9.75	10255.36	5.51	34425.36	7.93
3.	Energy	66795.00	26.95	48766.09	26.19	115561.09	26.62
4.	Industry and Minerals	37539.00	15.14	9382.75	5.04	46921.75	10.81
5.	Transport	40977.00	16.53	14948.57	8.03	55925.57	12.88
6.	Social Services	34445.45	13.90	44566.45	23.93	79011.90	18.20
7.	Others (*)	31320.55	12.64	9191.12	4.94	40511.67	9.33
8.	Area Programmes			6750.16	3.62	6750.16	1.56
	Grand Total	247865.00	100.00	186235.00	100.00	434100.00	100.00

($) Include Agriculture and Irrigation sectors.

(*) Include Communications, Science Technology & Environment, General Economic Services and General Services

ANNEXURE-2

Eighth Plan Outlay and Progress of Expenditure : Centre, States & UTs.

(*Rs. crore*)

Sl. No.	Sector	Eight Plan Outlay at 1991-92 prices	Annual Plan at 1991-92 Prices					Anticipated Expenditure Eighth Plan (1992-97)
			1992-93 Actual Exp.	1993-94 Actual Exp.	1994-95 Actual Exp.	1995-96 R.E.	1996-97 R.E.	
1	2	3	4	5	6	7	8	9
1.	Centre	247865	39903	46517	44823	52424	50915	234582 (94.6)
2.	States	179985	25495	26538	28432	30261	33118	143844 (79.9)
3.	Union Territories	6250	1134	1149	1256	1617	1678	6834 (109.3)
	Total	434100	66532	74204	74511	84302	85711	385260 (88.8)

Note : Figures in brackets indicate as percentage of the Eighth Plan Outlay.

Annexure-3

Plan Outlay by Broad Heads of Development for Annual Plan, 1997-98

(*Rs. crores*)

Sl. No.	Heads of Development	Centre		States & UTs@		Total @	
		Outlay	%age to total	Outlay	%age to total	Outlay	%age to total
1.	Agriculture & Allied Services ($)	3292.23	3.58	14908.74	23.33	18200.97	11.69
2.	Rural Development	5800.75	6.32	5449.41	8.53	11250.16	7.22
3.	Energy	24234.53	26.39	12878.99	20.15	37113.52	23.83
4.	Industry and Minerals	11199.80	12.20	2119.30	3.31	13319.10	8.55
5.	Transport	15015.96	16.35	5573.61	8.72	20589.57	13.22
6.	Social Services	15707.01	17.10	18514.50	28.97	34221.51	21.97
7.	Others (*)	16588.43	18.06	3686.78	5.77	20275.21	13.02
8.	Area Programmes	0.00	0.00	780.85	1.22	780.85	0.50
	Grand Total	91838.71	100.00	63912.18	100.00	155750.89	100.00

($) Include Agriculture and Irrigation sectors.

(*) Include Communications, Science Technology & Environment, General Economic Services and General Services.

@ Provisional

12

STATE OF INDIAN ECONOMY*

GENERAL REVIEW

Review of Developments

Macro-economic Overview

Economic developments in India in 1998-99 have to be viewed against the backdrop of an exceptionally turbulent and unfavourable international economic environment. The year saw significant declines in the GDP of a number of East Asian Countries (over 15 per cent in Indonesia and 5-7 per cent in S. Korea and Thailand), continuing recession in Japan, severe financial crisis in Russia, unusual volatility in capital and forex markets of industrial countries, continuing drought in capital flows to developing countries and a sharp devaluation in Brazil in January 1999 as a result of capital flight triggered by continuation of unsustainable fiscal weakness. The extension of the East Asian crisis to countries in other continents ensured slowdown of world growth to less than 2 per cent in 1998 with little prospect of recovery in 1999. World trade growth also decelerated sharply, commodity prices fell and deflation affected much of the world economy. India was not wholly immune to these unfavourable developments.

The new, 1993-94 based GDP series recently released by the Central Statistical Organisation (CSO) shows that GDP growth decelerated significantly in 1997-98 to 5.0 per cent from 7.8 per cent in 1996-97 (Table 1.2a). The deterioration in growth was perhaps even worse, if one takes into account the fact that fully one percentage point of growth is attributed to the 20 per cent increase in real value added in the 'public administration and defence' sub-sector arising chiefly from pay increases to government servants. The economy recovered to an estimated growth of 5.8 per cent in 1998-99. The recovery, from the cyclical downturn that started towards the end of 1996-97, would have been firmer but for the East Asian crisis and its effect on world import demand and on international capital markets. Domestic uncertainty arising from non-economic factors also played a role in slowing recovery. Inflation rose sharply during 1998-99, because of an exceptional spurt in prices of a handful of agricultural commodities. The pressure from this source has, however, begun to abate during the last quarter of 1998-99. The inflation rate which peaked at 8.8 per cent in late September dropped steeply from December to below 5 per cent in January. Average inflation for the whole of 1998-99 will, however, be higher than the 4.8 per cent registered in 1997-98.

---

* Based on Economic Survey 1998-99 of the Ministry of Finance, Government of India, New Delhi.

Table 12.1 : Key Indicators

	1995-96	1996-97	1997-98	1998-99	1995-96	1996-97	1997-98	1998-99
	Absolute Values				Per cent change over previous period			
Gross national product (Rs. thousand crore)								
At current prices	1089.8	1272.2 P	1413.2 Q	NA	17.1	16.7 P	11.1 Q	NA
At 1993-94 prices	913.8	988.3 P	1038.7 Q	1099.7 A	7.8	8.1 P	5.1 Q	5.9 A
Gross domestic product (Rs. thousand crore)								
At current prices	1103.2	1285.3 P	1426.7 Q	NA	16.9	16.5 P	11.0 Q	NA
At 1993-94 prices	926.4	999.0 P	1049.2 Q	1110.0 A	7.6	7.8 P	5.0 Q	5.8 A
Agricultural production[1]	160.7	175.4	164.9	171.3 P	-2.7	9.1	-6.0	3.9 P
Foodgrains production (million tonnes)	180.4	199.4	192.4	195.3 P	-5.8	10.5	-3.5	1.5 P
Industrial production[2]	122.3	129.1	137.6	139.2 #	12.8	5.6	6.6	3.5 #
Electricity generated (Billion, KWH)	379.9	394.5	420.6	329.4 #	8.4	3.8	6.6	6.6 #
Wholesale price index[3]	299.5	320.1	337.1	353.9 *	4.4	6.9	5.3	4.6 *
Consumer price index for industrial workers[4]	319.0	351.0	380.0	429.0 @	8.9	10.0	8.3	15.3 @
Money supply (M3) (Rs. thousand crore)	604.0	701.8	825.4	934.7[5]	13.7	16.2	17.6	13.2[6]
Imports at current prices								
(Rs. crore)	122678	138920	151553	132447 #	36.4	13.2	9.0	23.2 #
(US $ million)	36678	39133	40779	31583 #	28.0	6.7	4.2	7.1 #
Exports at current prices								
(Rs. crore)	106353	118817	126286	101850 #	28.6	11.7	6.3	11.7 #
(US $ million)	31797	33470	33980	24287 #	20.7	5.3	1.5	-2.9 #

Table 12.1 : *(Contd.)*

Foreign currency assets[7]								
(Rs. crore)	58446	80368	102507	116515[8]	-11.5	37.5	27.5	13.7[8]
(US $ million)	17044	22367	25975	27429[8]	-18.1	31.2	16.1	5.6[8]
Exchange rate								
(Rs./US $) [10]	33.45	35.50	37.16	41.99[9]	-6.1	-5.8	-4.5	-11.5[9]

Note: Gross National Product and Gross Domestic Product figures are at factor cost (new series with base 1993-94).

Q—Quick estimates; A—Advance estimates; P—Provisional; NA—Not available

1. Index of agricultural production (of 46 crops, including plantations) with base triennium ending 1981-82=100.
2. Index of Industrial Production 1993-94=100.
3. Index with base 1981-82=100, at the end of fiscal year.
4. Indes with base 1982=100, at the end of fiscal year.
5. Outstanding as on January 15, 1999 for 1998-99 and end of financial year for previous years.
6. April 1, 1998 to January 15, 1999.
7. Outstanding at the end of fiscal year.
8. At the end of January, 1999.
9. April-January, 1998-99.
10. Per cent change indicates the rate of appreciation/depreciation (-) of the Rupee vis-a-vis the US dollar.

* As on 30-1-1999 (Provisional) @ Dec. 1998 # April-December, 1998.

The deceleration in the growth of India's exports (in US dollars) continued for the third year in succession and growth was negative for the first nine months of the year. Imports, on a BOP basis, have decelerated even more sharply, largely because of a decline in the prices of oil and other commodities, but also because of a slow down of non-DGCI&S imports. The current account deficit consequently fell from 1.6 per cent of GDP in 1997-98 to a projected 1.4 per cent of GDP in 1998-99.* Total net capital inflows in 1998-99 are expected to be lower than in 1997-98 as a result of a deceleration in the private inflows. The decline in Foreign Direct Investment (FDI) and commercial borrowing and outflow of portfolio investment by Foreign Institutional Investors (FIIs) had been only partly off set by the inflow under Resurgent India Bonds (RIBs). Despite these trends, foreign currency reserves (exclusive of gold and SDRs) continued to increase in 1998-99, though at a slower rate than in 1997-98. These reserves went up from US$26.0 billion at the end of March 1998 to $27.4 billion by the end of January, 1999.

Table 12.2 (a) : Sectoral Real Growth Rates

Industry	Percentage change over the previous year				
	1994-95	1995-96	1996-97 (P)	1997-98 (Q)	1998-99 (A)
I. Agriculture and Allied Sectors	5.4	0.2	9.4	-1.0	5.3
II. Industry	9.3	12.2	6.0	5.9	4.7
1. Mining and quarrying	9.2	7.4	1.2	2.7	0.1
2. Manufacturing	10.6	15.0	7.7	6.8	5.7
3. Electricity, gas and water supply	9.3	6.7	5.7	6.6	6.3
4. Construction	5.3	8.2	2.9	4.1	2.3
III. Services	**8.5**	**9.8**	**8.0**	**8.2**	**6.7**
5. Trade, hotels, transport and communications	12.8	11.5	8.6	5.7	6.8
6. Financial services	5.6	8.3	7.9	8.4	7.7
7. Community, social and personal services	3.4	7.8	6.7	13.3	5.8
IV. Total GDP at Factor Cost	7.8	7.6	7.8	5.0	5.8

A : Advance estimates P : Provisional Q : Quick estimates

The marked slowdown in GDP growth in 1997-98 was largely the result of the volatility in agricultural growth, which collapsed to –1.0 per cent in 1997-98 after soaring to 9.4 per cent in 1996-97 (Table 12.2a). This masked the equally sharp slowdown in growth of GDP from manufacturing to 7.7 per cent in 1996-97 (from 15 per cent the year before). This was followed by a more modest decline to 6.8 per cent in 1997-98. Industrial growth, however, remained almost unchanged in 1997-98 as this was compensated by an increase in other sub-sectors. The

* All ratios to GDP are noticeably lower using the new GDP series because the new series estimates GDP levels about 9 per cent higher on average than the old series for years for which both series are available.

increase in GDP from 'public administration and defence', arising from the decisions on the Pay Commission Report, which increased government employees' salaries substantially, compensated for the slowdown in growth of other services. The increased salary level of Central Government Employees since 1997-98 does not seem to have resulted immediately in a proportional increase in consumption. The growth of private domestic consumption (constant price) fell from 6.8 per cent in 1996-97 to 3.9 per cent in 1997-98 (Table 12.2b). The most important proximate factor in the growth slowdown in 1997-98 seems to be agriculture which affected household income, consumption and investment.

The recovery in 1998-99 was led by the rebound in 'agriculture and allied sectors', which is projected by the CSO to grow by 5.3 per cent (Table 12.2a). All other major sectors of the economy, with one exception, are estimated to have decelerated. The growth of GDP from manufacturing has slipped to 5.7 per cent, that from 'eletricity, gas and water supply' to 6.3 per cent, and mining to 0.1 per cent. 'Trade, hotels, transport and communications' was the only other category where growth accelerated from 5.7 per cent in 1997-98 to 6.8 per cent in 1998-99.

Although data on aggregate demand is not available for 1998-99, demand factors seem to have played a significant role in the slow recovery of manufacturing growth. The East Asian crisis and its reverberations on the world economy were an important reason for the slow recovery in industrial growth and the continuing deceleration in certain-sectors. The financial crisis in East Asia and the slowdown in world trade sharply reduced the growth in world demand for many commodities. This contributed importantly to the declining trend in export growth.

In addition to the direct impact on exports, the heightened imbalance between world supply and demand put intense competitive pressure on sectors producing homogeneous products The decline in global prices of oil by 25.7 per cent and of non-fuel commodities by 14.6 per cent in 1998, compared to a growth of -1.1 per cent and 5 per cent respectively in 1997, is one indication of this. The decline in production of mining sector and the slowdown in growth of basic goods and intermediate goods are at least partly a result of these developments in the global economy.

Total gross domestic savings declined to 23.1 per cent of GDP in 1997-98 from 24.4 per cent of GDP in 1996-97 (Table 12.3). Public saving contributed 0.5 per cent and Private saving 0.8 per cent of GDP to this decline. Public saving has declined progressively to 1 per cent of GDP from a recent peak of 1.9 per cent in 1995-96. Both household and corporate saving contributed to the decline in private saving rate. The most noteworthy aspect was the one per cent of GDP decline in household physical saving rate. Household financial saving bucked the declining trend in saving rates, by rising to 10.3 per cent of GDP in 1997-98 from 9.8 per cent in 1996-97. This is consistent with the hypothesis that the salary arrears received by Central Government employees consequent on the Pay Commission decision were largely saves.

Table 12.2 (b) : Disposition of Gross Domestic Product

Component	Percentage change over the previous year							
	(at current prices)				(at 1993-94 prices)			
	1994-95	1995-96	1996-97P	1997-98Q	1994-95	1995-96	1996-97P	1997-98Q
Total final consumption expenditure	15.7	15.2	16.5	10.1	7.2	7.8	7.5	6.4
Govt. final consumption expenditure	11.4	18.5	13.4	20.7	7.7	15.1	11.3	19.4
Pvt. final consumption expenditure	16.4	14.7	17.0	8.4	7.1	6.6	6.8	3.9
Gross domestic capital formation	34.1	19.3	15.1	7.1	23.0	8.9	8.5	3.0
Exports of goods and services	17.9	28.7	11.1	10.7	—	—	—	—
Less imports of goods services	21.8	38.4	11.1	12.7	—	—	—	—

Q : Quick Estimates P : Provisional

Table 12.3 : Savings and Investment

	1993-94	1994-95	1995-96	1996-97 (P)	1997-98 (Q)
	(As per cent of GDP at current market prices)				
Gross Domestic Savings	**21.8**	**24.2**	**24.1**	**24.4**	**23.1**
Public	0.5	1.5	1.9	1.5	1.0
Private	21.3	22.7	22.2	22.9	22.1
Household sector	17.9	19.3	17.4	18.8	18.3
Financial savings	10.8	11.6	8.2	9.8	10.3
Physical savings	7.1	7.7	9.3	9.0	8.0
Gross Domestic Investment*	22.4	25.4	25.8	25.7	24.8
Public	8.1	8.5	7.4	6.7	7.0
Private	12.7	14.4	18.2	16.5	16.4
Gross Domestic Investment*	**22.4**	**25.4**	**25.8**	**25.7**	**24.8**
GFCF	20.9	21.4	23.8	23.2	22.9
Change in stocks	-0.2	1.5	1.8	-0.1	0.5
Saving-Investment Gap@	**-0.6**	**-1.2**	**-1.7**	**-1.3**	**-1.7**
Public	-7.6	-7.0	-5.5	-5.2	-6.0
Private	8.6	8.3	4.0	6.4	5.7

Note : (i) Gross Domestic Investment denotes Gross Domestic Formation (GDCF)
(ii) Figures may not add up due to rounding off

* : adjusted for errors and omissions;
@ : refers to the difference between the rates of savings and investment
GFCF : Gross Fixed Capital Formation;
P : Provisonal estimates; Q : Quick estimates
Source : Central Statistical Organisation

Real Gross Domestic Capital Formation dropped marginally from 26 per cent of GDP (constant price) in 1996-97 to 25.6 per cent of GDP in 1997-98 (Table 12.4). This level is only 0.1 per cent of GDP lower than the average for 1994-95 to 1997-98, which represented a substantial step up from earlier levels. The main indentifiable factor in the decline was the 0.9 per cent of GDP decline in household investment rate to 8.2 per cent of GDP. The decline in household saving in physical form and decline in household investment are perhaps linked to the large fluctuations in agriculture. Corporate investment increased by 1.2 per cent of GDP to 9 per cent, while public investment increased marginally.

Somewhat surprisingly real Gross Fixed Capital Formation remained unchanged at 23.6 per cent of GDP a rate that is higher than the average for the same four years. Despite a drop in the household fixed investment rate to 7.8 per cent of GDP, the continuing up trend in corporate fixed investment kept overall fixed investment rate from falling. Corporate fixed investment increased from 7.9 per cent of GDP in 1995-96 to 8.3 per cent of GDP in 1996-97 and further to 9 per cent of GDP in 1997-98. This suggests that Indian corporate industry is responding to the challenge of domestic and global competition.

Production

After a decline in net agricultural output by 1.0 per cent in 1997-98, agricultural value added is expected to rebound by an estimated 5.3 per cent in 1998-99. Indications are that growth rate in production of agriculture would be about 3.9 per cent in 1998-99.

Foodgrain production estimated at 192.4 million tonnes in 1997-98 was quite a let down from the preceding year's record output of 199.4 million tonnes. Major setbacks were in wheat with production lower by 3.5 million tonnes and coarse cereals with production lower by over 3 million tonnes. The overall prospects of food grain output for 1998-99 are quite good mainly due to Rabi crops sown in November-December 1998. Rabi foodgrain output is likely to be 96.5 million tonnes, which would be higher than Rabi 1997-98 by 5.2 million tonnes. Thus 1998-99 food grain output is expected to be about 195.3 million tonnes.

Table 12.4 : Real Gross Domestic Capital Formation

	1994-95	1995-96	1996-97 (Q)	1997-98 (P)
	(As per cent of GDP at market prices, 1993-94 prices)			
GDCF*	**25.5**	**25.7**	**26.0**	**25.6**
Public	8.6	7.3	6.6	6.9
Private	14.5	18.2	16.9	17.2
Pvt. corporate sector	6.7	9.0	7.8	9.0
Household sector	7.8	9.2	9.1	8.2
GFCF	**21.6**	**23.8**	**23.6**	**23.6**
Public	8.6	7.5	6.5	6.8
Private	13.0	16.3	17.0	16.8
Change in stocks	**1.5**	**1.8**	**-0.1**	**0.5**
Public	-0.0	-0.1	0.1	0.1
Private	1.5	1.9	-0.2	0.4
	Growth rate in per cent			
GDFC*	**23.0**	**8.9**	**8.5**	**3.0**
Public	14.7	-7.5	-3.1	9.0
Private	23.2	35.6	-0.6	7.1
GFCF	**11.3**	**18.9**	**6.3**	**5.2**
Public	18.5	-6.4	-6.0	8.6
Private	7.0	35.8	12.0	3.9

Note : GDCF : Gross Domestic Capital Formation; GFCF : Gross Fixed Capital Formation:
Figures may not add up due to rounding off.
* : adjusted for errors and omissions; P : Provisional estimates; Q : Quick estimates

Source : Central Statistical Organisation

The 1998 monsoon turned out normal as predicted by the Meteorological Department. Despite this, fiscal 1998-99 experienced set-backs related to the weather. The first occurred in May-June when northern India experienced unprecedented heat wave conditions for many days with maximum temperature touching a high of 48°C. This unusual phenomenon caused extreme moisture stress in some crops, particularly fruits and vegetables. Second, there were severe floods and associated damage in Eastern India. The third weather related aberration occurred in late October 1998 when heavy rainfall resulted in damage to standing and matured paddy and cotton crops, as well as vegetables such as potato and onion.

As measured by the Index of Industrial Production (IIP) industrial growth revived slightly to 6.6 per cent in 1997-98 from 5.6 per cent in 1996-97. This revival however, faltered in 1998-99. The growth rate for April-December 1998 was only 3.5 per cent, down from a 6.7 per cent for April-December 1997 (Table 12.1). The mining sector (includes crude oil) has witnessed the greatest deceleration in growth, from 5.5 per cent for the first nine months of 1997-98 to -1.1 per cent in 1998-99 (same months). Manufacturing sector growth also fell from 6.9 per cent for the same months of 1997 to 3.7 per cent in 1998. Electricity growth on the other hand, improved from 6 per cent in 1997 to 6.6 per cent in 1998 over the same months.

The greatest decleration in 1998 was in basic goods, from 6.8 per cent growth in April-December 1997 to 1.4 per cent in 1998. The small recovery in consumer goods production from a growth of 5.2 per cent for 1996-97 to 5.7 per cent in 1997-98 was reversed in 1998-99. Consumer goods production increased by only 2.8 per cent during April-December 1998 compared to 4.6 per cent growth during the corresponding period of 1997. Though the recovery in 1997-98 had been led by consumer durables growth from 4.7 per cent in 1996-97 to 7.8 per cent in 1997-98, the reversal in 1998-99 (April-December) was due to a decline in both sub-sectors. Consumer durabies growth fell from 6.8 per cent in the first nine months of 1997-98 to 2.3 per cent in the same months of 1998-99 and non-durables growth fell from 4 per cent to 3 per cent.

The continuing slowdown in the manufacture of consumer goods suggests that an autonomous slowdown in the growth of private consumption has contributed to slower growth of aggregate demand. The decline in agriculture production affects the demand for industrial goods with a lag. The decline in asset prices, as reflected in stock prices and real estate, have probably brought the 'wealth effect' (on consumption) to Indian shores for the first time. Such negative effects on consumption are common in developed countries but have not previously been attributed to Indian consumers. The earlier boom in Non-bank Financial Companies (NBFCs) coincided with and was perhaps related to the increase in consumer credit for automobiles and other consumer durables. The subsequent difficulties of NBFCs may have contributed to the slowing of this credit, and consequently a decline in credit-financed consumption.

Greater global uncertainty, domestic uncertainty arising from non-economic factors and a heightened appreciation of risk and uncertainty may have also dampened demand. For instance the obverse of the high salaries offered to financial professionals in the boom years is the job uncertainty and job losses which follow in a downturn. This uncertainty combined with poor performance of stock markets since the boom of 1994 and lack of trust in issuing companies and market intermediaries has also led to a shift of retail investors from riskier investments into safe havens like bank deposits and post office saving.

The only industrial sub-sector, which bucked the trend of declining growth rates, was capital goods. Though growth in capital goods had declined to 5.2 per cent in 1997-98 (from 9.3 per cent in 1996-97), it seems to have staged a recovery. The growth rate of 9.8 per cent for April-December 1998 was significantly higher than the fairly respectable growth of 6.7 per cent in the corresponding period of 1997.

The import of capital goods (machine tools, mechanical and electrical machinery, transport equipment and project goods) in US $ value also increased substantially during April-November 1998. The growth rate of 7 per cent represents a large turn around from the 16.6 per cent fall in the corresponding period of 1997-98. This was despite a decline in foreign direct investment, and net FII outflows during 1998-99. On balance, total domestic investment has probably grown at a faster rate during the first eight months of 1998-99 than in the corresponding months of 1997-98.

The Government initiated several reforms for providing a stimulus to industrial growth (See Box 12.1). Coal and lignite, petroleum (other than crude) and its distillation products and bulk drugs were delicensed, as was the very important agro-processing industry, sugar. Coal and lignite and mineral oils were de-reserved from exclusive public sector production. The Budget also announced dis-investment of specified portions of equity from select Public Sector Enterprises like GAIL, LOC, CONCOR and VSNL and a separate policy package for the small-scale sector. Nine items (six from 'farm implements and tools' and three from 'leathr') and electronic toys, wre removed from the list of industries reserved for exclusive manufacture by the small sector. Companies were permitted to buy-back their own shares subject to restriction of buy-back to 25 per cent of paid-up capital and free reserves. The rules were changed to allow companies to make inter-corporate investments without prior approval of the Government.

A special additional duty of 4 per cent was levied on a large number of imports so as to offset the sales tax and other local taxes imposed by the States and provide a level playing field. Special 'Task Forces' were set up by the Government to look into the problems of steel, cement and capital goods industry. As recomended by them, seven imported inputs critical to steel manufacturing have been exempted from special additional duty and import of their seconds and defective have been allowed against specified c.i.f. values. Depreciation norms for income-tax purposes applicable to purchases of commercial vehicles have been relaxed.

Foreign investment norms were liberalised further :

- Scope of foreign direct equity investment under RBI's automatic approval scheme ha been enhanced. Indian companies have been permitted to accept investment under the automatic approval route without the prior permission of RBI.
- Requirement of prior approval from RBI for FDI/NRI/OCB investment and issue of shares to foreign investors after FIPB/Government approval has been done away with.
- Investment limit for individual NRIs/PIOs/OCBs in the total paid-up equity capital of a company has been increased to 5 per cent from 1 cent and the aggregate investment ceiling has been raised to 10 per cent from 5 per cent.
- NRIs/PIOs/OCBs permitted to invest in unlisted companies.
- Liberalisation of existing norms for NRI/PIO/OCB investment in health services sector.

Infrastructure performance during April-December 1998 has declined as compared to the corresponding period of 1997. Growth of six infrastructure and core industries (electricity generation, coal, steel, crude oil, refinery throughput and cement) decelerated to 2 per cent during April-December, 1998 from 4.1 per cent growth in April-December 1997. Crude oil and steel have displayed negative growth rates. Rates of growth have also declined for coal, refinery throughput and cement in 1998-99. Electricity generation recorded an increased growth rate of 6.6 per cent in April-December 1998 as compared to 5.6 per cent in April-December 1997 (Table 12.5).

Growth of sectors such as railways, ports and telecommunications, that do not appear in the IIP, showed divergent trends. Revenue earning goods traffic on railways in April-December 1998 was lower than in April-December 1997. The telecommunications sector, however, maintained the high levels of growth in the current year. The decline in many of these infrastructure and core sub-sectors seems to be primarily due to reduced demand from industry.

In keeping with the firm commitment of the government, and the growing consensus, a number of reforms were introduced in infrastructure, with a view to improving quality, availability and viability. These include the following:

- The Indian Electricity Act, 1910 and Electricity (Supply) Act, 1948 were amended to provide for private investment in power transmission.
- Following enactment of the Electricity Regulatory Commission legislation, the Central Electricity Regulatory Commission was set up, with an enabling provision for states to set up regulatory commissions. A few States have already established such commissions, while a number of them are in the process of doing so.
- Procedures for extending sovereign counter guarantees, to the Fast Track Power Projects which had been held up for some time, have been simplified and several counter guarantees issued.
- Foreign equity participation upto 100 per cent allowed for electricity generation, transmission and distribution (except those of atomic reactor plants) and in construction and maintenance of roads, highways, vehicular bridges, toll roads, vehicular tunnels, ports and harbours. This is subject to the provision that the total foreign equity in any such project does not exceed Rs. 1500 crore.
- The tax holiday, granted to the power sector, has been extended upto the year 2003.
- Inland waterways and inland ports according infrastructure status for fiscal concessions.
- The policy for issuing licenses for providing Internet services has been announced. There will be no license fee for the first 5 years and after 5 years a nominal license fee of Rupee 1 will be charged. Private Internet service providers can also set up international gateways after obtaining security clearance.
- Concessions to imports of equipment for construction of National highways extended to other road construction projects.
- The Companies Act was amended to designate IDFC as an All India Public Financial Institution with attendant fiscal incentives and the fund raising benefits.
- The Urban Land (Ceiling and Regulation) Act, 1976 was repealed by

Table 12.5 : Growth Rates of Core and Infrastructure Sectors

(*Per cent p.a.*)

Sectors	Weight (IIP)	1993-94	1994-95	1995-96	1996-97	1997-98^P	1997-98^P@	1998-99^P@
Infrastructure Sectors (IIP)								
1. Electricity generation	10.2	7.5	8.1	8.4	3.8	6.6	5.6	6.6
(a) Hydel		0.7	17.5	-12.2	-5.5	8.6	2.6	13.8
(b) Thermal (Incl. nuclear)		9.5	5.6	14.8	6.1	6.2	6.3	4.9
2. Coal production	3.2	3.3	3.2	6.4	5.7	3.6	4.9	0.0
3. Steel	5.1	6.2	8.3	8.9	1.6	0.6	-0.1	-2.6
4. Crude oil	4.2	0.3	19.3	9.1	-6.5	3.0	2.7	-3.6
5. Refinery throughout	2.0	1.5	4.1	3.9	7.2	3.5	3.5	3.2
6. Cement	2.0	5.7	9.9	6.6	8.6	12.8	9.0	3.7
Overall	26.7	5.0	9.1	7.9	2.6	4.8	4.1	2.0
Other Infrastructure Sectors								
1. Railway revenue-earning goods traffic	2.5	1.7	7.0	4.7	5.0	6.1	-2.5	
2. Cargo handled at major ports	7.6	10.0	9.1	5.6	10.6	12.4	0.0	
3. Telecommunications : New Telephone connections provided (DELs)	24.5	44.0	23.3	17.5	27.1	31.9	26.1	

P : Provisional @ April-December

Ordinance. This could contribute significantly towards the development of urban infrastructure including housing, especially in states, which have approved the repeal.

Money and Prices

Fiscal 1997-98 ended with an annual inflation rate of 5.3 per cent (point to point WPI) and an annual 52-week average inflation rate of 4.8 per cent. This decline in inflation from 6.4 per cent (average) in 1996-97 was consistent with increased availability of agricultural goods in the market (lagged supply effect) and lower international prices of imports The point-to-point annual rate of inflation in the WPI rose during 1998-99 to a peak of 8.8 per cent on September 26. It decelerated thereafter to 4.6 per cent (provisional) on January 30, 1999. The 52-week annual average rate was still about 6.9 per cent. In 1998-99 unexpected supply side effects arising from shortfalls in production of some agricultural commodities were overlaid on the earlier slowdown in aggregate demand. The shortfalls resulted in an unprecedented surge in the price of vegetables, especially onions and potatoes, which overshadowed the price behaviour of other sub-sectors.

Despite the steep, though temporary, flare up in the overall inflation rate during 1998-99, the underlying inflation rate remained modest. This is indicated by the subdued trends in wholesale prices of manufacturers (accounting for 56 per cent weight in the WPI) which has risen by only 3.4 per cent between end-March 1998 and, January 30, 1999. Fuel and power prices have actually declined over the same period, with the index dropping from 384.1 at the end of March 1998 to 374.1 by January 30, 1999. This contrasts with a rise of 10.2 per cent in the wholesale price index of primary articles over the same period. The steep fall in the rate of growth of primary goods prices, during the last quarter of 1998-99, is also consistent with the proposition of a smaller step-up in underlying inflation.

The year-on-year monetary (M3) growth at 19.8 per cent as of January 15, 1999 exceeded the corresponding growth in 1997-98 by 2.9 percentage points. It is also higher than the indicative target set by RBI of 15 to 15.5 per cent for 1998-99, which was explicitly based on a projected real GDP growth rate of 6.5 to 7.0 per cent and an assumed inflation rate of 5 to 6 per cent. Thus, *prima-facie* it could be argued that monetary policy accommodated the rise in inflation. The presence of excess capacity in the economy as well as the competitive pressure from outside has, however, ensured that the underlying inflation did not rise. It is only sub-sectors that are shielded from competition by internal controls or quantitiative restrictions on imports that have seen large increase in price. Some studies have estimated that about three-quarters of agricultural commodities remain on the restricted list of imports. It is therefore, not surprising that most of the inflationary surge was in these commodities, and that production shortfalls got translated immediately into price rises.

The rate of expansion in reserve money in the current financial year till January 15, 1999 was 10.7 per cent as against 4.1 per cent in the corresponding period of 1997-98. This reflected the sharp increase in the growth of Net RBI credit to the Government (NRCG) in 1998-99. Growth of NRCG accelerated from 2.5 per cent in 1997-98 to 13.4 per cent in 1998-99. This was only partly offset by a fall in the growth of RBI's net foreign exchange assets to 11.4 per cent in 1998-99 from 13.6 per cent in 1997-98. There was a rising trend in the cut-off yield of both 91-day and 364-day Treasury Bills during 1998, which suggests the possibility of crowding out of private credit in the last quarter of 1998-99, despite comfortable liquidity in the system during the first three quarters.

Private credit growth remained low during 1998-99, reflecting primarily the relatively low effective demand for funds from the corporate sector. Till January 15, 1999 in the current financial year, non-food credit expanded by 6.8 per cent as against 7.1 per cent in the corresponding period of 1997-98. The total flow of funds comprising non-food credit and investment in debt/equity instruments expanded by 9.7 per cent till January 15, 1999 as against 11.5 per cent in the corresponding period of 1997-98. Though nominal interest rates had fallen in 1997-98 relative to 1996-97, the trend seems to have reversed in 1998-99 (as measured by call money and Treasury bill rates). Real interest rates, however, continued to decline gradually. Thus, the slight rise in nominal rates reflected a partial adjustment to the higher inflation rate during 1998-99. With inflation beginning to subside, the downtrend in real rates may be reversed unless nominal rates fall during 1999.

The Monetary and Credit Policy of April 1998 reduced the Bank Rate to 9 per cent. The CRR was reduced to 10 per cent in April 1998 but it was raised to 11 per cent in August 1998 so as to reduce liquidity. This was needed to calm the heightened volatility in the foreign exchange market, following a rise in risk perception of emerging markets (including India) in the immediate aftermath of the Russian economic crisis. To facilitate mobilisation of long term external deposits, the interest rate ceiling on FCNR (B) deposits of one year and above, was raised by 50 basis points and for such deposits below one year and for floating rate deposits, the ceiling was reduced by 25 basis points.

Among the liberalisation measures announced in April 1998 were: (a) interest rates on loans upto Rs. 2 lakh were set so as not to exceed PLR applicable to prime borrowers of over Rs. 2 lakh. (b) All advances against term deposits were set at interest rates equal to or less than PLR, and (c) The minimum maturity period of term deposits was reduced from 30 to 15 days.

Fiscal Developments

The budget for 1998-99 was formulated in the backdrop of serious fiscal slippage and a deceleration in economic growth. Its objective was, to (a) restore the momentum of industrial growth, (b) ensure macroeconomic stability, (c) raise investment, particularly in infrastructure, (d) provide impetus to social sector developments (e) reverse the decline in agriculture production, and (f) calibrate the pace and character of integration with the world economy. The budget announced a modest reduction in the Gorss Fiscal Deficit (GFD) from 6.1 per cent of Gross Domestic Product (GDP) in 1997-98 (RE) to 5.6 per cent of GDP in 1998-99 (BE). Consequent to the release of new series of national accounts, the fiscal deficit as a proportion of GDP at current market prices is now placed at 5.5 per cent and 5.1 per cent for 1997-98 (RE) and 1998-99 (BE) respectively (Table 12.6). The Revenue deficit, which indicates the extent of borrowing required to finance current expenditure, was budgeted at Rs. 48068 crore (2.7 per cent of GDP) for 1998-99 compared with Rs. 43686 crore (2.8 per cent of GDP) for 1997-98 (RE). The primary deficit, which is an indicator of current fiscal operations of the Central Government, was estimated at Rs. 16025 crore (0.9 per cent of GDP) for 1998-99 compared with Rs. 20645 crore (1.3 per cent of GDP) attained in 1997-98 (RE).

The Central Government finances during the current year continue to be under stress. The fiscal deficit in April-December, 1998 was exacerbated on account of a higher growth in total expenditure at 26 per cent compared with a growth of only 4.7 per cent in total revenue receipts. Thus, preliminary estimates indicate that the fiscal deficit was higher by 77.1 per cent in April-December, 1998 over that in April-December, 1997, and accounted for about 80.7 per cent of the budgeted fiscal deficit for 1998-99. With continuing shortfalls in collections of indirect taxes due to sluggish growth in industrial production and imports, it is unlikely that the year end fiscal deficit would be contained within the budgeted amount.

Table 12.6 : Tax Revenue and Expenditure

	1990-91 Actuals	1994-95 Actuals	1995-96 Actuals	1996-97 Actuals	1997-98 Revised Estimates	1998-99 Budget Estimates
			(As per cent of GDP)			
1. Fiscal Deficit	7.7	5.6	4.9	4.7	5.5	5.1
2. Revenue Deficit	3.2	3.0	2.4	2.3	2.8	2.7
3. Primary Deficit	4.0	1.3	0.8	0.5	1.3	0.9
4. Gross Tax Revenue	9.9	8.9	9.1	9.1	9.1	8.9
(a) Direct Tax	1.9	2.6	2.8	2.8	3.3	2.8
(i) Income Tax	0.9	1.2	1.3	1.3	1.2	1.2
(ii) Corporation Tax	0.9	1.3	1.4	1.3	1.4	1.5
(b) Indirect Tax	7.8	6.3	6.4	6.4	5.8	6.1
(i) Union Excise Duties	4.2	3.6	3.3	3.2	3.1	3.3
(ii) Customs	3.5	2.6	2.9	3.0	2.6	2.7
5. Total Expenditure	18.1	15.5	14.6	14.3	15.0	15.1
of which						
(i) Interest Payments	3.7	4.2	4.1	4.2	4.2	4.2
(ii) Major Subsidies	1.6	1.1	1.0	1.0	1.2	1.1
(iii) Defence	2.6	2.2	2.2	2.1	2.3	2.3
(iv) Other Non-Plan Expenditure	5.2	3.3	3.5	3.2	3.5	3.4
(v) Budget Support For Plan	4.9	4.6	3.8	3.8	3.9	4.1

Note : 1. The ratios to GDP are based on new series of National Account Statistics with 1993-94 as base year released by the Central Statistical Organisation (CSO) on February 3, 1999. For the purpose of comparability GDP at current market prices for the year 1990-91, 1991-92 and 1992-93 have been interpolated by using an average link sector of 1.0878 obtained from the overlapping years viz. 1993-94, 1994-95, 1995-96 and 1996-97 for which both the old series and new series for the GDP at durrent market prices are available.

2. The estimate of GDP at current market prices for 1998-99 is based on CSO's advance estimates of real GDP growth of 5.8 per cent along with an assumption of an averaage inflation rate of 7 per cent for the year.

A number of measures were taken to strengthen the infrastructure and rural sectors. The plan outlay for infrastructure (comprising energy, transport and communications) was budgeted to go up by 35 per cent from Rs. 45252 crore in 1997-98 (RE) to Rs. 61146 crore in 1998-99. National Highways Authority of India (NHAI) was provided Rs. 500 crore to catalyse new road projects. To generate funds for development of roads, an additional duty at the rate of one rupee per litre on pertrol was introduced. This is expected to garner Rs. 790 crore in a year and will entirely go towards augmenting the corpus of NHAI. Housing was another thrust area. The allocation for the Indira Awas Yojna Programme was enhanced to Rs. 1600 crore, from Rs. 1144 crore in 1997-98 (RE). The budget provided more fiscal concessions to stimulate housing activity and an ordinance was promulgated for repeal of the Urban Land Ceiling Regulation Act.

A number of programmes were strengthened to enhance agricultural productivity i a sustainable manner. The plan allocation for Watershed Development Programmes was hiked to Rs. 677 crore from Rs. 517 crore in 1997-98 (RE). The outlay for Accelerated Irrigation Benefit Programme was enhanced by 58 per cent over the 1997-98. Rural Infrastructure Development Fund (RIDF)-IV was launched with an enhanced allocation of Rs. 3000 crore. The share capital of National Bank for Agriculture and Rural Development (NABARD) was further augmented by Rs. 500 crore with a contribution of Rs 100 crore from the budget and Rs. 400 crore from RBI. This will enable NABARD to leverage additional resources from the market to meet the credit needs of the agriculture.

The Infrastructure Development Finance Company (IDFC) was designated an all India public financial institution with all attendant fiscal incentives, to enhance long-term finance for infrastructure investment in the private sector. As Provident Funds can be an important source of funding for private sector infrastructure projects, the Union Budget has allowed investment upto 10 per cent of the new accretion in private sector securities which have an investment grade rating. Inland waterways and inland ports have also been included in the definition of infrastructure and given associated fiscal incentives of tax holiday. The budget proposed a guarantee scheme to cover the outstanding dues of Central PSUs such as NTPC and Coal India from SEBs. This would enable the former to raise resources either by securitising these debts or directly entering the market for tapping resources.

The effort to simplify and widen the personal income tax continued. Two additional presumptive tax indicators were introduced and the ambit of the presumptive tax effort extended from 12 cities to 35 cities. This has been accompanied by making it obligatory for assesses to quote their Permanent Account Number (PAN) or GIR number in respect of certain high value transactions. With a view to simplify the tax return, a one-page tax return called "Saral" was introduced for all non-corporate taxpayers.

To encourage industrial activity in backward areas, the tax holiday granted to industrial undertakings located in any industrially backward State or district was extended till March 31, 2000 and for power generating units till March 31, 2003.

On the excise side, the process of rationalisation and reduction of duty rates were carried forward so as to ensure convergence towards a mean rate of 18 per cent *ad-valorem*. Towards this end an excise duty of 8 per cent was imposed on a number of commodities. With a view to off set the State and Local taxes paid by domestic producers a special additional non-modvatable levy of 8 per cent was imposed on imports, which was subsequently scaled down to 4 per cent. However, this levy excludes a wide range of goods and categories of imports.

For the small-scale industries sector the exemption limit for excise purposes was enhanced from Rs. 30 lakh to Rs. 50 lakh. Furthermore, to reduce litigation in payment of direct and indirect taxes, a new scheme called "Samadhan" was introduced. This would offer waiver of interest, penalty and a part of tax and immunity from prosecution on payment of arrears. The scope of service tax was widened.

Financial Developments

There has been slow but steady improvement in the performance of public sector banks. The ratio of Non-Performing Assets to total advances in respect of public sector banks declined from 17.8 per cent in end 1996-97 to 16.0 per cent in end 1997-98. The ratio of net Non-Performing Assets to net advances also declined from 9.2 to 8.2 per cent in 1997-98.

Based on the recommendations of the Narasimham Committee (II) on Banking Sector Reforms, the Reserve Bank announced a number of decisions as part of its mid-term review of the monetary and credit policy released on October 30, 1998. These related to phased introduction of risk weight for Government/Approved Securities, risk weight for Government guaranteed advances, general provision for standards assets, higher Capital to Risk-Weighted Assets Ratio (CRAR, 9 per cent) for banks, etc. Based on the recommendations of the Task Force on Non-Banking Finance Companies (NBFCs), deposit acceptance norms have been rationalised by the RBI.

Sanctions and Disbursements by All India Financial Institutions continued their strong growth in 1998-99. During April-December 1998 Sanctions grew by 36.9 per cent and Disbursements grew by 12.5 per cent. This growth was consistent with the improved growth of production of capital goods.

Capital markets remained subdued during most of the year. Rs. 3929 crore was raised from the Primary Market during April-December, 1998 as against Rs. 3093 crore in the corresponding period of 1997-98. The bulk of the capital raised (nearly 80 per cent) was in the form of bonds, with very little in the form of equity issues. The Sensex, which had risen at the beginning of the year from 3893 on March 31, 1998 to over 4200 in April, declined thereafter to 2934 by end-August 1998. It crossed the 3000 mark in September, 1998 but declined to 2878 on October 5, 1998, and remained below 3,000 for nearly three months. The last quarter of 1998-99 has, however, seen a revival, with the Sensex crossing 3400 in January 1999. This is perhaps reflective of the declining level of uncertainty and improved risk perceptions.

The SEBI Board accepted most of the recommendations of the "Informal Group on Primary Markets". The recommendations accepted for immediate implementation were :

- Primary issues to be made compulsorily through the depository mode after a specified date.
- 100 per cent book building in respect of issues of Rs. 25 crore and above.
- Reduction in the number of mandatory collection centres in respect of issues above Rs. 10 crore to four metropolitan cities.

Measures taken to revive the secondary market included,

- The Companies (Amendment) Ordinance, 1998 dated October 31, 1998 (and January 7, 1999) empowering companies to purchase their own shares or other specified securities subject to SEBI regulations,
- Amendment of SEBI take-over regulations permitting easier consolidation by promoters,
- Publication of unaudited results by listed companies on quarterly basis,
- Rolling settlements in respect of dematerialised securities, and
- Stringent margin requirements to curb excess volatility in share prices.

To facilitate flow of funds to the infrastructure sector, the SEBI decided to grant specific relaxation to public issues by infrastructure companies, which are defined under Section 10 (23G) of the Income Tax Act, 1961.

Notable developments in the Government securities market include,

- Notifying issue size in respect of all Treasury bills,
- Exclusion of non-competitive bids from notified amounts,
- Permission for FII debt funds to invest in both Government dated securities and treasury bills.
- Amendments to RBI guidelines on tansactions by FIIs to facilitate investment by regular FII equity funds, in Government dated securities and treasury bills, in both the primary and the secondary markets, within their debt ceiling of 30 per cent.

Balance of Payments

The East Asian crisis, which continued to deepen and spread in 1998, led to tremendous volatility and uncertainty in global financial markets, and to a re-evaluation of emerging markets as investment destinations. The increased risk aversion of international capital has had an impact on all emerging economies, including to some extent, India. In spite of a turbulent international environment, India's balance of payments has remained moderately comfortable, with some reserve accumulation. The current account deficit widened to 1.6 per cent of GDP or U.S.$ 6.5 billion in 1997-98. In 1998-99, it is estimated to fall, as a per cent of GDP, below the level in 1997-98. Net capital inflows are expected to be lower in 1998-99 than in 1997-98 as a result of a deceleration in the inflows of foreign direct investment and commercial borrowing and outflow of portfolio investment by FIIs.

The trade deficit, on a BOP basis, increased from 3.7 per cent of GDP in 1996-97 to 3.9 per cent in 1997-98, despite the sharp deceleration in import growth. This is attributable to deceleration in export growth, which continued for the third year in succession in 1998-99. Export growth, in BOP terms, slowed from 5.6 per cent in US dollar terms in 1996-97 to 2.1 per cent in 1997-98. Performance continues to be a major source of concern in the current financial year with exports having declined by 2.9 per cent during April-December 1998, compared to a 3.3 per cent growth in the corresponding period of 1997 (DGCI&S data). This data does not include software exports which are shown under invisibles.

The weakness in export performance reflects various international and domestic factors, which include:

- A decline in the growth of world trade. Import growth into the advanced economies, which are India's major trading partners has decelerated sharply from 18.2 per cent in 1995 to 3.7 per cent in 1996 and to 2.5 per cent in 1997.
- A reduction in the export prices of major items of manufactured goods.
- An appreciation of the Rupee in real effective exchange rate terms in 1997 against the currencies of major trading partners. The movement of exchange rates during 1998, however, has largely corrected for this appreciation.
- The massive depreciation of the currencies of the East Asian economies. This has impacted the price competitiveness of our exports in sectors such as man-made yarn, finished leather; and fabrics and processed minerals. Other items like textiles, automotive parts, chemicals, iron ore, machinery and electronic goods have also been affected.
- Domestic factors such as growing infrastructure constraints, high trasnsaction costs, and restrictions on agricultural exports.

Total imports, on BOP basis, increased by only 4.4 per cent to US$ 51.1 billion in 1997-98 compared to 12.1 per cent growth in 1996-97, while non-oil imports, excluding gold and silver, grew by only 5 per cent in 1997-98. This marked deceleration was due to several factors, including weak domestic demand, lower industrial activity and lower unit values of imports. There has been a further deceleration of imports in the current financial year. Imports during April-December, 1998 increased by 7.1 pr cent compared to 7.4 per cent in the corresponding period of 1997-98 (DGCI&S data). This is largely due to a decrease in the dollar value of POL imports by about 26.3 per cent because of continued softening of prices. The increase of 15.7 per cent in non-POL imports over the same period is mainly a result of a shift in imports of gold and silver from baggage channel to the DGCI&S channel. This follows placement of these imports under a liberal import regime in October 1997. Lower international prices of gold in 1998 have also contributed to the increase in overall demand for gold.

The slowdown in global growth and international trade has also led to the introduction of protectionist measures in some countries. These have primarily taken the form of Non-tariff Barriers (NTBs) like more stringent quality, testing and labelling standards and increased investigations of dumping and subsidies. This has contributed to uncertainty in foreign trade and some market disruption.

Trade policy reforms have sought to eliminate various impediments to trade and to promote export growth. The EXIM Policy 1997-2002 continues this process. In the light of the continued slowdown in exports, various measures were announced in August/September 1998 which include:

- Exemption of exports under all export promotion schemes from Special Additional Duty (SAD) of 4 per cent;
- Reduction in interest rates on pre-shipment and post-shipment export credit in rupees from 11 per cent to 9 per cent;
- Extension of the zero duty Export Promotion Capital Goods scheme to bio-technology and small scale engineering;
- Promotional/procedural changes like,

— extension of tax holiday for EOU/EPZ to 10 years,
— sub-contracting facility for Domestic Tariff Area (DTA),
— permission to selected manufacturer-exporters to furnish legal undertaking instead of bank-guarantee against import of duty free raw materials.
— simplification of bond furnishing procedure for exporters.

In order to promote trade among SAARC countries, India has unitaterally removed all quantitative restrictions on imports of around 2300 items from SAARC countries with effect from August 1, 1998. A free trade agreement was signed between India and Sri Lanka which will reduce tarriff to zero by 2007 on most commodities. This will provide an impetus to the eventual creation of a South Asia Free Trade Area (SAFTA).

The net inflow on invisible account has continued to be a major support to the balance of payments. Invisible receipts have shown robust growth, reaching US $ 23.0 billion in 1997-98. This increase has been spurred by increased private transfer receipts, which have grown by 25 per cent per annum from U.S. $ 3.9 billion in 1992-93 to U.S. $ 11.9 billion in 1997-98. Tourism receipts have risen at a rate of 6.8 per cent per annum during the five years ending 1997-98. The receipts under the miscellaneous category in the invisible account, which include software exports rose from U.S. $ 1.4 billion in 1992-93 to U.S. $ 4.0 billion in 1997-98. Software exports continue to show exceptional growth rates, and increased by nearly 60 per cent in 1997-98. The net surplus earned under invisibles, excluding the Indian Development Bonds (IDB) return flow in 1996-97, is estimated to have increased from U.S. $ 9.3 billion in 1996-97 to U.S. $9.8 billion in 1997-98, financing about 60 per cent of the trade deficit in the BOP in 1997-98.

The capital account in the balance of payments, which had shown an impressive surplus of U.S. $ 10.4 billion in 1997-98, is likely to be lower in 1998-99. Total net capital inflows in 1998-99 are expected to be substantially lower than the levels in 1997-98, if the exceptional inflows under Resurgent India Bonds (RIBs) are excluded. Foreign Direct Investment (FDI), which had increased by 18.6 per cent in 1997-98, has fallen by 38 per cent in April-December 1998. Portfolio investment has continued to decline from U.S. $ 3.3 billion in 1996-97 to U.S. $ 1.8 billion in 1997-98, to an outflow of $ 0.7 billion in April-December 1998. The significant decline in portfolio investment was partly a result of contagion from the East Asian crisis that affected all emerging markets.

The Resurgent India Bonds (RIB) scheme, launched in the current financial year, was open to both NRIs/OCBs. The scheme opened on August 5, 1998 and closed on August 24, 1998, mobilising U.S. $ 4.2 billion. Net inflows under non-resident deposits declines from U.S. $ 3.3 billion in 1996-97 to U.S. $ 1.1 billion in 1997-98. The gross disbursements under external assistance have declined slightly from U.S. $ 3.0 billion in 1996-97 to U.S. $ 2.9 billion in 1997-98. Gross disbursements during April-September 1998 was lower at US $ 830 million compared to US $ 1066 million during the corresponding period of 1997.

External Commercial Borrowing (ECB) approvals up to 23-12-98 in 1998-99 have been placed at US $ 3.8 billion compared to U.S. $ 8.7 billion in 1997-98. Disbursements have fallen even more sharply from $ 4 billion in April-September 1997-98 to US $ 1.6 billion in the first half of 1998-99. This is due to the relative un-attractiveness of ECB from the perspective of borrowers. The increase in the cost of ECB funds is due to a general increase in the risk premium for emerging market borrowers, downgrading by international credit rating agencies and the rise in forward premia.

The ECB guidelines were revised in 1998-99 and include the following changes:

- Proceeds of ECB can now be deployed for project related Rupee expenditure in all sectors subject to certain conditions;
- The limit under the "US $ 3 million scheme" has been increased to "US $ 5 millon" with 3 years simple maturity.
- ECB eligibility under the scheme for exporters has been raised to three times the average export performance during the last three years subject to a maximum of US $ 100 million.

The foreign currency assets of the RBI rose from U.S. $ 22.4 billion at the end of March 1997 to U.S. $ 26.0 billion at the end of March 1998. The high surplus in the capital account in 1997-98 outweighed the current account deficit and resulted in an increase in foreign exchange reserves of U.S. $ 3.9 billion. Total foreign exchange reserves (including gold and SDRs) at the end of January 1999 amounted to U.S. $ 30.4 billion, which provides cover for about 7 months of imports in 1998-99.

After an 18 month period of stability, the exchange rate of the Rupee against the U.S. dollar came under downward pressure in August 1997, arising mainly from the East Asian crisis. At the end of January 1999, the exchange rate of the Rupee vis-a-vis the U.S. dollar was Rs. 42.50. The movements in the exchange rate have helped to largely correct the relative appreciation of the Rupee in real terms, which will help to offset the competitive disadvantages arising from the extensive depreciation of the East Asian currencies, and is expected to revive our exports and contain import growth.

India's stock of external debt at end-September 1998 stood at U.S. $ 95.2 billion as against U.S. $ 93.9 billion at end-March 1998. The debt service payments, as a ratio of current receipts, continued to improve over the years declining from 30.2 per cent in 1991-92 to 19.5 per cent in 1997-98. The share of short-term debt to total debt declined from 7.2 per cent at end-March 1997 to 5.4 per cent at end-March 1998 and further to 3.7 per cent at end-September 1998. The share of concessional debt has declined from 44.7 per cent in 1996 to 39.3 per cent at end-March 1998 and further to 37.7 per cent at the end of September 1998.

Social Sectors

The government has relied mainly on three approaches for reduction of poverty and unemployment viz., higher economic growth, antipoverty and employment programmes and priority to government expenditure on social sectors. The poverty ratio declined from 56.4 per cent in 1973-74 to 37.3 in 1993-94 in rural areas and from 49.0 per cent in 1973-74 to 32.4 per cent in 1993-94 in urban areas. For the country as a whole, the poverty ratio declined from 54.9 per cent in 1973-74 to 36 per cent in 1993-94.

The Planning Commission has estimated that, additional employment opportunities of the order of 29.74 million were generated during January 1, 1994 to March 31, 1997. This implies an average growth rate of employment of

2.47 per cent per annum compared with 2.31 per cent during July 1, 1983 to December 31, 1993 and 2.32 per cent during January 1, 1978 to June 20, 1983.

The government has decided to set up the Second National Commission on Labour with a view to provide protection to millions of workers. The main focus of the Commission would be to suggest rationalisation of the existing labour laws in the organised sector and an umbrella legislation for ensurng a minimum level of protection to the workers in the unorganised sector.

Increased availability of health care and family welfare services has resulted in reduction of all-India death rate, birth rate and infant mortality rate. The crude death rate declined from 14.9 per thousand in 1971 to 9.8 in 1991 and further to 8.9 in 1997. Similarly, the infant mortality rate per thousand declined from 129 in 1971 to 80 in 1991 and further to 71 in 1997. The birth rate per thousand also declined from 36.9 in 1971 to 29.5 in 1991 and further to 27.2 in 1997.

Average real wages for unskilled agricultural labour, which reflect the economic conditions of agricultural labourers, have increased by 0.72 per cent in 1995-96 (Agricultural year July to June), 4.67 per cent in 1996-97 and 4.88 per cent in 1997-98. These trends are consistent with the view that more rapid economic growth has brought about an improvement in living standards of people in general.

Several anti-poverty measures have been in operation for decades focussing on the poor as the target group viz. welfare of weaker sections, women and children, and a number of special employment rogrammes for self and wage employment in rural and urban areas. The Central Plan and non-Plan expenditure on social sectors comprise education, health, water supply, sanitation, housing, slum develoment, social welfare and nutrition, rural employment and minimum basic services. As a ratio to GDP at market prices these expenditures increased to a record high of 1.91 per cent in 1998-99 (BE) as compared to 1.33 per cent in 1991-92 and 1.75 per cent in 1997-98 (RE). The Central Plan allocation for social sectors and programmes show highest growth of about 36 per cent for family welfare and Women and Child Development in 1998-99 (BE) over 197-98 (BE). The outlay for health has gone up by about 25 per cent in 1998-99 (BE) over 1997-98 (BE).

Environment Sector

A country's environmental problems vary with its stage of development, structure of its economy, production technologies in use and its environmental policies. While some problems may be associated with the lack of economic development (e.g. inadequate sanitation and access to clean drinking water), others are exacerbated by the growth of economic activity (e.g. air and water pollution). Environmental changes may be driven by many factors including economic growth, population growth, urbanisation, intensification of agriculture, rising energy use and transportation. Poverty remains at the root of several environmental problems.

Large scale industrialisation, spread of transport, communication and other modern infrastructure combined with the pressure of population growth have added to the difficulties of preserving clean environment and healthy natural resource base. These have been exerting pressure on environment as witnessed in growing evidence of air and water pollution and land degradation. For instance Delhi is now classified as the fourth most polluted city in the world, with a suspended Particulate Matter (SPM) of 145.3 to 929.8 microgrammes/m^3 as against at the National ambient air quality standard of 70 to 360 microgrammes/

m³. Organic and bacterial pollution continue to be the predominant source of pollution in our aquatic reserves. The forest cover and globally recognised bio-diversity is also under threat.

Such degradation imposes a cost on the society, with the burden of such coasts being disproportionately high for the poor who live and depend on such natural ecological systems. Such costs need to be explicitly accounted for in economic policy and planning. The challenge of sustainable development remains formidable and requires Integration of country's quest for economic development with its environmental concerns. Choice of policies and investment has to be such which encourage cleaner production/consumption and practices that minimise the environmental impact.

Issues and Priorities

The most intractable and long-standing issue confronting us is that of the fiscal prudence. The various aspects of the fiscal problem, namely the fiscal deficit, the revenue deficit, un-productive expenditures and un-sustainable subsidies are now fairly well known. With the exception of the intitial success achieved in 1991-92 under the pressure of the balance of payments crisis, subsequent improvements have alternated with set backs and reversal. As a result, the position today is not significantly better than in 1991-92. There is, therefore, a clear need for building a political consensus on this issue in terms of both constitutional and administrative measures that need to be taken.

The fiscal deficit is the key parameter of macroeconomic policy, which has rofound implications for inflation, interest rates, investment, growth, the financial system, balance of payments and last, but by no means least, overall credibility of Government's macroeconomic policy. For the Central Government the fiscal deficit simply reflects the net borrowing requirement of the Government. A high fiscal deficits leads to excess borrowing from either the RBI or the market for loanable funds. Excessive borrowing from the RBI leads to high monetary growth, which fuels inflation and puts pressure on the exchange rate. When considering Government borrowing from the market, the fiscal deficits of Centre and State Governments need to be aggregated [in 1997-98 (RE) this was 7.4 per cent of GDP]. Such a high level of Government borrowing pre-empts funds which could otherwise have been used productively in industry, agriculture and services. High deficits also keep interest rates high and investment and growth low. Excess Government borrowing also places undue pressure on the domestic financial system and capital markets. There is also the long-term issue of sustainability of fiscal deficit.

Long-term fiscal sustainability generally requires brining down the Primary deficit (gross fiscal deficit minus interest payments) to below zero. For the Centre and States together, the primary deficit is estimated at 2.4 per cent of GDP in 1997-98 (RE), with little prospect of improvement in 1998-99. A reduction in the primary deficit to zero would, therefore, require at least a 2.4 per cent of GDP reduction in the fiscal deficit. If the entire adjustment falls on the Central Government, this would require a reduction of the Central fiscal deficit to about 3.3 per cent of GDP. This target assumes that the real interest rate in the economy is lower than the growth rate. If this condition does not hold for any reason, a primary surplus and consequently a greater reduction in the fiscal deficit would be required.

Quite clearly, fiscal consolidation is absolutely necessary for containing inflation, reducing interest rates, promoting investment and growth, and fostering reasonable stability in the financial system and the foreign exchange market. Experience from the rest of the world underlines the importance of fiscal deficit reduction in regard to reducing interest rates and inflation. It is, therefore, essential to put the fiscal deficit on an irreversible and unambiguously declining trend.

In a broader qualitative sense, sustainability also depends on the quality of the government expenditure and the nature of the tax system underpinning the fiscal system...

Box 12.1

Economic Reforms Continue

Industry

- Delicensing of coal and lignite, petroleum (other than crude) and its distillation poroducts and bulk drugs.
- Delicensing of sugar.
- Dereservation of coal and lignite and mineral oils.
- Companies were permitted to buy-back their own shares subject to restriction of buy-back to twenty five per cent of paid-up capital and free reserves.
- A National Task Force on Information Technology and Software Development submitted a 108 point Action Plan in July 1998. The recommendations have been accepted by the Government and directions for their implementation have been given to all concerned departments.
- Patent bill approved by Rajya Sabha and subsequently promulgated through an Ordinance.
- A number of items, including some farm implements and tools, have been removed from products reserved for exclusive manufacture by SSI sector.

Infrastructure

- The Indian Electricity Act, 1910 and Electricity (Supply) Act, 1948 have been amended to provide for private investment in power transmission.
- Following enactment of the Electricity Regulatory Commission Legislation, the Central Electricity Regulatory Commission was set up, with enabling provision for states to establish their own independent regulatory commissions.
- The Urban Land (ceiling and regulation) Act, 1976, repealed through an ordinance.
- The policy for issuing licenses for providing Internet services has been announced. There will be no license fee for the first 5 years and after 5 years a nominal license fee of Rupee 1 will be charged.
- A National Integrated Highway Project merging the golden quadrilateral connecting Delhi, Mumbai, Chennai and Calcutta with the East-West (Silchar to Saurashtra) and North-South (Kashmir to Kanya Kumari) corridors has been launched.
- A new Telecom policy is under preparation.

Trade Policy

- The April 1998 Exim policy delicenced 340 items of import by moving them from the restricted list to OGL.

- India unilaterally removed all quantitative restriction on imports of aroung 2300 items from SAARC countries with effect from August 1, 1998.
- A Free Trade Agreement was concluded on 28 December, 1998 between India and Sri Lanka which will result in zero import tariffs for most commodities on both sides by 2007.
- Payment of interest on dues to exporters for delays in duty drawback/refund of duty beyond two months.
- The scope of Export Promotion Capital Goods scheme at zero duty has been extended further to certain specified bio-technologies and small scale engineering industry.
- Extension of tax holiday for EOU/EPZ to 10 years.
- Permission to set up Private Software Technology Parks (STPs) for export.

Foreign Direct Investment

- Projects for electricty generation, transmission and distribution and construction and maintenance of roads, highways, vehicular tunnels and vehicular bridges, ports and harbours have been permitted foreign equity participation up to 100 per cent under automatic route. The automatic route is subject to a ceiling of Rs. 1500 crore on foreign equity.
- FDI permissible under Non-banking Financial Services now includes "Credit Card Business" and "Money Changing Business".
- Multilateral financial institutions have been allowed to contribute equity to the extent of shortfall in NRI holdings within the overall permissible limit of 40 per cent in private sector banks.
- FDI up to 49 per cent euqity has been allowed subject to license, in the companies providing Global Mobile Personal Communication by Satellite (GMPCS) services.
- Unlisted companies are permitted to float Euro issues under certain conditions.
- End-use restrictions on GDR/ADR issue proceeds have been removed except those on investment in stock markets and real estate.
- Indian companies permitted to issue GDRs/ADRs in the case of Bonus or Rights issue of shares, or on genuine business reorganisations duly approved by the High Court.

NRIs

- The aggregate ceiling for investment in a company by all NRIs/PIOs/OCBs through stock exchanges has been made separate and exclusive of the investment ceiling available for FIIs.
- Investment limit by a single NRI/PIO/OCB has been enhanced from 1 per cent to 5 per cent of the paid up capital.
- Aggregate investment ceiling for NRIs/PIOs/OCBs has been raised from 5 per cent to 10 per cent of the paid up capital of a company. In the case of listed Indian companies the ceiling can be raised to 24 per cent under a General Body Resolution.
- NRIs/PIOs/OCBs are permitted to invest in unlisted companies subject to the prevailing norms, procedures and ceiling applicable in case of listed companies.

- The Government is finalising a scheme for Persons of Indian origin (PIO) for issue of PIOs card which would facilitate a visa free regime to them along with same special economic, educational, financial and cultural benefits.

Foreign Institutional Investors

- FIIs permitted to buy or sell treasury bills and government securities in both primary and secondary markets within overall approved debt ceilings.
- Authorised Dealers have been permitted to provide forward cover to FIIs in respect of their incremental equity investment in India.
- Transactions among FIIs with respect to Indian stocks will no longer require post facto confirmation from the RBI.
- 100 percent FII debt funds have been permitted to invest in unlisted debt securities of Indian companies.

External Commercial Borrowing

- Proceeds of ECB can now be deployed for project related rupee expenditure in all sectors subject to certain conditions.
- The Government has delegated ECB approvals to RBI up to US$ 10 million under all the ECB schemes.
- ECB eligibility under the scheme for exporters has been raised to three times the average export performance during the last three years subject to a maximum of US$ 100 million.
- Average maturity requirement for ECB under the long term maturity window which is outside the ECB cap has been reduced.
- Domestic rupee denominated structured obligations have been permitted to be credit-enhanced by international banks/international financial institutions/ joint venture partners.
- Prepayment of ECB by Indian corporates has been allowed if this is met out of inflow of foreign equity.

Financial Sector

- Prudential regulations for banks tightened to require provisioning for Central and State Government securities, Government guaranteed loans, and general provision for standard assets.
- Risk weight of 2.5 per cent for market risk of government securities, 20 per cent for state government guaranteed advances in default and 100 per cent for foreign exchange open position.
- Minimum Capital to Risk-weighted Asset Ratio (CRAR) for banks to rise to nine per cent by April 2000.
- Assets in the substandard category to be classified as doubtful after 18 months instead of 24 months, by March 31, 2001.
- Regulatory framework for NBFCs rationalised Companies which solicit public deposits to comply with revised norms.
- Number of companies whose shares must be traded in de-materialised form increased. Rolling settlement introduced for de-materialised shares.
- Conditions for public issue by infrastructure companies eased.
- Primary issues to be compulsorily through depository mode.
- 100 per cent book building permitted for issues above 25 crore.
- Bill for strong independent Insurance Regulatory Authority, and opening of Insurance and Pension funds to private companies introduced in Parliament;

proposed to allow 26 per cent foreign equity and additional 14 per cent NRI and FII holding.

- Bill introduced in Parliament for amending the Securities Contracts (Regulation) Act, 1956 so as to widen the definition of "Securities" to cover derivative contracts.
- New bill for Foreign Exchange Management, to replace FERA, introduced in Parliament.

Taxation

- All the gifts made on or after 1-10-98 exempted from payment of gift tax by Finance (No. 2) Act, 1998.
- Tax holiday increased from 5 to 10 years to industrial undertakings set up in the free trade zones and units in the software technology parks.
- Tax holiday benefits extended to inland waterways, inland ports, radio-paging, trunking and EDI Network and domestic satellite service.
- Administrative measures to improve reporting and widening the tax base include: (i) introduction of a simple one page taxpayer-friendly return form called, 'SARAL', applicable to all non-corporate tax payers; (ii) making it obligatory for assesses to quote their PAN or GIR number in respect of certain high value transactions; (iii) the presumptive taxation scheme, introduced in 1997-98 budget in 12 cities, extended to 23 more cities in India taking the total coverage to 35 cities and two additional economic criteria added; and (iv) introduction of a new scheme called "KAR VIVAD SAMADHAN SCHEME" to recover the money locked in litigation both in direct and indirect taxes.
- Reduction in import duty on 75 specified machinery from 25 per cent to 15 per cent to encourage investment in the information technology sector.
- Reduction in basic import duty to a level of 5 per cent *ad valorem* on many items related to information technology.
- A number of items which were earlier exempted from excise duty, would now attract nominal duty of 8 percent.
- Excise duty on a number of products, which were attracting a low rate of duty raised by 5 percentage points.
- The coverage of service tax was widened to cover 12 more services.

VIEWS ON INDIAN ECONOMY BY PRESIDENT OF INDIA, PRIME MINISTER OF INDIA, NCAER AND WORLD BANK

(a) President of India

President K.R. Narayanan on January 25 underlined the need to bridge economic disparities in order to make India a better place to live in. In his address to the nation on the eve of Republic Day, the President said there was a consensus in the world today that "economic development is not all and the GDP is not necessarily a measure of progress of a society". The President said India ranked among the major economies advanced in modern industry and occupying the forefront of scientific and technological development—in the world. "Out GNP is one of the biggest in the world and our growth rate and other economic parameters have been affected only marginally by the economic crisis in other parts of Asia.

This has emphasised the basic strength of the Indian economy and the validity of the policies the country has pursued", he added.

However, in the midst of these remarkable economic achievements "we have to recognise that economic disparities in the country have also increased. For example, the number of people living below the poverty line is estimated a little larger than the size of India's population at the time of independence". The President said Republic Day was an appropriate occasion for us to evaluate the facts of "our society and economy, and to examine our hearts to find out how far we have succeeded in overcoming these contradictions in our minds and in the objective conditions of the life of our people". Mr. Narayanan said India was once stalked with famine but thanks to the green revolution, the country had achieved self-sufficiency in foodgrain. It was no mean achievement, he stressed, to be able to feed a population now nearing the one billion mark without having to depend on others.

He said in the era of liberalisation, this enterprising middle class had become a potent force imparting momentum to the develomental process and to the wheels of commerce. Commending the democratic structure of the country, the President said political freedom in India was vibrant and unconfined, but the pursuit of social and economic freedom was still on and the nation's efforts were focussed on "justice social and economic". The President also expressed satisfaction over the fact that the Ninth Plan had given priority to the spread of elementary education in India.

(b) Prime Minister of India

The Prime Minister, Mr. Atal Behari Vajpayee, on November 10 reassured foreign investors that instability in Indian politics would have no fundamental impact on economic reforms in the country even as he outlined a 12-point medium term agenda to raise GDP growth to about 7-8 per cent annually. "My Government has depoliticised the economic agenda", he said, noting that the reform process had become irreversible. In his first public address after the Bharatiya Janata Party's debacle in the four State Assembly polls, he stressed that whatever was happening now was a sign of the vibrancy of Indian democracy. Mr. Vajpayee was addressing a galaxy of India and foreign corporate leaders at the three-day annual India Economic Summit organised by the World Economic Forum (WEF) and the Confederation of Indian Industry (CII). "Do not be overly influenced by the democratic drama of the day," he urged them. Instead, Mr. Vajpayee said, they should look at the inherent strength of the country and the huge opportunities it offered for mutual benefit. "These opportunities will grow irrespective of political vagaries," he said, while commenting in a lighter vein that with so many things happening outside, he was happier to be inside at the conference. He conceded he pace of change needed to be faster and assured the corporate leaders that the BJP Government would act a lot faster and firmer on its economic agenda in the coming months. He also recognised that with global shortage of capital, nations must compete in creating a milieu that attracted foreign investment, "India would be second to none in establishing a transparent framework in which such investment can flourish," he said...

Mr. Vajpayee took the opportunity to outline a 12-point medium term economic agenda aimed at preparing the country to face the challenges of full liberalisation and globalisation. It seeks to achieve a 7-8 per cent GDP growth annually through a strategy of ensuring low inflation and high employment generation.

Domestic savings are sought to be raised to 30 per cent of the GDP while public sector enterprises would be restructured. He said the financial and banking sectors would be strengthened by introducing transparency, accountability and non-interference by the Government. The fiscal deficit would also be reined in through a combination of measures like expenditure control and increased revenue buoyancy. Infrastructure constraints would be addressed and information technology promoted as a high priority. The plan envisaged an increase in the country's share of world trade through long-term export growth. The other elements of the agenda include ensuring sustainable agricultural growth and creating widespread rural prosperity by encouraging massive private investments in agriculture and agro-processing industry. Similarly, it is proposed to generate massive employment through small scale industries, village and khadi industries and housing construction while social sectors would be strengthened.

(c) NCAER

The National Council for Applies Economic Research (NCAER) painted a gloomy picture of the economy, pegging overall growth at 5.7 per cent, much below the government's estimate of 6.4 per cent. Industrial production was projected to slow down to 5.2 per cent and agriculture production fall to 3.4 per cent against the earlier estimate of 4.6 per cent. "Overall performance of agriculture sector will remain below normal due to deviation from normal rainfall in some regions of eastern, western and southrn, NCAER Director General, Rakesh Mohan said while presenting the mid-term review of the economy on Nov. 28. Fiscal deficit would be higher at 5.8 per cent against the government's target of 5.6 per cent, mainly due to lower indirect tax collection and roll back of key budget proposal like urea price hike, Mr. Mohan said. However, inflation based on Wholesale Price Index (WPI) would be hovering around 8.2 per cent mainly due to increase in the prices of primary goods. NCAER projected a further increase in trade deficit to five per cent of GDP in the current fiscal primarily due to increased import dependence and decline in exports. Exports have been targetted to grow at 14 per cent, while the imports would be at 15.3 per cent in the remaining fiscal, Mr. Mohan said. Elaborating on the fall in agriculture production. Mr. Mohan said, the government target of 204 million tonnes of foodgrain production during 1998-99 was unlikely to be achieved. NCAER said country should reduce its excessive dependence on rainfall, improve its infrastructure and deregulate the sector for capitalising the opportunities offered by the WTO in agriculture. On the industry front, it said, consumer goods continued to suffer due to lack of domestic demand and intense competition from foreign manufacturers with the manufacturing sector making a marginal growth of only two per cent. It said, their has been a continuous decline in the index of industrial production for general goods, manufacturing goods, mining and electricity.

(d) World Bank

The World Bank has made a depressing forecast for India, warning that failure to achieve its stipulated growth target of over six per cent for the current year would represent one of the biggest challenges for the country's economy. Its Ninth annual report on the world economy released in Washington on Dec. 2 says that "policy drift" and weak industrial performance have slowed India's economy. Besides, depressed export markets in East Asia and Japan are a blow since they had come to account for a significant share, and consequent growth, of South Asia's exports. Competition from East Asia in other markets will slow the growth of exports, especially from India and Pakistan, it adds. The report, titled "Global Economic Prospects", complains about the lack of any "concrete proposal" in India's budget for 1998-99 for further substantial reductions in the public sector deficit. The Bank calls India's alternative strategy to increase revenues through higher excise collections and import tariffs as "potentially a step in the wrong direction". "If growth targets of over six per cent do not materialise, the total public sector deficit could well persist at more than nine per cent of GDP (Gross Domestic Product), representing one of the biggest challenges for the Indian economy," it warns.

It notes that the Indian economy slowed to five per cent in fiscal 1997-98, following three years of rapid advances averaging 7.5 per cent. While a decline in agricultural output was a contributing factor, non-agricultural GDP growth had begun to slow down in 1996-97. Indeed, industrial output has fallen from 12.5 per cent in 1995-96 to 6.4 per cent in 1996-97 and then further to 5.7 per cent in 1997-98. Contributing to the slowdown was the persistence of large public sector deficits (crowding out private investment), a decline in export growth since 1995-96 and cutbacks in investment because of uncertainty about reforms, the report notes. It draws attention to the slight fall in the public sector deficit to 9.1 per cent of GDP thanks to a cut in subsidies on petroleum products that brought domestic oil prices closer to world prices. But it faults the 1998-99 budget for absence of any provision for further reduction. Stiglitz and Senior Economists Mick Riordon and Milan Brahmbhatt, says domestic financial weaknesses remain a concern and will need to be addressed if the financial system is to be a source of strength rather than a drag on longer-term growth—as evidenced most recently by a run on deposits with the state-owned investment corporation, Unit Trust of India (UTI). "Domestic stock markets, already depressed, slumped further in response", it added.

SPECIFIC ISSUES

(a) Banking and Financial Institutions

(i) RBI Annual Report, 1997-98

The Reserve Bank of India (RBI) has hinted that the fiscal position of the government would continue to be under considerable pressure in 1998-99 even though the overall GDP growth of 6.5 per cent may be attainable on account of favourable prospects for agriculture, industry and the services sector. In its annual report for 1997-98, the RBI has made a special mention of addressing the issues like reduction of subsidies, expenditure prioritisation and widening of the tax base, and the need to give appropriate signals to the market regarding government's commitment to fiscal deficit reduction. The growing reliance on market borrowings to bridge the gap between receipts and expenditures has posed a serious challenge to monetary management. The RBI has warned on recurrence of market borrowing in excess of planned amounts in view of the risk this bears on rates of interest. "Market would closely watch the evolving fiscal position and in particular the progress in respect of disinvestment programme and collection of revenue receipts. Any indication of slippage in this regard could trigger unfavourable market expectations", the report states.

The fiscal management thus should give appropriate signals to the markets since interest rates have impact on investment decisions, as well as on capital flows. The gross market borrowings are likely to go up sharply by over 33 per cent to Rs. 79,376 crore in 1998-99, "which would have to be accommodated by a substantial rise in household sector's financial saving", states the report. Moreover, corporates are also lining up to enter the market for raising funds from the domestic market. "There could be expectations of severe pressure on market interest rates but such expectations could be moderated by the fact that by August 18, 1998, 73.87 per cent of net borrowing programme of the government has already been met," according to the report. The RBI has further stated that the revenue deficit is estimated at 3.0 per cent of DGP in 1998-99, suggesting continued constraints on feasibility of fiscal correction. Added to this, the high revenue deficit of state governments in recent years have placed high burden on the fiscal position. The gross fiscal deficit has been pegged at 5.60 per cent of the GDP in 1998-99.

The report is critical of states' failure to meet their growing expenditures in view of insufficient collection of taxes. The RBI has suggested complete rationalisation of their tax structure and harmonisation of taxes (e.g. moving to VAT from sales taxation), s also to explore newer avenues for raising resources (e.g. taxes on services). Similarly, on the expenditure side, there is need for reduction on subsidies in non-merit goods.

(ii) Privatisation of Banks, FIs

Strict control on the Government expenditure, privatisation of banks and financial institutions with a thrust on disinvestment are among major recommendations by a working group of the Prime Minister's Advisory Council on Trade and Industry. The group on capital markets and financial sector initiatives, headed by industrialist Mr. Mukesh Ambani, has recommended that there should be an overall cap on the amount the Government can borrow. The recommendation to cap Government finance assumes significance in the wake of predictions by economists that interest rates would jump in the markets, making borrowing expensive if the Government had a heavy borrowing programme. As per budget estimates, the Government borrowing has been pegged at Rs. 79,000 crore for 1998-99 fiscal, but reports indicate that the targets have already been exceeded. The group submitted its report to the Prime Minister on Dec. 15 where the recommendations were discussed at the second meeting of the council. The report is one among six submitted by different working groups.

Other reports are on infrastructure by Mr. Ratan Tata, food and agro industreis management policy by Mr. Nusli Wadia, service industries by Dr. A.C. Muthiah and knowledge-based industries by Mr. Narayana Murthy. The working group has advised that high repayments pressures should be avoided by borrowing long term and swapping securities issued to pension and provident funds with deep discount bonds. While stressing that financial sector intermediaries function on commercial principles, the group wanted the Government to dilute its ownership in banks, financial institutions (FIs) and insurance companies.

Specialist institutions should be designated to perform the development role with systems for Government support, it said. Referring to banks, the group said that prudential norms should be strigent and there should be tight supervision. The group suggested the Government to sell real assets and aggressively disinvest its equity in public sector undertakings even at discounts to market prices and use the proceeds to retire debt and reduce the interest bill...

(iii) No Major Change In Monetary, Credit Policy

The Reserve Bank of India (RBI) on Oct. 30 accepted a host of recommendations of the Narasimham Committee on banking sector in its mid-term review of monetary and credit policy 1998-99, even as it left alone the short-term measures like bank rate, CRR and repo rate. The Central Bank has decided to raise the capital adequacy ratio (minimum capital to risk asset ratio) for banks from the existing 8 per cent to 9 per cent which would take effect from the year ending March 31, 2000. With a view to further improving the quality of the asset portfolio and enhancing the financial soundness of banks, income-recognition and provisioning norms on Government guaranteed advances are being brought on par with those on other advances with effect from the financial year 2000-2001. Provisions on existing and old Government guaranteed advances which would consequently become NPA are to be fully provided for over a period of four years beginning March 31, 1998.

- Capital adequacy ratio hiked from 8 per cent to 9 per cent.
- Restrictions of 3 days period for repo rate withdrawn.
- Foreign exchange open positions to carry 100 per cent risk weight.
- Risk weight for Government-guaranteed advances which go into default introduced.
- Public sector banks encouraged to raise tier 11 capital.
- Government-guaranteed advances which have turned stisky to be classified as NPAs.
- Government-guaranteed advances on par with other advances.

In a measure aimed at further strengthening the inherent strengths of banks balance sheets, provisioning requirements are being introduced for standard assets with effect from financial year ending March 31, 2000. Regarding Government securities, the RBI has stated they by the end of the century Government-approved securities will have to provide a risk weight of 2.5 per cent. The balance of 2.5 per cent risk weight on Government-approved securities will be announced at a later date. Going a step beyond the recommendations of the second Narsimham Committee on introduction of risk weight of 20 per cent on investments in the Government guaranteed securities of Government undertakings which do not form part of the market borrowing programme is also to be introduced.

(iv) Financial Institutions' Disbursals in 1997-98

The combined sanctions and disbursements by IDBI, ICICI, IFCI, UTI and LIC in 1997-98 aggregated Rs. 79,947 crore and Rs. 51,855 crore showing an increase of 48.7 per cent and 28.5 per cent respectively over the year. The Report on Currency and Finance, 1997-98, released by the Reserve Bank of India on Dec. 28 has said that while disbursements of IDBI, ICICI, LIC and GIC went up sharply during the year, those by IFCI and UTI grew at a much lower rate than that of the industry. The report has also pointed out that funds have moved to the core sectors in a big way and private sector continued to garner a larger share of the sanctions pie. According to the report, IDBI sanctions and disbursements aggregated Rs. 24,199 crore and Rs. 15,165 crore registering an increase of 41.9 per cent and 32.6 per cent respectively over the year. Industry-wise analysis of IDBI's financial assistance reveals that during the year, core and other manufacturing sectors accounted for bulk of the assistance sanctioned and disbursed. "Core sector industries such as iron and steel, oil exploration and refining, cement and fertiliser together accounted for 18.7 per cent of overall assistance sanctioned," the Report says.

During 1997-98, financial assistance sanctioned and disbursed by ICICI aggregated Rs 25,532 crore and Rs. 15,807 crore, registerng increase of 81.3 per cent and 41.4 per cent respectively over the year. The sector-wise assistance sanctioned by ICICI during the year reveals that the private sector accounted for bulk of the sanctions amounting to Rs. 21,679 crore (84.9 per cent). Sanctions made by IFCI amounted to Rs. 10,983 crore indicating a growth of 52.3 per cent over the Rs. 7,212 crore during the previous year. Disbursements at Rs. 5,650 crore recorded a growth of 9.6 per cent over the year.

(b) Budgetary and Fiscal Developments

1. Budget for 1999-2000

Finance Minister Yashwant Sinha on Feb. 27 attempted a please-all Budget for 1999-2000 which sought to impart a major thrust to the rural sector. He slapped taxes worth Rs. 9,334 crore to trim the fiscal deficit to 4.4 per cent of the GDP in an attempt to restore fiscal discipline. The FM imposed a 10 per cent surcharge on the tax paid for those earning Rs. 60,000 per annum and above. Even for corporates, the levy of 10 per cent across the board surcharge on income tax has been levied. The decision to exempt all income from UTI and other mutual funds sent the BSE sensex soaring by 165 points at the end of trading this evening. A new gold deposit scheme has been announced to mobilise the idle gold from households, various charitable institutions and religious institutions in the country.

Diesel will become costlier as the Finance Minister has imposed an additional duty of one rupee per litre. By doing so the Finance Minister seeks to raise an additional revenue of about Rs. 5,000 crore on both domestically produced and imported diesel. The Rs. 5,000 crore accrual will be over and above the Rs. 9,334 crore sought to be raised through new taxes and levies. In Delhi, cooking gas will now cost Rs. 146 per cylinder for domestic use. This is Rs. 6 lower than its exiting price. A litre of petrol in the capital will now cost Rs. 23.80, which is 14 paise less than what it currently costs. Diesel goes up by Rs. 1.05, to cost Rs. 9.94 per litre in the Capital.

The Finance Minister has allowed 74 per cent Foreign Direct Investment (FDI) in the pharmaceutical industry, through the automatic route. He also proposed special facilities for the information technology industry and measures for spurring housing and construction sectors. A special package for small scale units has also been announced by extending the SSI benefits to cosmetics, refrigeration, air-conditioner, cotton yarn units. In a bid to humour the Swadeshi lobby, the Financial Minister has continued with 4 per cent "protectionist" Special Additional Import Duty (SAID). This also pleased the Bombay club which has a pronounced swadeshi tilt. Continuing with the indirect tax reforms started by Dr. Manmohan Singh, the Finance Minister realigned and simplified the customs and excise rates. While the excise slabs have been reduced to three from the existing 11 rates, he also simplied the customs duty structure by pruning the rates to five from seven slabs. Following this, condensed milk, supari, malt, solf drinks, cosmatics and ice creams would be costlier.

There was some bad news for the smokers as the excise duty on small cigarettes has been hiked. However, some respite was granted to the housewife, who will now pay less for cooking gas, kerosene, tea and toilet soaps...

Budget Highlights

- Surcharge of 10 per cent on Corporate Tax, and also a 10 per cent surcharge on all other categories of assessees.
- In respect of individuals and Hindu Undivided Families, the applicability of the surcharge is limited to those having total income of Rs. 60,000 or more.
- All income from UTI and other Mutual Funds received in the hands of the investors exempt from income-tax.
- 3 years exemption from dividend tax to US-64 Scheme as also for all open-ended equity-oriented schemes of UTI and mutual funds — with more than 50 per cent investment in equity — from dividend tax. However, income distributed by Mutual Funds, where the equity investment is less than 50 per cent, will become subject to the 10 per cent dividend tax.
- Pension received by the recipients of the different gallantry award winners, and the family pension received by their heirs, exempted from income tax.
- External commercial borrowing of undertakings under section 10(15) to be exempt in certain cases.
- Modification in the provisions of section 10 (23G).
- Exemption of Commodity Boards and Authorities from income-tax.
- Expenditure made on hostel projects for working women eligible for deduction from taxable income under Section 35AC.
- Tax deduction at source on payment of compensation relating to compulsory acquisition of a capital asset.
- Computation of actual cost of asset in the case of Non-Residents.
- Taxing profits and gains arising from insurance claim received for damage or destruction of a capital asset as capital gains.
- Amendments of sections 44AD, 44AE and 44AF to provide for claiming lower profits.
- Extension of provisions of section 43D to Housing Finance Companies.
- Long-term capital gains tax for resident Indians at the rate of 10% on transfer of shares and securities.
- Stock options and sweat equity will be taxed as a perquisite at the time of exercise of the option by the employee, and later as capital gains at the time of sale of the security.
- On buy-back of shares, the shareholders will not be subject to dividend tax, and would only be liable to capital gains tax.
- Expenditure incurred in making computer systems Y2K compliant allowed as revenue expenditure in the next financial year.
- Ceiling on interest on a loan for a self-occupied property exempt from tax increased from Rs. 30,000 to Rs. 75,000.
- Ceiling on approved housing projects enjoying a tax holiday increased from

1000 sq. ft to 1500 sq. ft at all locations except Mumbai and Delhi.

- Depreciation rate to be increased from 20 to 40 per cent on new dwelling units purchased by the business sector for its employees.
- Concession for in-house R&D available to corporate houses upto 31-3-2000 extended upto 31-3-2005. Similar concession of permitting a weighted deduction of 125 per cent of expenditure allowed for R&D Projects entrusted to research laboratories and universities.
- 'Doubtful debts' made tax deductible subject to a maximum of 5 per cent of such aggregate 'doubtful debts', in any one year.
- Tax concession will be available to a loanee on interest payment to a co-operative bank on actual basis rather than accrual basis.
- In the case of amalgamation of companies, the existing requirement of routing the proposal through Board of Industrial and Financial Reconstruction is being removed.
- In the case of de-mergers, the carry forward of accumulated losses and unabsorbed depreciation from the de-merging company to the resultant company permitted. All fiscal concessions will survive for the unexpired period in the case of amalgamation and de-mergers.
- Section 80HHC benefit extended to Indian entertainment industry, which includes films, music and television software.
- Tax holiday benefits to cold chains for agricultural produce.
- Activities of State Electricity Boards of transmission and distribution of power, set up after 1-4-1999, eligible for tax holiday available to infrastructure units.
- Tax exemption period given under Section 80IA to the infrastructure sector and other core sectors made uniform for a maximum period of 15 years in which units can avail of the tax concessions.
- 10 years tax holiday for all industries set up in Growth Centres, Industrial Infrastructure Development Corporations, and for other specified industries in the North Eastern Region.
- Deduction for medical insurance premia for senior citizens raised from Rs. 10,000 to Rs. 15,000.
- Tax deduction for treatment of specific diseases increased to Rs. 60,000.
- "One by Six" scheme to be extended to 19 more cities in the country having a population of more than 5 lakh.
- Full deductions under section 80G to donations to the Fund for Technology Development and Application.
- Incentives for Investment in Tourism Sector.
- Tax holiday for processing of bio-degradable waste.
- Concessional rate of tax for income from certain Global Depository Receipts.
- Exemption of leave salary of non-government employees revised to the limit of salary of ten months.
- Simplification of procedure of processing of return under sub-section (1) of section 143 and doing away of *prima facie* adjustment.
- Receipts of money in convertible foreign exchange to be considered for deduction under sections 80HHB, 80HHC, 80HHD, 80HHE, 80-O, 80R, 80RR and 80RRA when received beyond the period of six months with the approval of the Reserve Bank of India.
- Amendments in provisions for deduction for donations made to funds or institutions for charitable purposes.

- Modification of the definition of small scale industry under section 80HHA.
- Exclusion of two-wheelers from the purview of the motor vehicle for the purpose of filing return under proviso to section 139(1).
- Amendment of section 139(6) to provide for particulars of bank account and credit card in prescribed form of return.
- Self-assessment tax to be paid while filing returns for the block period in search cases.
- Omission of Sections 180 and 180A relating to assessment of income from royalties and copyright fees and consideration for know-how.
- No deduction of tax from interest on securities in certain cases.
- Provision for certificate for collection of tax at a lower rate.
- Rationalisation of interest chargeable from the assessees.
- Filing of tax collected at source returns on magnetic media.
- Provision of appeal against orders relating to Registration of Trusts.
- Replacement of scale of amounts by a definite amount as penalty imposable under 272A (2).
- Rationalisation of provisions relating to reduction of litigation and other allied issues.
- Time limit for disposal of appeals by the Commissioner (Appeals) and the Appellate Tribunal and empowering the latter to award costs.

2. Fiscal Deficit

(a) For the first time since his Budget presentation on June 1 this year the Union Finance Minister, Mr. Yashwant Sinha, conceded that the fiscal deficit would exceed the target of 5.6 per cent of the Gross Domestic Product (GDP). The Finance Minister's admission about a possible slippage came during a meeting he had with the PHD Chamber of Commerce and Industry in New Delhi. In a somewhat angry reaction to the Chamber's contention that the fiscal deficit would reach a level of seven per cent, Mr. Sinha said it would miss the 5.6 per cent target but would not end up at 7 per cent. "There has to be some basis for your pegging the fiscal deficit at seven per cent. You are an apex chamber and people will tend to believe whatever you say. So, is it right on your part to say such things," the Finance Minister asked in a sharp reaction to the Chamber's outgoing President, Mr. O.P. Vaish's contention that the fiscal deficit would end up at 7 per cent in 1998-99.

Mr. Sinha conceded that the deficit was under pressure because of the shortfall in indirect taxes. This was because the industrial growth has been low and exports had been negative, Mr. Sinha said adding that though the target would be missed. "I am not in a position to give you a specific number at this time...But it will not be 7 per cent." The Finance Minister pointed out that in the early '80s, the deficit averaged around 6.2 per cent per annum and later slipped to levels around 8.2 per cent. Between 1991-92 and 1995-96, the deficit was in the range of 6 per cent and in 1997-98 reached 6.1 per cent. "This trend shows that it has been a difficult problem for successive Governments. It is easy to say cut subsidies, reduce non-Plan expenditure, but very difficult to implement them in actual practice. If these steps had been so easy, the previous Governments would have taken them and the fiscal deficit would have averaged at three per cent of the GDP," he added. However, the Finance Minister still maintained that he would try to check the growth of the fiscal deficit.

The Finance Minister said the Government would focus on indirect taxes in the next Budget with a view to rationalising them and probably reducing them. "Major initiatives would be taken in the next Budget to rationalise the indirect tax structure. We will be reducing the level of indirect tax rates besides restructuring the rules and regulations governing them. We have taken the steps to restructure direct taxes, why can't we do the same with indirect taxes," Mr. Sinha said. Some steps would also be taken to recreate the confidence of the small investor in the capital markets. "If we can bring back the small investor, we can bring back the buoyance which we had witnessed in the past," the Minister said and pointed out that people were saving their money but not investing it in the stock markets. The money was instend being parked in small savings and the swelling small savings collections were putting pressure on the fiscal deficit.

(b) Fiscal Deficit in 9th Plan at 5.1 per cent

Minister of State for Planning and Programme Implementation Ram Naik has said that the fiscal deficit during Ninth Plan period (1997-02) would be contained at an annual average rate of 5.1 per cent. Replying to supplementaries in the Rajya Sabha during the question hour on Dec. 17, the Minister said the Ninth Plan formulations incorporating the new priorities of the BJP led coalition would be decided by the end of December. He added, "we have changed some priorities in the 9th plan which would be decided by this month-end by the cabinet and go to National Development Council thereafter." Raising the supplementary, senior Congress member Pranab Mukherjee wanted to know how the government would be able to contain the fiscal deficit to 5.1 per cent during the 9th Plant period when the first two years of the plan period would end with an average deficit of over 6 per cent.

Mr. Mukherjee expressed skepticism that the fiscal deficit during the current financial year would be kept at the targeted level of 5.6 per cent in the backdrop of huge shortfall in revenue collections till November this year. He said as in the previous year, the current fiscal year would also end up with a fiscal deficit of 6 per ent. In reply to the main question raised by Ms Lakshmi Sagar and Ms Kamla Sinha (both JD), Mr. Naik said the gross fiscal deficit of the Central Government during the Eighth Plan period stood at around 5.9 per cent of GDP and would be substantially brought down to an average fiscal deficit of 5.1 per cent during the current Plan period. "The experience gained so far in the first two years of the Plan with regard to the financial position of the government and the existing economic situation has been kept in view in working out this projection," he said.

The Minister stressed, "we are confident of arresting the deterioration," and added that the special advisory group set up by the government had deliberated on this and formed strategies to arrest the deterioration. Mr. Naik also expressed confidence that the targeted GDP growth at an annual average of 6.5 per cent would be achieved during the Ninth Plan. The Minister also lauded the work of former Deputy Chairman of the Planining Commission Madhu Dandavate and said he had done a good job in the Commission.

(c) WEF Chief On Fiscal Deficit

World Economic Forum (WEF) Managing Director Claude Smadja on Nov. 30 warned that after seven years of economic reforms India was almost back to where it stood in 1991 with respect to fiscal deficit. The present government had based its budget projections on a fiscal deficit of 5.6 per cent of GDP, but the forecasts are now oscillating between 6 and 7 per cent, he said. Speaking at the 1998 India Economic Summit, organised by the Confederation of Indian Industry (CII) and WEF, he said there was a need for a strategy, a broad framework which would provide orientations of what the Indian economy would look like 10 years from now. "To start with, there is the need to define a clear strategy for dealing with the fiscal deficit not as such but for what it reflects with respect to structural problems in the Indian economy. For instance, the issue of subsidies and the need to replace this culture by the notion that all commodities have their price," he added.

The WEF Managing Director stressed the need to restructure public sector enterprises as they constituted a drag on the resources by the extremely low return on investment. "Linked to the issue is the problem of labour law which is definitely no longer adapted to the new conditions of the economy. No Government since 1991 has dared to address this extremely sensitive issue and talks about an exit policy have remained just talk," he asserted. Mr. Smadja said the labour policy had to represent the optimal trade-off between the need for flexibility and the necessity to provide an appropriate level of protection. He pointed out that a major drawback was the lack of a broad and organised constituency of reforms which was able to combine enough elements of the fledgling middle class, media and intellectural elite as well as a sufficient majority of the business community.

Referring to issues that may be immediately taken up by Parliament, WEF Managing Director stated that there should be a legislation on the Foreign Exchange Management Act as it basically freed all transactions which were not capital in nature. The bill replacing the present Urban Land Ceiling Act should be approved. "In addition to this unfinished agenda, it is crucial that the Insurance Regulatory Authority (IRA) Bill, which will open the sector to private competition and foreign investors be carried through," he observed.

(c) Gross Domestic Product in 1998-99

Based on advance estimates of national income put out by the Central Statistical Organisation (CSO) on Feb. 9, the Union Government claimed that things were looking up on the economic front with the Gross Domestic Product (GDP) expected to grow by 5.8 per cent during 1998-99. In 1997-98, the GDP growth rate was five per cent. Briefing press persons on the CSO data, the Union Minister of State for Planning, Mr. Ram Naik, said the push to the GDP growth rate was provided by the agriculture sector which was expected to grow by 5.3 per cent against a negative growth of one per cent last year. The other "over five per cent growth" sectors were manufacturing, electricity, gas and water supply and the services sector. Also, to press home the point about the accuracy of the CSO data, Mr. Naik pointed out that the organisation had projected the GDP growth rate in 1997-98 at 5.1 per cent and the actual growth at the end of the year had turned out to be five per cent. "The difference is just 0.1 per cent, which reflects the reliability of the advance estimates."

As per the CSO data, the agriculture, forestry and fishing sector is expected to grow by 5.3 per cent during 1998-99 (against negative 1.0 per cent growth last year), mining and quarrying by 0.1 per cent (2.7 per cent last year), manufacturing by 5.7 per cent (6.8 per cent last year), electricity, gas and water supply by 6.3 per cent (6.6 per cent last year), construction 2.3 per cent (4.1 per cent), trade, hotels, transport and communication 6.8 per cent (5.7 per cent), financing, insurance, real estate and business services 7.7 per cent (8.4 per cent) and community, social and personal services 5.8 per cent (13.3 per cent last year due to the award of the Fifth Pay Commission). Therefore, the total GDP at factor cost (1993-94 prices) is expected to grow at 5.8 per cent.

The estimates at the aggregate level reveal that the Gorss National Product (GNP) is expected to grow 5.9 per cent, the net national product by 5.7 per cent, the GDP by 5.8 per cent and net domestic product by 5.6 per cent. The country's population is estimated to reach 975 million by the end of the financial year which will mean a 1.7 per cent growth rate and the per capita income will, therefore, work out to Rs. 10,047. The CSO date reveals that production of food-grains during 1998-99 will be around 195.25 million tonnes as compared to 192.43 million tonnes during 1997-98, showing a growth rate of 1.5 per cent. During 1997-98, foodgrains recorded a negative growth rate of 3.5 per cent. While production of wheat is expected to rise by 4.9 per cent this year, that of rice and coarse cereals is expected to decline by 0.1 per cent and 6.6 per cent respectively during 1998-99. However production of pulses is expected to show a growth rate of 13.1 per cent during the current year and is placed at 14.78 million tonnes, compared to the previous year's production of 13.07 million tonnes.

In the case of commercial crops, production of oilseeds, sugarcane and cotton are expected to register growth rates of 10 per cent, 4.9 per cent and 25.8 per cent, respectively, during 1998-99, compared with the previous year's negative growth of 9.7 per cent, 0.5 per cent and 21.7 per cent. In the industry segment, the Index of Industrial Production (IIP) for mining, manufacturing and electricity registered negative growth rates of 1.2 per cent, 3.7 per cent and 6.2 per cent during April-November 1998. The figures for the corresponding period of 1997 were 5.2, 6.9 and 6.4 per cent, respectively. Based on past trends, the GDP for mining, manufacturing and electricity during 1998-99 is expected to show growth rates of 0.1 per cent, 5.7 per cent and 6.3 per cent, respectively. Here, the Minister explained that while the IIP reflected the growth trends, for calculations of the GDP, the value added factor is considered. Also, the GDP calculation is based on the Annual Survey of Industries and not on the IIP. The CSO data also reflects that the construction sector is expected to show a decline in growth rate at 2.3 per cent during 1998-99 against a 4.1 per cent growth in the previous year, mainly on account of less growth in production of cement and steel during the current year.

On the services side, the higher growth of 6.8 per cent during 1998-99 in the trade, transport and communication sectors against 5.7 per cent last year is said to be mainly on account of increase in the GDP of the trade sector, estimated on the basis of volume of goods transacted. At the same time, the anticipated lower growth of 7.7 per cent in financing, insurance, real estate and business services against 8.4 per cent last year is said to be because of the higher inflation during 1998-99 compared with 1997-98 since this factor is used for deflating the aggregate deposits and banks credits to arrive at real prices. The net national product (national income) at 1993-94 prices is likely to be Rs. 9,79,573 crore during 1998-99 against the quick estimates of Rs. 9,26,420 crore. The per capital income in real terms (at 1993-94 prices) during 1998-99 is likely to reach a level of Rs. 10,047 whereas quick estimates made at the beginning of the 1998-99 fiscal year had estimated it to be Rs. 9,660. The growth rate in per capital income is estimated to be four per cent against three per cent in 1997-98. In response to a specific question, it was put out by the Government side that the estimates of GDP growth this year would be the same if calculations were based on the earlier base year of 1980-81 instead of the current base year of 1993-94.

(d) Inflation, Prices and Public Distribution System

(i) Inflation Rate Dips Further

After an year plagued by unprecedented rise in agriculture products, 1999 began on a sound note with annual rate of inflation falling to a 42 week low of 5.03 per cent in the first week of the year, inflation, based on Wolesale Price Index (WPI), fell by 0.31 percentage points to 5.03 per cent (provisional) for the week ended January 2, from 5.34 per cent (p) in the previous week. In comparison, inflation was at 5.63 per cent during the same week last year. The rate of increase in prices has been falling persistently in the last two months as prices of agriculture products eased on arrival of kharif crops. It has fallen by about 3.8 per cent since November first week when it touched a three-year high of 8.85 per cent.

Inflation had gone up in September and October, mainly on account of unprecedented rise in prices of vegetables and edible oils. In the reference week, vegetable prices fell by about 11 per cent, while edible oils were cheaper by about 1 per cent. The index for 'all commodities' (base: 1981-82 = 100) during the week, however, remained unchanged at its previous week's level of 354.8 (p). Despite the fall in inflation based on WPI, the rate of increase in prices based on CPI-W stood at an all-time high of 19.7 per cent in November. This is the highest inflation recorded ever on CPI-IW. The previous highest was in October 1998 at 18.6 per cent. Compared to 19.7 per cent on CPI-IW, the average inflaton on WPI in November was only 8.34 per cent.

(ii) 11-Point Plan to Check Prices

Contrary to expectation, the meeting of the Chief Ministers convened by the Prime Minister, Mr. Atal Behari Vajpayee, in New Delhi on Nov. 27 to review the general price situation turned out to be a tame affair. The only fireworks were provided by the West Bengal Chief Minister, Mr. Jyoti Basu and, suprisingly, the Rajasthan Chief Minister, Mr. Bhairon Singh Shekhawat, who were both forthright in pointing out that the Centre had delayed taking action to control prices. Mr. Basu sought an explanation for the onion crisis. But Mr. Shekhawat said the meeting should have been called much earlir, causing ripples in BJP circles. Even the Prime Minister was visibly taken aback by Mr. Shekhawat's statement. Later, talking to presspersons, the Maharashtra Chief Minister, Mr. Manohar Joshi, too said the meeting should have been convened earlier.

The conference adopted a 11-point resolution on measures to check rise in the prices of essentials. Giving the details, the Prime Minister said a Joint Monitoring Mechanism would be set up for prices and production under the chairmanship of the Cabinet Secretary, which would hold quarterly meetings with the Chief Secretaries of States and Union Territories. He said the Cabinet Committee on Price (chaired by the Finance Minister) would be restructured "to make it more functional for enabling timely and monthly reviews on prices and corrective action". The States and Union Territories would initiate urgent steps to implement a programme to set up efficient and cost-effective cold storages to minimise the high percentage of waste. Programmes relating to development of food processing industries were also in the offing. The Union Finance Ministry would examine the possiblity of providing soft loans to the States/UTs from the banking system.

A Group of Officials would be constituted under the Cabinet Secretary to make recommendations on amending the Essential Commodities Act and examine how State Governments and Union Territories could be empowered to take effective actions against hoarders and those responsible for causing artificial shortages. A Special Cell would be set up under the Cabinet Secretariat to monitor and analyse price data and trends relating to essential commodities. It would provide inputs to the Cabinet Committee on Prices, which would take decisions on imports and exports of essential commodities. The cell would establish a mechanism for obtaining crop price and production data from various centres and share this information with the States. In the event of an abnormal increase in the prices of perishable essential commodities, the State Government/ UTs would intervene to distribute these commodities at reasonable prices till the situation returned to normal. States would be given funds for these operations.

Referring to fiscal deficit of the Central Government, as well as the States, it was resolved that efforts would be made by both to augment revenues, realise user charges fully and curb unproductive expenditures. It was resolved that the items included by the Centre and States under the Public Distribution System (PDS) would be reviewed from time to time. The Prime Minister said a National Crop Forecasting centre would be immediately set up under the Ministry of Agriculture which would make full use of the satellite-based remote sensing capabilities of the Department of Space and the computer network set up by the National Informatics Centre.

(iii) Roll Back of PDS Food Prices

The Prime Minister, Mr. Atal Behari Vajpayee's announcement on Feb. 2 to roll back the issue prices of foodgrains in the Public Distribution System, sent the Food Ministry into a tizzy. The major apprehension was that the wide gap between price of foodgrains for Below Poverty Line (BPL) and Above Poverty Line (APL) populations would only increase leakages and diversion of foodgrains from ration shops. After the Union Cabinet clears the roll back, the issue price for BPL would remain Rs. 2.50 per kg for wheat and Rs. 3.50 paise per kg for irce. For APL, the new rates will, however, be Rs. 6.50 paise per kg for wheat and Rs. 9.05 per kg for rice. There has been no going back on the price of levy sugar, which will be sold at Rs. 12 per kg for all consumers under the Targetted Public Distribution System (TPDS), as announced. The sugar price revision will be effective from February 15.

The revision of issue price which came about after four years, was only to the tune of Rs. 0.75 paise per kg for rice and Rs. 1 per kg for wheat for the poor BPL sections. This would have brought a burden of only between Rs. 7.50 to Rs. 10 per month per BPL family of four, as under TPDS a family of four can draw only 10 kg of foodgrains—either rice or wheat—per month at BPL rates. The subsidy saving, which was estimated at about Rs. 2,900 crore earlier, with overall increase of issue price for APL and BPL, would now be at about Rs. 2,200 crore, depending upon the lifting. Of a total allocaton of 175 lakh tonnes of foodgrains for TPDS per annum, 72 lakh tonnes is meant for the poor APL population. A large chunks—103 lakh tonnes—goes for the non-poor (APL) population. The central issue price of wheat and rice were last revised in 1994, after Assembly elections in Andhra Pradesh, Karnataka and North-East. Then in 1996 when TPDS was introduced, the prices were "adjusted" so as to give a concession to BPL populations, against APL populations, keeping the rates at the same level as 1994. This adjustment had not brought about any change in the subsidy component, Food Ministry sources said.

In the meantime, the minimum support price of wheat and rice was revised every year from 1994 till now. Wheat MSP went up from Rs. 350 per quintal to Rs. 540 in 1998. Not only that, a tradition of giving Central bonus over and above the recommendations of the Cabinet Committee on Prices has been set from 1997, further widening the gap with issue price. This fact is not lost on the State representatives who clamoured for a roll back because many of them have initiated subsidised schemes back home. A revision in Central issue price would increase their own subsidy burden, besides being an unpopular step during the year when Assembly elections are due in several States.

(e) Foreign Investment

(i) FDI Inflow Expected at $4 billion

Foreign direct investment to the tune of $4 billion is expected to flow into India as against the previous year's $3.71 billion. Of this, around $3.1 billion have already made its way into the country in the first 10 months, Secretariat of Industrial Assistance (SIA) source said. This would represent a mere 7.81 per cent growth in foreign direct investment inflow over the previous year. The figure for this year, sources said, does not include global depository receipts. Of the total inflows, 80 per cent has gone into setting up greenfield unit. Mauritius led the list of countries infusing capital into India followed by the United States, Japan, Germany and South Korea. Telecom, transport, including automobiles, chemicals, service sector and fuel were the major sectors where FDI flowed into. India, sources said, was the only nation besides China to record a positive growth in FDI inflow last year. "This year too, we expect the trend to be the same." However, $1.3 billion worth of capital outflow from the country was witnessed during the year.

The sources further pointed out that approval trend during the year has been lower as most of the mega projects and multinationals have already set up bases in India. They further refuted reports that the nuclear blasts earlier this year were responsible for the lower FDI inflow. "Had that been true, the country would not have witnessed Rs. 1,600 crore worth of FDI inflows during June this year, the month the tests were conducted. For a reaction to every such internatinal action, we have to wait for at least six to eight months to see the reactions." Moreover, had the Tata domestic airline project been cleared by the FIPB in time, the inflow might have increased by at least another Rs. 500 crore. The major proposals cleared by the board during the year include a Rs. 200 crore joint venture proposal of AB Electrolux of Sweden for producig domestic appliances and a $600-million investment by Gaz de France Internatinal (GDF) of France for LNF transportation terminals.

AB Electrolux has been given the go ahead to set up a joint venture with Voltas to manufacture domestic appliances other than air-conditioners and equipment like industrial catering appliances. The company intends to cater to the large restaurants through this joint venture. The board had also approved ford motor corporation's proposal to hike its equity in Mahindra Ford India Ltd. (MFIL) from the existing 50 per cent to 92 per cent, besides allowing Mercedes Daimler-Benz to hike its stake in Mercedes Benz India Ltd. and Honda Motor Company to pump in fresth equity to buy out stake in Honda Siel Cars India Ltd. The board had also approved a Rs. 19.50 crore proposal by Sanyo Electric of Japan to set up an export-oriented software development centre in Bangalore.

(ii) Modifications of FDI Guidelines

The Govt. has decided to allow foreign corporations through automatic route in areas where applicants have already got permission to operate joint ventures. Modifying the guidelines pertaining to approval of foreign or technical collaborations under the automatic route, a statement of the Industry Ministry said automatic route for direct foreign investment or collaborations would not be available to those who have or had any previous joint ventures in the same or allied field in India. The restrictions apply to technology transfer and trade agreement also. It would now be left to the Reserve Bank of India to stipulate necessary declaration before application for automatic route are taken on record. In view of the new restrictions, those investing in technology would have to seek Foreign Investment Promotion Board approval for joint ventures of technology transfer agreements, including trade mark, the communication said. While seeking the approval, these companies would have to give the circumstances under which they find it necessary to set up a new joint venture or go in for a new technology transfer.

The communication said the onus to justify approval for new ventures was on the investors and technology supplies. They would also have to satisfy Foreign Investment Promotion Board that the new venture would not jeopardise interest of existing joint ventures or technology or trade market partner or other stake holders. The Foreign Investment Promotion Board and Projects Approval Board had the discretion to approve application for fresh proposals with or without conditions. They could also reject in toto duly recording reasons for the decision, it said. The restriction would form part of approval procedures of industrial policy and procedures in India, it said. Reacting to the guidelines, industry sources said it could mean that fresh ventures could be stopped if any Indian project partner objected to the new proposal. Stating that the foreign firms already having tieups would now be at the mercy of their Indian partners, they said it could also lead to "influencing" at government machinery to get the approval.

(f) Foreign Trade

(a) Reconstitution of Board of Trade

In order to lift sagging exports, the government has reconstituted its high-level Board of Trade and its first meeting will be held on Feb. 18. The board advises the government on short and long-term export policy measures, Headed by Commerce Minister Ramakrishna Hegde, the board, re-constituted on Feb. 5, will have 44 members including top government functionaries and corporate leaders. The board was initially set up in May 1989 to ensure continuous dialogue with trade and industry on major developments in international trade with particular reference to formulation of export strategies, a government statement said on Feb 10. The other terms of reference for the body were to review export performance of various sectors, identify constraints, suggest measures to maximise export earnings, examine existing institutional framework for exports and re-examine policy instruments, incentives and procedures for exports. Commerce Secretary, Revenue Secretary, Secretary (Economic Relations) in the External Affairs Ministry and Textile Secretary were members of the board while Director General of Foreign Trade would be the Member-Secretary; it said. Other prominent members of the board include Federation of Indian Chambers of Commerce President Sudhir Jalan, Confederation of Indian Industry president Rajesh V. Shah, Federation of Indian Exporters Organisation president Navratan Samdria. Chemexil Chairman Ramu S. Deora, Larson and Toubro Chief Executive Officer S.D. Kulkarni, Anil Ambani (Reliance), Dr. Anji Reddy (Reddy's Laboratories), Mallika Srinivasan (TVS Suzuki) and L.M. Thapar (BILT). The Board will be meeting in the backdrop of the dismal export performance during the last nearly two years due to the sluggish international market and South-East Asian meltdown. India's exports in the first nine months of the current fiscal declined by 2.88 per cent compared to the same period last year. However, during December 1998, exports increased by 6.73 per cent to $2.79 billion against $2.61 billion compared to the same period in 1997.

(b) Exports

(1) *Further Simplification of Export Procedures* : The Director General of Foreign Trade (DGFT) has further simplified the procedure contained in Handbook of Procedures (Vol. I) (RE-98) 1997-2002. The exporters can obtain advance licence based on ad hoc norms fixed by technical committees without any limit till the same is modified/notified by Special Advance Licence Committee (SALC). The grant of Export House Certification has been decentralised and regional licensing authorities have been authorised to issue the certificates. According to an official release, Post Export Duty Entitlement Pass Book (DEPB) can be claimed in respect of shipments made prior to issuance of pre-export DEPB as well as in respect of shipments made from a port other than port mentioned under pre-export DEPB. All airports/sea ports/inland container depots (ICDs) in a particular district have been declared as a single port under DEPB. A number of agencies have been added in the list of agencies empowered to issue IS/ISO 9000.

(2) *Exports Growth in 1997-98* : The country's export growth rate in dollar terms during 1997-98 nose-dived to an abysmally low of 2.64 per cent pushing the overall trade deficit to a high of $6.79 billion compared to $5.44 billion in 1996-97. As per the trade data made available by the Commerce Ministry, the country's export during 1997-98 is estimated a $33.97 billion compared to $33.10 billion in 1996-97 thereby reflecting an export growth rate of 2.64 per cent, which is the lowest so far, compared to 4.01 per cent in the previous fiscal year. This export growth rate is still too low compared to a high of 21.38 per cent in 1995-96. However, in rupee terms the export during 1997-98 grew by 3.06 per cent.

Imports during 1997-98 are estimated at $40.77 billion which is 5.79 per cent higher than the level of $38.54 billion during 1996-97. Import growth rate during 1996-97 was 5.99 per cent compared to a high of 28.74 per cent in 1995-96. Due to poor export performance, trade deficit during 1997-98 swelled to $5,798.84 million compared to $5,442.09 million in 1996-97. Average monthly trade deficit during 1997-98 has been about $567 million. Oil imports during

1997-98 are valued at $7,627.09 million which is 20.59 per cent lower than oil imports valued at $9,604.81 million in the corresponding period last fiscal year of 1996-97. Non-oil imports during 1997-98 are estimated at $33,151.69 million which is 14.54 per cent higher than the level of such imports valued at $28,943 million during 1996-97. Imports during March this year are valued at $3,519.51 million representing a growth of 1.59 per cent over the level of imports valued at $3,464.40 million in March 1997. Exports during March, 1998 are valued at $3,085.06 million, which is 6.42 per cent lower than the level of $3,296.59 million in the conesponding month in the last year.

(3) *Export Growth Target in 1998-99* : Commerce Minister Ramakrishna Hegde has indicated that he had cut the export growth target for 1998-99 (April-March) to 15 per cent from 20 per cent because of the depressed global trade scenario. "If we achieve 15 per cent growth (in exports) I'll be happy because the Asian crisis is still continuing and global trade has shrunk by 2 per cent this year," Mr. Hegde told a gathering of businessmen in the southern city of Madras. Indian merchandise exports fell by 3.28 per cent of $16.27 billion in April-September 1998 from $16.82 billion in the same period of 1997. In September, Mr. Hegde told a conference of economic editors that the country's export target for 1998-99 appeared "improbable". His Ministry had targetted an export growth of 20 per cent in the current fiscal year ending on March 31, 1999.

Mr. Hegde said that the growth target set in April, though "very, very ambitious," had been based on two factors—that export performance would perk up after two years of very poor growth, and the hope that the Asian crisis would abate by mid-1998. "My hope that the Asian crisis would come to an end by middle of this year did not happen, unfortunately. "He said that there was an overall decline in exports of goods that had been India's mainstay, particularly readymade garments and engineering products. "Barring software, most of our traditional exports have been declining. Engineering goods saw minus 45 per cent growth."

(4) *Export Credit Refinance Rate* : The RBI on Aug. 6, announced lowering of refinance rate for export credit to 7 per cent from 9 per cent. This follows Commerce Minister Ramakrishna Hegde's announcement of a two percentage-point cut in export credit to 9 per cent as part of a package of measures meant to boost the sagging export sector. The new refinance rate is lower by two per cent to RBI's bank rate, which is at present pegged at 9 per cent. The revised rate will be effective from Aug. 6 and valid upto March 31, 1999. "The new rates of interest will be applicable up to March 31, 1999 after which status *quo ante* will be restored automatically, unless otherwise notified," an RBI release said. In keeping with the government announcement on Aug. 5, RBI has effected concomitant changes in interest rates of various other export financing schemes of commercial banks. The pre-shipment credit upto 180 days has been brought down to 9 per cent from 11 per cent, beyond 180 days and upto 270 days to 12 per cent from 14 per cent and against incentives receivable from government covered by ECGC guarantee upto 90 days from 11 to 9 per cent.

Interest rates for all other export credit schemes have also been lowered by an identical margin—two percentage points. The 7 per cent export credit refinance rate will be temporary in nature in tandem with the new export credit rate which is effective only till March 31, 1999. The lower interest rate 6.5 per cent incremental export credit scheme announced by the Central Bank in June. The RBI was forced to withdraw it following oppostion from banks and exporters. The incremental export credit scheme of June was meant only for incremental export over and above export houses' export value in 1997-98. The scheme was abandoned soon after its announcement as it was found full of loop-holes and operationally difficult to implement.

(5) *Revamping of Export Credit Scheme* : Reseve Bank of India (RBI) on Feb. 28 announced a major simplification and revamping of scheme of export credit in foreign currency for exporters with the view of make available export credit at pre-shipment and post-shipment stages at internationally competitive rates. As per the existing instructions, interest to be charged for export credit under the scheme would be directly related to London Inter Bank Offered Rate (LIBOR), according to a RBI release in Mumbai on Feb. 28. This follows the Finance Minister, Mr. Yashwant Sinha's budget proposal to devise a new scheme to enable exporters to get credit at rates prevailing in the world markets and to bring about major simplification of export procedure. The interest rate to be charged by Indian banks over 'LIBOR' for such credits would not exceed 1.5 per cent. On fresh transactions, banks would be allowed to use *euro libor/euribor* (wherever applicable) as benchmark for prupose of determining the applicable interest rate.

Under the scheme, export credit was expected to be made available to exporters without any exchange risk and at rates which were internationally competitive, the release said. The other highlights of the revamped schemes include, assessment of export credit limits being 'need based' and not dirctly related to an availability of collateral security. In case of established exporters having satisfactory track record, banks would consider sanctioning "line of credit" for a longer period with an inbuilt flexibility to step up/step down the quantum of limits within the over-all outer limits assessed, the release said. The step-up limits would become operative on attainment of predetermined performance parameters by exporters Banks would also obtain security documents covering the outer limit sanctioned exporters for such longer periods.

(6) *FIEO Task Force to Boost Exports*: In a bid to reverse the slump on the foreign trade front, the Federation of Indian Export Organizations (FIEO) has set up a task force to assist state governments to aggressively promote exports. Working directly under the supervision of FIEO President Ramu Deora, the task force has been advised to work out state-specific export strategies in coordination with officials. New avenues would also be identified to fully realize the export potential of various states, according to a press note issued in New Delhi on Nov. 25 by FIEO. Mr. Deora had written to all chief ministers seeking support for the bid to revive trade and industrial activity across the country. He has stated states could play a crucial role in boosting the country's exports which have been going through a sluggish phase.

In his letter to chief ministers, the FIEO Chief has called for special attention to make export production cheaper even while maintaining high quality. State governments should help exporters to achieve these two key elements. In this connection, the export policy of Uttar Pradesh, announced last month by Chief Minister Kalyan Singh, has been cited as an example. Describing the policy as exhaustive and bold, Deora has urged other states to emulate this model. While the Central Government was responsible for formulating export policies, states have ample scope to provide impetus to growth.

(c) Imports Lifting of Curbs on Import Products

The Government on Aug. 17 further liberalised import trade, removing quantitative restrictions on 148 import products. The products are allowed to be imported against Special Import Licence (SIL). A notification to this effect was issued by the Directorate General of Foreign Trade, according to an official release. The products are primarily related to consumer goods, electronics and plastics. They include uncut ruby, sapphire, emperalds and precious stones like uncut aquamarine, chrisobaryle and topaz. Import of tape recorders, compact discs (CDs), mustard oil, essence of ambrettolide and flavouring essences of all types, including those for liquors, are allowed under SIL. Pocket knives, garage tools in sets, screwdrivers and other knives having fixed blades of a kind classified as consumer goods besides cookers and kitchen stoves have been moved to the SIL list, the release said.

This move has been initiated as part of the Government's commitment towards gradual removal of quantitative restrictions on imports. It may be recalled that India agreed to remove quantitative restrictions on imports with countries like Japan, European Union, Australia and New Zealand, over a priod of six years. The differences with the United States over the removal of quantitative restrictions continue, with Washington dragging New Delhi to the dispute Settelment body of the World Trade Organisation. Earlier, India scrapped quantitative restrictions over 2000 import products for the SAARC member countries as part of its commitment to make SAPTA into a SAFTA by the beginning of the next decade.

(d) Exports and Imports

Trade Deficit at New High : India's trade deficit touched a new high of $7.295 billion during April-December 1998, with a fall in exports and rise in imports. The trade deficit during the corresponding period in 1997 was $4.478 billion. In December 1998, however, exports increased by 6.73 per cent to $2.78 billion and imports fell by 3.37 per cent to $3.39 billion, according to an official release. The total exports during the first nine months of the current fiscal stood at $24.28 billion as against $25 billion in the corresponding period of 1997, a fall of 2.88 per cent. In rupee terms, exports grew by 11.69 per cent to Rs. 101850.15 crore during the same period. The imports in the April-December period amounted to $31.58 billion compared with $29.48 billion during the corresponding period of 1997, an increase of 7.12 per cent. In rupee terms, the imports increased by 23.18 per cent to Rs. 132446.84 crore. Of the April-December 1998 import basked, oil imports dropped by 26.32 per cent to $4.42 billion and non-oil imports increased by 15.67 per cent to $27.15 billion.

In case of exports, textiles and agriculture showed a sharp fall in their shipments during the same period. The Commerce Ministry, however, is confident of achieving positive growth in exports during the current fiscal. Commerce Minister Ramakrishna Hegde said recently at an exporters' meet that the sluggish trend on the export front was over and would pick up in the remaining months of the current fiscal. The sluggish export growth was primarily due to the prolonged South-East Asian economic crisis. "We were expecting that the South-East Asian crisis would end in the middle of the year, but that was not the case," the Minister said. He expressed happiness that Indian exports survived because of their strong economic base, while many Asian economies were swept away. Many countries including China and Japan, have sealed down their targets on the export front, following recessionary trends in many countries.

(g) Taxation

(i) Kar Vivad Samadhan Scheme

Kar Vivad Samadhan Scheme (KVSS) which was launched by the Union Government to recover a portion of Rs. 30,000 crore locked up in about 6.5 lakh cases pending at various stages of disputes provides hosts of incentives for voluntary settlement of disputed cases. Originally it was to remain open to eligible persons and companies from September 1 to December 31, 1998. But it was extended till January 31, 1999.

(ii) Samadhan to mop up Rs. 5,000 Cr.

The Union Government was expected to mop up more than Rs. 5,000 crore under the Kar Vivad Samadhan Scheme, proposed in the Budget. According to a study undertaken by the Centre for Monitoring Indian Economy Pvt. Ltd (CMIE), major cooperates like ITC, ONGC, IG Petrochemicals, Maruti Udyog and Indian Oil Corporation have disputed excise liabilites aggregating Rs. 2,305 crore. The respective compaines' liabilities stood at Rs. 876 crore, Rs. 740 crore, Rs. 302 crore, Rs. 211 crore and Rs. 176 crore during 1996-97. The disputed excise liability of 25 major companies, including 10 public sector companies, worked out to Rs. 3,896 crore. Similarly, the disputed corporate tax liability of ONGC, Punjab National Bank, GTC Industries, BHEL and Tata Chemicals aggregated Rs 2,670 crore. The respective liability of these companies stands at Rs. 1,417 crore, Rs. 485 crore, Rs. 266 crore, Rs. 262 crore and Rs. 240 crore respectively. The disputed tax liability of Bank of America and Deutsche Bank amounted to Rs. 165 crore and Rs. 52 crore respectively at the end of March 1997. The tax liability disputed by other Indian banks are Allahabad Bank, Indian Bank and IDBI touched Rs. 217 crore. Total disputed corporate tax liability of 25 companies/ banks worked out to Rs. 4,260 crore.

The CMIE conducted a quick study of a sample of 6,500 companies, where around 906 companies have disputed excise labilities to the tune of Rs. 5,851 crore during 1996-97 and disputed corporate tax liabilities of 1,140 companies aggregate to Rs. 6,271 crore. On the assumption that all the companies are persuaded to go in for the scheme, which provides a quick and voluntary settlement' of tax dues outstanding as on March 31, 1998, the revenue to the Government would be close to Rs. 2,900 crore on the indirect tax front and Rs. 2,194 crore on direct taxes. Thus, the total amounts up to more than Rs. 5,000 crore. Samadhan Scheme offers waiver of a part of the arrear taxes and interest as also immunity against prosecution and penalty. Under indirect taxes, the assesse seeking redressal under this scheme will be allowed a waiver of 50 per cent of the tax arrears, including interest payable, fine or penalty levied. The scheme will be in force from Sept. 1, 1998 to Dec. 31, 1998.

(iii) Collection of Rs. 2,000 Crore from Samadhan

Government has collected around Rs. 2,000 crore from the Kar Vivad Samadhan Scheme, the centrally sponsored scheme designed to collect tax locked-in disputes. the amount collected from more than 66,000 declarations filed by litigants aggregates to Rs. 4,900 crore by Jan. 31, the last date for filing declarations, said an official communque released recently. More than 47,000 declarations were filed under the direct tax, valued at a gross amount of Rs. 2,800 crore, and more than 18,500 declarations were field under indirect tax amounting to Rs. 2,100 crore, the release added. The revenue expected to accure to the Government on the basis of these declarations will be about Rs. 2,000 crore. 'Mumbai' zone has performed exceptionally well where 10,000 declarations were filed in both direct and indirect side aggregating to an amount of Rs. 1,400 crore locked-up in litigation. The Kar Vivad Samadhan Scheme was launched in September 1998 with the objective of collecting revenue locked-up in disputes. The scheme was also designed to reduce the burden of litigation. The period of filing declarations under the scheme was extended till Jan. 31, 1999.

(iv) Estimates Committee Report on Kar Vivad Samadhan Scheme

The Government should review and amend provision of Kar Vivad Samadhan Scheme (KVSS) in order to make it more attractive to increase revenue collection, a parliamentary committee said on Dec. 9. "The Government may review the scheme to achieve the projected collection in the light of suggestions received from various business and industry groups," the first report of the Estimates Committee of 12th Lok Sabha on Kar Vivad Samadhan Scheme said. The report presented to the Lok Sabha on Dec. 10 said that the scheme could have been made more simpler by amending the present definition of tax arrears. It said that tax arrears should cover the show cause/demand notices issued after March 31, 1998.

The committee felt that the scheme could have been appropriately made applicable to tax arrears in cases of show cause/demand notices. The 30-member committee suggested suitable amendment in the scheme for removing the personal penalty clause. "No data is readily available regarding number of cases where personal penalties on directors/senior executives of companies have been imposed and the amount involved in such cases," it said quoting the Finance Ministry. The committee also criticised the Government for not doing enough background work while formulating legal provisions in the scheme. The committee has recommended existing provision of the scheme be modified to eliminate the discretion which has danger of misuse.

(v) Three-fold Increase in I.T. Assessees Number

New personal income tax assessees have increased by nearly three fold this financial year vindicating the Government's new three-pronged strategy that low rates, simple procedures and friendly approach leads to better tax compliance. "Our efforts in the last two or three years to have low tax rates, simplified procedures, helpful attitude of tax officers have paid dividends this year and Delhi recorded an unprecedented rise of 290 per cent in the number of new assesses," Central Board of Direct Taxes (CBDT) Chairman Ravi Kant said on Nov. 20. "This trend is true of not only Delhi, but other cities as well," he said. The figures for other cities were being compiled and the number of new assessees would be much higher by the end of this year, he said.

The tax collections from these new assessees might not be very large, but the trend is welcome as more people were coming forward on their own to file returns, which in the long run would increase revenue from I-T substantially, he said. With this, the total personal I-T assessees in the country was expected to go up to 1.5 crore this year from last year's figure of 1.2 crore, he said, adding that the personal income tax base would be widened by at least 25 per cent in 1998-99. Asked if the simplified tax form 'Saral' contributed to the increase in new assessees, Mr. Kant said that though Saral was introduced only a few weeks back, its acceptance was generally good but its impact could be fully gauged only next year.

He did not agree with the general perception that there was unusual delay in refund of the excess income tax paid by individuals. In most of the cases, refunds were despatched promptly but in some cases there was some administrative delay which gets "magnified and distorted" bacause of the "hue and cry" raised by the victims and particularly the media, he said. He however, said that CBDT was looking into the issue and "soon we will have a mechanism to monitor such delays."

He said that direct tax collections were buoyant this year with corporate tax registering a reocrd 31.7 per cent growth and personal I-T 9 per cent upto October 1998 as against the coresponding period last year. The year-on-year overall direct tax growth upto October was 19 per cent. The direct tax collections has been targetted at Rs. 48,000 crore in 1998-99, he said, adding that corporate tax collections up to October 1998 was Rs. 10,300 crore as against Rs. 7,800 crore in the corresponding period previous year. The corresponding figures for personal I-T were Rs. 8,700 crore and Rs. 7,930 crore.

13

AGRICULTURE

Crop Production

The highest ever producton of 199.32 million tonnes of foodgrains was achieved during 1996-97. The production of wheat, reached a new high of 69.27 million tonnes and that of coarse ceereals 34.28 million tonnes during the year. Production of cotton, oilseeds and jute and mesta also reached record levels.

Rainfall Situation

1997 was the tenth successive normal monsoon year. Country-wide seasonal rainfall was 102 per cent of the long-term average.

During 1997, the South-West monsoon set in over Kerala on June 9, against the normal date of June 1. The onset of monsoon was delayed in most parts of the country by about 8-10 days. The monsoon covered the entire country by July 19, four days later than the normal date of July 15. At the end of South-West monsoon season (1st June to 30th September). 32 out of 35 meteorological sub-divisions received excess to normal rainfall. The rainfall was deficient only in three sub-divisions viz., Marathawada (-32%), Telangana (-27%) and Vidarbha (-22%). Vidarbha was only marginally deficient. About 80 per cent districts covering about 92 per cent area of the country received excess to normal rainfall. On the whole, the country has received 102 per cent of its long period normal rainfall of 90.9 cm. The total rainfall was normal for the tenth year in succession.

Foodgrains Production

Targets

Ministry f Agriculture has proposed a target of 200 million tonnes of foodgrains production for 1997-98 with its break-up of 105.50 million tonnes for Kharif and 94.50 million tonnes for Rabi/Summer seasons. Crop-wise targets are indicated below:

Table 13.1 : Targets of Food grains Production

(*Million tonnes*)

Crop	Kharif	Rabi	Total
Rice	72.00	11.00	83.00
Wheat	—	68.50	68.50
Coarse Cereals	27.50	6.00	33.50
Pulses	6.00	9.00	15.00
Total foodgrains	105.50	94.50	200.00

Achievements

Rice: Rice is the most important foodgrain crop. During 1996-97, the production of rice was 81.31 million tonnes. The production of Kharif rice (1997) is estimated to reach a peak level of 73.76 million tonnes as compared to 71.41 million tonnes during Kharif, 1996. However, Rabi/Summer rice production during 1997-98 is estimated to be less than the target of 11.0 million tonnes.

Wheat: Wheat is one of the most important winter cereals in India contributing more than 34 per cent of the total foodgrains basket of the country, in terms of area (25.9 million hectares) as well as production (69.27 million tonnes), as estimated for 1996-97, India ranks Second in the world. Ministry of Agriculture proposed a target of 68.5 million tonnes for 1997-98. Rainfall during November-December delayed the sowing and affected the standing crop. There may be a marginal shortfall in production against the target fixed.

Coarse Cereals: Coarse Cereals are cultivated over an area of about 32.3 million hectares with a production of 30.43 million tonnes. Coarse cereals include the crops of jowar, bajra, maize, ragi, barley and small millets. The production of coarse cereals fluctruates widely depending on quantum of rainfall and its distribution pattern. During 1996-97, the production of coarse cereals is estimated at 34.48 million tonnes. During Kharif 1997 the production is likely to be 25.21 million tonnes as against 27.48 million tonnes during Kharif 1996. Shortfall is attributed to aberrant weather conditions prevailed during Kharif season in some of the important coarse cereal growing States like Maharashtra and Karnataka. Crop-wise production target and estimated production of coarse cereals during Kharif 1997 is indicated below:

Table 13.2 : Production Target of Coarse Cereals than 1997-98

(*Million tonnes*)

Crop	Kharif		Rabi	
	Target	Likely achievement	Target	Likely achievement
Jowar	7.20	4.93	3.50	3.23
Bajra	7.00	7.67	—	—
Maize	10.00	9.81	1.00	1.34
Ragi	2.50	2.17	—	—
Barley	—	—	1.50	1.37
Small Millets	0.80	0.63	—	—
Total	27.50	25.21	6.00	5.94

Table 13.3 : All India Estimats of Foodgrains Production

(*Million tonnes*)

Crop		1990-91	1991-92	1992-93	1993-94	1994-95	1995-96	1996-97	1997-98 Target	1997-98 Likely
1	2	3	4	5	6	7	8	9	10	11
Rice	Kharif	66.32	66.37	65.24	70.72	72.60	67.88	71.41	72.00	73.76
	Rabi/Summer	7.97	8.31	7.62	9.58	9.21	9.10	9.90	11.00	9.76
	Total	74.29	74.68	72.86	80.30	81.81	76.98	81.31	83.00	83.52
Wheat		55.14	55.69	57.21	59.84	65.77	62.10	69.27	68.50	66.38
Jowar	Kharif	8.33	5.71	9.38	7.28	5.87	5.66	7.01	7.20	4.93
	Rabi	3.35	2.39	3.43	4.13	3.10	3.67	4.08	3.50	3.23
	Total	11.68	8.10	12.81	11.41	8.97	9.33	11.09	10.70	8.16
Bajra		6.89	4.67	8.88	4.97	7.16	5.38	7.91	7.00	7.67
Maize	Kharif	8.96	6.96	8.94	8.53	7.64	8.34	9.33	10.00	9.81
	Rabi		1.10	1.05	1.07	1.24	1.19	1.28	1.00	1.34
	Total	8.96	8.06	9.99	9.60	8.88	9.53	10.61	11.00	11.15
Ragi		2.34	2.58	2.53	2.60	2.34	2.50	2.47	2.50	2.17
Small Millets		1.19	0.88	0.87	0.92	0.80	0.78	0.76	0.80	0.63
Barley		1.64	1.70	1.51	1.31	1.73	1.51	1.44	1.50	1.37
Coarse Cereals	Kharif	27.71	20.80	30.60	24.30	23.81	22.66	27.48	27.50	25.21
	Rabi	4.99	5.19	5.99	6.51	6.07	6.37	6.80	6.00	5.94
	Total	32.70	25.99	36.59	30.81	29.88	29.03	34.28	33.50	31.15

Table 13.3 : *(Contd.)*

1	2	3	4	5	6	7	8	9	10	11
Cereals	Kharif	94.03	87.17	95.84	95.02	96.41	90.54	98.89	99.50	98.97
	Rabi	68.10	69.19	70.82	75.93	81.05	77.57	85.97	85.50	82.08
	Total	162.13	156.36	166.66	170.95	177.95	168.11	184.86	185.00	181.05
Tur		2.41	2.13	2.33	2.69	2.14	2.31	2.70	2.90	2.27
Other Kharif Pulses	3.00	2.29	3.30	2.69	2.52	2.27	2.83	3.10	2.46	
	Gram	5.36	4.12	4.42	4.98	6.44	4.98	5.76	6.00	5.42
Other Rabi Pulses	3.49	3.48	2.77	2.95	2.94	2.75	3.17	3.00	2.93	
Total Pulses	Kharif	5.41	4.42	5.63	5.38	4.66	4.58	5.53	6.00	4.73
	Rabi	8.85	7.60	7.19	7.93	9.38	7.73	8.93	9.00	8.35
	Total	14.26	12.02	12.82	13.31	14.04	12.31	14.46	15.00	13.08
Total Foodgrains										
	Kharif	99.44	91.59	101.47	100.40	101.07	95.12	104.42	105.50	103.70
	Rabi	76.95	76.79	78.01	83.86	90.43	85.30	94.90	94.50	90.43
	Total	176.39	168.38	179.48	184.26	191.50	180.42	199.32	200.00	194.13
Groundnut	Kharif	51.2	49.9	66.6	57.1	60.6	60.5	72.7	67.0	56.9
	Rabi	23.9	21.0	19.0	21.2	20.0	15.3	17.5	22.0	17.7
	Total	75.1	70.9	85.6	78.3	80.6	75.8	90.2	89.0	74.6
Castorseed		7.2	5.8	6.3	6.3	8.5	7.8	8.9	8.0	9.1
Sesamum		8.4	7.1	7.6	5.6	5.9	5.3	6.7	8.0	6.1
Nigerseed		1.9	1.8	1.6	2.0	1.9	1.9	1.6	2.0	1.4
Rapseed & Mustard		52.3	58.7	48.0	53.3	57.6	60.0	69.4	67.0	62.1

Table 13.3 : *(Contd.)*

1	2	3	4	5	6	7	8	9	10	11
Linseed		3.3	2.9	2.8	3.3	3.2	2.9	3.3	3.0	2.9
Sunflower	Kharif	3.3	3.6	4.3	5.0	3.3	4.5	4.1	5.0	2.5
	Rabi	5.4	8.3	7.5	8.5	8.9	8.1	9.1	10.0	9.4
	Total	8.7	11.9	11.8	13.5	12.2	12.6	13.2	15.0	11.9
Soyabean		26.0	24.9	33.9	47.5	39.3	50.9	52.0	59.0	65.2
Total Nine	Kharif	98.0	93.1	120.3	123.5	119.5	130.9	146.0	149.0	141.2
Oilseeds	Rabi	88.1	92.9	80.8	91.5	93.9	90.1	103.6	106.0	95.7
	Total	186.1	186.0	201.1	215.0	213.4	221.0	249.6	255.0	236.9
Cotton#		98.4	97.1	114.0	107.4	118.9	128.6	142.5	148.0	114.2
Jute $		79.2	89.4	75.0	73.5	80.0	76.7	97.5	81.0	87.0
Mesta $		13.1	13.5	10.9	10.7	10.8	11.3	12.4	16.5	11.2
Jute & Mesta $		92.3	102.9	85.9	84.2	90.8	88.0	109.9	97.5	98.2
Sugarcane (Cane)		2410.5	2540.0	2280.3	2296.6	2755.4	2811.0	2772.5	2800.0	2601.6
Potato		152.1	163.9	152.3	173.9	174.0	188.4	250.7		
Onion		32.3	35.8	34.9	40.1	40.4	40.8	44.3		
Coconut @		97.3	100.8	112.4	119.8	133.0	139.7			
Tobacco		5.6	5.8	6.0	5.6	5.7	5.4	6.0		

Lakh bales of 170 kgs each.
$ Lakh bales of 180 kgs each.
@ In hundred million nuts.

Programmes for increasing production and productivity of careal crops on the basis of cropping system approach was continued during the year under these programmes emphasis is laid on the use of bio-pesticides and Integrated Pest Management (IPM), useof organics and soil ameliorants in problem soils to improve soil health and soil productivity and development of blocks/areas with low productivity levels. Incentives are provided to farmers for use of seeds of location specific high yielding varieties and improved implements. Field demonstrations on farmers' holdings and training of farmers and far labourers are organised for effective transfer of technology.

Programmes for increasing productivity of cotton, sugarcane and jute and mesta were also continued.

Technology Mission on Oilseeds and Pulses

The Technology Mission is responsible for the development of oilseeds, pulses and maize through its four Mini Missions on production technology, post harvest, handling, input supply and support services, marketing and credit aspects. In addition, the National Oilseeds and Vegetable Oils Development Board is also working as a precursor to the Technology Mission for opening of new areas and non-traditional seasons for promotion of oilseeds cultivation.

The Oilseeds Production Programme was implemented by the Technology Mission in 22 States in 361 districts during the year. The National Pulses Development Project was implemented in 26 States/Union Territories covering 277 districts. An accelerated Maize Development Programme has been taken up in 23 States covering 255 districts. Assistance has been provided under these programmes for key inputs.

Oil Palm has been recognised as the highest yielder of edible oil producing 3-5 tonnes of oil per hectare. An Oil Palm Development Programme has been taken up in identified areas in Andhra Pradesh, Karnataka, Tamil Nadu, Gujarat, Goa, Tripura, Assam and Orissa. An area of 33245 hectare has been brought under oil palm cultivation in these states. Processing units have been set up at six places in Andhra Pradesh and Karnataka with a capacity of 20 MT Fresh Fruit Bunches (FFB) per hour to ensure processing of oil palm within 24 hours of harvesting.

Horticulture

There has been a substantial increase in area and production of horticultural crops during the Eighth Five Year Plan. The area under horticulture crops has gone up from 123 lakh hectares in 1991-92 to 150 lakh hectares in 1996-97 with estimated production which increased from 96.00 million tonnes to 141.00 million tonnes during the period. India has emerged as largest producer of fruits and the second largest producer of vegetables in the world. In Ninth Five Year Plan, a production target of 183.9 million tonnes of horticulture crops is envisaged.

Multifaceted programmes taken up for promotion and development of horticulture include promotion of fruits, vegetables, spices, coconut, cashew, Cocoa, floriculture, root and tuber crops, medicinal and aromatic plants, mushrooms, bee-keeping and use of plastics in agriculture.

Major thrust for development of horticulture is proposed in expansion of area, supply of better planting material, seed rejuvenation/rehabilitation of existing plantations, installation of drip irrigation system, popularisation of green house cultivation, infrastructure for post-harvest handling and marketing and development of market intelligence etc.

New direction given to development of floriculture to satisfy growing domestic and export demand. Eleven model floriculture centres being established as focal points for promoting floriculture.

Special programmes of rehabilitating diseased/senile coconut and pepper gardens implemented through attractive incentive schemes and support for essential inputs.

Major thrust given to popularising new technologies viz. True Potatio Seed in Potato, Tissue culture for multiplication of planting material, etc.

A network of spawn production and pasteurised compost units being established to promote rapid growth in mushroom production.

Ambitious programme for promoting use of plastics in agriculture through drip irrigation, green house, mulching, new plasticulture application taken up. A subsidy of 90 per cent in the case of SC/ST and small marginal farmers and women and 70 per cent in the case of other farmers with a ceiling of Rs. 25000 per ha. provided. Over 29,000 ha. was covered with drip irrigation during 1997-98.

Integrated development of horticulture in North-Eastern region and tribal areas of the country to receive particular emphasis during the Ninth Five Year Plan period.

New initiatives such as intervention for human nutrition, human resource development in horticulture, and market intelligence identified for the Ninth Five Year Plan.

Rainfed Farming Systems

About 4.30 million hectares rainfed areas spread over 2554 micro Watersheds in 25 States and two Union Territories have been developed during the Eighth Five Year Plan under the National Watershed Development Project for Rainfed Areas at a cost of Rs. 97152,00 Thousand. Significant achievements have been made under the programme in creating basic infrastructure in the form of establishment of 2040 Barani Chetna Kendras and 4334 Composite nurseries as well as organising about four lakh training programmes at various levels to benefit the project beneficiaries.

Areas contiguous to the existing areas are being taken up for development during the Ninth Five Year Plan. During 1997-98, the programme was implemented with the same components and approach as in the Eight Five Year Plan, pending finalisation of the new guidelines for Ninth Five Year Plan.

Multisectoral Development Projects with World Bank assistance were implemented in Assam, Bihar, Rajasthan and Tamil Nadu. The project for Uttar Pradesh, Andhra Pradesh and Haryana is in an advanced stage of finalisation.

Soil and Water Conservation

The schemes for Soil Conservation in the catchments of the River Valley Projects and Flood Prone Rivers were continued. Priority delineation of catchments under River Valley Project and Flood Prone Rivers scheme has been carried out by All India Soil and Land Use Survey Organisation and an area of 55.7 lakh hectare has been covered.

The Scheme for Watershed Development Project in Shifting Cultivation

Areas was continued in 210 micro watersheds in seven North Eastern States during 1997-98 to cover an area of 0.30 lakh hectares.

The scheme for Reclamation of Alkali soils in Haryana, Punjab, Uttar Pradesh, Gujarat, Madhya Pradesh and Rajasthan was continued during 1997-98. Another scheme for Reclamation of Alkali Land in Bihar and Uttar Pradesh was also implemented with EEC assistance. Due to reclamation of alkali land, land productivity has been improved, thereby a production of 3.5 tonne/ha. for paddy and 2.5 tonne/ha. for wheat has been achieved in the project areas.

Participation of the beneficiaries under various programmes at each level of planning, implementation and operationalisation of the project has been ensured. In the formation of self help groups and water-user groups, women have played vital role in the project and also improved their socio-economic status.

Employment opportunities have been generated for the rural community through their active involvement in the reclamation programmes.

Agriculture Minister has been notified as Chairman of the National Land use and Conservation Board.

Fertiliser

Fertiliser consumption which was 138.77 lakh tonnes of nutrients (NPK) during 1995-96 increased by 3.1 per cent and stood at 143.08 lakh tonnes of nutrients during 1996-97. During 1997-98, it is estimated at 163 lakh tonnes of nutrients.

The scheme for concession on decontrolled phosphatic and potassic fertilisers was continued. The rate of concession on decontrolled fertilisers were raised to Rs. 3750 per tonne for indigenous DAP, Rs. 2250 per tonne for imported DAP, Rs. 2000 per tonne for MOP, Rs. 600 per tonne for SSP (16%) and Rs. 1630-3320 per tonne for indigenous complexes with effect from 1-4-1997 for the Kahrif 1997 season. For the Rabi 1997-98 season, the rates of concession on indigenous and imported DAP were Rs. 3500 and Rs. 2000 per tonne while those on complexes range from Rs. 1522-3130 per tonne. The rate of concession on MOP and SSP remained the same as that in Kharif 1997 season. Prior to 1-4-1997 the rate of concession on these fertilisers was Rs. 3000, Rs. 1500, Rs. 1500, Rs. 500 and Rs. 1304-2633 per tonne of DAP (indigenous), DAP (imported) MOP, SSP and complexes respectively. The process of payment under the scheme has also been streamlined during 1997-98. It has been decided to provide additional freight support for movement of decontrolled fertilisers in the North Eastern region including Sikkim and Jammu & Kashmir w.e.f. 1-4-1997.

The price of urea which continues to be under statutory control, was raised by 10 per cent w.e.f. 21st Feb., '97. It is now being made available to the farmers at a uniform price of Rs. 3660 per tonne as against the earlier price of Rs. 3320 per tonne.

The National Project on Development and use of Bio-fertilisers was continued. A quarterly news letter for popularisation of Bio-fertilisers has also been introduced.

Seeds

Production of Breeder and Foundation seeds maintained a steady growth. Distribution of certified/quality seeds is to go up from 70.00 lakh quintals in 1996-97 to 75.50 lakh quintals in 1997-98.

In order to encourage export of seeds in the interest of farmers, the procedure for export permission for seed has been simplified. Privately developed varieties/ hybrids are allowed to be exported freely except where there is any emergency caused by the national calamities and seed is required for meeting the demand in the country. Export against orders for which production of seed is organised, is allowed without restriction. In other cases, appropriately high quantitative ceilings have been prescribed upto which export is permitted freely subject to the provisions of EXIM Policy.

During 1997-98, 163 varieties of different crops have been notified for the purpose of the Seeds Act to make available newly evolved superior and high yielding varieties to the farmers for general cultivation in the regions for which it is adopted. 49 varieties were denotified because they have become very old and obsolete.

The following schemes to increase the production and distribution of seeds were continued:

(i) National Seeds Project-III with the objective of restructuring of States Seeds Corporations and strengthening of Seed Certification agencies.
(ii) Transport Subsidy on Seeds with the objective of ensuring timely availability of seeds to the farmers of North Eastern States including Sikkim.
(iii) Streamlining certified seed production of important identified vegetable crops with the objective of increasing production of certified seed of vegetable crops.
(iv) Quality control arrangements on seeds with the objective of strengthening quality control arrangements in order to ensure that farmers get good quality seeds.
(v) National Programme on Varietal Development with the objective to strengthen infrastructural facilities for multiplication of various categories of seeds.

Plant Protection

The Central Integrated Pest Management Centres are promoting biological control of crop pests by encouraging conservation and augmentation of naturally occurring bio-agents and large scale laboratory rearing and release of beneficial organisms. A total of 920 million laboratory reared bio-control agents have been released in the field during April-October, 1997.

Five Plant Quarantine Stations at Delhi, Mumbai, Chennai, Calcutta and Amritsar were upgraded with new laboratory facilities and modern equipment under a UNDP/FAO Project. Plant Quarantine techniques have also been simplified. Officers numbering 106 were notified for issue of Phytosanitary Certificates.

Issue of Import Permits has been decentralised and the certificates are now being issued from Delhi, Mumbai, Calcutta, Chennai and Amritsar. Notification for issue of import permits from Bangalore, Hyderabad, Lucknow, Patna and Indore are under issue.

Ban on movement of Potato tubers was lifted except in seven blocks in Darjeeling District to help potato growers in West Bengal.

The Registration Committee for registration of pesticides continued its activities during the year. The Committee simplified data requirements for neem based pesticides and bio-pesticides. During 1997-98, 1997 pesticides have been registered. Priority is given for registration of pesticides for export.

The Ventral Insecticides Laboratory analysed 854 samples and two Regional Pesticide Laboratories 496 samples for monitoring the quality of pesticides.

Yellow mature swarms of locust which entered some areas of Jaisalmer were controlled effectively by the Locust Warning Organisation.

Agricultural Implements and Machinery

Farm Machinery Training and Testing Institutes that have been set up at Budni (Madhya Pradesh), Hissar (Haryana), Garladinne (Andhra Pradesh) and Biswanath Chariali (Assam) imparted training in proper selection, repair, maintenance and management of farm machinery and testing of farm equipment. A total number of 3367 personnel were trained, and 60 equipments tested by the institutes, during the year.

The scheme for promotion of agricultural mechanisation was continued. Subsidy @ 30 per cent, limited to Rs. 30,000 is provided to farmers, registered cooperative societies, agricultural credit societies, etc. thereunder for purchase of tractors up to 30 PTO HP and their matching implements. Rs. 166930 thousand were released to the states for subsidising 5564 tractors against the annual target of subsidising 5333 tractors.

Extension

Integrated Extension Delivery is being pilot tested at district level under technology dissemination component of forth-coming National Agricultural Technology Project (NATP) in six States namely, Andhra Pradesh, Bihar, Punjab, Himachal Pradesh, Maharashtra and Orissa.

With a view of increasing the coverage and efficiency of extension services, the efforts made by Non-Governmental Organisations (NGOs) have been dovetailed through a Central Sector Scheme.

To have a strong interaction between Department of Agriculture and Cooperation (DAC) and Indian Council of Agricultural Research (ICAR) and to develop joint strategies, interfaces are organised on pre-Rabi and pre-Kharif.

He Hon'ble Agriculture Minister had dedicated permanent Agriculture Pavilion to the Nation, 4 National level Fruit Shows on mango, citrus, ber and guava organised at Lucknow, Shillong, Jodhpur and Allahabad respectively. 14 National Productivity Awards were given through National Productivity Council to Agro-based Institutions/organisations.

A TV news *Krishi Times* has been started on DD-1 on every Sunday at 8.50 P.M. The farm Information Unit brought out 4 bi-monthly journals namely Intensive Agriculture and Agricultural Extension Review in English, Unnat Krishi and Krishi Vistar Samiksha in Hindi. Farm Information Unit have participated in International Agriculture Exhibition at Muscat and National level Exhibitions at Nagpur, Durgapur and Calcutta.

Training Courses and Workshops organised to upgrade knowledge and skill of senior and middle level extension managers and grass-root level extension functionaries in Extension Management Communication and Subject Matter Areas.

Training Support for strengthening Extension Services in the North-Eastern States, Union Territories and other small States strengthened.

Extension Services for Women further strengthened through Central Sector Scheme, externally aided projects and by establishing a National level Expert Committee on Women in Agriculture.

Agricultural Credit

The flow of agricultural credit continued to register a constant and steady growth. The total agricultural credit increased by 30.05 per cent to reach a level of Rs. 28,653,00,00 thousand during the year 1996-97 as against its estimated flow of Rs. 22,032,00,00 thousand during 1995-96. The flow of agricultural credit is likely to reach a level of Rs. 34,2,74,00,00 thousand during the year 1997-98.

Crop Insurance

The existing comprehensive Crop Insurance Scheme (CIS) continued in 15 States and two Union Territories during 1997-98.

As a first step towards coverage of non-loanee farmers under the Crop Insurance Scheme, the Government has decided to implement an Experimental Crop Insurance Scheme (ECIS) covering all small and marginal farmers (both loanee and non-loanee) growing cereals, pulses and oilseeds crops in 24 selected districts of eight States for one year from Rabi 1997-98.

Cooperation

The cooperative movement has been recognised as an instrument of socio-economic change in the country, particularly in the rural economy. Cooperatives have been playing an important role in the disbursement of credit, distribution of inputs such as fertilisers, seeds and pesticides, and production, processing storage and marketing of agricultural produce. The total number of cooperative societies increased from 1.81 lakh during 1950-51 to 4.48 lakh as on 31-3-1996. The total membership of cooperative societies has registered an impressive growth from 1.55 crore during 1950-51 to 27.59 crore as on 31-3-1996.

The main organisations at the national level which are implementing various programmes for the development of cooperatives are the National Cooperative Development Corporation (NCDC), National Agricultural Cooperative Marketing Federation of India Limited (NAFED) and National Cooperatives Union of India (NCUI).

The main objectives of the NCDC are to promote, stengthen and develop cooperatives of farmers with a view to increasing production and productivity.

14

COMMUNICATIONS

Report on National Telecom Policy

In a clear departure from the present licensing regime, the report of 'national telecom policy—five year horizon', has suggested two alternate models to the government. Under the first model the license fee or revenue share should cover administrative and regulatory costs. Companies can divert committed license fees toward network expansion and provide cheap services more rapidly. Or, alternatively, the government can pursue its budgetary goals rationally by improving its own prospects of expanding long term revenues by allowing the industry to establish itself and more become profitable. The report on the national telecom policy emphasizes that "the government will also undermine its own long-term budgetary goals of receiving enhanced revenues from the companies on a sustained basis".

It analyzes the merits of revenues per line model and for weightage based upon the Singapore model. On the problem of qualifying the technical experience front because of lack of a foreign partner, the report suggested that this requirement can be compensated through operations and management contract, technical service agreement, full contract with consulting firms specializing in telecom engineering procurement and construction contracts and also ticups with vendors, etc. It will then be possible to meet all conditons as per the weightage requirement of the Singapore model without getting into the difficulties of the "highest bidder syndrome" in the absence of a foreign partner.

The following reproduces the text of the New Telecom Policy in respect of a few features:

Importance of Telecommunications

The Government of India (Government) recognises that provision of world class telecommunications infrastructure and information is the key to rapid economic and social development of the country. It is critical not only for the development of the Information Technology Industry, but also has widespread ramifications on the entire economy of the country. It is also anticipated that going forward, a major part of the GDP of the country would be contributed by this sector. Accordingly, it is of vital importance to the country that there be a comprehensive and forward looking telecommunications policy which creates an enabling framework for development of this industry.

NTP 1994-Objectives and Achievements

In 1994, the Government announced the National Telecom Policy which defined certain important objectives, including availability of telephone on demand, provision of world class services at reasonable prices, ensuring India's emergence as major manufacturing/export base of telecom equipment and universal availability of basic telecom services to all villages. It also announced a series of specific targets to be achieved by 1997. As against the NTP 1994 target of provision of 1 PCO per 500 urban population and coverage of all 6 lac villages, DoT has achieved an urban PCO penetration of 1 PCO per 522 and has been able to provide telephone coverage to only 3.1 lac villages. As regards provision of total telephone lines in the country, DoT has provided 8.73 million telephone lines against the eighth plan target of 7.5 million lines

NTP 1994 also recognised that the required resources for achieving these targets would not be available only out of Government sources and concluded that private investment and involvement of the private sector was required to bridge the resource gap. The Government invited private sector participation in a phased manner from the early nineties, initially for value added services such as Paging Services and Cellular Mobile Telephone Services (CMTS) and thereafter for Fixed Telephone Services (FTS). After a competitive bidding process, licenses were awarded to 8 CMTS operators in the four metros, 14 CMTS operators in 18 state circles, 6 BTS operators in 6 state circles and to paging operators in 27 cities and 18 state circles. VSAT services were liberalised for providing data services to closed user groups. Licences were issued to 14 operators in the private sector out of which only nine licencees are operational. The Government has recently announced the policy for Internet Service Provision (ISP) by private operators and has commenced licensing of the same. The Government has also announced opening up of Global Mobile Personal Communications by Satellite (GMPCS) and has issued one provisional license. Issue of licenses to other prospective GMPCS operators is under active consideration.

The Government recognises that the result of the privatisation has so far not been entirely satisfactory. While there has been a rapid rollout of cellular mobile networks in the metros and states with currently over 1 million subscribers, most of the projects today are facing problems. The main reason, according to the cellular and basic operators, has been the fact that the actual revenues realised by these projects has been far short of the projections and the operators are unable to arrange financing for their projects and therefore, complete their projects. Basic telecom services by private operators have only just commenced in a limited way in two of the six circles where licenses were awarded. As a result, some of the targets as envisaged in the objectives of the NTP 1994 have remained unfulfilled. The private sector entry has been slower than what was envisaged in the NTP 1994.

The government views the above developments with concern as it would adversely affect the further development of the sector and recognises the need to take a fresh look at the policy framework for this sector.

Need for a New Telecom Policy

In addtion to some of the objectives of NTP 1994 not being fulfilled, there have also been far reaching developments in the recent past in the telecom. IT, consumer electronics and media industries world-wide. Convergence of both markets and technologies is a reality that is forcing realignment of the industry. At one level, telephone and broadcasting industries are entering each other's

---

Source : *The Hawak*, March 31, 1999

markets, while at another level, technology is burring the difference between different conduit systems such as wireline and wireless. As i the case of most countries, separate licences have been issued in our country for basic, celluiar, ISP, satellite and cable TV operators each with separate industry structure, terms of entry and varying requirement to create infrastructure. However this convergence now allows operators to use their facilities to deliver some services reserved for other operators, necessitaiing a relook into the existing policy framework. The new telecom policy framework is also required to facilitate India's vision of becoming an IT superpower and develop a world class telecom infrastructure in the country.

Objectives and targets of the New Telecom Policy 1999

The objectives of the NTP 1999 would be as under:

Access to telecommunications is of utmost importance for achievement of the country's social and economic goals. Availability of affordable and effective communications for the citizens is at the core of the vision and goal of the telecom policy.

Strive to provide a balance between the provision of universal service to all uncovered areas, including the rural areas, and the provision of high-level services capable of meeting the needs of the country's economy; encourage development of telecommunication facilities in remote, hilly and tribal areas of the country; create a modern and efficient telecommunications infrastructure taking into account the convergence of IT, media, telecom and consumer electronics and thereby propel India into becoming an IT superpower, convert PCO's, wherever justified, into Public. Teleinfo centres having multimedia capability like ISDN services remote database access, government and community information systems etc. Transform in a time bound manner, the telecommunications sector to a greater competitive environment in both urban and rural areas providing equal opportunities and level playing field for all players.

Strengthen research and development efforts in the country and provide an impetus to build world-class manufacturing capabilities and Achieve efficiency and transparency in spectrum management. Enable Indian Telecom Companies to become truly global players. In line with the above objectives, the specific targets that the NTP 1999 seeks to achieve would be: Make available telephone on demand by the year 2002 and sustain it thereafter so as to achieve a teledensity of 7 by the year 2005 and 15 by the year 2010, encourage development of telecom in rural areas making it more affordable by suitable tariff structure and making rural communication mandatory for all fixed service providers increase rural teledensity from the current level of 0.4 to 4 by the year 2010 and provide reliable transmission media in all rural areas.

Achieve telecom coverage of all villages in the country and provide reliable media to all exchanges by the year 2002, Provide Internet access to all district head quarters by the year 2000, Provide high speed data and multimedia capability using technologies including ISDN to all towns with a population greater than 2 lac by the year 2002.

New Policy Framework

The New Policy Framework must focus on creating an environment which enables continued attraction of investment in the sector and allows creation of communication infrastructure by leveraging on technological development. Towards this end, the New Policy Framework would look at the telecom service sector as follows:

Cellular Mobile Service Providers, Fixed Service Providers and Cable Service Providers, collectively referred to as 'Access Providers'

Radio Paging Service Providers

Public Mobile Radio Trunking Service Providers

National Long Distance Operators

International Long Distance Operators

Other Service Providers

Global Mobile Personal Communication by Satellite (GMPCS) Service Providers

V-SAT based Service Providers

Corporatisation of Do'T Cleared

In a significant move, the government announced its in-principle clearance for corporatisation of the department of telecommunications (DoT). DoT employees will, however, be given the option to remain in government if they so wished. Disclosing this to newspersons in New Delhi on June 26, Union Minister for Communications Sushma Swaraj said that under the corporatisation plan. DoT will get a new name—India Telecom—which will be a 100 per cent government-owned PSU in the initial phase. Before the announcement, Mrs. Swaraj held a meeting with Union Finance Minister Yashwant Sinha during which she got the nod for a final go-ahead for the corporatisation plan.

She said that the department would prepare a draft Cabinet note within a fortnight. On his part, the Finance Minister would consult the expenditure department of his Ministry to complete other details. The corporatisation plans of DoT would involve an extra burden of Rs. 12,000 crore on the government's part on account of pensionary funds and gratuity. The Communications Ministry has placed three options before the Finance Ministry to prepare the balancesheet for the new corporate identity. Though there will be no cash transaction involved between the Communication Ministry and the Finance Ministry, but one had to wait for the latter's decision to see whether the corporation gets an interest holiday, equity or loan amount, Mrs. Swaraj stated.

Mrs. Swaraj further said that with the corporatisation of DoT, the deemed deputation staus of the Mahanagar Telephone Nigam Ltd, (MTNL) would be abolished. In the first phase the Group C and D employees would be transferred to DoT. The Secretary DoT would meet the expenditure Secretary to finalise the financial implication of the corporatisation proposal. She also announced that the Ministry had decided to allow authorised Interest Service Providers (ISP) to set up international gateways for data transmission. Currently the department of telecommunication (DoT) has six gateways for the purpose.

The newly-appointed Minister for Communications Mr. Jagmohan Singh, indicated on Dec. 6 that corporatisation of the Department of Telecommunications (DoT) might be deferred in view of employee unions' opposition. Addressing newsmen in New Delhi immediately after assuming office, Mr. Jagmohan said that he would proceed in that direction only after assessing the views of different parties and financial implications of corporatising the DoT. Besides, the views of employees' union, including the Bharatiya Mazdoor Sangh which had opposed the move, would be taken into consideration before arriving at a final decision, he said.

Mr. Jagmohan's views are, notably, in total consonance with that of the Communications Secretary Anik Kumar who had, at an Assocham-organised seminar on telecommunications on Dec. 5, ruled out immediate corporatisation of the DoT because of the imperative of balancing the growth of high returns market with the obligation to increase teledensity and reach out to the rural areas. Though Mr. Jagmohan reiterated that "we will stick to the national agenda with regard to the corporatisation," he made it clear that corporatising DoT was a matter which needs further study and close examination.

When asked about the controversy over the corporatisation of DoT, the Minister said that the Government would stick to the national agenda of the ruling alliance which promised corporatisation of the department. The Minister said that an indepth study would be made on the overlapping of powers between the telecom regulatory authority (TRAI) and the DoT before taking any decision. Earlier, Minister of State for Telecommunications Kabindra Purkayastha and senior officials briefed Mr. Jagmohan about various issues before the Ministry. Mr. Jagmohan said that he would pull every stop to make India a global superpower in telecommunications.

4.5 Million GSM Subscribers

India expects to increase its Global System of Mobile (GSM) communication subscribes from 3 to 4.5 million subscribers by 2001 from 0.9 million subscriber base today. According to T.V. Ramachandran, Chairman, India Interest Group, GSM is the fastest growing standard in the world. The subscribers have increased from nil in 1992 to 80 million subscribers today and is headed to 100 million subscribers the world over. The standard has been developed by the original group of 14 countries in 1982 that was commercially launched in 1992. Today, any country offering the cellular service by the GSM standards has to be a member of the GSM MoU. India is hosting 40th GSM plenary wherein 125 countries are expected to take part in the GSM MoU association from Oct. 20-23. The agenda of the meet covers the technical aspects, roaming, fraud, enhanced code security and IT aspects. "By 2005 all the countries will physically phase out analog systems," says Mr. Ramachandran. The first generation technology that most of the developing countries adopted were analog. India started its foray in mobile telephony by starting with digital technology by adopting the GSM standard in 1992. The third generation standard is expected to be launched in 2001 in Japan by NTT Dcomo, with the universal mobile telephone service that will be based on the GSM Platform.

Nineth-eight per cent of the GSM world has adopted the "calling party pays" principle, points out Mr. Ramachandran. The Telecom Regulatory Authority of India (TRAI) has recently suggested that India also introduce the "calling party pays principle" as it would boost the usage of cellular phones. India, USA, Hong Kong are some of the countries where the CPP principle has not been adopted. This is on account of several reasons like the presence of electro-mechanical exchanges that cannot facilitate billing in the CPP regime. In order to introduce the CPP the electro-mechanical exchanges will have to be phased out. USA decided on a time-frame of two years as late as last year for phasing out the electro-mechanical exchanges. The number of GSM millions in the USA stands at 1.5 million.

MTNL, VSNL Tie Up

Telecome giants Mahanagar Telephone Nigam Ltd. (MTNL) and Videsh Sanchar Nigam Ltd. (VSNL) signed a memorandum of understanding (MoU) on Jan. 8 to make a foray into high technology areas, overseas markets and domestic long distance telephony. According to a joint press statement, the MoU envisaged that "the partners will pool their resources and expertise in India and abroad to deliver telecommunication solutions and form joint ventures for emerging market leaders in the rapidly emerging competitive environment." VSNL acting Chairman and Managing Director Amitabh Kumar and MTNL Chairman and Managing Director S. Rajagopalan said that they planned to leverage from each other's strengths and jointly look for opportunities in India and abroad, and diversify into new ventures.

MTNL Finance Advisor S.D. Saxena told *The Observer of Business and Politics* that to begin with, the two companies would work together to provide high speed data transfer services to buiness customers. MTNL would provide its network for data transfer in Delhi and Mumbai, VSNL would carry it to overseas destinations. Among overseas markets, the companies would be looking for business opportunities in African and Latin American countries which are in the process of opening up their telecom sector for competition. The immediate targets of the companies would be countries like Mozambique, Kenya and Mauritius.

Source : *The Hawk*, March 31, 1999.

15

DEFENCE

National Security Council (NSC)

The Prime Minister, Mr. Atal Behari Vajpayee, on Nov. 19 approved formation of the National Security Council (NSC), a new high powered hub which will give policy directions to safeguard the country's security. The NSC, formed 8 months after the BJP-led Government assumed office, will be headed by the Prime Minister. The Home Minister, the Defence Minister, the External Affairs Minister, the Finance Minister and the Deputy Chairman of the Planning Commission will be its other members. Other Ministers will be invited to attend the NSC meeting as and when required. The Principal Secretary to the Prime Minister will play the key role of the National Security Advisor. He will be the lynchpin connecting the NSC with an elaborate three-tiered backup structure.

The three-tiered body comprises the Strategic Policy Group, the National Security Advisory Board and a Secretariat represented by the Joint Intelligence Committee (JIC). The JIC will be suitably revamped to meet the demands of its new role, an official Press statement said. A new Chairman of the JIC will be named shortly. The Strategic Policy Group will be the nucleus providing inter-ministerial coordination and backup for the NSC. This group will consist of the Cabinet Secretary, the three service chiefs, the Foreign Secretary, the Home Secretary, the Defence Secretary, Secretary (Defence Production), Finance Secretary, the Secretary (Revenue), the RBI Governor, the Director (Intelligence Bureau), the Secretary (Research and Analysis Wing), the Secretary (Department of Atomic Energy), Scientific Advisor to the Defence Minister, the Secretary (Space) and Chairman (JIC). Other invitees will be brought in as and when required.

The Strategic Policy Group will undertake a strategic defence review, a blueprint of short and long term security threats as well as possible policy options on a priority basis. Significantly, the formation of detailed nuclear command control is linked to the strategic defence review, the sources added. The National Security Advisory Board will form the third element of the NSC set up. It will consist of persons of eminence outside the Government with expertise in external security, strategic analysis, foreign affairs, defence, the armed forces, internal security, science and technology and economics.

India's High Commissioner to Pakistan, Mr. Satish Chandra has been appointed Chairman of the Joint Intelligence Committee (JIC), which will serve as the Secretariat to the National Security Council (NSC). The formation of the NSC, which will be headed by the Prime Minister was announced on Nov. 19. Mr. Chandra, a 1965 batch officer of the Indian Foreign Service, will now head the Secretariat. The JIC is one of the three wings of the NSC. Its other two tiers are the Strategic Policy Group and the National Security Advisory Board. According to the official spokesman, the JIC would be suitably revamped to perform its new role. The NSC will undertake a strategic defence review which is part of the national agenda of the BJP-led Government.

India Missile Power

India will emerge as a full-fledged missile power by the turn of the century, with all its indigenous missiles ready for induction by 2000, the Scientific Adviser to the Defence Minister, Dr. A.P.J. Abdul Kalam, has said. 'By 2000, all the strategic and tactical missiles will be made in the country', Dr. Kalam said at a Press conference in Bangalore on Dec. 9. The induction of these missiles will boost India's capability to deter an external attack. They would also spin off knowhow to help fulfil the country's ambitious plans for indigenisation. India wanted to produce 70 per cent of its military hardware requirements on its own by 2005. India had already developed the nuclear capable. Prithvi ballistic missile. It was working on an extended range Agni Intermediate range Ballistic Missile (IRBM). Besides, it was building the Trishul and Akash ground-to-air projectiles. The four-km range tank-busting missile, Nag, was also under development.

Elaborating on the induction time-table, Dr. Kalam said the highly agile Trishul missile, with a short target range, would be inducted in all the three services next year. The radar-guided Akash missile, which could track and engage several high flying targets simultaneously, would be ready to enter service between 1999 and 2000. The Nag anti-bank missile would be inducted in 2000. The presence of the indigenous ground-to-air missiles would greatly enhance India's air defence capability. At the moment, the core of India air defence capability revolved around the static Soviet origin Pechora missile and the OSAAK mobile systems. According to experts, both these missiles were prone to jamming as the frequency on which their radars function had become known. The induction of indigenous missiles could largely resolve this problem. The Trishul's presence was also expected to add punch to mobile armoured columns. The Trishul, which would be fired from a moving armoured vehicle, could prevent an aerial attack on mobile tank columns.

44 DRDO Awards

The Defence Research and Development Organisation (DRDO) on Aug. 22 instituted 44 new annual awards totalling Rs. 1 crore in a bid to accelerate the pace of critical technology development, technology transfer and production of state-of-the-art defence technology. Defence Minister George Fernandes said that the 44 awards would be given annually and the awardees would be selected by a committee headed by Dr. A.P.J., Abdul Kalam, Scientific Advisor to the Defence Minister. The Minister recalled that during his visits to the DRDO laboratories, he was deeply touched by the sense of patriotism dispalyed by defence scientists and the dedication to meet the obstacles imposed by the controlled regime of the western powers denying them access to critical technology. He urged those scientists who have been askd to leave the United States to come back to their country and said the doors of the DRDO were open for them.

The awards, to be started this year, would be given to DRDO scientists, laboratories, academic institutions, industries, organisations, armed forces and certifying agencies. The awards would be carrying a sum varying from Rs. 25,000 to Rs. 10 lakh each. There would be five AGNI award for excellence in self-reliance, each carrying a sum of Rs. 2 lakh. The DRDO award for path-breaking research would be carrying a sum of Rs. 10 lakh. A similar amount would be given to each of the two awardees for excellence in performance. Two awards, carrying a sum of Rs. 10 lakh each, would be given for defence technology absorption while another Rs. 10 lakh has been earmarked for academy excellence award. Other awards include Rs. 2 lakh each for two technology leadership awards, Rs. one lakh each for 10 scientists of the year, Rs. 50,000 each for eight young scientists, Rs. 25,000 each for eight best performances and Rs. five lakh each to five organisations for defence technology spin-off.

Revision of Pension for Defence Forces

The Defence Ministry on June 24 announced a revision of person in for the armed forces personnel who retired on or after Jan. 1, 1996 and for those who attained superannuation before 1986 or prior to 1996. The Ministry order states that in both the cases, the pensioner has to apply for revision by filling up a prescribed form in duplicate to the Pension Disbursing Authority. The last date of submission is Feb. 28, 1999. In case of personnel who retired on or after 1996, the revised pension would be based on the revised pay following the implementation of the Fifth Pay Commission recommendations. According to the order, pension would be paid at a uniform rate of 30 per cent of the last pay drawn for all categories instead of the earlier slab system. The minimum limit for all kinds of pension, including ordinary family pension, has now been fixed at Rs. 1,275 per month. The arrears on account of the revision of pension would be paid in cash in two instalments.

The order states that the rates for calculation of all types of gratuities remain unchanged but from now on full dearness allowance admissible on the date of retirement/death would be taken into account for the calculation of gratuity. The maximum ceiling on gratuity has been enhanced to Rs. 3.5 lakh. Further, there would be no change in the percentage of the commutation of pension. The commuted portion of the pension would continue to be restored after 15 years. The difference in the amount of gratuity and the commuted value of pension would be calculated automatically by the Pension Sanctioning Authority and paid in lump sum.

16

EDUCATION AND CULTURE

1. EDUCATION

Introduction

Education is the key to all processes of development especially human development. Catalytic action of education in this complex and dynamic growth process needs to be planned meticulously and executed with great sensitivity. Education is fundamental to all-round development of human potential—material and spiritual. It refines sensitivities and perceptions that contribute to national cohesion, a scientific temper and independence of mind and spirit—thus furthering the goal of socialism, secularism and democracy enshrined in our Constitution. Education develops manpower for different levels of economy and empowers the poor masses to become self-reliant enough to participate in the process of national development. Education is thus an instrument for developing an economically prosperous society and for ensuring equity and social justice.

The education scenario at the time of independence was structurally flawed with inequities characterised by gender, social and regional imbalances. Even though the post-independence period saw significant achievements in the field of education, the structural flaws continued and, to a certain extent, got accentuated. An attempt to take a holistic view was made in 1986 through the National Policy on Education.

The National Policy on Education (NPE), 1986 is a landmark in the history of Indian education. The NPE visualised education as a dynamic, cumulative, life-long process, providing diversity of learning opportunities to all segments of society. It envisaged improvement and expansion of education in all sectors; elimination of disparities in access and stresses on improvement in the quality and relevance of education at all levels—from primary to higher education along with technical and professional education. The National Policy on Education (NPE) also emphasised that education must play a positive and interventionist role in correcting social and regional imbalances in empowering women and in securing a rightful place for linguistic and minorities.

The nation is now firmly committed to provide Education For All. Overriding priority to provide compulsory primary education, coverage of children with special needs, eradication of illiteracy, vocationalisation, education for women's equality, special focus on the education of SCs/STs and Minorities are the major strategies to achieve the national goal of Universalisation of Elementary Education (UEE). The educationally backward areas are given special attention to remove regional disparities. Emphasis has been laid on the improvement of infrastructural facilities in the primary schools to make the school environment more attractive. Flexible and innovative programmes in the form of Non-Formal Education (NFE) have been launched to cater to school dropouts, girls, working children, etc. The National Literacy Mission (NLM) was set up to represent a national and political commitment on the need to harness all social forces to achieve the objective of eradicating illiteracy and effecting a qualitative change in the lives of the people. It has made it possible for the country to set a target of marking 100 million non-literates in the age grop of 15-35 years functionally literate.

Vocationalisation has been given emphasis to develop healthy attitude among students towards work and life, to enhance individual employability to reduce the mismatch of demand and supply of skilled manpower, and to provide an alternative for those intending to pursue higher education without particular interest or purpose.

Secondary Education has its importance in the national development as it provides large skilled manpower for the economy and prepares for higher, technical and professional education. It is the stage where a proper understanding of work ethos and values of a humane and composite culture is provided to future citizens of the country.

There is great demand for expansion of higher education on account of increasing expansion of primary and secondary education and rising social expectations. Consequently, emphasis has been on the removal of disparities and to equalise educational opportunities attending to the specific needs to those who have been denied equality so far. The country is passing through major economic developments with liberalisation and globalisation of the economy. The universities are also expanding their territorial boundaries through distance education. In all these areas, quality assurance has become a major focus.

Educational development is a participatory process. Education was incorporated in the Concurrent List to facilitate evolution of all-India policies in the field of education. The concept of concurrency implies a meaningful partnership between the Union Government and the States. While the role and responsibility of States to provide education continues to remain essentially unchanged, the Union Government has assumed a larger responsibility to reinforce the national and integrated character of education, to look after the international aspects of Education, Culture and Human Resource Development; and, in general, to promote excellence in all sectors of education throughout the country.

Having regard to the size of the population, diversity and economic frailties the challenges are enormous. This realisation has resulted in steadily rising levels of budgetary allocations, and resource transfer for educational initiatives to the States. Given in the succeeding paras is a resume of the current state of education in some of the areas of fundamental concern.

(i) Elementary Education

The Elementary Education system in India is one of the largest in the world. There has been massive expansion of Elementary Education (EE) during the post-independence period, however, the goal of Universalisation of Elementary Education (UEE) is yet to be achieved.

Universal access, universal retention and universal achievements are broad parameters to achieve UEE. Considering the magnitude and the complexity of the problem, meticulously formulated strategies have been adopted in the form of Operation Blackboard (OB), Non-Formal Education (NFE), Teacher Education (TE). District Primary Education Programme (DPEP) to address the specific problem areas, gender and regional disparities.

Special focus has been laid on the access to education for millions of girls and working children, who cannot participate in the school system on account of socio-economic compulsions. These segments largely constitute girls, SCs/STs and the other deprived sections of the society.

Unattractive school environment, unsatisfactory conditions of buildings and insufficiency of instructional material acting as major demotivating factors for enrolment and retention of children in primary schools called for a drive called Operation Blackboard for substantial improvement in the infrastructural facilities at the primary stage. The physical targets for the Eighth Plan were achieved with remarkable success. The scheme has been expanded to cover upper primary schools as well. A national evaluation of the scheme has been entrusted to NIEPA recently.

A large and systematic programme of Non-Formal Education (NFE), which is an integral component of the strategies to achieve UEE has been taken up to cover children who cannot attend formal school due to socio-economic compulsions. Girls, working children, dropouts and those belonging to SC/ST and deprived sections of the society stand to benefit from this approach. NFE has enough flexibility to provide education at their doorsteps to enable them to learn at their own pace and convenience. The major challenge is for NFE to maintain quality comparable with the formal system.

The National Programme of Nutritional Support to Primary Education is intended to boost enrolment, attendance and retention in primary schools and also to supplement nutritional requirements of children. The scheme covers the children studying in primary classes in the Government, local body and Government-aided schoosl throughout the country. Total beneficiaries are estimated to be 9.75 crores in nearly 6.88 lakh primary schools in the country during the period under report.

The District Primary Education Programme provides sepcial thrust to achieve Universalisation of Primary Education (UPE) through decentralised planning and management, disaggregated target setting, community mobilisaton, district and population specific planning. The programme mainly aims at providing access to primary education for all children, reducing dropout rates to less than 10 per cent, increasing level of achievements of primary students by at least 25 per cent and reducing the gap among gender social groups to less than 5 per cent catering to the needs of special target groups like tribals, SCs, women and other marginalised sections.

The Teacher Education scheme envisages setting up of DIETs in each district to provide academic and resource support of elementary education teachers and non-formal and adult education instructors. It also envisages establishment of CTEs/IASEs to organise pre-service and in-service training for secondary teachers and provide extension and resource support service to secondary schools. IASEs are expected to conduct programmes for preparation of elementary teacher educators; conduct in-service training for elementary and secondary teacher educators and principals of secondary schools; engage in advanced level fundamental and applied research especially of inter-disciplinary nature; and provide academic guidance to DIETs and support services to CTEs. 448 DIETs, 76 CTEs and 34 IASEs have been established under the scheme till the end of January 1999.

Some areas-specific externally aided projects in the field of primary education are also being implemented. Shiksha Karmi Project (SKP) aims at universalisation and qaulitative improvement to primary education in remote and socio-economic backward villages of Rajasthan with focus on girls. It identifies teacher absenteeism as a major problem in primary schools and in inaccessible areas. Mobilisation and participation of the community to improve primary schools is an important feature of the project. Lok jumbish is an innovative peoople's movement for education. Bihar Education Project (BEP) is meant to provide education for all through people's mobilisation and participation. It is a basic education project which aims at bringing out qualitative improvement in the educational system and overall socio-cultural situation in Bihar.

Although special programmes have been taken up to improve upon specific deficiencies in the educational system, no strategies can succeed in achieving UEE without specifically addressing its gender and regional dimensions. Gender disparities are conspicuous in India. Recognising this gender bias, most programmes have specific components for ameliorating the condition of the girl child.

(ii) Adult Education

Literacy is an important tool for communication, learning and information. It is a virtual pre-condition for individual and national development. The National Literacy Mission represents a national and political commitment on the need to harness all social forces to achieve the objective of eradicating illiteracy and effecting a qualitiative change in the lives of the people. It has made it possible for the country to set a target to make 100 million persons in the age group of 15 to 35 years functionally literate in the foreseeable future.

The Total Literacy Campaign (TLC) is the principal strategy adopted by NLM for eradication of illiteracy in the country. The Literacy Campaigns are area-specific, time-bound, delivered through voluntarism, cost effective and outcome-oriented.

After completion of the TLC in a distruct, Post Literacy Programme (PLP) is launched to mop up the leftover illiterates and also to consolidate the gains accrued during TLC. This enables the neo-literates to develop abilities for self-learning and skill upgradation. A total of 450 districts have been covered by TLCs. Of these, 250 districts have moved into the Post Literacy phase.

The ultimate objective is to carry forward the literacy programmes in the district to the third phase of life-long learning which is conceived under the scheme of Continuing Education. In this final phase the Centre-based approach in a revitalised and restrengthened form is brought back to the centre-stage of adult education activities. The Continuing Education Centres would aim to create a learning environment in the villages and habitation which they serve. There would be opportunities here for addressing the residual non-literates and for providing neo-literates with Equivalency Programmes, Income Generation Programmes, Quality of Life Improvement Programmes and Individual Interest Promotion Programmes.

The NLM takes special care to emphasise linkages between literacy and life and in so doing provides enhanced opportunities for skill development and improved income generation. This attempt is operationalised through the scheme of Shramik Vidyapeeths. The basic idea behind the multi-dimensional or polyvalent education approach to the education of urban working community in Shramik Vidyapeeth is to meet the various inter-related needs of target groups which mainly constitute the socially and economically deprived sections of worker communities with specifically tailored programmes. This provides knowledge and imparts vocational and technical skills in an integrated manner. The programme helps in enhancing employment opportunities and supplementing their income.

The NLM also lays emphasis on involving voluntary agencies. Several of them have been provided with assistance to take up innovative programmes on adult education in various parts of the country.

The NLM also has set up 25 State Resource Centres which provide academic input, improved training practices and opportunities for creation of imaginative literature for neo-literates.

Under Adult Education Programmes 72.56 million persons have been made literate so far, 60 per cent of them are women; 22.40 per cent are SCs and 13.20 per cent belong to STs.

The NLM has a system of concurrent and external evaluation of literacy campaigns and post-literacy programmes by reputed research agencies in the field of social sciences.

According to the National Sample Survey Organisation (NSSO) the percentage of literacy has increased from 52 in 1991 to 62 in 1997 and projected at 64 for 1998.

The quantum jump of 10 per cent between 1991 and 1997 and 12 per cent between 1991 and 1998 thus compares extraordinarily favourable with the decadal trends of previous years which are at an average of 8.5 per cent since Independence. The urban-rural differential in literacy rates has also shown a marked decline of 4 per cent, this is faster than in any previous decade. The rise in female literacy between 1991 and 1997 has been 11 per cent whereas the male literacy rate has risen by 9 per cent. This is a tribute to the special emphasis laid by NLM on women's participation. With annual rate of literary growth of 2 per cent revealed by NSSO survey, India could be expected to touch sustainable threshold level of 75 per cent by 2005.

Although the literacy campaigns are being implemented with varying degrees of success, it is certain that remarkable progress has been achieved. The focus is now on the four low literacy Hindi-speaking States which together account for nearly 50 per cent of the total number of illiterates in the country. Now that the process has begun in these States as well, the goal of universal literacy appears closer.

Some of the spin-offs of TLCs have been improved enrolement at primary level; social empowerment of women; improvement in immunisation and acceptance of the small family norms and organised correction of superstitions and social evils. This has generated a great demand for adult education projects throughout the country.

The National Literacy Mission has undertaken a number of new initiatives in adult education. These include rigorous system of monitoring of literacy campaigns; transparent and more effective evaluations; sensitising Panchayati Raj representatives to ensure mass participation in literacy programmes and decentralising of financial and administrative powers to State Literacy Mission Authorities.

(iii) Secondary Education

Secondary Education which serves as a bride between primary and higher education serves a step towards preparation for higher and professional education. Socio-economic imperatives and initiatives taken during the Eighth Plan to provide learning facilities to school going children upto elementary stage, has necessitated that the perspective for Secondary Education Sector in the Ninth Plan would be, besides vocationalisation, substantial expansion of infrastructure, innovation in harnessing technology for improved teaching/learning and quality upgradation. This visualises the maximum expansion requirements of the secondary education infrastructure during the Ninth Plan without diluting the quality.

The schemes initiated during the Eighth Plan such as Vocationalisation, Improvement of Science Education, Computer Literacy, Educational Technology, special interventions for girls, Integrated Education of Disabled Children, etc. have been made fully functional during the Ninth Plan. Besides, applications of available communication technology to promote school education at all levels and in all areas figure prominently in the deficient and remote areas. For this, open learning system (Distance Education) has been emphasised.

The key issues in Secondary Education apart from access are quality, relevance, modernisation and diversification. The norms developed by the NCERT for standards of minimum facilities for schools are being provided. The concept of Minimum Levels of Learning is being extended to the secondary stage as well. Emphasis has been laid on programme in Value Education. Population Education and various newly emerging concerns such as Human Rights, Adolescence Education. Greater diversification and flexibility, proper education materials, capacity building in the schools to gradually eliminate the domination exercised by the public examinations are some of the aspects of modernisation of curriculum. The NCERT continues to play a nodal role in evaluation of textbooks from the standpoint of national integration and incorporation of core elements outlined in the National Policy on Education (NPE). More transparency and authenticity is being visualised as a part of examination reforms.

Teacher Education is being strengthened to provide quality pre-service and in-service training to secondary school teachers to update their competency and professional skills.

The thrust on Vocational Education is continuing to meet the increasing demand of skilled manpower in the context of chaning economic environment with globalisation and consequent induction of new and emerging technologies. Given the complexity and magnitude of the task a multi-pronged strategy has been adopted with multiple entry and exit options to vocational students. Almost 35 per cent of children drop out before reaching Class V and over 50 per cent reach Class VIII. Finally, only about 6 per cent reach the degree level and hence, intervention at each stage in the form of vocational education is necessary to enable the potential dropouts with some skills. The programme is being strengthened and expanded.

Kendriya Vidyalayas and Navodaya Vidyalayas are promoting excellence in education with a national identity throughout the country. Navodaya Vidyalayas have an added objective to provide opportunities to talented rural children particularly girls of deprived sections of the society. These schools are intended to become pace-setters of a nationwide programme of school improvement with innovation and experimentation.

The National Open School has been providing flexible life-related education through distance education mode to deprived and socio-econimcally backward sections of the society in the remotest parts of the country. It designs, develops and offers flexible courses at secondary/senior secondary stage and is equipped to meet the growing demand of those who find it difficult to attend full time school and the working people, who could not complete secondary stage. The major beneficiaries are women. SCs/STs and other deprived sections of the society. The technological advancement has increased its potential substantially.

The National Council of Educational Research and Training (NCERT) continues to provide major resource support to school education in the form of various experimental innovative programmes; to diversify and make qualitative improvements in secondary education and also reducing the burden of school bag. The NCERT textbooks have the unique distinction of being attractive and inexpensive. These books are widely adopted by schools throughout the country. 'Persons with Disability Act, 1995' has placed responsibility on the Government to ensure that every child with disability has access to free education until the age of 18 years. The integration of disabled children in the ongoing and evolving schemes is in progress to achieve additional coverage.

(iv) Higher Education

Higher Education has a crucial role to play in the process of progress and modernisation. There has been considerable expansion of higher education with its role for economic and social development. The expansion of the system has been affecting the quality to a great extent. The Government, during the year, has tried to focus upon the initiatives to address the quality issues in higher education.

There has been consistent efforts to improve upon the salaries and service conditions of University and College teachers so as to attract talents in the teaching profession. Accordingly, the recommendations of the Fifth Central Pay Commission were extended to the University and College teachers with further improvement and modifications in the scales suggested by the committee earlier set up by the UGC for this purpose. As a result, the expenditure on account of the salaries to Central University teachers increased over Rs. 300 crores during the year 1998-99. The Government also agreed to meet 80 per cent of the expenditure incurred by the State Government towards implementation of the improved pay scales, for a period of five years.

The country made significant contribution to setting up the world agenda for higher education in the twenty-first century. A high power delegation led by the Minister for Human Resource Development attended the UNESCO World Conference on Higher Education held at Paris between 5-9 October 1999. India's amendments to the World Declaration on Higher Education were highly appreciated by the Conference. One such accepted amendment said:

Ultimately, higher education should aim at the creation of a new society—non-violent and non-exploitative—consisting of highly cultivated, motivated and integrated individuals, inspired by love for humanity and guided by wisdom.

The Government took concrete measures to reform Higher Education and initiated steps for restructuring the UGC to achieve the purpose, during the year. A Task Force, headed by Prof. Amrik Singh submitted its report and has recommended amendments in the UGC Act so as to provide for wholetime members in the Commission, increase the penalty for running fake universities and awarding unrecognised degrees and make the laws more stringent, regulate the operation of foreign universities, encourage the setting up of self-financing institutions that could award degrees also and allow colleges and universities to determine the tuition fees within a broad policy framework and guidelines.

By the end of Ninth Plan it is expected that at the rate of 5.5 per cent compound rate of present growth there will be 8.5 per cent million students, and 10,000 colleges. Innovative initiatives have been taken up in the form of distance education to cater to the unprecedented expansion. It is expected that reforms initiated in Higher Education during the year would go a long way to meet the needs and challenges of the system in terms of quantity as well as quality.

(v) Technical Education

Technical Education which includes Management Education as well, is the main vehicle of social and economic transformation in the country. It is one of the most vital and significant components of the human resource development spectrum with great potential for adding value to products and services, for contributing to the national economy and for improving the quality of life of the common man. It has also been instrumental in making significant contribution to India's economic development by way of manpower production and relevant activities suiting to the needs of the industry and society and adapting to the vast changes in the global economy.

Background and Growth

The rapid industrialisation during the post-independence period witnessed phenomenal growth of technical education facilities in the country. The first three Five Year Plans were devoted to expansion of technical education to meet the growing demands for technical pesonnel at Diploma, Degree and P.G. levels. From the Fourth Five Year Plan onwards, emphasis was on the improvement of quality and standards of technical education. Apart from the Government Sector, involvement of private and voluntary organisations in setting up of Technical and Management Institutes helped in the expansion of the system. From 43 Polyteclynics with an intake of 3,400 students at the time of Independence, the number has grown to 1,128 Polytechnics with the intake of 1.90 lakh students in 1997. Similarly, the number of Degree level institutions and the corresponding intake figure rose from 38 and 2940 in 1947 to 552 and 1.36 lakh in 1997. 185 institutions today conduct P.G. courses in Engineering and Technology with an annual intake capacity of 16,800. Facilities for Doctoral Studies in Engineering, Technology and Applied Sciences have also been created in a number of Technical Institutions.

This quantitative increase had its repercussion on the quality of technical education. A mushroom growth of self-financing private Enginnering Colleges/ Technical Institutions in the country, particularly in the southern region was causing concern to the policy makers, throwing to the winds all norms and standards for ensuring quality technical education. Accordingly, AICTE which was an advisory body since 1945, was given statutory status with the introduction of AICTE ACT, 1987 with a view to the proper planning and co-ordinated development of technical education system throughout the country. The AICTE issued Regulations in October 1994 relating to grant of approval for starting new technical institutions, introduction of courses or programmes and approval of intake capacity of seats for the courses for programmes. These were subsequently amended in May 1997.

The technical education system was to enhance its coverage and accessibility suiting to the needs of organised as well as unorganised and rural sectors with its relevance to productivity. Several initiatives were taken to revamp the technical education system by modernising the laboratories, etc. in technical institutions, promoting industry-institution interaction, providing continuing education for upgrading the skill and knowledge of technical personnel working in industry and services sector, transfer of technology to the rural sector and setting up of Technology Development Missions to meet the emerging challenges in the field of engineering and technology with active participation of industries. A major project was undertaken with the assistance of the World Bank to upgrade the technician education system for enabling the Polytechnics to improve their capacity, quality and efficiency. The scheme of Community Polytechnics was launched that aims at sustainable community development without environmental degradation by way of science and technology applications for socio-economic uplift and improvement in the quality of life of the common man through micro-level planning and people's participation at the grassroot level. The scheme lays stress on poverty alleviation, employment generation and removal of drudgery for the women through location-culture specific non-formal need-based short-term training in skill oriented technical/vocational trades.

To upgrade the Technician Education System in the Polytechnics, in the terms of capacity, quality and effiiency, a massive World Bank aided State Sector Project was launched in two phases starting in 1990. The fall-out of the project created increase in women's participation in Technician Education from 12 per cent to 27 per cent through establishment of new Women's Polytechnics and Women's Wings in the existing Polytechnics. To render the benefits of techno-economic advances in Technical Education towards rural/community development, the scheme of Community Polytechnies with Extension Centres are functioning all over the country today including hilly, desert, coastal, remote, difficult and minority concentrated areas. Meaningful and relevant Apprenticeship Training is being provided under the apprentie Act, 1961 (amended) to a large number of Engineering Degree, Diploma and 10+2 (Vocational) Passouts to bridge the gap between the world of Academics and the Industry and to help them achieve better employment prospects.

Development of appropriate technical manpower with assured quality in technology and management areas, was sought to be achieved through establishment of six Indian Institutes of Technology and six Indian Institutes of Management at different places in the country. Two specialised institutes with flexible academic design and non-conventional modular courses at Certificate, Diploma and Degree levels in Engineering/Technology/Applied Sciences, viz. (i) North Eastern Regional Institute of Science and Technology (NERIST), Itananagr, Arunachal Pradesh and (ii) Sant Longowal Institute of Engineering and Technology at Village Longowal, Sangrur, Punjab were also set up for appropriate manpower development in technical areas. An Institute for Information Technology and Management for development of specified technical manpower in the emerging area of Information technology has also been set up at Gwalior.

It may thus be seen that India has a large infrastructure of technical institutions spread all over the country which qualitatively and quantitatively can compete with the best available facilities in the world. The Indian Institutes of Technology (IITs) are premier centres of Education and training in engineering and applied sciences at under-graduate level and provide facilities for post-graduate studies and research. Indian Institutes of Management (IIMs) have been functioning as centres of excellence with the objective of providing education, training, research and consultancy in management. Indian Institute of Science, Bangalore has earned recognition as centre of research in basic and engineering sciences and allied fields. Excellence and creativity in research and development and learning programmes have characterised academic activity of the Institute. The Institute has also set up Super Computer with an Internet Hook-up.

The National Policy on Education has laid emphasis on modernisation and removal of obsolescence of laboratories and workshops of engineering colleges and polytechnics in order to enhance functional efficiency. The scheme covers IITs and Regional Engineering Colleges (RECs) and other Engineering Colleges, Technical Faculties of Unversities and Polytechnics.

Priority is being given to bring industrial commercial system and institutions closer. Technology missions in seven identified generic areas of strategic significance have been set up on the basis of their relevance to the Indian economy through IITs and IISc. These missions have earned wide acceptance and confidence among industries for development and know-how transfer of various technologies/products by them and as such a unique example of industry-institute partnership have been established. The technical education system is vibrant even in the remote areas of North East (including Sikkim), Andaman & Nicobar Islands, Jammu & Kashmir and the Union Territories of, *inter alia*, Daman and Dadra & Nagar Haveli. Towards promotion of overall societal development in such areas through technological inputs, expansion of technical education facilities is always encouraged through establishment of newer technical institutions and strengthening of the existing ones through all sorts of academic, technical and managerial support, co-operation and guidance.

As such, while we have higher level technical institutions like (i) I.I.T. Guwahati, (ii) NERIST, Itanagar, (iii) R.E.C., Silchar and scores of Diploma level Polytechnics in the North East, the Union Territories of Delhi, Chandigarh and Pondicherry offer high quality technical education through Degree and higher level technical institutions as well as Diploma level Polytechnics which are there even in the other UTs of A&N Islands, Daman and Dadra & Nagar Haveli. The State of J&K does not lag too far behind with one Regional Engineering College at Srinagar, one Government College of Engineering and Technology at Jammu and a large number of Polytechnics in the State.

In spite of this massive and cumulative build-up of a diverse infrastructural base, technological capability and institutional growth stand threatened from the sudden and complex change in the industrial base of the country and the advent of global competition in the wake of economic liberalisation.

To face new challenges the thrust during the Ninth Plan is envisaged on the following four dimensions:

1. Sustaining and consolidating the infrastructures and initiative with visible gains developed during the Eighth Plan and expanding the scope of such infrastructures for additional gains.
2. Strengthening system of management and governance at all levels, networking between institutions and developing effective new linkages.
3. Introducing new and innovative schemes which shall enhance the vibrancy of the system and help it conform to the emerging demands of industrial growth and societal development in terms of new technologies as well as quality enhancement.
4. Expanding the research base amongst technical institutions to effectively tackle the industrial problems related to product, process and technology developments and also the manpower need.

(vi) Monitoring and Evaluation

Under the scheme of Teacher Education it has been decided to undertake an assessment of the technical and infrastructural capacity of DIETs with a view to critically assessing the adequacy and quality of various training resource functions being carried out and to recommend immediate and long-term actions aiming towards strengthening of capacity of DIETs thereby enabling them to discharge their critical functions as nodal district level training institutions and as a vital link in achieving the national goal of Universalisaton of Elementary Education.

The first in-depth review of District Primary Education Programme generally commended the progress of programme implementation and has observed that the impact of DPEP on the entire Primary Education system is visible. There has been increase in enrolment in the DPEP districts, gender and social inequities have been substantially reduced and preliminary signs of increased learning achievements are in evidence.

In the scheme of Vocational Education, a network of external agencies have been used for the evaluation of the scheme on a state-wise basis.

The National Literacy Mission (NLM) has a system of concurrent evaluation by which each literacy campaign district is subject to external evaluation by the end of the Project. The NLM has identified agencies capable of undertaking external evaluation. Efforts have been made to provide substantive funding for strengthening the programme of modernisation and removal of obsolescence in order to upgrade the infrastructural facilities and thereby improving the overall quality of Technical Education all over.

2. CULTURE

(i) Archaeological Survey of India

The Archaeological Survey of India (A.S.I.) was established in 1861. It functions as an attached office of the Department of Culture, Ministry of Human Resource Development. Under the Ancient Monuments and Archaeological Sites and Remains Act of 1958, the Archaeological Survey of India has declared 3601 monuments to be of National importance in the country. In the last 136 years of its existence, the A.S.I. has grown from a humble beginning to a large organisation with an organised work force at the base and the Director General at the apex. With the passage of time, its major activities have expanded manifold to include *inter-alia*:

- Maintenance, Conservation and Preservation of Centrally protected monuments/sites;
- Conducting archaeological explorations and excavations;
- Chemical preservation of monuments and antiquarian remains;
- Architectural survey of monuments;
- Development of epigraphical researches;
- Setting up and re-organisation of site museums;
- Training in Archaeology; and
- Creating awareness of the heritage of the country.

The A.S.I. takes up nearly 500 monuments annually for special conservation, preservation and environment development apart from executing routine annual maintenance on the monuments under its charge. Besides taking up conservation work on unprotected monuments as deposit work, it also provides assistance for the conservation of the unprotected monuments.

Another important assignment of the A.S.I. is archaeological exploration, surveys and scientific excavations in the country. New sites are being explored and excavations are carried out strictly in accordance with archaeological principles.

The A.S.I. is running a two year graduate diploma course in its Institute of Archaeology where young archaeologists are imparted practical and theoretical training in the multifarious discilines in the field of archaeology. This is the only institution in the country where extensive training in archaeology is imparted.

(ii) Museums

Indian Museums and Art Galleries are the repository of the nation's valuable treasures. The Department of Culture feels that they play a positive and important role in moulding people's tastes and making them aware of the history and creative talent available in India. The emphasis in the Ninth Plan, therefore, is to overcome generally held perceptions that the Museums are only the 'store-house' of curiosities. We are striving to change the Museums into multi-cultural complexes engaged in promoting art, education, research and appreciation.

At present the Department of Culture administers four general Museums of national importance. These are: the National Museum, Delhi; The Indian Museum, Calcutta; the Salar Jung Museum, Hyderabad and the Allahabad Museum. In addition, the Department also administers National Gallery of Modern Art, Delhi with a branch at Mumbai. The National Council of Science Museums, which is a group of 26 Science Centres and Science Museums also falls under the Department. The Victoria Memorial Hall, Calcutta, which is a period museum, also gets grants from the Department.

National Museum

The National Museum was set up in 1960 as a subordinate office under the Department of Culture. It began in 1949 at the Rashtrapati Bhawan when art objects, which returned from an exhibition in London, where put on display for the public. It later moved to an exclusive building. At present there are about 2 lakh works of art objects covering the last 5000 years of our heritage in the National Museum. The main activities of the National Museum are in the fields of Acquisition, Exhibition, Education, Public Relations, Publication and Conservation.

During the year, the National Museum undertook numerous activities in improving the displays and strengthening conservation activities. One of the major exhibitions organised by the Indian Museum was a special exhibition entitled Treasures of Indian Art: Germany's Tribute to India's Cultural Heritage which was inauguratedby the Hon'ble President of India on 14th August, 1998. The exhibition comprising 92 exhibits, was loaned for the first time ever from the collecton of the Museum of Indian Art, Berlin, State Museum Prussian Cultural Foundation. Coinciding with the six-week long exhibition a series of ancillary events was also organised at the National Museum in collaboration with the National Museum Institute, the Centre for Cultural Resources and Training and the Max Muller Bhavan.

National Gallery of Modern Art

The National Gallery of Modern Art (NGMA) was established in 1954 by the Government of India with the objective of developing and promoting modern art in India. It has acquired a unique place in the growing landscape of Indian art. It is a repository of contemporary visual art and has been implementing a number of schemes for strengthening its activities and spreading art education amongst the public. NGMA represents the evolution of changing art forms through the passage of time. At present the NGMA owns a permanent collection of more than 14,000 works of art, both Indian as well as Western modern art.

NGMA has a branch at Mumbai at the Sir Cowasji Jehangir Public Hall and is also in the process of acquiring Manikyavelu Mansion from the State Government of Karnataka for opening its branch at Bangalore.

NGMA has undertaken a number of exhibitions, lectures, seminars and general awareness programmes during 1998-99.

National Council of Science Museums (NCSM)

The NCSM which was set up in April, 1978 in Calcutta, is primarily engaged in the task of popularising science and technology through a wide range of programmes, and by establishment of science parks and science Museums through out the country. The NCSM is an autonomous organisation under the Department of Culture and has 26 constituent units. State Govts/UTs etc. Most of the recommendations of the Committee are proposed to be implemented during the year 1999-2000 in the programmes of Zonal Cultural Centres.

The Centre for Cultural Resources and Training (CCRT) is an autonomous organisation under the Department of Culture. The broad objectives of the Centre is to revitalise the education system by creating an understanding and awareness among students and teachers about the plurality of regional cultures in India and integrating this knowledge with school education in India.

Orientation courses and workshops are conducted for primary and high school teachers in various activities to provide a practical training in arts and crafts by the CCRT. During the period from April 1998, to Novemeber 1998, 1193 teachers and 1055 studnets were trained in 19 Workshops organized in and outside Delhi.

(iii) National Akademies and the National School of Drama

The three National Akademies, namely the Sangeet Natak Akademi (National Akademi for performing Arts), the Lalit Kala Akademi (National Akademi for Visual Arts), the Sahitya Akademi (National Akademi for Literary Arts) and the National School of Drama (a National training school for theatre) were brought together by interaction between them so as to create a concerted effort to promote these arts.

Sangeet Natak Akademi

The Sangeet Natak Akademi — the National Akademi of Music, Dance and Drama — an autonomous organisation funded by the Ministry of Human Resource Development, is devoted to the furtherance of the peforming arts of India. The Akademi seeks to achieve this by arranging performance by renowned veterans as well as by talented artists of the younger generation, through training programes, award of scholarships, documentation, etc. The Akademi also bestows honours annually on outstanding artistes in the field of performing arts.

The Akademi runs two teaching institutions — Kathak Kendra (New Delhi) and Jawaharlal Nehru Manipur Dance Akademi (Imphal) — for Training in Kathak dance and music and Manipuri dance and alied art). The Akademi also looks after the management of the Rabindra Rangshala in New Delhi.

Sahitya Akademi

The Sahitya Akademi was founded in March 1954 to promote the cause of Indian Literature and promote national integration through literature by way of publications, translations, seminars, workshops, cultural exchange programmes and literary meets organised all over the country. The Sahitya Akademi recognises eminent writers through Awards of 22 Indian languages for creative writings, 22 translation prizes, fellowships for distinguished contributions to literature, Bhasha Samman meant to promote peripheral languages, the Ananda Coomaraswamy Fellowship for South Asian scholars and Honorary fellowships for foreign scholars who have done significant work in Indian literature. The Akademi publishes books in 22 languages and has three journals — Indian Literature (in English), Samakalena Bharatiya Sahitya (in Hindi) and Samskrita Pratibha (in Sanskrit). Besides, it holds various literary programmes in different parts of the country.

Lalit Kala Akademi

The Lalit Kala Akademi (National Akademi of Fine Arts) was estalished by the Government of India at New Delhi in 1954, to promote and propagate an understanding of Indian Art, both within the country and abroad. The Akademi has regional Centres at Lucknow, Calcutta, Chennai and Bhubaneswar was well as a small office at Mumbai where it has set up Community Artists, Studios with workshop facilities in painting, sculpture, print making and ceramics. There is a similar studio centre at Garhi in New Delhi.

Since its inception, the Akademi has been organising National Exhibitions of Contemporary Indian Art during which 10 National Awards, each of Rs. 25,000 are awarded. Special exhibitions are also organized every three years. The Akademi organises Triennale India, an International exhibition of contemporary art at New Delhi.

To propagate Indian art, the Akademi participates in International Biennales and Triennales abroad and also organises exhibitions of works of art from other countries. To foster contacts with artists abroad, it sponsors exchange of artists with other countries under the various Cultural Exchange Programmes and Agreements of the Government of India.

The Lalit Kala Akademi extends financial assistance to State Akademies and artists through prizes in exhibitions organized by them. The Akademi also brings out publications of art works and multi-colour reproductions and portfolios for sale.

From the Artists Aid Fund, Financial assistance is given to ailing artists.

(Iv) National School of Drama

The National School of Drama, one of the foremost theatre training institutions in the world, and the only one of it's kind in India was set up by the Sangeet Natak Academy in 1959. In 1975, it became an independent entity, fully financed by the Department of Culture, Ministry of Human Resource Development. Over the years, the School has made rapid strides on various fronts including a rapid expansion of its activities in all parts of the country. It has produced a galaxy of talents — actors, directors, script writers, designers, technicians, and educationists who work not only in theatre but also in films and television— winning several awards national and international.

Training in the Schools is based on a thorough comprehensive, carefully planned syllabus which covers every aspect of theatre in which theory is related to practice, and in which all work is ultimately put to test before the public. The syllabus takes into account the methods of great threatre personalities who have shaped contemporary theatre, in all its facets of expressional forms. The systematic study and practical performing experience in Sanskrit Drama, Modern Indian Drama, Traditional Indian theatre forms, Asian drama and western drama gives the students a solid grounding and a wide perspective in the art of theatre. In order to establish linkages between the traditional theatre forms of India and modern expressions, the School invites experts to train the students in these forms and also sends students to regional centres for training in traditional theatre. The School has also attached to its teaching faculty, some of the finest creative talents from within the country and abroad.

The National School of Drama has a faculty of 14 members. To provide a varied and wide ranging syllabus the school regularly invites professoors, theatre personalities and experts from India and abroad to supplement the teaching process. The school admits 20 students per year in the first year of the three-year diploma course. The selection is on an all India basis. All students admitted are awarded a scholarship of Rs. 2,000/- for meeting their academic and other expenses.

The School has a Repertory Company, which is the performing wing. It consists of a group of artists and technicians who are mainly alumni of the school. The Repertory Company staged 58 shows during the period.

(v) National Archives of India

The National Archives of India (NAI), an attached office under the Department of Culture, houses Central Government records of enduring value for permanent preservation and use by administrators and scholars. It has in its custody, private papers of eminent personalities of India and microfilm copies of records acquired from abroad. During 1998-99, regular programmes of the National Archives of India, viz. assisting various Ministries/Departments of the Government of India in their record management programmes, extending research facilities to scholars visiting the Department from all over India and abroad and providing financial assistance to various voluntary organisations for the preservation of manuscripts in their custody as also to State/Union Territory Administration Archives for their development programmes, etc. were carried out. It also continued to tender guidance to various Government Departments, voluntary institutions and individuals regarding technical know-how for preservation of valuable records and papers.

17

ENERGY (COAL, GAS, POWER AND PETROLEUM)

COAL

Coal Production

Coal production has grown by 4 per cent touching a record 296 million tonnes during 1997-98. This was stated by Coal Minister Dilip Ray while addressing the 17th meeting of the standing committee on safety in coal mines in New Delhi on May 20. The Minister informed the committee that Coal India Ltd. exceeded its targets while Southern Coalfields Ltd. saw a marginal shortfall in its targets, an official release said. The provisional profit of these companies is estimated at Rs. 1,400 crore and Rs. 100 crore, respectively. Coal off-take stood at 296 million tonnes during this period. Meanwhile, for the first time power stations nation-wide have a record stock of nearly 17 million tonnes, equivalent to over 25 days consumption per station, Mr. Ray said.

Coal production in the country is slated to increase by 74 million tonnes over the next five years and would touch 370 million tonnes by 2001-02, the Rajya Sabha was informed on July 13. Replying to supplementaries during question hour, Coal Minister Dilip Ray said that the increase in production is largely due to modernisation measures initiated by the government. He added that by the end of the Ninth Plan period the country would have a surplus of 12 million tonnes of Coal. Reorganisatiton of existing mines, introduction of modern technology and opening of new mines are some of the measures initiated by the centre, Ray told the House. Referring to the century-old fires in some coalfields in Jharia district of Bihar, the Minister said a study was being conducted by foreign experts and government would soon come out with measures to douse the blaze.

He said that 17 mining projects costing over Rs. 100 crore each are currently under implementation, of which 14 are in Coal India Ltd. (CIL) and two in Singreni Collieries Company Ltd. (SCCL). The Minister pointed out that Eastern Coalfields Ltd. (ECL) and Bharat Coking Coal Ltd. (BCCL) had accumulated losses worth about Rs. 2,700 crore till end of fiscal 1996. The two subsidiaries of CIL alongwith North Eastern Coalfield (NEC), a unit under direct control of the coal PSU, had incurred combined losses of Rs. 2,761.46 crore at the end of 1996-97, he said adding the annual accounts for 1997-98 of these undertakings were not yet audited.

India's coal production is expected to double at 600 million tonnes in the next decade, the Minister of State for Coal Mr. Dilip Ray, said on Oct. 11. To realise this impressive growth, optimum utilisation of modern tecnologies like

Geographic Information Services (GIS) and Global Positioning Systems (GPS) in all facets of mineral exploration was essential, he said. Inaugurating a workshop on 'GIS application in mining in industry', Mr. Ray said that sustained development of all facets of the coal industry was required for overall economic development of the sector. GIS was a sophisticated computer-aided facility and could play an important role in the mining industry in organising and storing large amounts of valuable data available in the form of paper media, the official statement said.

Sale of Coal in Open Market

The Centre is planning to kickstart retail distribution and open market sale of coal to clear inventories in coal companies. The centre is taking it up as a short-term measure, Union Minister of State for Coal Dilip Ray said. "We plan to sell coal through Open Sale Scheme and Localised Sale Scheme. We may start retail sales of coal to reduce stocks," Mr. Ray said. Besides, he said the coal companies are opening dumps in different parts of the country adding that 15 dumps would be opened to begin with. These are part of short term measures being contemplated by the Ministry to overcome huge stock pile-ups in coal companies, which is likely to affect their financial performance in the current fiscal year. In the first quarter of 1998-99, the lifting of coal is down by one million tonnes compared to last year.

ADB Aid for Coal Washeries

The Asian Development Bank (ADB) has decided to give the coal sector a loan of Rs. 675 crore for setting up to coal washeries in the country. The funding of $160 million by ADB is for purchase of plant and machinery an for development activities in nine coal washeries, an official statement said in New Delhi on Oct. 9. The ADB proposal for funding the coal sector is part of a Government plan to invest Rs. 3,546 crore for setting up 24 coal washeries by the year 2001-02. The Government has decided to establish new washeries to cope with the Ministry of Environment requirement for the use of washed coal of ash content not exceeding 30 per cent. The ADB has also sought private investment in coal washing and internalisation of environment costs by a properly enforced system of fees and fines reflecting economic costs of pollution.

These are the findings of a study carried out by ADB in conjunction with the Coal Ministry. The Ministries of Power and Environment and Forests too were involved in the study. The ADB recommendation has found favour with the Power Ministry. In its study, the ADB has advocated implementation of an economically-sound pricing system as a necessary precondition for attracting commercial investment in coal washing. The study holds the view that because of contractual complexities the build-own-operate (BOO) route for setting up washeries has not been found to be very satisfactory and that operation through the build-own-operate-transfer (BOOT) mode will have fewer complexities. It has also recommended that washed coal be used as such use would result in environmental benefits like reduced carbon dioxide and sulphur dioxide emissions along with cost cuts. The bank has also urged the Government to change the pricing of power station coal from Useful Heat Value (UHV) system to Gross Calorific Value (GCV) system. The Ministry of Coal has circulated the study recommendations of Ministries of Power and Environment and Forests.

Coal India to Invest Rs. 13,000 Crore

The Coal India Limited (CIL) will invest a whopping Rs 13,000 crore in 15 ongoing projects in the country in the Ninth plan period to raise the annual coal production from the present 251 million tonnes to 314 million tonnes, according to Minister of State for Coal, Mr Dilip Ray. The Company, which earned a profit of Rs 1,800 crore during 1997-98 againt Rs 1,100 crore in the previous year, would meet 60 per cent of the fund requirement from internal resources while a World Bank assistance of $1 billion would take care of the rest, Mr. Ray told a news conference. Six other projects, 3 taken up by the Neyveli Lignite Corporation and 3 by the Singareni Collieries Ltd. funded by the state government, were also under various stages of implementation, he said.

Privatisation of Coal Sector

The Cabinet decided on Feb. 17 to allow participation of domestic companies in mining and exploration of coal and lignite by amending the Coal Mines Nationalisation Act. Briefing the press after the Cabinet meeting, Minister for Information and Broadcasting Pramod Mahajan, said that following the passage of the Bill in Parliament it will only be private Indian companies which will be able to enter the hitherto closed sector of coal and lignite mining.

Mines which were nationalised in 1973 will continue to be under the public sector companies, he underscored. Mr. Mahajan ruled out allowing any international or multinational companies in the area of exploration of coal and lignite in the country. He said there would be no change on the nationalisation of the original mines. "The private companies will be allowed participation in mining of coal and lignite in new areas" Mr. Mahajan said adding the rules will be framed after parliamentary approval was given for the amendment in the act.

GAS

Natural Gas Prices

Natural gas prices became cheaper by Rs. 7 per 1000 Standard Cubic Metre (SCM) with effect from Jan.1, taking a cue from the continued downtrend in the global prices of fuel oil. Gas consumers like power, fertiliser and sponge iron plants, will pay Rs. 2215 per 1000 SCM for natural gas, if at a calorific value of 10,000 Kilo Calories per SCM. Since the Oil and Natural Gas Corporation (ONGC) and Oil India Limited's (OIL) gas fields yield a fuel with a calorific value of roughly 9000 Kilo Calories, the effective price for the consumer will be Rs. 1993 per 1000 SCM. The concessional price for gas guzzling industries in the north-east is Rs. 1274 per 1000 SCM. The actual price will, once more be lower, since the calorific value of the Oil India gas is roughly 9000 kilo calories. The dip in gas prices, though marginal, now takes the effective consumer price down to almost the administered gas price levels prevailing three years ago. It is also very close to the Rs 2150 per 1000 SCM floor price fixed for consumers.

The partial decontrol of gas prices in September last year allows gas to be priced within a range of Rs. 2150 per 1000 SCM and Rs 2850 per 1000 SCM. Since then, gas prices only came close to the ceiling once in January. The 12 per cent increase in natural gas prices for the January to March quarter, after the nearly 20 per cent hike in the previous three months, resulted in a selling price of Rs. 2411 per 1000 SCM (for gas of 10000 kilo calories per SCM). The worldwide tumble in oil prices since, resulted in a crash in fuel oi' prices and natural gas has cost less every three months since then. Natural gas prices slide by nearly six per cent in the April to June quarter, dropping to Rs. 2271 per 1000 SCM. Since then gas prices have knocked off a few rupees at every quarterly revision.

GAIL Plan for Longest Pipeline

The Gas Authority of India Ltd (GAIL) is contemplating the world's longest LPG pipeline, traversing 1,250 km, connecting Kandla in Jamnagar to Lone, near Delhi GAIL Chairman C.R. Prasad said on Jan. 12. "With rising demand for Compressed Natural Gas (CNG) pipeline is the most viable means of transporting it," he tole the Petrotech conference in New Delhi. Plans were also afoot to lay pipelines in the east and south India, to connect ports and refineries, Mr. Prasad said, noting that this ensured both safety and movement of the product. At present, piped gas was supplied in parts of Mumabi and Delhi as well as Ferozabad area of Agra, he said. Natural gas would take on greater importance in the future from the environment point of view. To meet the country's vast needs of an additional 80 million cubic metres of natural gas, he said the international pipelines were the only solution.

POWER

SERCs in All States

All the states will have State Electricity Regulatory Commission (SERCs) by the year 2000 AD for fixing the power tariff for their respective states. This was announced by the Power Secretary, Mr V.K. Pandit, while inaugurating a seminar on "India Power agenda beyond 2000" organised in New Delhi on Sept. 8 by the Associated Chambers of Commerce and Industry (ASSOCHAM). According to Mr. Pandit 10 states would have already established the SERCs by March end 1999. The Centre has this kind of feed with it, Mr. Pandit pointed out. Referring to coal sector in the context of thermal power generation, Mr. Pandit suggested that this sector be opened up for private participation keeping in view the increasing clectricity demand in the country. "The power sector has to expand at a much faster pace and in view of the growing demand for fuel (coal) to generate electricity, the coal sector should be thrown open for private sector participation," the Power Secretary said.

He pointed out that demand for crude oil was likely to increase in the future and more blocks should be explored and used for meeting the requirements of the power sector. Mr. Pandit said technology upgradation and large scale research and development activities should be stepped up to cater to the growing demand for electricity. Speaking on the occasion Secretary to the Prime Minister's Office (PMO) N.K. Singh said. "A sensible policy for financing power projects in the medium term should be worked out so as to reap benefits of privatisation". A model framwork for financing power projects has to be framed and should state the debt: equity ratio structure for public and private sector projects and the extent of External Commercial Borrowings (ECBs) that could be tapped by them, Mr. Singh said.

Mega Power Policy

The Union Cabinet, at a meeting on Oct. 30, cleared the mega power policy for creation of up to about 20,000 mw capacity through large projects which would be allowed duty free equipment imports, Power Minister P.R. Kumaramangalam said. Under the new policy, thermal power projects of 1,000 mw and hydroelectric projects of 500 mw would be promoted during the Ninth Plan period. A Power Trading Company (PTC) would be set up jointly by public sector power utilities—NTPC, NHPC and PGCIL, along with FIs to buy power from the mega projects, which in turn would be sold to State Electricity Boards (SEBs). The Cabinet also cleared a Rs 517-crore VRS for about 11,000 workers of eight sick PSUs identified by the Department of Heavy Industry for sell-off.

Six Mega Power Projects

The Union Power Ministry is planning to award contracts for six mega power projects to private power producers latest by March next year, stated the Union Power Minister, Mr P.R. Kumaramangalam, on Dec. 2. The Standing Independent Group (SIG), set up under the erstwhile United Front Government under the chairmanship of former justice P.N. Bhagwati, has already identified the projects to be taken under the proposed plan and is likely to finalise the names by the end of March next year, the Minister hinted. The Minister, who was addressing the World Economic Forum meeting, said that the proposed power projects would add a total capacity of about 7,000 mw. According to Mr. Kumaramangalam, as many as 27 private producers had evinced interest in the mega projects and the SIG is negotiating with them on tariff and other related issues.

Identified sites for the mega projects include Pipava in Gujarat, Krishnapatnam in Andhra Pradesh and Cuddalore in Tamil Nadu, the Minister pointed out. The SIG was also talking to various domestic and international financial institutions to make these projects bankable, Mr. Kumaramangalam said adding these projects are an 'indirect' form of counter-guarantee. The power generated by these mega projects would be taken by the Power Trading Corporation which would sell that to various state electricity boards. Mr. Kumaramangalam called on the foreign investors to invest in India as the potential for the power sector was growing at a faster pace and assured them good returns for their investments.

12-Year Plan to Ease Power Crisis

In a major announcement to meet the country's power requirements, the Centre on Nov. 6 introduced a 12-year plan title "Power Vision-2010" having a provision of *de facto* counter-guarantee for mega power projects. Presenting the plan for boosting power generation in the country, the Minister of Power, Mr. P.R. Kumaramangalam, said "the objectives of this policy are to develop mega sources of power utilising economies of scale with less efforts on project development and obtain lower tariffs, produce power at the most economical locations and transmit to needy areas and add capacity quickly to bridge the large deficits in power". "We will give power on demand by the year 2010 and put in place a national grid to improve supply", Mr. Kumaramanagalam said adding that the securitisation procedures to retrieve the coloss dues from the State Electricity Boards (SEBs) would soon be placed before the Union Cabinet.

The Ministry has also proposed access on generation to be used for power sector development as a part of its blueprint which has a target of capacity addition of 80,000 mw over the next 12 years besides creation of a transmission and distribution network, the Minister said. A Bill for cess would be introduced in the winter session of Parliament and it could be operational by the next Budget Session, Mr. Kumaramangalam said adding that two third of the collected money would be diverted to states for improving thermal power generation. The remaining one-third would be kept aside for development of hydel sector, he said declining to divulge full details of the proposed cess. The Minister further clarified that the earlier proposal of imposing a cess on consumer for hydel power development for 1997-98, registering a 28 per cent increase. This was decided at a meeting between the Deputy Chairman Planning Commission, Jaswant Singh and Chief Minister J.H. Patel in New Delhi. Briefing newspersons, Deputy Chief Minister Siddaramaiah said the 1998-99 annual plan would be financed by budgetary support of Rs. 3,522 crore and Internal and Extra Budgetary Resources (IEBR) of Rs. 1,831 crore. While the State will mobilise resources to the tune of Rs. 4,157 crore the Central plan assistance would be of Rs. 1,196 crore. Loans on small savings will be Rs. 750 crore and Nabard assistance for roads and irrigation works is expected to be Rs. 357 crore, he said.

With the 1998-99 annual plan being fixed at Rs. 5,353 crore, the State hopes to achieve almost 39 per cent of the Ninth Plan outlay of Rs. 23,400 crore (at 1996-97 prices) in the first two years, Mr. Siddaramaiah, who holds the finance portfolio said. Planning Commission officials said significantly the State would be permitted to draw additional funds from the Rural Infrastructural Development Fund (RIDF). Additional funds to the tune of Rs. 35.19 crore have also been provided to Karnataka this year under the Accelerated Irrigation Benefit Programme (AIBP). Deputy Chairman Planning Commission, Jaswant Singh assured the Chief Minister that after reviewing the performance of AIBP towards the end of this year the Commission might provide a fund of Rs 200 crore under that head. Mr Singh said the Commission was aware of the problems faced by the State in infrastructure development and finance management.

Deadline for Power Projects

The Prime Minister, Mr. Atal Behari Vajpayee, on Dec. 18 set a deadline of March 31,1999 for at least 10 power projects to complete all formalities (financial closure) and get off the ground. To achieve this, he suggested the creation of a crisis resolution group to resolve the so-called "last mile" problems holding up these projects. Addressing a meeting of the Chief Ministers on power in New Delhi on Dec. 18, the Prime Minister urged them to set up regulatory commissions soon as five months after the enactment of the Central legislation in this regard, only 10 State Governments were in the process of setting them up. He said the time had come to launch a national energy saving campaign. Later, briefing presspersons on the outcome of the meeting, the Minister for Power, Mr. Rangarajan Kumaramangalam, said the Chief Ministers decided that new initiatives were needed to push India's power sector into the next phase of reforms. Reforms in the power sector were essential to woo additional investments and improve the availability of reasonably priced power to the common man.

Consequently, the meeting decided that each State or Union Territory would constitute the regulatory commission before March next year and also announce a power sector reform policy and initiate steps to draw up appropriate legilsation to give effect to the policy. The meeting also decided that the States would endeavour to take steps to corporatise and commercialise power generating, transmission and distribution companies so that they are able to operate on commercial principles and generate the required resources and ensure availability of reasonably priced power to the common man. It was also decided to reform the power distribution system by establishing distributing companies in different regions of each State in a phased manner. The entry of the private sector would be encouraged wherever feasible. Each State would take steps to facilitate the setting up of mega power projects in accordance with Central Government guidelines.

The meeting decided that all States will adopt commerical arrangements like opening a letter of credit for the required amount to pay the generating companies and promptly settle all dues. As for the outstandings, the Power Ministry's proposal for an alternative scheme was discussed and the decision was that "State Governments will take steps to facilitate orderly securitisation of such debt." However, there were some differences on the amount of dues and it was decided that the States would reconcile their accounts first before going in for securitisation of outstandings. In case of the hydel power projects. Mr. Kumaramangalam said the proposed cess on power generation would be initiated once the Union Cabinet formally decided on the issue. Necessary legislation would then be introduced in Parliament, he added. Another important matter which came up at the meeting was the need to maintain the liability of the Railways and the State Electricity Boards. Consequently, it was decided that the States would rationalise railway traction tariff and the Railway Ministry would simultaneously look into the rationalisation of tariff on coal movement for power plants.

Limiting Subsidy on Power

Prime Minister Atal Behari Vajpayee on Jan. 17 hinted at limiting the subsidy on electricity to domestic and agricultural consumers across the country. Addressing a meeting at Kayamkulam (Kerala) after the commissioning of the first unit of Kayamkulam combined cycle power project, the Prime Minister said that his government would vigorously pursue tariff reforms in the power sector. Citing the massive losses being posted by State Electricity Boards (SEBs) and the heavy burden on industry as a result of cross-subsidisation, the Prime Minister said that the tariff would be restructed and rationalised, "It is my view that our farmers are willing to pay a reasonable tariff, provided they get assured, adequate and quality power" said the Prime Minister. He justified the limiting of the subsidy on power by citing the fact that the SEBs incur Rs. 6,000 crore losses annually.

The Prime Minister commissioned the first unit of 350 mw naphtha-fired power plant of central power utility, National Thermal Power Corporation (NTPC). The associated 220 KVA lines put up by the Power Grid Corporation of India Ltd. (PGCIL) were also simultaneously put into operation. Mr. Vajpayee pinpointed "excessive cross-subsidisation" as the major reason for the financial ill-health of SEBs. Overall inefficiency and poor realisation of bills, he said, were also responsible for things coming to a sorry pass. Mr. Vajpayee dwelt at length on his agenda for power reform, particularly about the need to end tariff-related subsidies and rationalisation of electricity rates. He said that only when all consumers pay their share, more capacities could be set up and states can access more power for industry and agriculture to enhance the pace of economic growth. He also asserted that non-conventional energy resources would be harnessed in a big way.

Crisis Group on Power Meeting

The Crisis Resolution Group (CRG) set up by Prime Minister Atal Behari Vajpayee for sorting out glitches in the power sector met for the first time on Jan. 13 amidst uncertainty over meeting the March 31 deadline to achieve financial closure in 18 projects. At the meeting spread over three hours, the NTPC and NHPC chairmen demanded that all the six projects that have been enlisted as mega power ventures be immediately notified and provided benefits, incentives and concessions accordingly. The bankers and FIs have been asked to commence disbursement of loans in cases where financial closure has been achieved, pending completion of documentation work. Escrow account cover far the private power projects came up for discussion at the CRG especially in states like Tamil Nadu and Madhya Pradesh. At this point, the SBI Chairman categorically stated that the bank has agreed to forego the first charge on revenues from SEBs allowing elbow room for the board to extend escrow cover for private power projects including the Videocon Power promoted 1050 mw and ST-CMS's Neyveli Lignite project envisaging a capacity of 250 mw. In the case of Madhya Pradesh, the CRG decided to wait for the verdict of High Court on the escrow cover. The High Court is expected to decide the issue in a day or two. The Maheshwar Hydroelectric Power Project being promoted by Soros Fund and S. Kumars is stuck for want of escrow cover owing to the high court case.

The CRG headed by Power Minister Rangarajan Kumaramangalam set about the task of sorting out the problems faced by state-owned power utilities and cooporates promoting these projects. Secretaries in the Ministries of Coal, Petroleum, Environment & Forests, Chairman of the Railway Board, Chiefs of SBI, IDBI, IFCI and PFC were present at the meeting that lasted for over two hours. Chairmen of the Central Electricity Authority (CEA), NTPC and NHPC were also present at the meeting of the CRG. The onus would be on NTPC to achieve financial closure as four projects at Anta, Auriya, Kawas, Gandhar with envisaged capacity addition of 650 mw each as well as 1,000 mw have been lined up for the same. NHPC's Chamera-II is expected to line up debt and equity funds by March 31.

9,000 MW Power Shortage

Power Secretary V.K. Pandit said on Feb. 3 that power capacity addition during the Ninth Plan period would fall short of the target by about 9,000 mw due to procedural delays and fiscal constraints. The total capacity addition during the Ninth Plan would be 31,000 mw as against the targetted 40,000 mw, Mr. Pandit said while delivering a lecture on the occassion of the platinum jubilee of Railway Electrification. "The public sector would add a total capacity of about 24,000 mw while the private sector was expected to generate about 5,000 mw to 7,000 mw duirng the plan," he said adding the shortfall would be mainly due to fiscal constraints and procedural and implementation delays.

To attain and sustain seven per cent GDP growth rate, the power sector must grow at 10 per cent per annum as against the present level of three to six per cent, he said. The major problem facing Indian power sector was the financial ill health of various State Electricity Boards which were incurring huge losses, Mr. Pandit added. "SEBs were inefficient, lethargic and unresponsive," he said adding their accumulated losses have reached a whopping Rs. 22,650 crore.

Huge subsidies and excessive transmission and distribution losses were the main reasons for the poor financial health of these SEBs, he said.

Renewables to Add 1,500 MW Power

Additional power generating capacity of 1,500 mw would be created from renewables in the country during the Ninth Plan, C.R. Kamalanathan, Secretary, Mines, said on Feb. 2. This is based on reduced Budgetary support indicated for the plan," he said. Greater thrust was being given to commercialisation of the sector in the Ninth Plan (1997-2000), Mr. Kamalanathan told a seminar on 'Photovoltaic Technoloy in India and Japan'. Under the solar energy programme, 1.25 lakh solar hot water systems and quarter million square meters of solar collectors area is expected to be installed in homes and commercial establishments and industry respectively. Further, solar photo-voltaics capacity of 70 mw would be added including five lakh solar lanterns, 1.5 home lighting systems and 5,000 solar pumps. Mr. Kamalanathan said renewable energy was expected to play in key role in accelerating development and sustained growth in the second half of the next century accounting for 50 to 60 per cent of the total global energy supply.

Fossil fuels will reach their maximum potential by 2020-2050 and their price will become higher than that of renewable energy, he said. Mr Kamalanathan said challenges in the energy sector were daunting in terms of increasing demand, supply constraints, capital requirement and environmental aspect. The demand for electricity was growing at the rate of eight per cent, which required capacity addition of about 8,000 mw per year during the Ninth Plan and 12,000 mw during the Tenth Plan. The per capital consumption of electricity was only 350 kwh per annum. Only one-third of the total electricity supply was consumed in rural areas despite three fourths of the population.

State Power Boards

A whopping 69 per cent of industrial units across the north find the supply of electricity insufficient. The shortfall is between 15 and 50 per cent in some cases even more. These figures were the result of an annual survey by the PHD Chamber of Commerce and Industry (PHDCCI) on infrastructure in Punjab, Haryana, Himachal Pradesh, Uttar Pradesh, Rajasthan, Jammu and Kashmir, Delhi and Chandigarh. The survey was carried out to analyse reasons for deficient infrastructure which hampers routine operations besides discouraging investments. It covered power, fuel, water, transport and communications.

Almost 80 per cent of respondents found the quality of power unsatisfactory. Seventy-three per cent said the average frequency of tripping was upto 10 times a day, in the remaining cases it was even higher. Such irregularity in power supply adversely affects businesses. Depending upon the size of the unit, the loss of production ranges from Rs. 10 to Rs. 20 crore per annum. Capacity is under-utilised by 20 to 30 per cent and sometimes even upto 40 per cent. The attitude of State Electricity Board officials towards consumers has been rated by more than 50 per cent of respondents as bad or poor. Unannounced load-shedding and illegal tapping of power by slums and unauthorised commercial complexes are also matters of concern. To keep their industrial units running almost all respondents are forced to rely on standby sources such as generator sets.

PETROLEUM

New Exploration Policy in Force

The New Exploration and Licensing Policy (NELP), now pending for 22 months since it was first announced in Parliament in February 1997, becomes effective at last. The last hitch in offering the package of fiscal sops to oil exploration companies has been cleared now with the Ministry of Law accepting the Petroleum Ministry's interpretation of Section 42 of the Income Tax Act. Union Petroleum Minister Vazhapadhy K. Ramamurthy told newspersons on Dec. 24 that the Petroleum tax guide, the model production sharing contract, the notice inviting offers and other documents had been finalised. The Minister announced a series of New Year resolutions, including roadshows for 48 exploration blocks that are being offered as part of the NELP, by the last week of January. He also hinted at a roll-back of some of the subsidy on Liquefied Petroleum Gas (LPG) and resolved to keep the subsidy on kerosene.

The Minister hinted at a reduction in diesel prices in the New Year. Petroleum Secretary T.S. Vijayaraghavan explained that diesel prices could not be brought in parity with international rates so long, because of the frequent fluctuations in oil prices. Diesel prices were last revised in May. "There is no going back on the Administered Price Mechanism (APM)," Mr. Ramamurthy said firmly, adding, "except on subsidy on kerosene." The roughly 40 per cent subsidy of kerosene and LPG was scheduled to be rolled back in phases, beginning April, till only 15 per cent subsidy remained on LPG and 33 per cent on kerosene by the year 2002. The subsidies, that now come from the oil pool account, were to be passed on to the Union Budget then. The BJP-led coalition government, however, decided to skip the subsidy roll-back scheduled for this fiscal.

Joint Ventures for Oil Exploration

The Government will permit national oil companies to set up joint ventures for exploration in India as part of a new strategy to be announced soon, the Petroleum Minister, Mr. V.K. Ramamurthy, said in New Delhi on Jan. 9. "This programme will set into motion a new initiative where exploration risks, managerial efficiency, application of modern technologies and attendant benefits would be shared between national oil companies and joint venture partners," Mr. Ramamurthy said. Addressing Petrotech-99, organised by the Indian Oil Corporation, the Minister said to supplement the efforts of the oil companies in the upstream sector downstream oil companies had been allowed to invest in both production and exploration in India and abroad. "To meet the country's fast increasing demand for hydrocarbon and reduce the dependence on imports, there is a need to accelerate efforts on the upstream front," he said. Mr. Ramamurthy said an effort of such dimension required capital, technology, and managerial skills of high order which would come through internatinal cooperation. A close interaction between the Government and industry, he said, was essential to ensure that exploration and production efforts were not dictated by merely short-term profit considerations but by the need for a sustainable growth. The New Exploration Licensing Policy (NELP) would offer a total of 48 exploration sites of which 10 would be onshore, two offshore and 12 deep water blocks.

No Plan to Privatise Oil Companies

The Government has no intention of privatising any of the oil sector companies, including the Oil and Natural Gas Corporation and Oil India Limited, the Petroleum and Natural Gas Minister, Mr. K. Ramamurthy informed the Lok Sabha on Dec. 2. "I say here on behalf of the Government that it has no intention of privatising any of the oil companies," Mr. Ramamurthy said in an intervention during a discussion on the Oilfields (Regulation and Development) Amendment Bill, 1998. The Bill seeks to replace the Oilfields (Regulation and Development) Ordinance 1998 promulgated by the President on Sept. 3, 1998. Earlier, moving the Bill the Minister said that demand had overtaken indigenous production and the country was dependent on imports to the extent of 54 per cent for crude and other petroleum products. Among other things, the Bill seeks to confer upon the Central Government the powers to notify more than one rate of royalty in respect of the same mineral oil produced from different classes of leased areas.

It also seek to empower the Government to grant partial or full exemption from the payment of royalty in respect of offshore areas and make consequential amendments for laying the notifications before Parliament. Mr. Ramamurthy said the Government had approved the new exploration licensing policy to encourage exploration of oil and natural gas. Participating the discussion, some Opposition members were apprehensive that there was scope for misuse by giving away too much authority to the executive. Mr. Satyapal Jain (BJP), supported the Bill and observed that there was no scope for misuse. He said the measure would boost exploration of oil and natural gas. Mr. T.R. Balu, DMK, who was the Petroleum Minister during the United Front Government, gave details of the seismic surveys conducted during his tenure and said huge deposits had been identified in the Andamans and several other areas.

IOC, ONGC Strategic Alliance

National Oil giants ONGC and Indian Oil Corporation have entered into a strategic alliance in which they will offer each other the right of first refusal in any new project that either of them takes up as a joint venture. The decision has come as a sequel to the 10 per cent cross-holding in each other's equity that the two oil companies will now come to have following the Cabinet clearance. Each of them will also have one director on the board of the other company. ONGC Chairman Bikas C. Bora and LOC Chairman M.A. Pathan told journalists today that the strategic alliance would result in "a national oil entity" that would have the characteristics of a vertically integrated oil major of global standing. Mr. Bora said that the alliance would help to pool the resources of both the oil majors to take on the competition of multinational companies and exploit opportunities abroad on the basis of their combined strength. While ONGC is engaged in the exploration and production of gas (upstream sector), IOC is an oil refining and marketing company (down-stream sector).

Mr. Pathan said while retaining the focus on respective core business and competencies both Indian Oil and ONGC would explore investment options for securing assured growth and profitability. Mr. Bora and Mr. Pathan further stated that the strategic alliance would operate through project-wise joint ventures constituted as non-government companies. Mr. Bora disclosed that several upstream opportunities in India and abroad have been identified where IOC can come in with ONGC. Mr. Pathan in turn said that IOC "is inviting ONGC participation in several ventures in refining, power generation and petrochemicals. On specifics. Mr. Bora talked about joint participation in under the New Exploration Licensing Policy (NELP) including deep waters as well as in exploration and production ventures in Central and South Asia. Mr. Pathan pointed out that the IOC refinery project in South India, power project at Panipat and Gujarat refineries, petrochemical project at Panipat and marketting and consultancy services abroad have been identified in addition to shipping and offshore services.

Both Mr. Bora and Mr. Pathan expressed the view that "today's global oil business favours big organisations with financial strength and capability to withstand competition and absorb price volatility. In the recent past oil majors in the world have been opting for alliances, mergers and acquisitions. The petroleum industry of tomorrow is heading towards smaller number of players and strategic alliances among survivors. Under the new strategic alliance ONGC would be spending around Rs. 1,600 crore for a 10 per cent stake in IOC while the latter will be shilling out about Rs. 2,600 crore for 10 per cent of the former. The exact amount would depend on the exact price of the shares of each company that the government decides to fix.

IOC, US Firm for Oil Exploration

Public Sector Indian Oil Corporation has signed an agreement with the US oil company Premier and is negotiating with Malaysian Petronas to jointly bid for oil blocks uner the New Exploration Licensing policy. "We have already signed an agreement with Premier Oil to bid for the blocks in the north-eastern region. We are still negotiating with Petronas for others," IOC Chairman M.A. Pathan said. The corporation is awaiting government approval for the agreement with Premier Oil. IOC is also open to form joint ventures on successful bidding for the new blocks, he said adding that these would be on equal footing. Asked about the deep sea blocks, Mr. Pathan said that IOC would limit its exposure in this arena as it did not have the requisite expertise. "We will prefer to be minority partners here," he added.

Oil and Natural Gas Corporation Chairman Bikas C. Bora said that his corporation was also negotiating with four global oil companies, including three from the US to jointly bid for the new blocks. The government is starting road shows globally from January 22 for 48 onshore, offshore and deep sea blocks under the NELP that promises a host of fiscal incentives. "We are going for deepwater exploration and ONGC is talking to multinationals like Mobile, Shell, Petronas and Unocal for jointly bidding for these blocks," Mr. Bora said. ONGC and the selected partner would initially set up an unincorporated company that could be converted into joint venture in case of discovery of oil, he said. Mr. Bora said the funds for exploration of blocks would not be a constraint as the corporation has enough internal resources to fund these ventures. ONGC has cash reserves of over Rs. 3,500 crore, Mr. Bora said. In case of joint ventures, Indian Oil and the two multinationals would have a 26 per cent stake each in the two new companies with the rest being offered to financial institutions and the public.

MNCs Keen on Oil Exploration

Leading multinationals in oil sector like Enron Corporation, Unocal, Total. British Gas and Marubeni have shown keen interest in bidding for oil exploration blocks to be offered under the New Exploration Licensing Policy (NELP). As many as 200 participants, including 45 international oil majors and national companies, on Jan. 22 participated in the roadshows for the 48 blocks to be offered by the Government. Out of these 48 blocks, 12 selected on the basis of surveys in the East Coast are situated in deep waters. The roadshows for these blocks started here and similar exercises would be repeated in London, Houston, Calgary and Singapore. Roadshows in London are scheduled for Jan. 27 and 28 while the same in Houston would be from Feb. 1 to 3.

The Calgary roadshow would be on Feb. 9 and 10 followed by Singapore on the 11th and 12th. Indian companies like Reliance, L&T, Indian Oil and ONGC participated on Jan. 22 roadshow. Earlier, Petroleum Minister V.K. Ramamurthy said the fiscal and contractual packages provided under the NELP were globally competitive. "The NELP provides tax holidays for seven years after the commencement of commercial production and there would be no customs duty on goods imported for petroleum operations," he said. State Minister for Petroleum and Natural Gas Santosh Kumar Gangwar said that the Government had already sent notices inviting offers from both the domestic as well as overseas oil majors for oil exploration. The notices were sent on the 8th of this month and the last date for the receipt of the bids under the offer has been fixed as 18th May, 1999. The purpose of the roadshows is to create an awareness about the investment climate and also to inform the participating companies about the initiatives taken by the Government in the oil sector.

Technical presentation were made during the roadshow here in which features of the NELP were explained in great details. NELP provides several fiscal incentives which includes no up-front payments like signature, discovery or production bonuses, nominal rates of royalty chargeable upto 12.5 per cent on *ad valorem* basis and no custom duties on goods imported for petroleum operations. There will be no mandatory state participation and the cess on crude oil has been abolished and there will be complete freedom for marketing oil and gas in the domestic market, he said.

Eighteen Oil Exploration Blocks Awarded

The Government has decided to sign production sharing contracts for 18 oil exploration blocks covering an area of around 50,000 square km with 16 private companies, five of which belong to the US, one each to Australia and Ireland while nine are Indian. According to an official statement on May 15, the Petroleum Ministry issued letters on May 14 to these companies to convey the Government's decision and the firm proposals for signing the contracts. The finalisation of the contracts is expected to bring in $40 million in investment including $25 million of foreign investment in the first phase itself. Clearly the Vajpayee Government has got into action to lure as much foreign investment as it possibly can, in order to counter the climate of uncertainty that has been created by the announcement of economic sanctions by most of the developed countries led by the US and Japan.

Sources disclose that the Government expects the profit incentive to foreign capital to go a long way in neutralising the effect of the economic sanctions that have been imposed in the wake of the nuclear tests at Pokhran. The companies that have been awarded the contracts include Okland Oil Company, Samson International, Opesis and Medallion Oil Company, all from the USA. Command Petroleum of Australia and the Irish Company Tullow Oil Plc are the other foreign companies to have been conveyed the firm proposal for signing the contract. Prominent Indian companies that have been awarded the contract include Essar,

Larsen and Tubro, Tata Petrodyne, Videocon, Hindustan Oil Exploration Company and Assam Oil Company.

Crude Production from Discovered Oilfields

The crude production from discovered oilfields allotted to the private sector nearly doubled last year to 2.47 million tonne from 1.34 million tonne in 1996-97, just as industry leader Oil and Natural Gas Corporation's (ONGC) yield from its much-flogged oil well's began to stagnate. Even as oilfields operated by private sector oil companies and their joint ventures with national oil companies showed an 84 per cent growth in output, ONGC's production dropped marginally by 1.5 per cent to 28.24 million tonne from 28.68 millon tonne the year before. The drop in oil output was particularly evident in ONGC's offshore fields, at which efforts have begun to arrest the decline in crude production.

The public sector company, which accounts for 88 per cent of the country's crude output, produced 19.86 million tonne of oil at its offshore fields in 1997-98, compared to 20.18 million tonne the year before. Onshore, ONGC's output dipped gently to 8.38 million tonne from 8.50 million tonne in 1996-97. Oil India Limited's output went up by eight per cent to 3.10 million tonne last year, from 2.87 million tonne the previous year. Higher output from Oil India and the oilfields allocated to the private sector increased the total crude output of the country to 33.86 million tonne last year from 32.9 million tonne in the year before. The million tonne jump in output actually came from the unincorporated joint ventures and other private sector operated oilfields. The five medium-sized oilfields and 15 small-sized fields offered to private sector companies in August 1992, first reported 6.5 lakh tonne of crude production in 1995-96.

Oil, Gas Strike in Bombay High

Oil and Natural Gas Corporation (ONGC) and Oil India Ltd. (OIL) have struck gas and oil in Bombay offshore basin and in the central part of the Upper Assam basin, repectively. According to an official release isssued in Mumbai on March 19, ONGC made a significant gas strike in B-105 prospect in Bombay offshore basin. The structure is located abour 34 km north-west of Bombay High field. In this area, as on date, four prospects have been probed, all of which have yielded gas. Total find is about 5-6 billion cubic meters.

The well was spudded on January 27, 1999, completed on March 6, 1999, and was drilled to a depth of 2,660 meters. Two interesting horizons have been identified—one in the Foegne formation where the pay zones are 27 meters thick, and the other in the value of the formation about a much of pay. All made a fairly large and promising discovery of oil in the Eocene sandstone reservoirs within the concession areas in central part of upper Assam basin in January 1999. This find affords possibilities of much brighter prospects in future and has given considerable impetus to OIL's exploration programme in new areas and already existing oilfields.

ONGC Oil Target

The Government has set a production target of 28.10 million tonnes of crude oil for the Oil and Natural Gas Corporation of India Ltd (ONGC) for the fiscal 1998-99. According to an MoU signed between the Ministry of Petroleum and Natural Gas and ONGC, the company has been asked to achieve sales of 18.54 BCM.

The indexing of prices of crude oil, natural gas and other products to international market with effect from April 1, 1998, will see a significant improvement in the company's profitability compared to last year's, an ONGC press release said. However, no details are available about the financial results of the oil major.

A high-powered committee, an independent body which evaluates the performance of Public Sector Undertakings (PSUs) vis-a-vis the MoUs they sign, has accorded a rating of 'excellent' to ONGC for its performance in 1996-97. On the basis of provisional data, the company hopes to repeat the performance for 1997-98, the release said. In line with the Government's policy for Navratna PSUs, ONGC has now stepped up its efforts on international operations by going for acreages over-seas.

Panipat Refinery by March 1999 End

After a delay of nearly one year, state-owned India Oil Corporations' (IOC) six million tonne refinery is expected to go on stream within the current financial year. However, there would be no cost overruns in the Rs 3,868 crore project, IOC Executive Director Surinder Singh Saini told visiting newsmen from Delhi. The company is also drawing up a Detailed Financial Report (DFR) to get clearance for its expansion project for enhancing its capacity to nine million tonnes a year, he said. "The project has been delayed due to the inability of contractors and suppliers to adhere to their schedule", Mr. Saini said. Even certain multinational corporations besides public sector and Indian private sector companies were responsible for the project going behind schedule, he said but ruled out any cost overruns due to the delay. "The contractors were chosen on the basis of their performance in earlier IOC projects and a databank maintained by Engineers India Limited (EIL). In future we will be more careful in selection, particularly for the expansion project", Mr. Saini said.

18

INDUSTRY

INDUSTRIAL POLICY REFORMS—DEREGULATION AND DELICENSING

Industrial Policy and Promotion

Major policy changes were initiated by the Department in July, 1991 to provide competitive stimulus for accelerated industrial growth. The thrust of the new policy has, therefore, been to provide free access to capital technology and markets in order to induce greater Industrial efficiency and international competitiveness. Domestic competition has been introduced by delicensing of industries and by liberalising the policy related to foreign direct investment. The new Industrial policy is also designed to enable entrepreneurs to take investment decisions based on commercial judgement with reduced regulatory role of the Government. The Policy initiatives have focussed on changing the basic orientation of industry to bench mark itself against global standards.

The process of reform was continued in 1997-98. Five more Industries were taken out from the list requiring a prior licence, viz. Animal fats & oils; Asbestos and asbestos based products; Chamois leather and tanned or dressed fur skin; Paper and newsprint and Entertainment electronics reducing the number of Industries requiring prior licence to only nine. Even in these nine Industries, it is the safety, security or environment requirements, and not the capacity regulation which was the prime guiding objective for continued licensing. Currently, less than 10 per cent of manufacturing activities require a prior licence. Sugar Industry was also brought almost at par with a delicensed industry as new capacities conforming to the guidelines were liberally permitted.

The response to the policy initiatives has been overwhelming as it has allowed the investment decisions to be made on commercial perception rather than for regulatory rent seeking. The policy initiatives have imparted perceptible buoyancy to new Industrial investments in all sectors. The total number of Investment Intentions received in the post policy period upto March, 1998 has been 36,045 with a projected investment of Rs. 7,10,958 crores.

REFORMS IN THE FDI POLICY REGIME

Foreign Direct Investment (FDI) Policy was considerably liberalised in 1996-97. The list of Industries where foreign equity participation of 51 per cent is permitted under automatic route was expanded to include 14 more Industry groups. In 9 industry groups the equity particiation upto 74 per cent is permitted on automatic basis. In mining sector, automatic foreign direct investment approval of 50 per cent was also introduced. For FDI which is not covered under the automatic route clearance through Foreign Investment Promotion Board (FIPB) has been in existence since 1991. FIPB was thoroughly revamped and transferred to Ministry of Industry in 1996-97. New guidelines have been issued regulating the working of FIPB. This has made the overall FDI approval system more accountable, transparent, efficient and expeditious. Further, the automatic approval list has been recast in terms of National Industrial Classification, 1987 to remove any ambiguity in classification of Industrial activity. A new Foreign Investment Promotion Council (FIPC) was also constituted to undertake promotional activities and established institutional contact with potential investors.

The New Industrial Policy and other economic reforms have catalysed foreign investment which is evident from the buoyancy in approvals for Foreign Direct Investment. The total amount of Foreign Direct Investment approvals was Rs. 530 crores in 1991 and Rs. 3,890 crores in 1992, increased to Rs. 8,860 crores in 1993 and further to Rs. 14,190 crores in 1994. In 1996, there was significant acceleration in the approvals. The overall approvals reached Rs. 36,150 crores. In 1997 total FDI approved reached Rs. 54,891 crores. Over 80 per cent of the approvals of FDI are in priority areas like power, oil refineries, electronic and electrical equipment, chemicals, food processing industries, telecommunications etc. The consumer industries sector, which attracts dividend balancing obligation accounts for only 11 per cent of total FDI approvals. Food processing, consumer electronics and passenger cars account for nearly 75 per cent of the approvals in this category. In the passenger car segment, some of the major investors, are envisaging indigenisation of over 70 per cent from the start of their production which indicates that even in these industries, domestic industries would immediately benefit by way of forward and backward linkages and additional employment creation.

With a view to improving technology levels in the Indian industry access to technology has been liberalised. Automatic approval is now available for foreign technology collaboration with the lumpsum payment upto US $ 2 millions and/or royalty payments within the stipulated limits. Nearly 40 per cent of the total foreign collaboration approvals are purely technical collaborations. The distribution of technology collaborations approved according to size of the proposed investment indicates that small and medium enterprises have taken considerable advantages of the technical collaboration route to obtain improved technology.

There has been continuous and steady increase in FDI inflows, though overall inflow to approval ratio is still around 0.22, which is due to the longer gestation period of many infrastructure and core sector projects. Overall infows during 1997 reached a level of US $ 3.44 billions as against US $ 2.42 billions in 1996.

INDUSTRIAL PERFORMANCE

Industrial growth after being moderate in 1991-93 increased to 9.4 per cent in 1994-95 and 12.1 per cent in 1995-96. However, since second-half of 1996-97 there has been moderate deceleration in the industrial growth. In the fiscal year 1997-98, overall industrial growth was 4.6 per cent during April-Februry of 1997-98. The manufacturing sector with a weight of 77.1 per cent has shown a growth of 4.2 per cent during this period compared to a growth of 9.3 per cent in the corresponding period of last year. An analysis of the performance shows that under-performance is confined to some sectors whereas there is relatively better performance in other sectors. Sectors like fertilizers, tractors, railway wagons and jute products, etc. have shown a significant growth rate of more than 10 per cent. Positive growth rate has also been recorded in electricity generation, cement, crude oil, cotton yarn, cotton cloth in decentralised sector, varios items of steel, diesel engines and several consumer non-durable products. Production has been stagnant or negative in respect of commercial vehicles, sugar, some of the capital goods industries, scooters and some varieties of tyres.

This under-performance is mostly ascribed to inadequate investment in infrastructure sectors like power and transport and slow down of investment in creation of new capacities. Under-performance has also been due to the sluggish export growth. Industrial performance was also initially constrained due to high rates of interest and inadequate availability of credit. This under-performance has been recognised by the Government and two high level meetings were taken by the Prime Minister with the Industrialists and representatives of the infrastructure sectors on 22nd July, 1997 and with Industrialists and Associations of manufacturing sector on 14th October, 1997. Several initiatives have already been taken in pursuance of the decisions taken at these meetings to expedite the clearance and implementation of the projects in power and infrastructure sectors and also to provide immediate support to the manufacturing sector. With the announcement of the credit policy by Reserve Bank Of India in April, 1997 and October, 1997 availability of credit has considerably improved and there has been decline in the interest rate. These factors are expected to favourably impact on the investment. Significant step-up of foreign direct investment would also supplement the domestic resources for capital formation.

Government also constituted an Expert Group under the Chairmanship of Dr Arjun Sengupta, Member, Planning Commission to examine the issue of imports of capital goods at zero duty and make appropriate recommendation. The Report of the Group is expected shortly.

To protect domestic industry from dumping and excessive imports, safeguards and anti dumping mechanisms have been approved and constituted in Department of Revenue and Ministry of Commerce.

Regular sector specific meetings were convened by Industry Minister with the Industrialists and Industry Associations to identify specific problems hindering growth and take timely corrective actions.

Industrial Stagnation Continued during 1998-99

Industrial output registered a meagre 2 per cent growth in October 1998 thus pushing down the April-October growth to 3.6 per cent as against a growth rate of 6.2 per cent during the corresponding period last year. Performance during October was even more dismal when compared to the 7 per cent growth in industrial production during the corresponding month last year. Performance of the indices of industrial production (IIP) for mining, manufacturing and electricity sectors for October also showed abysmal growth, fuelling the overall decline for the period April-October.

The IIPs of mining, manufacturing and electricity sectors in October stood at 118, 140.1 and 129.5, respectively, showing 2.8 per cent growth in case of manufacturing and 0.1 per cent growth in case of electricity, while it was (-) 2.6 per cent in the case of mining during October. Cumulative growth during April-October 1998 over the corresponding period last year in the three sectors also paints a poor picture. While the mining sector saw a cumulative growth of (-) 0.7 per cent in April-October this year, the manufacturing sector saw a cumulative growth of 3.8 per cent. However, due to larger production in electricity, the cumulative growth in April-October in electricity was a more respectable 6 per cent over the same period last year.

Industrial growth for the fiscal ending March 1999 would be only 4.5 per cent and the increase in agricultural production would not be more than 1.2 per cent, Centre for Monitoring Indian Economy (CMIE) has said. The first five months have registered a growth of only 3.5 per cent in the index "For Industrial production (IIP), requiring an IIP expansion of more than five per cent in the remaining six months of the year. The growth in consumer goods has been particularly poor, CMIE stated in its monthly review of the Indian economy, adding that production expanded by a mere 1.7 per cent in the first five months of financial year 1998-99. The energy sector has also recorded a major slowdown in Sept. with coal production declining by 1.4 per cent due to poor offtake in the current year.

Crude oil production reduced by 7 per cent, while power generation which grew by eight per cent in previous months recorded a growth of only 2.6 per cent in Sept. Hydel power generation also declined by 5 per cent. The damage due to heavy unseasonal rains, witnessed in Karnataka, Andhra Pradesh, Maharashtra and Gujarat would, however, not affect its projections of 1.2 per cent growth, CMIE said. The interim results of over 1,300 companies also indicate a continuation of the depressing performance, it added.

The corporate sector recorded a sales growth of 11.5 per cent, while profits declined by 6 per cent. Expenses of manufacturing companies grew at a faster pace compared to their sales. Profits of these companies declined by 12.6 per cent, while those for manufacturing companies was down by a whopping 30 per cent. The performance of the Indian private sector was much worse, CMIE said adding that the private sector recorded 17 per cent lower profits. However, multinational companies, excluding Non-Resident Indian owned companies recorded a 14 per cent increase in profits.

DEVELOPMENT OF BACKWARD AREAS AND INFRASTRUCTURE DEVELOPMENT

For development of infrastructure, a Centrally Sponsored Scheme of Growth Centres was conceived to be implmented in the VIII Five Year Plan. The scheme envisages setting up of 71 centres. So far, 66 centres have been approved. Each growth centre is estimated to cost Rs. 25 to 30 crores. The original schematic pattern of funding of the Growth Centres envisaged fundings from Central Government, State Governments, Financial Institutions and market borrowing. However, since no funding support has been forthcoming from the financial institutions and market borrowing was not considered feasible, the scheme is being funded by Central and State Governments. The release of Central assistance for the Growth Centres was significantly stepped up in 1994-95 and Rs. 80.39 crores were released. In 1996-97, Central assistance to the tune of Rs. 28.96 crores and during 1997-98, Rs. 25.00 crores had been released.

Government has also extended the Transport Subsidy Scheme for a further period of 5 years upto 31.3.2000. This scheme has been particularly helpful in industrialisation of the hilly, remote and other inaccessible regions. Since its inception an amount of Rs. 360 crores (approximately) including Rs. 64 crores during the current year, has been reimbursed to States/Union Territories.

PERFORMANCE OF MAJOR INDUSTRIES

(a) Automobile Industry

Transportation sector is responsible for movement of manpower and material and a good transportation system is the life blood of the economy and a vital pre-requisite for the country's economic development. The Indian automotive industry is well developed and produces a wide range of personal vehicles, commercial vehicles etc. The industry has been growing at an average growth rate of 20 per cent from 1993-94 onward. However, due to a fall in demand arising out of a slow down in the economy the industry has been passing through a phase of sluggish growth. But this is only a temporary phase and with the expected increase in investment in infrastructure and the expected economic revival in the near future the industry is projected to be back on high growth track.

All segments of vehicles industry except commercial vehicles and cars are expected to register marked growth in production during 1997-98 over 1996-97 as a shown below:

Table 18.1

S. No.	Item	Estimated growth in production during 1997-98 over 1996-97
1.	Commerical vehicles	-23.4%
2.	Cars	0.0%
3.	Jeeps	2.0%
4.	Two Wheelers	1.0%
5.	Three Wheelers	7.0%

The automobile industry is also contributing to the export effort of the country. Export has been growing consistently over the years. The details of import and export in 1995-96 and 1996-97 are given below:

Import & Export Statistics

Table 18.2

(Rs. in lakhs)

S. No.	Classifi-cation	Item	1995-96 Imports	1995-96 Exports	1996-97 Imports	1996-97 Exports	% Growth in export during 1996-97 over 1995-96
1	2	3	4	5	6	7	8
1.	8702	Public Transport type Passenger Vehicle	114.8	18027	112.86	16386.63	-9.09%

2.	8703	Motor Cars and Other Motor Vehicle	15954	60876	12386.30	84941.09	39.53%
3.	8704	Motor Vehicles for Transport of Goods	86.4	12090	53.65	19977.63	65.24%
4.	8711	Two Wheeler	41.27	30703	88.84	32935.97	7.27%
5.	8714	Parts for 2 Wheeler	6740	63424	5890.84	39644.55	-37.49%
6.	8708	Parts of 4 Wheeler			183848.58	62528.06	

In view of the continued growth of the passenger car segment new models, particularly in the small and mid-size segment with latest designs are expected to be introduced in market in the near future. It is expected that during 1998 TELCO, Daewoo and Hyundai will introduce their small cars.

Suzuki Agreement with Govt. of India

The Government and Suzuki Motor Corporation (SMC) of Japan on June 8 inked an agreement to end the internecine battle over the appointment of Mr. R.S.S. L.N Bhaskarudu as the Managing Director of Maruti Udyog Ltd. under which the tenure of the incumbent MD would be curtailed almost half and the Suzuki side would be offered the company chairmanship with immediate effect. The salient features of the MoU signed by the Government and SMC include:

The term of the present MD, Bhaskarudu, will be up to the end of Dec. 31, 1999, and from January 1, 2000, Mr Jagdish Khattar, currently MUL Executive Director, will be appointed as the next MD.

The nominese of SMC will be appointed as the MUL Chairman. In future, all appointments of Chairman and Managing Director by either the Government of India or SMC will be only in consulation and with the concurrence of the other party.

Announcing the pact between Government and SMC at a Press conference, Industry Minister Sikander Bakht said that Mr. Khattar would be appointed as the MUL Joint Managing Director from June 9. Subsequently, the Suzuki side also announced the nomination of SMC Executive Vice-President Y. Saito for the post of MUL, Chairman. Mr Saito is expected to take charge on June 9. Significantly, the appointment of Mr Saito will be for a five-year term.

That means the Suzuki side will hold both the crucial positions in the joint venture—managing directorship and chairmanship—from 2000 onwards for almost two-and-a-half years. Commenting on this, Mr Bakht said that since the functions of the two were totally different, it would not have any major adverse impact. An extraodinary general meeting (EGM) and a meeting of the board of directors of MUL have been called for Tuesday to ratify the decisions in the MoU. The new Oppointments to the posts of Chairman and the joint MD will also be ratified at Tuesday's meetings.

Suzuki to Introduce New Models

Suzuki Motor Corporation (SMC) would introduce new models and technology in Maruti Udyog Ltd (MUL) as the out of Court settlement with government has come in "good time", its President Osamu Suzuki said. "All the technologies that Suzuki owned would be open and available to Maruti," Suzuki said in an exclusive interview to PITI on June 17. Maruti's owners came to realise they could "no longer waste time quarrelling", and SMC on its part was determined to do its best to strengthen the company with all the latest and best technologies owned by it, Suzuki said.

Last week the government and SMC, 50:50 partners in the car company that commands over 80 per cent of the market, signed a memorandum of understanding to end the managerial dispute in the company. The two partners had been fighting a board room and court battle at the International Courts of Arbitration (CA) over the government appointing R.S.S.I.N. Bhaskarudu as Managing Director of the company in August 1997. Under the agreement, dubbed as a sellout by opposition parties in Parliament, the term of Mr Bhaskaradu has been halved and SMC Vice President Yoshio Saito became the Chairman. And, in exchange SMC dropped the case at ICA. Expressing happiness at settling the dispute "bilaterally", Mr Suzuki said the Japanese company would "throw open" all is technologies, including the "very latest and the most modern" to Maruti Udyog. "There is no question of which and what technologies. All the technologies that Suzuki owned would be open and available to Maruti," he said.

Mr. Suzuki said this would equip Maruti to face the tough competition posed by international auto majors and make the company" capable of beating competition not only within India" but also competition from elsewhere. He said car makers from around the work entered the Indian market making the competitive environment "very severe" for Maruti and the settlement reached had therefore come "in good time". "Both partners are now aware of the hard realities and are determined to defend Maruti on the road by introducing latest models and developing new designs to stay ahead of the market," he said.

Car Wars Leading to Price Crash

Maruti Udyog Ltd and Tata Engineering and Locomotive Co. Ltd triggered off a car price war on Dec. 30. The only winner of the tussle between the two, it appears, is the consumer. MUL reduced the prices of its popular 800cc car and some other models hours before Telco announced prices for Indica. Maruti has slashed the price of its standard 800 model by Rs. 24,632. Barely an hour after MUL slashed prices, Telco announced that its 1,400cc Indica standard petrol model would cost Rs. 2,59,000, its diesel version Rs. 2,85,000, and the diesel deluxe version Rs. 3,90,000.

The price of the Maruti 800 deluxe variant has been reduced by Rs. 11,127 to Rs. 2.35 lakh and will have additional feature like radial tyres. The company has also introduced a new variant, the Maruti 800 EX, priced at Rs. 2,09,627. Maruti has also reduced the price of the diesel version of Zen by Rs. 36,808 to Rs. 4.26 lakh. The prices of Zen VX, Esteem and Gypsy, however, have not been touched. "It's the market leader who redefines the pricing strategy," MUL Managing Director R.S.S.L.N. Bhaskarudu told reporters.

Maruti Turnover

Despite the major price cuts and sales promotion initiativestaken during the current fiscal, Maruti Udyog Ltd. has projected to close the year with a 7 per cent drop in turnover. According to an internal assessment by the car major's finance department sales of its vehicles are also likely to drop by over 5 per cent during the year against 3,27,240 units sold in the domestic market in 1997-98, company sources said. The turn-over during 1997-98 amounted to Rs. 8,133,75 crore against Rs. 7,662.9 crore the previous year. With the turnover now set to take a dip, it is most likely, to rest at around Rs. 7,600 crore at the end of the current fiscal, sources added.

The net profit is likely to record a greater fall which might result in a lower payout to both the equal partners—government of India and Suzuki Motor Corporation of Japan. The MUL board and announced a 30 per cent dividend last year having earned Rs. 977.31 crore as gross profit against Rs. 807.57 crore in the previous year. Maruti's contribution to the Central exchequer had in 1997-98 increased to Rs. 2,652.4 crore against Rs. 2,540.6 crore in the previous year. Last year, Maruti had recorded a 27.6 per cent growth in net profit and 6.3 per cent increase in total income. However, its growth rate had declined by 4 per cent on a year-on-year-basis. The company's bottom-line would be squeezed this year because of the major price reductions which it had effected on almost all its models in December.

Toyota to Launch Multi-utility Vehicle

Japanese auto major Toyota Motor Corp. has chalked out an ambitious plan which includes the launch of an eight to ten seater multi-utility diesel passenger vehicle next year, followed by the introduction of a small car. "The proposed family car, to be launched in January 2000, would be priced very competitively and is being developed exclusively for the Indian market, "Toyota Corp. executive vice-president Fujio Cho said. The multi-utility vehicle (MUV) will be built on the platform of Kijang. Over $170 million have been invested till now on the joint venture project between Toyota Corporation and Kirloskar group, Toyota Director, Hideaki Otaka said. Toyota Kirloskar Motors is a joint venture with 76 per cent held by the Japanese major and the balance by the Bangalore-based Kirloskars. The company is studying the existing small cars for launching a suitable model keeping in mind the Indian road conditions, he said.

Toyota Kirloskar Motors Vice-president Vikram Kirloskar said Rs. 600 crore has been invested on the assembly line for producing the MUV and Rs. 200 crore in the four other companies which will supply auto components to the company. Toyota is also planning to develop an exclusive dealer network comprising 25 dealers in 22 major cities of the country. The plant at Bidadi will have an annual capacity to produce 50,000 units, but plans to sell 20,000 cars in the first year of its commercial operation. Initial indigenisation level would be 50 per cent which would be increased progressively, company sources said.

Fiat, Toyota Investment Cleared

Foreign Investment Promotion Board (FIPB) on Aug. 22 cleared Foreign Direct Investment (FDI) proposals worth Rs. 525 crore, including those of Fiat, Toyota Motor Corporation and Siemens. A proposal by Tamil Nadu Industrial Development Corporation (TIDCO), amounting to FDI of Rs. 245 crore from two American companies for setting up hi-tech industrial park also got the FIPB nod, sources said. TIDCO proposal, which was the largest cleared at today's meeting, envisages a total investment of Rs. 850 crore where the American Companies will hold 89 per cent stake and the rest by TIDCO. Two proposals of Toyota Motor Corporation (TMC) for investment in the auto component sector were also approved. In the first proposal with their joint venture partner Kirloskar Systems, the Japanese auto giant will invest Rs. 16.25 crore for manufacturing components for steering wheels. A novel idea of an industrial park for Toyota's auto component manufacturers at Bidadi near Bangalore with foreign investment of Rs. 45 crore also got the approval.

(b) Cement Industry

Cement, which is a key infrastructure industry, has been growing since the decontrol of price and distribution with effect from 1st March, 1989 and several policy reforms thereafter, including delicensing of the industry on 25th July, 1991. At present, there are 115 large cement plants with an installed capacity of 96.25 million tonnes and more than 310 mini cement plants with an estimated capacity of 9 million tonnes per annum. Thus, the total installed capacity in the country is 105.25 million tonnes. The actual production in 1996-97 was 76.22 million tonnes as against production of 69.55 million tonnes in 1995-96. The industry has, therefore, achieved a healthy growth rate of 9.6 per cent in 1996-97.

Keeping in view the trend of growth of the industry, a production target of 81 million tonnes has been fixed for 1997-98. In spite of demand recession in the industry and infrastructural constraints like acute shortage of power, power cuts in major cement producing States and non-availability of good quality coal, a production of 74.84 million tonnes has been achieved against the target of 73.50 million tonnes for the period April, 97-Feg., 98. Keeping pace with the physical growth of the industry, it has also made tremendous strides in technological upgradation and assimilation of latest technology. 89 per cent of the total capacity in the industry is now based on the modern and environment friendly dry process technology. Only 9 per cent of the capacity is based on old wet process technology and the remaining 2 per cent is of semi-dry technology. A large number of mega plants with capacity of one million tonnes and above with latest technological features like roller process, vertical roller mills, process control equipments and efficient pollution control devices have come up in different parts of the country. The induction of advanced technology has helped the industry immensely to conserve energy and fuel and to save materials substantially. India is producing different varieties of cement like Ordinary Portland Cement (OPC), Portland Pozzolana Cement (PPC), Portland Blast Furnace Slag Cement (PBFS), Oil Well Cement, Rapid Hardening Portland Cement, Sulphate Resisting Portland Cement, White Cement etc. All these varieties of cement are produced strictly conforming to the BIS specifications and maintaining high quality of product.

Apart from meeting the entire domestic demand, the industry has also started exporting cement and clinker. After steadily increasing to a level of 3.2 million tonnes in 1994-95, the pace of export of cement had slowed down a bit to a level 2.4 million tonnes in 1995-96 and 2.7 million tonnes in 1996-97. This is mainly attributable to lack of infrastructural facilities like rail/road support, port congestion and consequent high sea freight, duties and levies etc. With availability of better infrastructural facilities at port and facilities for bulk handling, the export performance of the industry is likely to improve further. The export during 1997-98 (April, 97 to Feb., 98) is about 3.76 million tonnes.

The Cement Industry has been permitted to own and operate captive coal mines for their cement plants as well as thermal power plants. A number of cement plants have applied for availing of this opportunity. Some cement plants have also opted for "own your wagon scheme" introduced by Railways, in order to tackle their transportation problems to the extent possible.

To meet the requirements of trained man power to maintain the quality standards, Cement Industry has taken an initiative to implement the innovative "Cement Industry - Human Resource Development Project" assisted by the

The product ranges cater to all sectors of the Indian economy. Many multi-crore projects have been established in thermal, hydro, nuclear power stations, docks, chemical, petrochemical complexes, metallurgical units like integrated steel aluminium complexes etc. The industry has also kept pace with technology and has now the capability to even offer/undertake turnkey contracts. The industry is well equipped not only to meet the entire domestic requirements but is also capable of exporting. The industry is de-licensed.

The domestic industry has established a capacity for manufacturing and supplying around 4,500 MW of thermal, 1,345 MW of Hydro and about 1,000 MW of gas based power generating equipment per annum. Facilities and expertise for manufacture of nuclear sets have also been established. The share of domestic equipment in the present installed power generating capacity is around 66 per cent.

The domestic industry has established a capacity for the manufacture of transmission and distribution equipment upto 400 KV AC and high voltage DC. The domestic industry has also taken steps to upgrade the technology for the next higher system voltage of 800 KV.

The status of various products covered under Heavy Electrical Industry is given below:

(h) Iron and Steel FDI for Steel, Minining Sectors

The steel and mines sector has received Rs. 800 crore worth of foreign direct investment (FDI) since its liberalisation, the Steel Secretary, Mr. Ashok Basu said on Oct. 7. Speaking at the inaugural function of the second international metals and metallurgy exposition, he stated that of the Rs. 800 crore of foreign investment, Rs. 400 crore each was in the ferrous and non-ferrous metals. Extensive mineral reserves and their low per capita consumption in the country provided the sector with good growth prospects, the Steel Secretary said. The opportunity for tapping the potential of this sector, by both domestic and foreign investors, he felt, should not be ignored, especially when the government was prepared to render all requisite assistance for investment.

Answering queries about liberalisation in this sector, Mr. Basu informed that the legislation pertaining to the sale of steel had been revamped and private investment permitted in 13 minerals earlier earmarked exclusively for the public sector. The government had also permitted automatic approval of foreign investment, besides permitting 100 per cent foreign equity under specified conditions. Describing the prevailing recessionary trend in the steel sector as a pssing phase, he expressed confidence that the industry would shortly witness a turnaround. "The slowdown," he affirmed, "is temporary and with the economy picking up, the demand for steel will increase. Regarding new investments in the steel sector, Mr. Basu said that 19 new steel plants were scheduled to be commissioned in the next few years, entailing an investment of Rs.25,000 crore. These plants, he said, would increase steel output by 13 million tonnes, with two-thirds of this coming from the private sector.

SAIL Running Into Loss

The public sector giant, Steel Authority of India Ltd (SAIL), has run into a loss of Rs. 616.91 crore despite a higher sales turnover in the first half of 1998-99. The steel major had made a profit of Rs. 54 crore in the corresponding period of the previous year. According to the unaudited provisional financial results released by the company today, the second quarter loss of Rs. 305.9 crore was marginally lower than the Rs. 311 crore posted in the preceding quarter. The corporation has attributed the loss to a glut in the market combined with the dumping of unfairly priced imports which caused sales realisations to fall by over 4 per cent this wiped out the gains of the increase in the sales turnover of 4.7 per cent.

According to the company press release, the world-wide recession led to a sharp drop of about 20 per cent in the international prices of steel during April-Sept. 1998. This is reported to have adversely affected SAIL's main exports of items like plates, slabs and billets. Despite the glut in the market the company managed to achieve a higher level of sales as a result of which its steel inventory was reduced by nearly 3 lakh tonnes during the period April-September, 1998, with a closing inventory at 9.4 lakh tonnes. In fact, for the first time in the last 18 months, stocks have fallen below one million tonnes. Apart from the sluggish demand which prevented higher realisations for the tenth successive quarter, the higher burden of interest and depreciation on account of the huge investments in the recently modernised units continued to have an impact on the financial results of the company. Depreciation and interest in the first ended September, 1998, stood at Rs. 1,415 crore as against the Rs. 1,096 crore in the corresponding period of last year which represents an increase of Rs.319 crore.

SAIL to Reduce Costs

Steel Authority of India Ltd. (SAIL) is aiming for a cost reduction of Rs. 1,000 crore in all its six plants by saving on fuel and power, better utilisation of raw materials, standardisation of equipment and other techno-economic parameters SAIL is also aiming at hither capacity utilisation of its modernised units at Durgapur and Rourkela and all these measures will have an "immediate impact" on improving the financial picture of SAIL, according to a SAIL spokesman. SAIL is also planning on long-term measures, which include a 10 per cent reduction in manpower, the official told PTI. SAIL employs 1.70 lakh people in all its plants and subsidiaries in the country. "We are also aiming at better utilisation of inhouse facilities. Closing down of uneconomic divisions within plants is also being thought of, but such uneconomic divisions are yet to be identified," he said.

He said SAIL is serious in bringing about a change in terms of its opertions and functioning due to the changes in business environment that have come about in India. For the last two or three years, there has been a decline in SAIL's profit ...

TISCO Sales in 1997-98

Tata Iron and Steel Co. Ltd. (TISCO) said on April 9 that its sales of steel climbed 8.7 per cent to 2.63 million tonnes in 1997-98 (April-March) from 2.42 million tonnes the previous year. "Total steel sales last year (1997-98) were 2.63 million tonnes, which is an increase of 8.7 per cent over the previous year," TISCO Managing Director J.J. Irani told a news conference in Calcutta. He said that TISCO sold 2.42 million tonnes of steel in 1996-97 (April-March). Dr. Irani said that TISCO's domestic sales in 1997-98 increased to 2.21 million tonnes from 2.02 million in the previous year, while steel exports climbed to 420,000 tonnes in 1997-98 from 400,000 tonnes in 1996-97. "Domestic sales increased by 9.4 per cent and exports increased by 5 per cent over the previous year," he said, addition that hot metal production increased by 2 per cent over the previous year, and saleable steel production by 7 per cent over 1996-97. "We actually sold 9 per cent more saleable steel (in 1997-98), but we produced 7 per cent more....This surpassed all previous records," he said.

TISCO's hot metal production climbed to 3.51 million tonnes in 1997-98 from 3.44 million tonnes in 1996-97. The firm's saleable steel output climbed to 3.01 million tonnes in 1997-98 from 2.82 million last year. Dr. Irani said that crude steel production had also risen. "Crude steel production in 1997-98 was 3.23 million tonnes, up from 3.11 million in the previous year," he said. Dr. Irani said that TISCO's third stage of modernisation has been totally completed, and the fourth stage would be completed this year. On capital projects, Dr. Irani said that TISCO had spent Rs. 680 crore for constructing battery no. 8 and 9 and another Rs. 450 crore was being spent for the expansion of hot strip mill. Another Rs. 1,800 crore was earmarked for setting up cold rolling mill in Jamshedpur, but the company was hopeful of completing it with an investment of Rs. 1,600 crore.

Tata Steel to Invest Rs. 3,000 Cr.

Tata Steel will invest Rs. 3,000 crore in the next three years under its fourth phase of modernisation programme. This was stated by the Managing Director of Tata Steel J.J. Irani at a Press conference in Jamshedpur on Sept. 2. Dr. Irani said "The fourth phase of the modernsation programme is going on at present in which the company has decided to spend Rs. 1,000 crore every year for the next three years." Under this phase of the modermisation programme, the hot strip mill is already being upgraded and will be commissioned within the next two months. "Once the hot strip mill is commissioned, the production capacity will increase from one million tonne to two million tonne," Dr. Irani stated and added that the ID-II is also being modernised.

On the Rs. 1,600 crore cold rolling mill (CRM) project, Dr. Irani said that the future of the company would depend much on the success of the project which is likely to be commissioned by June 2000. "The product of CRM will be of high quality in fact of export quality," Dr. Irani stated and pointed out that once the CRM project becomes a success, the future of Tata Steel will become secured for the next 15 years. According to the Tata Steel MD, the product that CRM will manufacture is at present imported. "The finished product of CRM will be unparallel" he claimed. Dr. Irani said that the company would close a number of units in the near future, and would reduce its workforce by 2000 to 3000 every year. Dr. Irani said that to give impetus to the steel industry, the Government should spend more on housing and infrastructure.

(i) Leather Industry

Indian leather and leather product industries have made significant progress during the past years. The improved production and export performance during this period has been on account of:

— Introduction of technological changes in leather production;
— Impact of export stimulating policie; and
— Gradual shift into leather products manufacture.

Export Potential

Though traditionally, the Indian leather industry has been an exporter of tanned hides and skins, it had, in the early seventies itself, set its sight on becoming a major player in the leather products segments. Over the period of last twenty years and particularly so in the last ten years, it has become the fourth largest foreign exchange earner in the country. The Industry has become an area of export thrust with footwear having been identified as an area of extreme focus. Exports from leather sector today account for 6 per cent of India's exports. Given its potential, exports by the turn of the century has been projected at Rs. 11,000 crores. The industry uses primarily indigenous natural resources with little dependence on imported resources.

At the same time, while this has been a traditional industry in India with a reasonable share in total exports, the Indian leather industry still accounts for only 3 per cent of the global market. Obviously, there is need for a larger share of the global market.

Policy in Leather Sector

The industry is spread over organised as well as the unorganised sector. The small scale, cottage and artisan sectors account for over 75 per cent of the total production. Leather goods industry being reserved for manufacture in the small scale sector, organised sector units can, therefore, enter this area only with the minimum stipulated export obligation of their total production. Non-SSI units can, however, take up manufacture of finished leather from semi finished stage without any export obligation.

Units in the small scale and unregistered cottage sectors are encouraged to export leather footwear and leather products. This policy is designed to meet the twin objectives of safe-guarding the interests of the small scale and cottage sectors and of increasing exports.

A number of policy initiatives have been taken up by the Govt. to encourage value added exports of leather products. Imports of raw materials and machinery have been liberalised. Manufacture of finished leather has been de-licensed with effect from April 28, 1993. Tanned or dressed fur skins, Chamois leather have also been removed from the list of industries requiring compulsory licensing with effect from 17th July, 1997. Domestic manufacture of components for the shoe industry has been encouraged by promoting joint ventures and by duty rationalisation on inputs required for the manufacture of such components.

National Leather Development Programme

The National Leather Development Programme (NLDP) is being implemented by Govt. of India since April 1992 in association with the United Nations Development Programme (UNDP). UNDP had contributed US dollars 15.05 millions for the Programme. The Govt. of India has provided counterpart funding of about US dollars 11.065 millions. The programme seeks to strengthen the industry in the areas of human resource development, technical training, research and development, pollution control, export promotion and enhancement, product improvement, enhancement of value addition through increased flows of investment and technology and coordination with a specific focus on the micro and artisan sector. This Programme is aimed at integrated development of leather industry through select institutions/agencies in the country. The country has already been able to establish linkages with some of the reputed international organisations such as AFPIC (Association Nationale Pour La Formation Et La Promotion Professional Dans L'industry Et Le Commerce De La Chaussure Et Ets Cuirs Et and Peaux), Paris; Melbourne Textiles Institute (MTI), Melbourne; Clothing and Footwear Institute (CFI), London, in the areas of education and training. The Indian institutions have been able to upgrade the training systems for design & manufacture of footwear, garments and leather goods with the help of modern techniques including Computer Aided Design (CAD) facilities established under the Programme. These institutions are directly assisting the industry in developing various models of footwear and other products. With the setting up of footwear testing laboratories at Central Leather Research Institute, Chennai and Footwear Design & Development Institute, NOIDA, international standard testing facilities are now available in India which are acceptable overseas.

The Programme has been also successful in up-grading training systems for design and manufacture of footwear garments and leather goods. Research and development work has got a fillip under the Programme. The Programme which was to conclude in March, 1997, was extended till March, 1998, with an additional outlay of US$ 2.18 Millions by the UNDP. This has further been extended till August 1998, with no additional allocation of funds.

The response from the artisan communities and small enterprises clusters has been extremely encouraging towards the Programme. The recent reorientation of the NLDP has demonstrably resulted in sustainable employment and higher income generation through product up-gradation. The Terminal Evaluation Mission, which was fielded by UNDP in January 1997, observed that overall the Programme has been a considerable success in terms of outputs achieved.

Based on the perceived needs of the leather sector, it has been decided, in principle, to launch a follow-up Phase (namely Phase-II of the NLDP).

Indian Leather Development Programme

To complement and supplement the ongoing NLDP, a new scheme titled Indian Leather Development Programme (ILDP) has been approved under the Ninth Five Year Plan with a total allocation of Rs. 250 lakhs and Rs. 115 lakhs for the year 1997-98. The objectives of ILDP are mainly to bridge critical gaps in the infrastructure for integrated development of leather industry, activate national agencies towards tackling perceived gaps in the industry to promote and accredit productivity, value addition and employment, to undertake investment/trade development activities and build up an information base for leather industry.

Export Performance

The export performance of the leather sector has improved considerably during the Eighth Plan period. The value of exports went up from Rs. 3,036 crores during 1991-92 to Rs. 5,517 crores during 1996-97. Exports for the year 1997-98 are targeted at approximately Rs. 6,590 crores (about US$ 1780 millions).

(j) Rubber Goods Industry

Rubber goods manufacturing industry is a de-licensed industry. Several rubber goods like cycle tyres and tubes, canvas hoses, rubber wahsers etc. are reserved for the small scale sector. The industry has today 36 tyre producing units spread in 13 States, about 220 medium scale units, over 5500 units in the small scale sector and an equal number in the tiny sector with an annual turn-over of about Rs. 7,500 crores. It directly employs about 3.3 lakhs people.

The rubber goods manufacturing industry covers a wide range of items like tyres, tubes, conveyor belts, rubber hoses, rubber cots and aprons, contraceptives, examination and surgical gloves, rubber moulded goods, automative components etc. The growth of the rubber industry is indicated by the following trends of production and consumption of all types of rubber (natural, synthetic and reclaimed) during the last 5 years:

Table 18.5

Year	Production (Tons)	Consumption (Tons)
1991-92	4,24,448	4,85,800
1992-93	4,51,626	5,21,545
1993-94	4,96,000	5,62,000
1994-95	5,32,351	6,73,215
1995-96	6,40,913	7,25,325
1996-97	6,80,658	7,71,160
1997-98*	5,85,000	6,19,000

* Estimated

The import content in the various rubber goods produced in the country has, on an average fallen from approximately 30% in the sixties to nearly 2-3% at preasent. The total exports of rubber goods has increased from Rs. 313 crores in 1991-92 to approximately Rs. 1217 crores in 1996-97.

(k) Sugar Industry

Delicensing of Sugar Industry

In a major policy decision, the Centre on Aug. 20 announced delicensing of the sugar industry. With this, the incentives to new industries on levy sugar for five to eight years, also goes. A decision to this effect was taken at a meeting of the Cabinet Committee on Economic Affairs, chaired by the Prime Minister, Mr. Atal Behari Vajpayee. Announcing the decision, the Union Minister of State for Agriculture, Mr. Som Pal, said there was no proposal for de-control of the sugar industry before the CCEA today. The Minister was authorised to brief mediapersons in the absence of the Industry Minister, Mr. Sikander Bakht. Mr. Some Pal said the Industry Ministry's proposal on delicensing, had recommended a mandatory distance of 15 kilometres between two sugar units, which was accepted. This was done to ensure assured price to millers who are being asked to pay minimum statutory price to cane growers.

The policy will come into being from the day it is notified by the Industry Ministry. While recommending that the existing policy of licensing of new sugar mills be continued 'with modifications', the high-powered Mahajan Committee on Sugar Industry had recommended that a mandatory radial distance of 25 km be maintained betwen two licensed units. The distance at present is 15 km. It had recommended that there should be no need for a licence for expansion in capacity. Such an expansion may only be registered with the Centre and the concerned State Government. It said that insistence on minimum economic capacity of 2,500 tonnes crushed per day for a new unit should be given up and the size of the unit to be set up should be left to the entrepreneurs and financial institutions. The validity of the letter of intent be raised from one year to three years in case of cooperative units.

Earlier, the Government's proposal to delicense was described as "non-issue" by Indian Sugar Mills Association, but the National Federation for Cooperative Sugar Factories had wanted that the zoning and distance between sugar units be maintained. Mr. Som Pal described the decision to delicense the sugar industry as 'historic' and said there would be no obligation on sugar producing units to earmark a portion of their produce for selling to the Government. Presently sugar producers have to mandatorily keep 40 per cent for supplying to the Government for the public distribution system, he added.

The sugar industry is sorely disappointed with the Union Government's announcement of delicensing as it would serve little purpose either towards deceleration of prices for common consumers or progress of the industry as a whole if one cares to take into account the fact that the country is already saddled with huge imported stocks despite overproduction. In fact, the country needs no fresh licenses till the year 2010 as with 664 licensed and 450 installed factories having an annual licensed capacity of 283.7 lakh tonnes and annual installed capacity of 141.67 lakh tonnes, there will be a carry over stocks of more than 50 lakh tonnes when the new crushing season begins in October. Added to this will be 150 lakh tonness production in the new year even as per conservative estimates against an indigenous demand of about 165 lakh tonnes.

More significantly, as many as 235 letters of intent for setting up new factories are now pending for implementation. Besides, 236 letters of intent issued for capacity expansion of many existing units may well be carried through depending upon the demand-supply and price situations. Corroborating these estimates in the course of an interview of "*The Hindustan Times*", Mr. O.P. Dhanuka, a leading manufacturer and former president of Indian Sugar Mills Association (ISMA) strongly asstailed delicensing terming it a "non-issue and diversionary tactic."

Duty on Sugar Import Raised

The Government on Jan. 14 increased customs duty on sugar to 20 per cent but left the domestic sugar industry quite disappointed as the levél is considered inadequate to stem the dumping of the commodity that is taking place, especially from Pakistan. Sources disclose that Food Minister Surjit Singh Barnala had recommended that the duty be increased to 40 per cent but the Cabinet settled for 20 per cent under pressure from the Finance Minister. Reacting to the decision the Indian Sugar Mills Association (ISMA) Director General, Mr. S.L. Jain said that "it is unfair for the Govrenment to claim that the 15 per cent increase in customs duty on sugar would provide an adequate level of protection to domestic producers as Pakistan was giving a Rs. 4.50 per kg subsidy to its exporters." Mr. Jain said that there was no need for imports at the present juncture as indigenous industry was saddled with excess stocks. He said that with domestic prices slumping to Rs. 1,430 per quintal the indian Sugar Industry was running into huge losses as it has to supply 40 per cent of its output as levy for the public distribution system at a price that is 20 per cent below the cost of production.

Export of Sugar Likely in 1999

Union Food Minister Surjit Singh Barnala said in New Delhi on Feb. 4 that the country might be in a position to export sugar by the end of the current crushing season as the stock position was very comfortable. Mr. Barnala told newspersons that the country had a stock of 61 lakh tonnes of sugar as on December 31, 1998. The expected production in the ongoing season was 150 lakh tonnes while the total consumption was not expected to exceed 145 lakh tonnes. He said that the increase in price of PDS sugar from Rs. 11.40 per kg to Rs. 12 per kg would reduce the annual subsidy bill by Rs. 275 crore. While earlier the subsidy on sugar was Rs. 647 crore each year, this would now come down to Rs. 372 crore. He said that it costs the Government Rs. 12.22 per kg to supply sugar through PDS.

Mr. Barnala said that he had received several complaints from indigenous sugar producers about the dumping of sugar and had therefore increased the duty on sugar by 20 per cent foodgrains for people below the poverty line would entail a subsidy of Rs. 700 crore. The annual subsidy on foodgrains was to the tune of Rs. 8,500 crore which would now come down to Rs. 6,300 crore following the increase in PDS issue price, he added. Mr. Barnala said that the country had 25 million tonnes of foodgrains in stocks which was higher than the buffer stock requirement of 18 million tonnes.

Sugar Production

Union Food and Consumer Affairs Minister Surjeet Singh Barnala has admitted that the country's sugar production is likely to be less than the 150 lakh tonnes as anticipated by government in view of largescale damage to sugarcane crop. He said that imposition of additional import duty on sugar is on cards, but failed to spell out the timeframe. He denied that the Union Finance Minister was opposed to such a move of hiking import duty. Inaugurating the 64th AGM of Indian Sugar Mills Association in Capital on Dec. 19, Mr. Branala said that late heavy rains during the last season have affected various areas of the country. In many areas, waterlogging has caused extensive damage to sugarcane crop, which has reduced the yield as well as sucrose content. Initial reports received from factories indicated that there was a drastic fall in recovery of cane ranging from 0.5 per cent to 1.6 per cent, he said.

Mr. Barnala, however, said the production would be sufficient to meet the requirement of sugar for the next 12 months. Departing from his prepared speech. Mr. Barnala said that his Ministry would consider the industry appeal for review of the stipulation reducing the distance between two sugar factories from 50 km to 15 km. While announcing delicensing of the sugar industry, government also said the distance between sugar factories should be 15 km instead of 50 km earlier. Mr. K.K. Birla said in Parliament that in effect the distance between two sugar factories would be only 7.5 km and that a representation has been sent to the Industry Ministry. It has not come to the Food Ministry. Food Ministry will look into it after it was referred to it and see if remedial measures can be taken, he said. Referring to be arrears due to cane growers, he questioned the industry on why farmers should be made to wait so long for their dues.

(I) Textiles Industry

(a) Textile Policy to be Reviewed

Textiles Minister Kashiram Rana said on April 21 that the Government would review its textile policy in line with the BJP-led coalition's primary goal of checking unemployment. Priority attention would be accorded to revival of all viable units of the National Textile Corporation (NTC) while working out amicable settlement for the non-viable mills. The Government has already spent around Rs. 4,400 crore to pay idle wages for NTC workers and persisting with the practice would amount to wasting national wealth. The Government can ill afford to continue spending over Rs. 360 crore towards idle wages, Mr. Rana said. Therefore, the best option is to revive all viable mills by modernising them while closing down non-viable units by providing an attractive voluntary retirement scheme (VRS) which will take care of the interests of the labourers.

Eight out of the nine subsidiaries of NTC are sick and the Centre's efforts to encourage State Government to take over the mills have not met with any success. Employing a workforce of around 1 lakh, the 119 mills of NTC represent a monolith which needs major rehaul to be in a position to carry out economically viable operations. While noting that previous Government's had made only major claims about reviving NTC, Mr. Rana said the BJP-led Government would definitely turn-around the sick units of the ageing textile giant.

(b) Textiles Upgradation Fund

The Cabinet Committee on Economic Affairs on Jan. 20 cleared the setting up of Rs. 25,000 crore technology upgradation fund for textile from April 1, 1999 to modernise the weaving and processing sectors of the textile industry, besides jute, cotton ginning and pressing units. Textile Minister Kashiram Rana said told Press conference that the five-year fund, to be set up by April 1, 1999, will be available for spinning units in composite mills, however, stand-alone units would not be eligible as they were covered under a Rs. 750 crore modernisation fund during 1987-1991.

Under the scheme, government would give an interest subsidy of five per cent on loans availed from financial institutions. Guidelines for the fund would be framed by an interministerial steering panel, which would monitor it, the Minister said, additing TUF was expected to prepare Indian textile industry to face global competition after the phase out of Multi-Fibre Agreement on Dec. 31, 2004. The government would soon come out with a special package for revival of the 117 sick National Textile Corporation Mills and the Cotton Technology Mission, aimed at raising cotton productivity from the percent 280 kg per hectare to at least the global average of 580 kg and improving quality. The package would be approved by the Cabinet soon, he said. Elaborating on the scheme, Mr. Rana said the five per cent interest subsidy would be reimbursed by the Textile Ministry to the financial institutions on a half-yearly basis. The subsidy burden would be Rs. 3,000 crore during the first five years and subsequently Rs. 3,000 crore during the Tenth and 11th Plan.

Units availing the modernisation fund would be given a two-year moratorium and the period of repayment would be 10 to 12 years, he said. The funds would be available to those units which were "economically viable, bankable and technologically upgradable," Textiles Secretary Shyamal Ghosh said. He said the fund could benefit 1,700 textile mills, 15 lakh powerlooms and 40 lakh handlooms. The Industrial Development Bank of India would be the nodal agency for funding textile industry, excluding powerloom and hosiery sector, while Small Industries Development Bank of India would finance powerlooms and garment units and cotton ginning and pressing sectors.

(c) Textile Exports

India's textile exports increased by 4.6 per cent during 1997-98, but fell short of the $13.36 billion target by 7.3 per cent, Textile Minister Kashiram Rana has said. Textile exports during 1997-98 was $ 12.39 billion against $ 11.84 billion last year, he said chairing a meeting of senior textile industrialists in New Delhi on April 29. Textile exports not meeting the set target had made it imperative for the industry to take urgent steps to strengthen export capabilities of textiles and cloth in order to attain an ambitious export growth target of 20 per cent during 1998-99. Urging the industry to draw action plans to strengthen the industry's export capabilities, he said the 1997-2002 EXIM policy, modified recently, had a number of measures to provide fillip for exports.

Facility for zero import duty for machinery under export promotion capital goods scheme for garment and sericulture sector at a lower threshold value of Rs. 1 crore, allowance of 5 per cent special customs dury in DEPB rates, provision of private bonded warehouses for stock and trade and refining of producers were some of the measures which the industry could take advantage of, he said. There were better possibilities for accelerated growth of Indian textile and clothing exports in the future quota free regime. India should try to draw upon its inherent strengths but also systematically overcome its weaknesses. The Textiles Ministry would lay emphasis on technological upgradation and modernisation of weaving and processing industry.

Improving availability of raw cotton for export units by encouraging use of blends, enriched design capabilities and strengthening training network for skilled manpower were proposed to be initiated by the government, Mr. Rana said. Synthetic and Rayon Textiles Export Promotion Council Chairman R.L. Toshniwal said value cap to calculate DEPB entitlement for some synthetic textile items was a retrogade step as it would discourage high-value items export. He said export credit for packing and post-shipment should be reduced to 7 per cent. Indian Silk Export Promotion Council Chairman Sri Nath said silk exports could be increased only through a right policy ensuring availability of adequate quantity of raw materials.

(d) Textile Exports to European Union

India's textile exports European Union are set to fall further with the latter's decision to withdraw preferential tariffs under Generalised System of Preferences (GSP) from January 1 next year. Under GSP tariff scheme, EU offers 15 to 20 per cent discount on its tariffs for textile imports originating from developing countries like India. Brussels will withdraw the GSP scheme for Indian textile products on the ground that the Indian textile industry had attained better manufacturing skills and competing strengths. The scheme introduced in January 1995, has a provision of graduation, a mechanism to channel benefits from the more developed to less developed beneficiary countries.

As India is the second largest beneficiary of the scheme, the withdrawal of preferential duties was expected to affect the Indian products significantly, said Textile Ministry sources. Abour 40 per cent of Indian textile exports are destined to the EU. The Textile Ministry officials feel that the withdrawal would hit India's textile exports. Though the total garment exports registered a nominal growth in April 1998, garment exports to most of the European countries registered a negative growth.

19

RESEARCH AND DEVELOPMENT

ATOMIC ENERGY

(a) Nuclear Explosion

Twenty-four years after its first and only "peaceful nuclear explosion", India on May 11 decisively moved towards exercising the nuclear option by conducting three underground tests, including that of a thermonuclear device, in the Pokhran range in Rajasthan. Two more nuclear tests were conducted at Pokhran on May 13. With this move, India has risked potential global repercussions. However, the Government officially justified the action in the light of the "dangerous nuclear environment", claiming that the people of India now had a "credible nuclear deterrent". At the same time, the Government appeared to offer the world, particularly the United States, an olive branch by offering to consider "being an adherent to some of the undertakings in the Comprehensive Test Ban Treaty". New Delhi has thus far refused to sign the Nuclear Non-Proliferation Treaty (NPT) and the CTBT on the ground that the treaties discriminated between the nuclear haves and have-nots.

The tests on May 11 were conducted at 3.45 p.m. and the announcement, made this evening by Prime Minister Atal Behari Vajpayee, took the world by surprise. The Prime Minister, who was accompanied only by his political advisor and officials, read from a prepared text and did not entertain any questions from over 100 domestic and international media persons assembled at his offcial residence. Though the Government did not release any technical details, the Prime Minister spoke of the success of the tests. "The measured yields are in line with expected values. Measurements have also confirmed that there was no release of radioactivity into the atmosphere. These were contained explosions like the experiment conducted in May 1974," he said, congratulating the scientists and engineers who accomplished the task. In a symbolic link with the 1974 explosion, today's tests also coincided with Buddha Purnima. The coded message for the successful completion of the earlier test had read: "Buddha is smiling." Indira Gandhi was then the Prime Minister.

Welcome By President

President K.R. Narayanan led the nation in hailing the Indian scientists while the Opposition parties, barring the Left, generally welcome today's nuclear tests as demonstration of India's technological advance. "This event is a major break-through in the realm of national security. I extend my felicitations to all scientists and technologists who have made this possible and say to them India is proud of you," the President said in a message.

US Sanctions

US President Bill Clinto said on May 13 that he had imposed economic sanctions against India for conducting nuclear weapons tests this week. Mr. Clinton told a joint news conference with Germany's Chancellor Helmut Kohl the tests could lead to "dangerous instability in the region." He added that India should not conduct more tests and urged its neighbour Pakistan to remain calm. US officials said that Mr. Clinton, who was visiting Berlin, had decided to impose sanctions and signed them on May 13 morning before leaving for his meeting with Mr. Kohl. The sanctions are to be imposed under a 1994 US non-proliferation law that mandates strict penalties for countries not recognised as nuclear powers that receive or detonate a nuclear device. The sanctions cover the International Millitary Education and Training (IMET) programme, other military exchanges and training exercises for conducting nuclear tests, defence spokesman Ken Bacon said.

Japanese Sanctions

Japan's decision to freeze grants to India will affect some of the ongoing infrastructure projects and will also hinder India's economic underdevelopment, according to Mr. Noboru Kawagishi, Consul-General of Japan in Culcutta. However, he refused to name the projects which will be affected by the sanctions. The manner in which the grants to India will be frozen has not been finalised yet, Mr. Kawagishi said while addressing members of the Bharat Chamber of Commerce on May 15 on Indo-Japanese trade and economic cooperation.

Japan's direct investment into India had increased from Rs. 50 crore in 1991 to Rs. 600 crore in 1992 and finally to Rs. 1,500 crore in 1996. It is the fourth largest investor in India and this represents 0.5 per cent of Japan's entire overseas investment. Mr. Kawagishi pointed out that the total cumulative Official Development Assistance (ODA) to India from Japan is $5.4 billion. During 1996, Japan disbursed $580 million in the form of yen loans, grant-in-aid, technical cooperation and grant assistance for grassroot projects. Out of the total ODA India receives from donor countries 48 per cent is from Japan.

The United States administration has confirmed that the direct impact of the sanctions imposed against India will affect the flow of $142.3 million which this country receives as bilateral assistance. That apart, the US would also oppose loans and guarantees extended by the international financial institutions where India is expecting $3.8 billion as assistance. However, much would depend on whether the US just opposes the loans or actively mobilises support to block assistance to India as the US votes alone cannot stop the loans.

The other part of the sanctions would basically impact on US exports to India. For instance, the US Export-Import Bank (EXIM Bank) said its action of ceasing all new approvals of financing of US exports to India would immediately after approximately $500 million of such exports in pending transactions. Total US exports to India last year were placed at around $4 billion. It has also been clarified that financing for export transactions to India authorised prior to May 13, 1998, would not be affected by the sanctions.

Industry's Reactions

Even as India conducted two more nuclear tests on May 13, Indian industry reaffirmed its support to the Government's actions and reiterated that there was no reason to panic about global sanctions against the country. The Federation of Indian Chambers of Commerce and Industry (FICCI) has said that conductig two more nuclear tests at Pokharan by India has "become more of a diplomatic drill." Asserting that there was no need "to be unduly panicky," FICCI opined that while this period "could be the prime time for Indian business, but at the same time we should know how to face reality."

The chamber welcomed this decision by saying that India is a sovereign nation and has right to conduct nuclear explosions if it wishes to do so. FICCI says that imposing economic sanctions would affect multinational companies operating in India and it will still take some time to gauge its impact on Indian companies which are heavily dependent on technology and raw materials import from abroad. According to FICCI, economic sanctions might have some immediate impact but the dust will settle down soon.

The Confederation of Indian Industry (CII) also holds that there is absolutely no need to panic and the general feeling is of one stability and confidence within the industry. Reaching to second round of two nuclear tests at Pokharan on April 13, Secretary General CII Tarun Das said that India would face the situation with confidence and that Indian industry would not be unduly affected by sanctions, if imposed. It will be clear in next two days whether the sanctions would involve total cutting ... of financing of Government related.

(b) India Self-Reliant in Nuclear Field

The US sanctions will not affect India' nuclear programmes. India is self-reliant in the nuclear field. The infrastructure has been created and scientific and technological capability built up, Dr. Chidambaram, Chairman of the Atomic Energy Commission, said at Kaiga on Nov. 17. He told presspersons that the US sanctions on the nuclear establishments had provided them an opportunity to demonstrate their capability. "We will be successful in it," he said. India would like to be treated by developed nations as an equal partner as far as the nuclear programmes were concerned. "We are no more a developing country, but a developed country in the nuclear technology," he said. Dr. Chidambaram said the Atomic Energy Commission was not unfamiliar with such sanctions. After the first nuclear test in Pokhran in 1974, the Canadians withdrew mid-way from the construction of the second reactor unit at Ravalbhata in Rajasthan. "But it was later completed with out own technology."

About the tests in Pokhran, he said they were conducted on the basis of a new technology and new knowledge on physices and electronics. The few tests were equal to several nuclear tests carried out by various countries. He said every test provided a new device. Three robust designs had been prepared for Pokhran tests and a fission device of 15 kilotons. Thermo-nuclear device and sub-kiloton device were tested. These tests were meant to provide credible nuclear deterrent to the country, he said. Asked whether national development was not more important than the nuclear tests which required large sums of money, he said national security was equally important. Security and development were two faces of the same coin. About the safety aspects, he said the nuclear establishments in the country were safe in all respects. The country had a comprehensive capability in nuclear fuel cycle which included the construction of plants, power generation, reprocessing and waste.

(c) 500-MW N-Power Project at Tarapur

The country's first 500-mw nuclear power project is coming up at Tarapur near Mumbai, which was the launching pad of nuclear power in India with the commissioning of the first nuclear power plant in 1969. So far India is operating 220-mw nuclear power plants. The new Tarapur project comprises of two units—Tarapur Atomic Power Project (TAPP) units three and four based on pressurised heavy water reactors (PHWRS). These would be at par with nuclear power plants built elsewhere in the world, says Mr. A. Sanatkumar, Director (Engineering), Nuclear Power Corporation India Ltd.)

According to him, enhancement to 500 mw has been possible due to extensive experience gained in the design and building of the smaller 220 mw pressurised heavy water reactor units. Eight of these are operating—two each in Rajasthan, Madras, Narora and Kakrapar Atomic Power Stations—and four are in final stages of construction. The Government has accorded the necessary financial assistance and approval for simultaneous construction of both units of Tapp- 3 and 4.

(d) Koodankulam Nuclear Power Deal

After nearly a decade of protracted negotiations, India and Russia on June 21 wrapped up a $2.5 billion deal to set up a nuclear power station at Koodankulam in Tamil Nadu. The agreement was signed by the visiting Russian Atomic Energy Minister, Mr. Yevgeny Adamov, and the Atomic Energy Commission Chairman, Dr. R. Chidambaram, this evening. The deal sends a powerful signal of the existence of special ties between India and Russia. With the signatures to this contract the first deal between India and a foreign supplier in nearly three decades—Russia has broken the Western nuclear technology blockade imposed against India since it exploded a nuclear device in 1974. The agreement also acquires greater political significance as it shows that Moscow is committed to building a close relationship with India despite the opposition by industrialised countries against its nuclear tests last month. India is the '60s had imported the nuclear reactor for the Trombay power station from the United States and had an active nuclear power cooperation agreement with Canada.

The Russian participation in the deal, is an express on of Moscow's definance against American pressures. The US was pressurising Russia not to go ahead with the deal, sighting a western agreement of 1992 to which Moscow was a party, prohibiting nuclear transfers to any country, including India, which had not placed all its atomic facilities under "full scope" safeguards. Russia, countered this insistence by pointing out that the "full scope" rule did not apply to Koodankulam which had been negotiated by New Delhi and Moscow in 1988, prior to the new understanding among the nuclear suppliers. Besides, Russia maintained that India had agreed to put the Koodankulam reactor to inspections by the International Atomic Energy Agency (IAEA), leaving no room for the diversions of nuclear material from the plants for atomic weapons. The import of the Russian reactors will fit into India's plans to produce 20,000 mw of atomic power by 2020. The Koodankulam sight is located along the gulf of Mannar, 25 km northeast of Kanyakumari. The sight provides good foundation because of its hardrock structure. The sight is not subject to severe cyclonic storms or tidal wave. It has good accessibility by road, rail and sea. The nearest sea-port is at Tuticorin while the nearest broadguage rail head and national highway are located at Kanyakumari. The import of this nuclear power station is to make up for the anticipated shortfall in the electricity generation of the southern regional grid, partiuclarly the Tamil Nadu grid by the turn of the Century.

SCIENCE AND TECHNOLOGY

(a) Indian Science Congress Association Annual Session

Invoking natinal pride while simultaneously underscoring the need for global collaboration, the Prime Minister, Mr. A.B. Vajpayee, on Jan. 3 called upon the scientific community to be prepared to "deliver the goods" if any country tried to "arm-twist us and deny us the opportunities of legitimate scientific cooperation." For more than three decades, India had figured on the technology control radar screens of advanced nations. But, attempts of technology denial had not been without benefits as they had spurred scientists to further strengthen national capability. "This has reinforced our belief in the maxim that strength respects strength." he said while inaugurating the 86th annual session of the Indian Science Congress Association, in Chennai. In this context, he mentioned the "achievements" of nuclear scientists at Pokhran which had "filled the entire Indian scientific community with self-confidence". However, in today's world of inter-dependence, and at a time when research and development had become a very costly activity, "our scientific community must forge the closest possible collaborations with the best institutions across the globe", he said. The scientific establishment must focus on quality which stood international scrutiny, he added.

The Prime Minister identified meeting the needs of industry, agriculture and services as another problem-solving area for scientists. "Food security, water management, energy and material conservation, low-cost housing, environment protection, maximising our exports by achieving cost and quality competitiveness in world markets, high-quality technical education leading to self-employment opportunities, all these are crucial for our national development," he said. Also, universities and R and D institutions must be freed from bureaucratisation for creating world class scientific research. In the future, science would have to strive for a new integration of knowledge systems that combined reasoning, ethics, individual behaviour, social relations and the environment. "The world will have to move towards harmonisation of science and spiritualism in order to attain peace, prosperity and happiness for all," he said. The effects of science and technology had been both positive and negative; scientists and non-scientists must be concerned about minimising the negative effects and maximising the benefits for the greatest good of the greatest number of people, he said. While calling for special measures to support women scientists, Mr. Vajpayee urged the Ministry of Human Resource Development to give high priority to the simplification of rules and regulations and encourage more women professionals to get involved in scientific programmes.

The Prime Minister gave away the annual scientific awards, including the Jawaharlal Nehru birth centenary award to the Union Human Resource Development Minister, Dr. Murli Manohar Joshi, and the Shatabdi Pursakar awards to eminent scientists such as Prof. M.S. Swaminathan, Prof. V. Ramalingaswamy and Prof. M.G.K. Menon. Among the distinguished foreign scientists honoured on the occasion were the Nobal laureate, Dr. James Watson, and the editor of the magazine *Nature*, Dr. Philip Campbell.

Rs. 15,000 Cr. for Biosciences

The India Science Congress, which focusses on biosciences, has asked the government for a Rs. 15,000 crore 10-year plan for ushering in a bioindustrial revolution in the country in the next millennium. This recommendation was made by Ms Manju Sharma, General President of the 86th Indian Science Congress and Sectetary of the Department of Biotechnology, in her presidential address at the inauguration of the Congress. Special incentives must be given for the proliferation of biotechnology industries, specially small-scale units, in terms of venture capital and other facilities, she said.

The Secretary called up on the biotech industries to develop close relationship with academic and research institutions. "It must be made mandatory for the industries to have leading technologists as advisors and consultants. Industry should promote indigenous R & D significantly". Scientists should make all efforts to educate and inform the public about biosciences to remove apprehensions about advancements in biosciences, she said. Outlining a series of recommendations to promote biosciences in the next decade, she asked states to give top priority to biotechnology in their plans and launch special biotechnology programmes for rural areas and weaker sections. Simpler administrative and financial procedures with full accountability without violation of biotechnology rules should be developed in national interest.

Jai Vigyan National Mission

The Union Minister for Human Resource Development, Dr. Murli Manohar Joshi, has said that scientific institutions would take up 21 important development projects as part of the Jai Vigyan National Mission with focus on science and technology. These projects would be in areas such as food security, energy conservations, health care, disaster management and bio-diversity. Scientific and R and D institutions would take up one project in 1999. All the projects would be given green channel treatment with procedures relaxed he said while participating at the annual sessions of the 86th Indian Science Congress in Chennai on Jan. 3.

The Minister said he had directed the Department of Bio-technology to institute 10 awards every year for outstanding young scientists in biosciences. This would encourage high quality research of excellence and relevance. As achieving excellence was dependent in innovative talents which in turn needed identification and nurturing from an early age, a new scheme to select under 18 youngsters of outstanding talent and to provide them with necessary ambience and opportunities for harnessing their talent had been instituted.

(b) 16 Projects Under Jai Vigyan Mission

Sixteen projects have been identified for the Jai Vigyan Mission at a meeting of secretaries of various scientific departments, presided over by Minister of Science and Technology, Dr. Murli Manohar Joshi in New Delhi on March 10, said on offcial release. The mission was announced by Finance Minister Yashwant Sinha in Parlimanet during his budget speech. The projects will be taken up as Jai Vigyan Science and Technology Missions on fast track and also as green channel schemes. They are in the areas of food security, sustainable plant genetic resource management, nuclear medicine, development of new generation vaccines, herbal product development, mirror site for genomic research design development,

World Bank, Danish International Development Agency (DANIDA), Denmark and the Government of India. The Project has been completed and formally launched in May 1997. The four Regional Training Centres (RTCs) under the Project at ACC, Jamul (M.P.), Dalmia Cement, Dalmiapuram (T.N.), J.K. Cement, Nimbahera (Rajasthan) and Gujarat Ambuja, Ambuja Nagar (Gujarat) have been equipped with all the training and class room equipments, special equipments, computers, books, manuals, etc. As on 31st December, 1997, 4084 persons have been trained in various technical courses, being conducted by the RTCs using the 49 high quality training packages developed for the projects on various aspects of the cement industry.

Another innovative pilot project for bulk transportation and distribution of cement is being implemented with World Bank Assistance at Kalamboli, New Bombay. Department of Industrial Policy & Promotion, M/s Associated Cement Companies Limited (ACC), IDBI and ICICI are participating in the project. Under this project, special high efficiency wagons would be developed for transportation of bulk cement from Wadi Plant of ACC to the Depot at Kalamboli where cement would be stored in silos and then distributed in bulk or bagged condition in and around Bombay. The project has started trial runs in November, 1997 and the project is likely to be operational by middle of 1998.

(c) Electronics Industry

Electronics is the fastest growing sector of the Indian industry. During the Eighth Plan, the electronics industry has achieved a cumulative annual growth of 20 per cent in production and over 40 per cnet in exports. The Electronics production during the year 1997-98 was Rs. 32,070 crores, as compared to Rs. 26,640 crores during 1996-97, registering a growth of over 20 per cent. The export performance of electronics industry is expected to be Rs. 9,500 crores during 1997-98, against Rs. 6,287 crores during 1996-97. An export target of about Rs. 49,000 crores has been set for the terminal year of Ninth Plan with a growth rate of about 52 per cent.

The principal strength of the country with abundant manpower of technical skills is well recognised in the software area. The Government is taking all necessary steps to make India, a global Information Technology power and one of the largest generators and exporters of software in the world within 10 years. Over the years, the Government has taken various measures to provide a conducive policy framework, as a result of which software industry has emerged as one of the fastest growing sectors in the economy with a CAGR exceeding 50 per cent. Currently, this industry is worth US$ 2.5 billion and is expected to be about US$ 15 billion by the year 2002. Indian software export has jumped to a level of US$ 1.6 billion in 1997-98. Software exports registered a growth of 68 per cent in rupee terms and 52 per cent in dollar terms during 1998. According to a survey conducted by the National Association of Software and Service Companies (NASSCOM), exports revenue for 1998 stood at Rs. 9,500 crore as against Rs. 5,640 crore reported in the previous year. Announcing the results of the NASSCOM survey on the export performance of the Indian software industry, at a Press conference in New Delhi on Feb. 5. NASSCOM President Dewang Mehta attributed the growth of software exports to the growth respect for Indian software industry in the international market. He said, "We have yet to see any other country in the world which has recorded a growth rate of 50 to 60 per cent in software exports continuously for the last seven years." The performance of the software industry was well reflected in the growing market capitalisation of the information technology companies. Current market capitalisation of the software industry is more than Rs. 100,000 crore which is almost 10 per cent of the Indian gross domestic product.

According to NASSCOM, during 1998 more than 158 of *Fortune* 500 companies outsourced their software requirements to India, Stating that the speedy implementation of the first report of the National IT task force had helped remove many of the bottlenecks faced by the industry, Mr. Mehta urged the Government to quickly implement many of the pending recommendations of the national IT task force. NASSCOM also attributed the handsome growth in exports to continuing increase in offshore services and the year 2000 date conversion opportunities, India has already bagged export orders of more than $2 billion for Y2K projects, and now many companies are offering a package deal to solve Y2K as well as Euro currency conversion. Euro currency conversion is the next big opportunity for India.

The principle strategy of the Ninth Plan is on Export, Employment and Productivity-led growth of Electronics and Information Technology. One rupee invested in this sector has the capacity to double every two years through the benefit of higher productivity in all other sectors through automated equipment, instrumentation and computer control systems. Electronics and Information Technology industry has the propensity to increase the overall growth rate to a higher level, and hence this industry should be given a special thrust during the Ninth Plan. Keeping this in view and the projected Export, Employment and Productivity-led growth of Electronics and Information Technology, the working Group on Electonics Industry has strongly recommended that the Electonics and Information Technology industry should be classified as basic growth infrastructure industry and thereby a special status be accorded to this sector.

In the liberalised economic scenario, the Department of Electronics (DoE) aims to bring the benefits of electonics to every walk of life, and is playing a catalytic role to make the Indian electronics industry a global player. This is being achieved through a three-pronged strategy of supporting technology development, setting up of critical infrastructure and formulating policies conducive to industrial growth.

In order to achieve the above goals, the strategic imperatives proposed are production levels at international cost and prices; market promotion and export thrust; quality of products at internationally competitive levels; rationalisation of procedures to ensure growth; identifying niche areas in the world market; strengthening R&D efforts; strengthening manpower base; computing in Indian languages; developing new applications of electronics relevant to India, etc. The penetration of computers in India, at present, at one per thousand of the population, is targeted to grow to ten per thousand by the year 2001.

VLSI Fabrication Facility

The new VLSI fabrication facility at Semiconductor Complex Ltd., Mohali, has been rebuilt with an investment of over Rs. 330 crores with a capacity of 20,000 six-inch wafers per annum and 1.2 micron technology. The facility was commissioned on April 29, 1997, and the first working chips came out in October 1997. The plant was dedicated to the nation by the then Prime Minister, Shri I.K. Gujral, on December 17, 1997.

Policy

The electonics industry as a whole, with the exception of aerospace and defence electronics, has been fully delicensed. Fiscal, investment and trade policies for the electronics sector have also been liberalised. DoE played a key role in the opening up of Internet Services for the Private Sector in order to support and stimulate the use of INTERNET in the country.

R&D Efforts

The Department of Electronics has been giving high priority for all-round development of technology in the country. The DOE supports and funds technology development through its councils set up in various fields. A major result of sponsored research has been the enhancement of technological base and capabilities in the country besides generating specific hardware. It has also produced strong pockets of specialised expertise which have been used as a spring board for launching major national projects besides providing the much needed trained manpower to man such national programmes.

National High Voltage Direct Current Project

After successful operation of 100 KV/100 MW HVDC link between Lower Sileru in Andhra Pradesh and Barsoor in Madhya Pradesh under Stage I of the National High Voltage Direct Current Project, Stage II of the NHVDC Project execution is in progress which upgrades the link to 200 MW/200 KV and incorporates state-of-the-art digital controls built indigenously with this, the total turn key capabilities in HVDC technology from design to Commissioning is being established.

Language Technology Development

DOE has intensified efforts in developing and promoting localized applications and system software for popular applications in Indian languages. As a result a project for development of Disk Operating System (DOS) in Hindi by Tata Information System Ltd. and IBM of USA has been started. Microsoft Corpn., USA, in collaboration with National Centre for Software Technology, has started development for supporting Indian languages in Windows NT operating system.

High Performance Computer System

C-DAC has built a massively parallel processing technology-based computer of 100 GFLOP peak computing power with an architecture scalable to 1 TFLOP.

Education and Research Network (ERNET)

ERNET has been providing network services to Indian academic and research community since 1990. There has been a steady growth in number of institutions availing the services of ERNET. Today, ERNET has over 80,000 users and has now been converted into an autonomous body.

Social Welfare for Blind

Computerised Braille transcription of text from English and some other Indian languages including automatic Braille printing interfaces has been developed under a project promoted by Department of Electronics at Ramakrishna Mission Blind Boys Academy, Calcutta.

National Information Infrastructure for National Development

The Department of Electronics has initiated a national focus on National Information Infrastructure with the aim of promoting use and proliferation of Information Technology. Some of the sectors proposed to be covered would include—literacy, education and life-long learning leading to increase in employment oppotunity, better health care, environment friendliness, opportunities for rural populace to acquire new skills, etc. It is expected to generate a new Mega Industry bigger than any sector known today. As such, it assumes both strategic and economic importance in the country. DOE is working very closely with the Andhra Pradesh Government on Electronic Governance. This experience could be used by other states for replication.

Under multimedia programme, a multi-institutional project on a Development-cum-Training Infrastructure as a National Resource for low cost multimedia Content Creation has been initiated.

An Inter-Ministerial Standing Committee has been set-up under the Chairmanship of Secretary (Electronics) to formulate Cyber laws in the country to facilitate the admissibility of electronic document as evidence. The Standing Committee has suggested amendments in the Indian Evidence Act, the General Clause Act, the Code of Criminal Procedure and the Indian Penal Code. Three new legislations viz., Digital Signature Act, Computer Misuse (Prohibition) Act and Data Protection Act, primarily to address the origin and authenticity of the electronic message/document/data have been identified. These legislations will cater to the legal requirements for implementation of electronic commerce/ electronic fund transfer in the country.

The department has initiated number of development programmes for manpower, infrastructure, quality upgradation, stimulation of software engineering and research (now called the National Software Capability Enhancement Programme). A National Institute of Advanced Software Education and Research (NISER) for providing high quality and specialised training for software professionals has also been initiated. DOE has also taken initiative in setting up of a JAVA Competency Centre at CMC R&D Centre, Hyderabad in collaboration with Sun Microsystems Ltd. and NASSCOM to improve and expand quality at high end of software capability, both in education as well as R&D sectors.

Manpower Development

The per capita investment creating a new job in the electonics sector is one of the lowest among all economic sectors. As this sector is one of the largest employer of skilled and educated persons, according higher priority to this sector helps to reduce the revolutionary tendencies and social unrest amongst the skilled and educated unemployed. This sector is also one of the largest employers of women and can go a long way in fulfilling the ideal of creating economic opportunities for women.

As a part of the initiative to promote development of electronics in the North-East, a Centre of Electronics Design and Technology at Tezpur is being set up with the assistance and support of University of Tezpur. A special programme has also been initiated to promote employment generation in the North East by assisting human resource development in this sector through selected institutions.

(d) Fertiliser Industry

Optimum fertilizer application plays a key role in improving the productivity of various crops. It is a critical component of the strategy for self-sufficiency in foodgrains to feed a rapidly growing population. Concerted efforts in this direction have resulted in a substantial increase in agricultural production and productivity. From a modest level of 52 million tonnes in 1951-52, the foodgrain production in 1996-97 rose to the level of 199.3 million tonnes but again decreased to 193.1 million tonnes during 1997-98. The increase in fertilizer consumption has contributed significantly to a more or less sustained improvement in the production of foodgrains in the country.

Although the average per hectare consumption of fertilizer nutrients has increased from less than 1 kg. in 1951-52 to about 86.1 kg. in 1997-98, even this level of fertilizer use is low with reference to the objective of accelerating the growth in the agriculture sector, as well as the consumption levels prevailing in other countries, including some of the developing countries in Asia. Moreover, the consumption of chemical fertilizers in the country is unevenly distributed, being much higher in regions with assured irrigation. In view of the limited scope for increasing the land area under cultivation, further increases in agricultural production can be achieved only through better water management, expansion of the area under irrigation, improved farming practices, research and development in the use of scientific inputs and seeds, and last but not the least, more extensive and balanced use of fertilizers through fertilizer education. Hence, the critical importance of the fertilizer sector in the Indian economy, expecially in creating a prosperous rural base.

Growth

The Indian fertilizer industry has been supplying a substantial portion of the growing demand of fertilizers. It had a very humble beginning in 1906, when the first manufacturing unit was set up in Ranipet near Chennai with a production capacity of 6000 Metric Tonne (MT) of Single Superphosphate per annum. The Fertilizer & Chemicals Travancore Ltd. (FACT) at Cochin in Kerala and the Fertilizer Corporation of India Ltd., Sindri in Bihar were the first large sized fertilizer plants to be set up in the forties and fifties with a view to establishing a base for industrialization and achieving self-sufficiency in foodgrains. The Green Revolution in the late sixties gave an impetus to the growth of the fertilizer industry in India. The eighties witnessed a significant addition to the fertilizer production capacity.

The installed capacity as on 30.11.98 has reached a level of 105.20 lakh MT of nitrogen (inclusive of an installed capacity of 192.92 lakh MT of urea) and 31.70 lakh MT of phosphate nutrients, making India the third largest fertilizer producer in the world. The rapid build-up of fertilizer production capacity in the country has been achieved as a result of a favourable policy environment and heavy investments made over the years in the public, co-operative and private sectors. Today, there are 63 large sized fertilizer plants in the country, manufacturing a wide range of nitrogenous, phosphatic and complex fertilizers. Nine of the units produce ammonium sulphate as a by-product. Besides, there are about 79 medium and small-scale single superphosphate units. The sector-wise intalled capacity is given in the table below;

Table 18.3 : Sector-wise, Nutrient-wise Installed Capacity of Fertilizer As on 30-11-98

Sr. No.	Sector	Capacity (Lakh MT)		% age share	
		Nitrogen	Phosphate	Nitrogen	Phosphate
1.	Public Sector	43.20	8.27	41.06	26.09
	i) Viable Units	33.09	8.27	31.45	26.09
	ii) Loss Making Units	10.11	-	9.61	-
2.	Cooperative Sector	22.68	3.09	21.56	9.75
3.	Private Sector	39.32	20.34	37.38	64.16
	Total	105.20	31.70	100.00	100.00

Table 18.4 : Sector-wise Installed Capacity of Urea and Its Percentage Share as on 30-11-98

Sr. No.	Sector	Capacity Urea (Lakh MT)	% age share
1.	Public Sector	75.95	39.37
	i) Viable Units	54.43	28.21
	ii) Loss Making Units	21.52	11.16
2.	Cooperative Sector	46.71	24.21
3.	Private Sector	70.26	36.42
	Total	192.92	100.00

Self-Sufficiency

Of the three main nutrients required for various crops — nitrogen, phosphate and potash, indigenous raw materials are available mainly for nitrogen. The Government's policy has aimed at achieving the maximum possible degree of self-sufficiency in the production of nitrogenous fertilizers based on utilisation of indigenous feedstocks. As of now, the country is self-sufficient to the extent of about 85 per cent in the case of nitrogen. Prior to 1980, nitrogenous fertilizer plants were based mainly on naphtha as feedstock. A number of fuel oil based ammonia-urea plants were also set up during 1978 to 1982. In 1980, two coal-based plants were set up for the first time in the country at Talcher (Orissa) and Ramagundam (Andhra Pradesh). With associated and free gas becomig available from offshore Bombay High and South Bassein basins, a number of gas based ammonia-urea plants have been set up since 1985. In view of the limitations on availability of gas, a number of expansion projects were taken up in the last few years with naphtha as feedstock with the flexibility for switching over to gas as and when it is available. Feasibility of a delivery system of Liquefied Natural Gas (LNG) to meet the demand of fertilizer units and projects is also being explored.

In the case of phosphates, the paucity of domestic raw material constrains the attainment of any degree of self-sufficiency. Recognising this, a deliberate policy-mix has been adopted which involves the modulation of three options:

(i) domestic production based on indigenous/imported rock phosphate and imported sulphur; (ii) domestic production based on imported intermediates, viz. ammonia and phosphoric acid; and (iii) import of finished fertilizer, viz. Di-Ammonium Phosphate (DAP) and very rarely, Mono-Ammonium Phosphate (MAP) and Nitrogen Phosphate Potash (NPK) complexes. Roughly 70 per cent of the requirement of phosphatic fertilizers is met through the first two options. Since indigenous rock phosphate supplies meet only 5 to 10 per cent of the total requirement of P_2O_5 , phosphatic fertilizers produced in the country are essentially based on imported raw materials and intermediates.

There are no known commercially exploitable reserves of potash in the country and per force, the entire requirement of potassium fertilizers for direct aplication as well as for production of complex fertilizers is met through imports.

While the country may have to continue to depend on imports to meet the requirement of phosphatic and potassic fertilizers, due to non-availability of indigenous raw-material, imports may have to bridge the gap between demand and domestic availability. This is desirable in view of strategic considerations as the international urea market is highly volatile to demand supply scenario.

Technological Advancements

India is one of the largest producers and consumers of chemical fertilizers in the world. To meet the growing demand of fertilizers in the country through maximum indigenous production, self-reliance in design engineering and execution of fertilizer projects is an important as autonomy in fertilizer production. This requires a strong indigenous technological base in planning, development of process know-how, design engineering and expertise in project management and execution of the project. As a sequel to the continuing support of the Government for research and development as well as design engineering activities over the years, Indian consultancy organisations in the field of fertilizers have grown steadily in tandem with the fertilizer industry. These consultancy organisations are today in a position to undertake execution of fertilizer projects starting with feasibility studies, basic and detailed engineering, to procurement, construction and commissioning of complete fertilizer projects, as prime engineering consultants.

The fertilizer plant operators have now fully absorbed and assimilated the latest in fertilizer technology and are in a position to opeate and maintain the plants at their optimum levels without any foreign assistance. The average performance of gas based plants in the country today is amongst the best in the world.

The country has also developed expertise for fabrication and supply of major critical equipment like centrifugal compressors, high pressure reactors, heat exchangers etc. required for fertilizer projects. The indigenous vendors are in a position to compete and secure orders for such critical equipment under stiff international competitive bidding procedure. Today, roughly 70 per cent of the equipment required for a major fertilizer plant can be manufactured indigenously.

Based on indigenously developed know-how, facilities have been installed for the manufactutre of a total range of catalysts required for production of nitrogenous fertilizers. Only a few organisations in the world have been able to develop and manufacture such catalysts. Likewise, expertise has been developed for undertaking complete health study of fertilizer plants and equipment using the latest sophisticated methods of non-destructive testing. Such health studies are essential for safe operation and preventive maintenance of plants.

Fertilizer Prices and Subsidy

The sale prices of controlled fertilizers are fixed by the Government of India (Department of Agriculture & Cooperation) under the Fertilizer (Control) Order, 1985 issued under the Essential Commodities Act, 1955. At present, only urea, which is the main nitrogenous fertilizer constituting about 60 per cent of the total fertilizer consumption in the country, is under statutory price control. The farmgate price of urea which is fixed at Rs. 4000 per tonne, excluding local levies is amongst the lowest in the region and is heavily subsidised.

The difference between the sale price and the Retention Price (the cost of production as assessed by the Government plus reasonable return on net worth) is paid as subsidy to the individual manufacturing units under the Retention Price-cum-Subsidy Scheme (RPS). The cost of production of various fertilizer units differ from unit to unit and even from month to month, depending upon the health and vintage of the plant, the feedstock used, the levels of capacity utilisation, energy consumption, distance from the source of feedstock/raw materials, cost of inputs, etc. In addition to the retention price subsidy, equity freight subsidy is paid to the manufacturers of controlled fertilizers to cover the cost of transportation from the production points to the consumption centres. Since the consumer prices of both indigenous and imported fertilisers are fixed uniformly, subsidy is also paid on imported fertilizers in order to bridge the difference between the cost of imports and the statutorily fixed consumer price.

Apart from the subsidy on controlled fertilizers, the Government has been giving a special concession on decontrolled fertilizers in order to promote the balanced use of plant nutrients. This scheme is being implemented by the Department of Agriculture & Cooperation.

Concessions/Incentives to Domestic Fertilizer Industry

To encourage investment in the fertilizer sector, the following concessions are available to the domestic industry :

(i) Nominal duty on import of capital goods for setting up of new plants/ modernisation of existing units.
(ii) Deemed export benefits to indigenous supplies of capital goods to fertilizer projects provided such supplies are made under the procedure of international competitive bidding.
(iii) Nominal duty on import of fertilizer raw materials and intermediates.

Important Developments — 1998-99

The high-powered Hanumantha Rao Committee has recommended total deregulation of the fertilizer industry which includes phased lifting of price controls, distribution and movement curbs. The seven-member committee which reviewed the fertilizer pricing policy and subsidies has, however, favoured an upper ceiling on the farm gate price to be notified annually under which the fertilizer companies will be free to sell the farm nutrients. The committee submitted its final report to the Union Fertilisers and Chemicals Minister Surjit Singh Barnala on April 3. It has also asked the Government to discontinue the present system of fixing the unit-wise retention price based on which subsidy is made available. Following an alternative methodology proposed by the committee, it was stated that a normative referral price (NRP) would be determined for existing fertilizer units to fix the subsidy component.

Right now, the committee has recommended a farm gate price of Rs. 6,500 per tonne for urea, Rs. 12,800 for DAP while fixing the ex-factory NRP of Rs. 6,050 and Rs. 11,900 per tonne respectively. It was also stated that the NRP and subsidy should be periodically revised apparently in tune with international price movement for inputs like ammonia and phosphoric acid. The committee asked the Government to remove distribution and movement controls on fertilisers from Rabi season of 1998-99 itself. In effect, there will not be allocation of various fertilizers—especially urea—to different states under the Essential Commodities Act except for inaccessable and remote areas. The Hanumantha Rao panel emphasised the need to continued canalised imports during next five years to allow the industry to switch over to fuel energy efficient technologies and feedstock like domestic natural gas and liquified natural gas from the prevailing naphtha, fuel oil and coal fired plants.

The production target for 1998-99 has been fixed at 106.32 lakh tonnes of nitrogen and 30.27 lakh tonnes of phosphate.This represents a growth rate of 5.9 per cent in nitrogen and 1.7 per cent in phosphate as compared to the actual production in 1997-98. Production of nitrogenous and phosphatic fertilizers in April-November 1998 was 68.45 lakh tonnes and 19.76 lakh, respectively. This represented a growth rate of 4.6 per cent vis-a-vis the corresponding period last year. In respect of urea (which is a controlled fertilizer), the production has been 126.60 lakh tonnes by the end of November which is 7.1 per cent higher over the corresponding period in 1997-98. Also, the production of DAP registered a growth of 4.1 per cent over the production in the corresponding period of the previous year.

At present 6 major fertilizer projects involving an estimated capital cost of approximately Rs. 4122.02 crore are under implementation in the country. When commissioned, they are likely to add an additional capacity of 9.75 lakh MTPA of urea, 7.90 lakh MTPA of NPK, 23.07 lakh MTPA of DAP and 1 lakh MTPA of NP fertilizers.

No new projects were being sanctioned for quite some time on account of differences in the perception of the demand supply scenario among different Departments.

Fertilizer Projects Cleared

The way has now been cleared for the approval of four new fertilizer projects at a total estimated cost of Rs. 7,000 crore by the Public Investment Board (PIB) with both the Union Agriculture Ministry and the Chemicals and Fertilisers Ministry resolving their difference over the projected demand-supply gap vis-a-vis the decline in global urea prices. These four new ammonia-urea projects are KRIBHCO's Hazira plant at an estimated cost of Rs. 1,203 crore, KRIBHCO's new plant at the existing site of FCI at Gorakhpur at an estimated cost of Rs. 1,445 crore, RCF's Thal expansion project at an estimated cost of Rs. 1,228.83 crore and IFFCO's Nellore project at an estimated cost of Rs. 1,568.70 crore. With considerable delay in getting approvals, the total cost of all these four projects in likely to exceed the stated initial estimate and is likely to escalate to over Rs. 7,000 crore, according to reliable sources.

Earlier, when IFFCO's Nellore project and other projects came up for consideration before the PIB, the Board was of the view that the Planning

Commission's projected demand-supply gap for nitrogenous fertilizers in the terminal year of the Ninth Plan did not justify the setting up of such high cost projects on grounds of food security of the nation. Since the Agriculture Ministry did not concur with the Planning Commission's demand estimates, the Ministry was asked to reconcile their differences with the Planning Commission and evolve a consensus over the demand estimate for nitrogenous fertilizers in 2001-02.

The initiatives undertaken to set up joint venture projects in countries with better resource endowments so as to meet the growing demand of fertilizers in the country have made significant progress. The Government has approved the investment of RCF/KRIBHCO to make an equity contribution of US $ 69 million each in a joint venture in Oman for production of 14.52 lakh tonnes of urea and 3.30 lakh tonnes of merchant ammonia per annum. The Joint Venture Company i.e. Oman India Fertilizer Company has been registered in Oman on 18.2.98. All major agreements have been finalised.

The joint venture company of 'Industries Chimiques du Senegal' (ICS) which started production in 1984 has taken up a project for doubling the production of its phosphoric acid plants and development of new rock phosphates mines at a cost of about US $ 215 million. The Government has approved equity contribution of US $ 20 million by IFFCO in ICS Senegal for financing the expansion project. The project is expected to be competed within 30 months from the zero date of 1.7.98. ICS proposes to sell a major portion of the phosphoric acid produced in the expanded plant to India.

In order to involve a strategy for use of Liquefied Natural Gas (LNG) as feedstock, the Government has set up a Core Group on Fertilizer Companies with a view to exploring the feasibility of a delivery system of LNG essentially to met the demand of fertilizer units and projects. The report of the Core Group is awaited.

The Disinvestment Commission has recommended disinvestment of shares of MFL, FACT, NFL and PPCL. Recommendations of the Commission are under process.

The revival package of HFC and FCI reformulated on the basis of a fresh technical appraisal by an expert group led by ICI from the stand point of the financial institutions were considered by the Government on 1.10.97. The Government has approved the proposal for the revamp of Namrup units of HFC at an estimated fresh investment of Rs. 350 crore. The project is to be implemented within 30 months of award of Engineering, Procurement and Construction (EPC) contract. The groundwork for launching the project has started. To ensure timely implementation of the scheme, a plan budgetary support of Rs. 70 crore has been made in the budget for 1998-99. The decision in respect of the other units HFC and FCI is still to be taken. Proposals in respect of the remaining units of HFC have been reviewed from the angle of unit-wise viability and tie-up of funding arrangements and are presently under inter-ministerial consultation.

The Government of India has continued the supply of urea to farmers at heavily subsidised prices. The farmgate price of urea, currently fixed at Rs. 4000 per tonne, continues to be one of the lowest in the region.

Under a scheme administered by Ministry of Agriculture, substantial special concessions are also being provided on decontrolled phosphoric and potassium fertilizers with a view to encouraging the farmers to optimise the use of the three plant nutrients. The revised rates of special concession for Kharif 1998 have been announced recently which recognises the nitrogen content in complex fertilizers while deciding the level of subsidy. This would give substantial benefits to the manufacturers of complex fertilizers.

The consumption of urea in terms of sales registered 4% growth during Kharif 1998. The trend is expected to be maintained during Rabi 1998-99 during which the area under sowing of wheat and other crops has been substantial on account of unseasonal rains and consequent availability of moisture over more than expected area. Adequate and timely availability of urea was ensured throughout the country during Kharif 1998. There is no State which complained of non-availability of urea. During Rabi also, the availability of urea would be adequate in all the States to meet the estimated requirement.

In respect of the decontrolled fertilizers, the requirement had registered a sharp increase following the unforeseen rains during October. All possible support was extended both to the indigenous manufacturers and importers in movement of these fertilizers to the States thus making them available as per their requirement. Nearly 1.5 million tonnes of DAP was cleared from JNPT and a same quantity from Vizag port by according priority berthing of DAP vessels at both these ports. This helped in meeting the requirements of DAP in the States of Punjab, Haryana, Rajasthan, Madhya Pradesh, Uttar Pradesh and Bihar. This considerably reduced the complaints in respect of decontrolled fertilizers which would otherwise have been unmanageable. For future, the Government has decided to maintain buffer-stock of decontrolled fertilizers to meet any eventuality arising out of sudden spurt in demand. The Buffer Stocking Scheme shall be operated through Indian Potash Limited (IPL) and necessary preparations for it are under way.

DAP Fertilizer Shortage

Shortfall in availability of di-ammonium phosphate (DAP) which has been created by indecision in finalising subsidy policies has delayed wheat sowing in the main surplus producing states of Punjab, Haryana and Uttar Pradesh, according to the fertilizer industry. In addition, fertilizer companies are facing serious liquidity problems as arrears of subsidy payments have mounted to over Rs. 800 crore. This was disclosed on Nov. 17 by the Chairman of the Fertilizer Association of India, Mr. V.N. Rai, who said the supply of fertilizers will be inadequate if import and home made production are not viable. As a result of the Goverhment's decision to reverse the policy on phosphatic and potassic fertilizers orginally announced at the end of the August, several companies have been forced to either cancel import contracts or put on hold plans for further imports. The reversal of policy has meant that the DAP prices are frozen at Rs. 8300 per tonne through subsidy has been raised to Rs. 4000 per tonne. The increase in subsidy by Rs. 250 per tonne over the previous season is not sufficient, however, to cover higher costs of importing phos acid and ammonia owing to rupee depreciation.

Addressing a Press conference, Mr. Rai said the turmoil and turbulence in the fertilizer sector will continue till a stable, long term and conducive policy is prepared for this vital sector of the economy. The possibilities of a significant revival in production and consumption had been dashed this year because of the Government's reversal of its original decision to allow manufacturers and importers of the DAP and single super phosphate (SSP) the freedom of fixing prices. It has once again restored controls and intervention by the Central and State

Governments in this sector. Regarding fertilizer consumption, he said this increased from 14.31 million tonnes during 1996-97 to 16.19 million tonnes in 1997-98, a record increase of 1.88 million tonnes. The previous highest rise in consumption was in 1988-89 when it rose by about 2.2 million tonnes. Production also recorded phenomenal growth during 1997-98 with output of nitrogen crossing the 10 million tonnes mark. It increased from 8.59 million tonnes during 1996-97 to 10.08 million tonnes during 1997-98, making it a record increase of 1.49 million tonnes. Apart from substantial additions to the installed capacity due to commissioning of the IFFCO, Anonla and NFL-Vijaiur, this was made possible by higher capacity utilisation. Production of phosphatic fertilizers also increased significantly from 2.58 million tonnes in 1996-97 to 3.06 million tonnes in 1997-98.

IFFCO to Raise Production

The Indian Farmers Fertilizer Cooperative Ltd. (IFFCO), has planned to increase its fertilizer production to over 50 lakh tonnes per annum by 2000-01 from the current production of about 40 lakh tonnes per annum, said Mr. R.V. Subba Rao, Joint General Manager, Marketing, IFFCO, Bangalore, in Truchi on Dec. 23. Speaking at the inaugural function of a three-day "Inservice training programme" for the field staff of IFFCO in Tamil Nadu and Andhra Pradesh, Mr. Subba Rao said that the IFFCO had proposed to set up an ammonia-urea complex at Nellore in Andhra Pradesh. The unit would have a capacity of producing 7.26 lakh tonnes of urea per annum and is expected to commence commercial production by the turn of the century.

The Rs. 1,568-crore project would help bridge the demand-supply gap in one of the richest agricultural areas of the country, he observed. In its pursuit of attaining global reputation as a fertilizer giant under its Vision-2000 programme, the IFFCO had already expanded its production units at Aonla Pulphur in UP and at Kalol in Gujarat in quick succession. Though the country's foodgrain production, which had touched 199 million tonnes in 96-97, had come down to 192 million tonnes in 97-98, fertilizer consumption has increased significantly. In 98-99, the country's foodgrain production is expected to be around 198 million tonnes. To meet the increasing demand for fertilizers, the IFFCO had already increased its production from 30 lakh tonnes in 96-97 to 40 lakh tonnes in 97-98, he said.

(e) Food Processing Industries

1. Recent Initiatives

To further liberalise the Indian food processing industry to make it globally competitive and facilitate further investment, the following initiatives were taken during the year by the Ministry of Food Processing Industries.

Repeal of Rice Milling Act

The Rice Milling Industry (Regulation) Act, 1958 (RMI Act) was enacted to facilitate modernisation of rice mills and to regulate the establishment of new rice mills. Considering the fact that nearly 65 per cent of the total paddy produced in the country is processed in modern rice mills and most of the commercial rice millers in the country are now aware of the advantages of setting up of modern rice mills and of modernising their old units which had been yielding high percentage of brokens and inferior quality by-products, the Government has repealed the RMI Act with effect from 28th May, 1997. In view of this, no Government permission is now required the setting up of rice mills.

Amendment of Fruit Products Order (FPO)

The Furit Products Order (FPO), 1955 which has been promulgated under the Essential Commodities Act, is implemented by the Ministry of Food Processing Industries. In view of the demands of the industry, the Act was amended with effect from 30th May, 1997. These amendments include renewal of FPO Licences for periods ranging from three, five or ten years instead of annual renewals, and removal of the requirement for specific approvals for labels for every packed food product.

Dereservation of Certain Industries

Ice Cream, Vinegar, Rice Milling, Dal Milling, Biscuits, Poultry Feed (except in pellet form) and Synthetic Syrups have been dereserved i.e. they have been deleted from the list of items reserved for exclusive manufacture in the small scale sector with effect from 3rd April, 1997. As a result, large scale production facilities can be set up to achieve economies of scale without any requirement for licensing.

2. Investments

In the era of economic liberalisation where the private, public and cooperative sectors are to play their rightful role in development of food processing industries, the Ministry acts as a catalyst for bringing in greater investments into this sector.

Since August 1991 till March 1998, 4375 Industrial Entrepreneur Memorandas (IEM) envisaging an investment of Rs. 51,825 crore and direct employment of 6.74 lakh persons (approx) have been received for various sectors of food processing. Out of the IEMs filed in the post liberalisation period 3738 IEMs envisaging an investment of Rs. 45,400 crore and direct employment of approximately 6.11 lakh persons are for non-urban areas. About 4 per cent of these investments are for backward areas. Of these, 556 IEMs envisaging an investment of approximately Rs. 6,876 crore and direct employment of 72,115 persons have already been implemented.

During the post-liberalisation period till March 1998, the Government has also approved 1071 proposals for joint venture/foreign collaborations/industrial licences/100 per cent export oriented units, envisaging an investment of over Rs.18,649 crore including foreign investment of Rs.8,756 crore and direct employment of approximately 2.69 lakh persons. Out of this, an investment of Rs.17,738 crore is for setting up of food processing industries in the non-urban areas. Of these, 206 proposals envisaging investment of Rs.2,010 crore and direct employment of approximately 0.86 lakh person have already been implemented.

3. Growth of the Industry

Grain Processing

Due to the constant efforts made by the Ministry from time to time, the number of modern/modernised rice mills has gone up from practically nil in 1970 to 34688 as on 01.01.1998. As a result of improved availability of bran from these modern and modernised mills, the processing of bran is estimated to be around 33 lakh tonnes in 1997-98 as against 32.70 lakh tonnes in 1996-97.

The Regional Extension Service Centres and the Post-Harvest Technology Centre at Indian Institute of Technology (IIT), Kharagpur, continue to provide requisite assistance to the milling industry and conducts short term training courses etc. 13 Regional Extension Service Centres provide necessary assistance to the machinery manufacturers and millers for testing of equipments, selection and operation and maintenance of machinery. The basic research work on different applied aspects of rice processing and by-products utilisation like drying, storage, parboiling, milling, bran stabilisation and oil extraction, etc., is being carried out at the Paddy Processing Research Centre, Thanjavur. Currently, the projects handled at that centre are:

(a) Quality Management in Storage of Milled Rice.
(b) Establishment of a pilot plant for treatment of rice mill effluent.

No licence is required for manufacture of wheat products. There are no controls on price and distribution of wheat products. The mills have been given a free hand to obtain their requirements of wheat from any source, thereby avoiding their dependence on Government for supply of faw materials. Nearly 10.5 million tonnes of wheat is converted into various wheat products by 812 roller flour mills in the country every year.

Consumer Food Industries

The consumer food industry mainly consists of ready-to-eat products or ready-to-cook products such as pasta products, cocoa based products, bakery products, biscuits, soft drinks, etc.

Bakery industry in India is probably the largest of the processed food industries, production of which has been increasing steadily in the country. The two major bakery industries, viz., bread and biscuits account for about 82 per cent of the total bakery products. The annual production of bakery products which includes bread, biscuits, pastries, cakes, buns, rusk, etc., most of which are in the unorganised sector is estimated to be in excess of 30 lakh tonnes. The production of bread and biscuits in the country both in the organised and unorganised sectors is estimated to be around 15 lakh tonnes and 11 lakh tonnes respectively. Of the total production of bread and biscuits, about 35 per cent is produced in the organised sector and the remaining is manufactured in the unorganised sector.

Another wheat based product known by its generic name, i.e., pasta products comprising of noodles, vermicelli, macaroni spaghetti is gaining popularity.

There are 20 units engaged in the manufacture of cocoa products like chocolates, drinking chocolates, cocoa butter, cocoa butter substitutes, cocoa based malted milk foods with a production of approximately 45 thousand tonnes.

The production of soft drinks during the period under review has increased from 4450 million bottles in 1996-97 to 4920 million bottles during the period under review.

At present, there are 33 units manufacturing beer under licence from Government of India having an estimated output of 3.75 lakh KL per annum.

Fruit and Vegetable Processing Industries

The estimated installed capacity of fruits and vegtables processing industries has increased from 19.1 lakh tonnes in 1996-97 to 20.4 lakh tonnes in 1997-98. However, the production of processed fruits and vegetables in the country has decreased from 9.6 lakh tonnes in 1996-97 to 9.1 lakh tonnes in 1997-98. During the period under review, there has been increase of licences under Fruit Product Order (FPO), 1955 to 4932 from 4674 in 1996-97.

Milk and Milk Products

The trend of milk production and milk procurement has been better during the current year in comparison to the last year. The milk production in the year 1997-98 is anticipated to be 72 million tonnes as against 68 million tonnes during 1996-97. There has been increase in the estimated production of milk powder including infant milk food from 2,10,000 tonnes in the year 1996 to 2,15,000 tonnes in the year 1997 and the estimated production of malted food product has increased from 53,000 tonnes in the year 1996 to 55,000 tonnes in the year 1997. Similarly, the production of cheese has also increased from 4,000 tonnes in the year 1996 to 7,000 tonnes in the year 1997. However, the estimated production of condensed milk has declined to 7,800 tonnes in the year 1997 from 9,300 tonnes in 1996.

Meat and Poultry Processing

The production of meat and meat products has been impressing growth. The details of production of meat and meat products from 1993 to 1996 is an under:

(Thousand Tonnes)

	1993	1994	1995	1996
Mutton & goat meat	623	636	647	669
Pork	366	366	420	420
Chicken (Poultry Meat)	382	442	578	480
Cattle (Beef)	1215	1290	1290	1292
Buffalo (Meat)	1182	1200	1204	1204

The total meat production in the country is to the tune of 4.06 million tonnes per annum. The slaughtered rate in relation to the population of animals is about 6 per cent in the case of cattle, 10 per cent in the case of buffalo, 99 per cent in case of pigs, 31 per cent in case of sheep and 39 per cent in case of goat.

Fish Processing

Sixty per cent of the production of fish in India is from marine sources with coastal fishing constituting the bulk and only 2 per cent coming from deep sea resources. Production of fish from both marine and inland sources has increased from 4.94 million tonnes in 1995-96 to 5.23 million tonnes in 1996-97.

Processing of marine products into canned and frozen forms is carried out almost entirely for the export market. In all, there are 399 freezing units, 13 canning units, 150 ice-making units, 16 fish meal units and also about 474 cold storage units.

4. Development Councils

During the period under review, two Development Councils have been constituted, viz, (i) Development Council for processed Fruits and Vegetables, Cereal Products and Beverages; and (ii) Development Council for Dairy Products, Marine Products and Meat & Poultry Products. These comprise of representatives who have knowledge of the subject, and those who can represent the interests of industry, consumers and the employees. The role of these Councils is to recommend targets for production, suggest norms for efficiency with a view to eliminate waste, obtain maximum production, improve quality, and reduce costs, recommend measures for optimum utilisation of installed capacity, promote standardisation of products, promote training of personnel, promote or undertake scientific and industrial research and promote and undertake collection and formulation of statistics.

5. Exports

Exports of processed fruits and vegetables in 1997-98 is estimated to be around Rs. 725 crores as against Rs. 473.8 crores in 1996-97. Export of animal products has also increased from Rs. 803.6 crores in 1996-97 to Rs. 900 crores in 1997-98. Export of processed foods (including cereal based products) has decreased from Rs. 7037.7 crores in 1996-97 to Rs. 5840 crores in 1997-98 whereas export of marine products has increased from Rs. 4121.4 crores to Rs. 4642.9 crores during the same period.

(f) Gems and Jewellery

Jewellery Exports

The Gem and Jewellery Export Promotion Council is estimating gold and studded jewellery exports to cross $900 million in the current fiscal against $850 million recorded in 1997-1998. "There is a 15 to 20 per cent growth in the gold jewellery sector and we can grow at a much faster rate, taking into account the world's total usage of $70 billion, if enough facilities are given," Council Chairman Praveenshankar Pandya said. Of the total export basket of over $6 billion, diamond constitutes 81 per cent, gold jewellery about 15 per cent and coloured gem stones exports comprise 4 per cent. In 1997-1998, cut and polished diamonds exports stood at $4.5 billion, while rough diamonds recorded a figure of $48.42 million. Nearly $132.16 million worth of coloured gemstones were exported. India processes 90 per cent of the world's diamonds. Technically, this industry is only value addition, which employs one million people and brings in foreign exchange of $4.8 billion. But, China has become very active since the last five years and India has to be competitive so that none of the business goes to China. "We are alarmed at the opening of the diamond bourge in China this year, where diamond is made duty-free. They have trained 40,000 workers that can more than match our skilled manpower", pointed out Mr. Pandya.

(g) Heavy Electrical Industry

Equipment used for generation, transmission, distribution and utilisation of power constitutes Heavy Electrical Industry. The items of manufacture include generators, boilers, turbines, transformers, switchgears etc.

fabrication and testing of the airworthiness light ransport aircraft, establishment of a national botanical garden both for recreation ad research purpose, language competing,medical electronics, tapping ocean thermal energy, a programme on thalassemia, rehumatic fever, technology for the visually handicapped, landslide management and biodiversity characterisation.

Dr. Joshi said that these projects would be targeted with a clear time schedule and milestones. It should be possible to demonstrate in a given time and fund and a given purpose, the results of our advancement in science and technology and its impact of society, he added. The Minister underscored the need for scientists to take up specified projects related to certain problems facing the country. The technological skills should be able to solve at least some of the major problems confronting the mankind. Food security, he said, must be given priority as it concerns the masses. All departments are connected with the production of food in one way or the other, so food security can be brought under one umbrella, Dr. Joshi added. He pointed out that the Prime Minister, the Finance Ministry and the Planning Commission are inclined to the Jai Vigyan Mission and have agreed to provide all help to achieve its goal. A number of scientific agencies and departments would come together for the implementation of these 16 projects and some more projects are also to be identified soon under this mission.

(c) Liberalisatoin of Technology Import Regime

The Union Cabinet on Jan. 20 decided to liberalise the technology import regime to facilitate inflow of appropriate technology with simplification of procedures and greater delegation of powers of approval. The Cabinet, which met in New Delhi on Jan. 20, also approved a proposal to merge four schemes to promote voluntary action for persons with disability, another to provide for an expenditure of Rs. 261 crore for the National Child Labour Projects over the Ninth Plan period, and a third to continue with the scheme of Maulana Azad Education Foundation. The cabinet also decided that specialists in medical or scientific fields may be granted extensions beyond their retirement age, but in no case beyond the age of 62, and approved the selection of M/s Maurbeni Corporation, Japan, as joint venture partner for the 301 mw power project at Panipat, Haryana.

The decision on liberalisation of technology imports envisages allowing projects appraised and funded by financial institutions to acquire technology through the automatic route without any restrictions. It would apply to public and private sectors projects. However, for the new norms to apply, in the case of public sector undertakings, projects must be approved by the competent authority...

(d) Biotechnology

The past four decades represent the age of modern biology. Supported by spectacular advances in the areas of computer-based information, communication and powerful instrumentation, biology has become the harbinger of new and hitherto unimagined products and processes in the areas of food, feed, animal productivity, human health, environment and energy. The Department of Biotechnology has, since its inception in 1986, provided sustained support to research, application and commercialisation of biotechnology products and processes. This year has been very exciting both from the view point of excellence in research, product development and technology transfer.

In India, ten years of concerted effort in research and development in identified areas of modern biology and biotechnology related to agriculture, human health, animal husbandry, environment and industrial biotechnology have given rich dividends. The proven technologies at the laboratory level have been scaled up and demonstrated in field. Patenting of innovations, technology transfer to industries and close interaction with them have given a new direction to biotechnology research. Initiatives have been taken to promote transgenic research in plants with emphasis on pest and disease resistance; nutritional quality; silk-worm genome analysis; molecular biology of human genetic disorders; brain research, plant genome research; development, validation and commercialisation of diagnostic kits and vaccines for communicable diseases; food biotechnology; biodiversity conservation and bioprospecting; setting up of micropropagation parks and biotechnology based programmes for SC/ST, rural areas, women and for different states.

A number of new projects were formulated and funded with the advice of Standing Advisory Committee - Overseas (SAC-O), Scientific Advisory Committee to DBT (SAC-DBT) and Task Forces. In order to speed up the processing time for major proposals (above Rs. 45 lakhs), a Biotechnology Research and Promotion Committee (BRPC) has been constituted in addition to the Task Forces.

During the current year, there were over 500 ongoing projects. Besides, about 450 fresh proposals were received in diverse areas ranging from agricultural biotechnology to bioprospecting. With the advice of BRPC and Task Forces about 190 projects have been approved during the year. The BRPC and the different Task Forces have met at least twice to consider new proposals/activities and to monitor the progress of the ongoing projects. Highlights of important activities during 1997-98 are presented below.

Basic Research and Emerging Areas

Significant achievements in the area of Basic Research include: determination of three dimensional structure of an iron binding protein, lactoferrin leading to a new use as an antibacterial or antifungial agent (AIIMS, New Delhi); demonstration of the potential of reconstituted sendai viral envelopes containing only the F protein of the virus as efficient and site specific vehicles for delivery of reporter genes into hepatocytes (Delhi University); designing, cloning, hyper-expression, purification and characterization of novel second genration derivatives of streptokinase that display improved fibrin clot specificity (IMTECH, Chandigarh); elucidation of structural polymorphism in DNA encompassing with standard structures and pH induced transitions, using a 600 MHz FTNMR (TIFR, Mumbai); development of a cross-linked efficient cellulose-based absorbent beads for expanded bed operations of chromoatography (UDCT, Mumbai); solving the three dimensional structure of a novel 122 amino acid-long protein of mosquito (University of Pune); and *Mycobacterium smegmatis* uracil DNA glycosylase shown to be an efficient enzyme for molecular biology applications (IISc., Bangalore). The automated DNA sequencing facility at IISc. Bangalore was fully utilised by the scientists from the Institute as well as from other laboratories of the region.

Agriculture Biotechnology

Cloning and sequencing of at least six genes has been achieved in JNU Centre.

The seed storage genes and amino acid biosynthetic genes can be utilized to get genetically engineered plants with enhanced nutritional value.

Full length *Cry IA (c)* gene from *Bacillus* thuringienstis was cloned and used for the construction of a direct transformation vector. The transgenics would be subjected to field trials soon. Transgenic tobacco plants containing trypsin inhibitor were developed. Also transgenic tomato containing coat protein gene of *TLCV* is under testing. In a project on development of molecular methods using barnase and baster genes for hybrid seed production in *Brassica juncea*, a number of transgenics have been made with different gene constructs. These plants have been put under controlled growth conditions and are being analysed for their respective phenotypes.

In the network project on transgenic cotton, two genes coding for larvicidal endotoxin protein *Cry IA (c)* and *Cry IE* were chemically synthesized through indigenous efforts. Transformation studies of Indian cultivars have been initiated. In wheat, efforts are underway for tagging quality traits like protein content, seed size as well as pre-harvest sprouting tolerance. Also, significant progress was reported on modification of triticin gene for higher expression and enhanced lysine content.

Biological Control of Plant Pests, Diseases and Weeds

The technologies for the mass production of candidate biocontrol agents-baculovirus, parasites, predators, antagonisties, fungi and bacteria for economically important crops have been transferred to industries through BCIL. Technologies of some of the biocontrol agents like *Trichhogramma* (developed by IARI) and *Trichoderma* (RRL, Jammu) are being patented. So far, five entrepreneurs have signed the technology transfer agreement. An area of 55,000 ha. have been covered in various field crops using biocontrol agents. Popularization of the biopesticide technology is an important component. About 20,000 farmers benefited by attending the training through various extension activities at different centres. The gap between the availability of biocontrol agents and their quality has been bridged significantly through the biocontrol networks.

Significant achievements have been made in the areas of microbial and other pesticides including transgenic BT. Insect cell lines, pheromones and botanical pesticides. Five selected pheromones have been synthesised by simple and economically viable processes for monitoring and control of insect pests of cotton, red gram, gram, maize, vegetables, potato, cabbage, sorbhum etc. Under the botanicals the nematicidal efficacy of various neem products against the major groups of phytonematodes has been established under field conditions. Extracts of leaves of *M. azadirach* are more than 80 per cent larvicidal against *H. armigera* as well as aphids. A very economic and effective methods for the management of Parthenium in non-cultivated areas was developed. A bioformulation of an antagonistic yeast (*Debaryomyces hansenii*) has been developed for the control of host harvest diseases of citrus and mango fruits.

Medicinal and Aromatic Plants

An Integrated programme on taxol has been initiated and five project launched on various aspects such as conservation of germplasm, *in vitro* studies for micropropagation and biotransformation of taxane derivatives such as 10-DAB (deacetyl baccatin) for production of anticancer compound-taxol. Active fractions have been isolated and purified from *Piper longum and Tinospora cordifolia* at NII, New Delhi and evaluated for immunomodulatory activities in animal models. A quick, simple and inexpensive thin-layer chromatographic densitometry method for determination of antimalarial artemisinin in *Artemisia annua* has been developed at CIMAP, Lucknow. New projects have been launched on : cardio-protective properties in *Terminalia arjuna*; isolation of active principles from *Azadirachta indica* for controlling gastric hyperacidity and ulceration; and production of podophyllotoxin by plant cell cultures.

A new immunomodulatory compound (NII-30) has been identified in *Piper longum* which can be further developed into a potential drug for cancer therapy in future. The evaluation of immunomodulatory properties and therapeutic potential of NII-30 against experimental tumour has been completed. Genotypes yielding very high levels of root- and leaf alkaloids have been identified in *Catharanthus roseus*.

Human Genetics and Genome Analysis

Fourteen genetic clinics, established for molecular diagnosis and counselling for the common genetic disorders like beta-thalassemia, Duchenne Muscular Dystrophy (DMD) and other haemoglobinopathies prevalent in the country are providing prenatal diagnosis and counselling to the affected families. A major project on genome diversity to study for the first time the genetic variations among different population groups in the country was initiated. A programme on "Functional genomics with an objective to develop technological capability and provide assistance to clinical scientists has been launched at CBT, New Delhi. It aims at identifying novel mutations in Indian population in known genetic disorders like beta-thalassemia, Down syndrome and other mental retardations, DMD, myotonic dystrophy, spinocerebellar ataxia, etc., and develop of novel diagnostics.

INFORMATION TECHNOLOGY

(i) The Government on May 22 set up a national task force on information technology and software development which will prepare and submit a draft National Informatics Policy to the Prime Minister within three months. The Planning Commission Deputy Chariperson, Mr. Jaswant Singh, has been appointed the Chairperson of the 16-member national task force while the Andhra Pradesh Chief Minister, Mr. Chandrababu Nadiu, and the former Union Minister for Science & Technology, Dr. M.G.K. Menon, have been named co-chairpersons. Significantly, Mr. Naidu, who had called on the Prime Minister during the day, presented a "submission paper" to him on the national informatics policy. The paper among other things had recommended constitution of a high-level committee for formulation of the policy.

The task force is expected to recommend to the Government within a month immediate steps needed to be taken to remove bottlenecks and give the IT industry a boost. With the new policy focussing on development of world-class software products and brands, the Government is otpimistic about a 20-fold increase in India's software and other IT service exports in the next 10 years. Along with drafting of the policy, the task force will also recommend an appropriate empowered institutional mechanism for its implementation as a national mission with the participation of Central and Sate Governments industry, academic institutions and the society. Making the announcement, an official spokesman said, the decision is a "millennium initiative" which, if given the right stimulus, would help the country to emerge as a software superpower. The Government is keen to become a key player in the IT-based international society and therefore, the new policy would look into how India can leverage its global competitiveness in Infotech to play a prominent role in the development of information technology in other countries.

(ii) The Department of Electronics has prepared an Action Plan called India Information Technology Mission 2010 to achieve the Prime Minister's mission on making India a global giant in information technology. This was stated by Mr. Ravinder Gupta, Secretary Department of Electronics, at a function held to give away awards for excellence in electronics. The Action Plan will cover important areas of infrastructure, skill and education, finance and marketing promotion and applications development having R and D policy support and indigenous manufacturing for self reliance, Mr. Gupta added.

He said that the national task force on information technology and software development constituted in May has submitted its 108-point information technology action plan, which is being considered by a group of four cabinet ministers. According to Mr. Gupta, except aerospace and defence electronics, the electronics industry has been fully delicensed. "India has also signed the Information Technology agreement excepting gradually reduced tariff to zero by the year 2000 for many information technology products and by 2005 for all the assigning products.

(iii) Tata Consultancy Services (TCS) has emerged as the number one information technology (IT) company in the country with its revenue touching Rs. 1,083.63 crore during 1997-98. Wipro systems (Rs. 481.65 crore) and HCL consulting (Rs. 345.50 crore) came second and third in terms of revenue achieved during the last fiscal year, says a study by national association of software and service companies (Nasscom). A major portion of revenue of it companies comes from exports with TCS clocking Rs. 955.27 crore through this route, the study said adding entire revenue of HCL came from exports. Out of the total exports of Rs. 6,530 crore from the country during the year, almost 59 per cent was to the United States, 22 per cent to Europe, 5 per cent to South East Asia, 4 per cent to Japan, 2 per cent to West Asia and 6 per cent to rest of the world, Nasscom said.

The other companies which came in the first six list includes NIIT (Rs. 325.40 crore), Pentafour Software Exports (Rs. 284.56 crore) and Infosys Technologies Limited (Rs. 257.66 crore), the study said. During the last year, about 73 companies have exported more than Rs. 10 crore worth of software. This is in comparision to 1992-93, when only eight companies exported software to the tune of Rs. 10 crore or above. This indicates an upswing, high proliferation and all-round proliferation and growth in the area, it noted.

(f) Satellite Communication Project

In a bid to consolidate its presence in the broadcasting industry, ASC Enterprise, is planning to kick-start an ambitious Rs. 3,300-crore satellite communication project by the first half of 2001. The Company is promoted by Mr. Subhash Chandra of Zee Television and by the Essel Group. The Board of Videsh Sanchar Nigam has also reportedly ratified its approval to invest Rs. 215 crore in the project and a final clearance is awaited from the Department of Telecommunications. Estimated at Rs. 3,300 crore, appraisal for the project has been completed by the Industrial Finance Corporation of India which has also given its nod. The debt-equity ratio of the project has been fixed at 1:1, with the debt component valued at Rs. 1,650 crore.

If the project takes off, ASC Enterprises would become the only Indian Company to lease satellite for broadcasting. It is also in talks with Russian-based Proton for the launch of the satellite. "A majr protion of the project would be funded through rupee term loans and some portion from the US Exim Bank," Company Director Vipin Garg said. The equity part would be promoted by Mr. Subhash Chandra and the Essel Group. Zee Television vendor Lockheed Martin which is reportedly keen on the project has also evinced interest in taking part in the equity of the project. ASC Enterprises is expected to come out with an initial public offering for the project towards the end of 2000. The project would be of a multi-media nature with a multi-mission payload. The focus would be on satellite transmission as the government is yet to give its nod to the direct-to-home service. "Our primary target is to provide three-fold connectivity," Mr. Garg said.

The satellite would equipped with an L-band to facilitate mobile satellite telephony and C and Ku bands for television broadcasting. The project would facilitate mobile satellite telephony through its vendor, Lockheed Martin. The project would cater to provide service in those areas where telecommunication is minimal and provide mobility to subscribers who face the out-of-range problem, he said. "It will also serve the long distance traffic, 500 km and above, and the international traffic," Mr. Garg added. "The rates will also be in conformity with those suggested by the Telecom Regulatory Authority of India on March 9," he said. Though rentals on basic and cellular services have gone up, the domestic long distance charges have been reduced 45 per cent on an average, while the international calls have been slashed by 50 per cent. According to ASC, the focus would also be more on the international traffic. Interestingly, the reduction of the ISD rates is expected to end the friction between India and the US as the later has not been happy with it.

(g) India Missile Power

India will emerge as a full-fledged missile power by the turn of the century, with all its indigenous missiles ready for induction by 2000, the Scientific Adviser to the Defence Minister, Dr. A.P.J. Abdul Kalam, has said. 'By 2000, all the strategic and tactical missiles will be made in the country', Dr. Kalam said at a Press conference in Bangalore on Dec. 9. The induction of these missiles will boost India's capability to deter an external attack. They would also spin off knowhow to help fulfil the country's ambitious plans for indigenisation. India wanted to produce 70 per cent of its military hardware requirements on its own by 2005. India has already developed the nuclear capable, Prithvi ballistic missile. It was working on an extended range Agni Intermediate Range Ballistic Missile (IRBM). Besides, it was building the Trishul and Akash ground-to-air projectiles. The four-km range tank-busting missile, Nag, was also under development.

Elaborating on the induction time-table, Dr. Kalam said the highly agile Trishul missile, with a short target range, would be inducted in all the three services next year. The radar-guided Akash missile, which could track and engage several high flying targets simultaneously, would be ready to enter service between 1999 and 2000. The Nag anti-Bank missile would be inducted in 2000. The presence of the indigenous ground-to-air missiles would greatly enhance India's air defence capability. At the moment, the core of India air defence capability revolved around the static Soviet origin Pechora missile and the OSAAK mobile systems. According to experts, both these missiles were prone to jamming as the frequency on which their radars function had become known. The induction of indigenous missiles could largely resolve this problem. The Trishul's presence was also expected to add punch to mobile armoured columns. The Trishul, which would be fired from a moving armoured vehicle, could prevent an aerial attack on mobile tank columns.

NATIONAL SPACE PROGRAMME

Introduction

The launch of Indian remote sensing satellite, IRS-1D, using the indigenously designed and built Polar Satellite Launch Vehicle, PSLV, on September 29, 1997, was a significant event, coming in the 50th year of India's independence; the event heralded the era of technological self-reliance in launching remote sensing satellites from within the country. With PSLV having proved its capability to place 1,200 kg class of satellites in polar orbits, all future satellites in the IRS series are planned to be launched by this vehicle. The next flight, PSLV-C2, will launch IRS-P4, meant for observations of oceans. A Korean Satellite and a German Satellite are also being flown on board PSLV-C2 along with IRS-P4 thus signifying the start of marketing of Indian launch services. A notable progress has been achieved in the development of India's Geosynchronous Satellite Launch Vehicle, GSLV, including the testing of its liquid propulsion strap on stage. An Indian sounding rocket has been procured and successfully launched by the Norwegian Space Agency for conducting atmospheric investigation in the north polar region.

The nation is now benefiting from the world's largest constellation of four Indian remote sensing satellites, IRS-1B, IRS-1C, IRS-1D and IRS-P3 for undertaking space-based remote sensing. That, the data from IRS satellites is also received and disseminated by several countries all over the world under commercial agreements, shows the leading edge that India has established in this advanced technology. The plan to launch the follow-on satellites in the IRS series—IRS-P4 for remote sensing of ocean in the current financial year, IRS-P5 for cartographic applications next year and IRS-P6 for resources survey by 2000-01—indicates that India is determined to increse the role of space-based remote sensing for its resources survey and management while continuing to play an important role in the international market for space-based data.

With the advent of high resolution satellites, IRS-1C and IRS-1D, newer applications in the areas of urban sprawl, infrastructure planning and other large-scale thematic mapping applications have been initiated. Use of spacebased remote sensing has also been extended to bio-diversity mapping. A data-base on the country's wet-lands is now available with the completion of mapping using IRS satellites. Other on-going remote sensing projects, including Integrated Mission for Sustainable Development (IMSD), are progressing.

The INSAT system continues to provide services in the areas of telecommunications, television broadcasting, meteorology and disaster warning. The services are now provided by five satellites, INSAT-1D, INSAT-2A, INSAT-2B, INSAT-2C and another satellite, INSAT-2DT, that has been acquired from ARABSAT Organisation. INSAT-2D, which was launched on June 4, 1997 and had gone through orbit raising manoeuvres and deployment of appendages, faced a power bus anomaly and has become inoperable since October 4, 1997. The INSAT-2DT is expected to partialily augment the INSAT system capacity depleted by the loss of INSAT2D. INSAT-2DT, which was already in the geostationary orbit, has since been moved to an INSAT location at 55 degree east longitude and its transponders are being loaded in a phased manner. The planned launch of INSAT-2E in 1998 will further augment the INSAT services. The Department of Space will be leasing eleven transponders on board INSAT 2E to the International Telecommunication Satellite Organisation (INTELSAT) under a commercial agreement. The capacity for use by INTELSAT is being additionally built into the satellite. Work on INSAT-3 series of satellites, which will have more advanced features than the present ones, has already commenced. New technologies of satellite communications like digital audio broadcasting will be demonstrated using experimental satellites, GSAT, which are planned for launch by GSLV during its developmental test flights.

Demonstration of new application of INSAT system is continuing. Under the two-year Jhabua Development Communications Project (JDCP) which started on November 1, 1996, developmental training and education is being provided via INSAT to 150 villages in the predominantly tribal district of Madhya Pradesh. Under JDCP, 150 direct reception television sets have been installed with talk-back provision in twelve block headquarters. It is planned to expand this system to 25 more districts in the Ninth Five Year Plan. The exclusive Training and Developmental Communication Channel of INSAT is being used effectively by several agencies for interactive training and education of Panchayat Raj workers, banking staff, industrial workers, management students, etc.

Considering the importance of satellite communication in the country, the government has approved a policy framework for offering transponder capacity on INSAT system to non-governmental users also on commercial terms. The policy is expected to regulate and ensure an orderly growth of the system.

Exciting scientific results on several types of celestial objects have been obtained from the X-ray astronomy experiment on board IRS-P3 satellite launched by PSLV in March 1996. The SROSS-C2 satellite launched by India's ASLV in May 1994 continues to provide scientific data for Gamma-ray astronomy and upper atmospheric research. The National Mesosphere, Stratosphere, Troposphere (MST) Radar at Tirupati continues to provide data for investigation of the atmosphere. Towards reviewing and exchanging ideas on the role of MST radars, the 8th International Workshop on technical and scientific aspects of MST Radar was hosted by India in Bangalore. Research in the areas of astronomy and astrophysics, planetary atmospheres and aeronomy, earth science, etc. is continuing. Global changes studies in the Indian region as part of the International Geosphere-Biosphere Programme, is progessing well.

Interface between the Department of Space and the academic and other research institutions in the country is being strengthened further. An educational programme on satellite technology and applications has been initiated during the year at Indian Institute of Science (IISc), Bangalore. The space technology cells set up at Indian Institutes of Technology and IISc continue to take up research and development in advanced areas of space technology. During the year, 23 new projects have been initiated at various academic and research institutions under the Sponsored Research (RESPOND) scheme. An ISRO Chair has been created during the year for space communications research at IIT, Kharagpur.

Commercial benefits have started accruing to the nation through marketing of Indian space capabilities. Acquisition of data from Indian remote sensing satellites by several ground stations all over the world including USA and Europe, agreement to lease transponders on INSAT-2E for use by INTELSAT organiation, agreements to fly a Korean and a German satellite on board PSLV-C2 as piggy-back payloads and sale of sounding rocket to Norway, besides supply of satellite subsystems to internationally renowned space industries, indicate the recognition for India's space capabilities in the international market. Indian industries continue to participate in the space programme by undertaking major fabrication jobs and supply of hardware. Four more technologies developed under the space programme have been transferred to Indian industries during the year for commercialisation; the total number of technologies transferred so far is 231.

The signing of a Memorandum of Understanding during the year by the Department of Space and Department of Science and Technology with the National Aeronautics and Space Administration (NASA) and National Oceanic and Atmospheric Administration (NOAA) of USA has paved the way for undertaking a number of joint projects in atmospheric sciences through exchange of meteorological data from India's INSAT and US research and operational satellites including GOES. The agreement is also expected to increase the level of scientific cooperation between the two countries. The data from the German instrument, Modular Opto-electronic Sensor, flown on board Indian remote sensing satellite, IRS-P3, will also be received by USA under another tripartite agreement signed by India, USA an Germany. Several activities are being pursued under the cooperative agreements that exist between India and other countries including China, France, Germany, Hungary, Indonesia, Mauritius, Russia, Sweden, Syria, The Netherlands and Ukraine. That, India has been elected Chairman of the United Nations Committee on Peaceful Uses of Outer Space, indicates that the country is held in high esteem by the international space community. India's role in promoting the role of space-based remote sensing for various applications has also been recognised by the world community with ISRO taking over the Chairmanship of the international Committee on Earth Observation Satellites (CEOS) in November 1997. India will host the next annual meeting of CEOS. The UN sponsored Centre for Space Science and Technology Education, started by India in November 1995, has completed two courses so far benefiting many students in the Asia Pacific region. The third course is now in progress.

As the Department of Space, set up in June 1972, is celebrating its Silver Jubilee, it is a matter of satisfaction that significant progress has been achieved in all aspects of space science, space technology and space applications. Space systems that have been established by the Department today form an important element of the national infrastructure, especially, in the areas of communication, broadcasting, meteorology, disaster warning and, monitoring and mangement of resources. The plans to launch more advanced satellites in the IRS and INSAT series and to place them in orbit using indigenously designed and built launch vehicles like the PSLV which has already entered into service and GSLV which is now under development, indicate the nation's commitment to further the development and application of space technology for the country's development in a self-reliant way.

20

RURAL DEVELOPMENT AND EMPLOYMENT

Planning has been one of the pillars of Indian policies since Independence and the country's strength is derived from the achievements of planning. The policies and programmes have been designed with the aim of allieviation of rural poverty which has been one of the primary objectives of planned development in India. It was realised that a sustainable strategy of poverty alleviation has to be based on increasing the productive employment opportunities in the process of growth itself. Since growth bypasses a few sections of the population, it is felt necessary for State's direct intervention and to formulate specific poverty alleviation programmes for generation of a certain minimum level of income for the rural poor.

Rural development implies both the economic betterment of people as well as greater social transformation. In order to provide the rural people with better prospects for economic development, increased participation of people in the rural development programmes, decentalisation of planning, better enforcement of land reforms and greater access to credit are envisaged.

The Ministry of Rural Areas and Employment through its various programmes endeavours to reach out to the last and the most disadvantaged sections of society, provide them with avenues for employment through special employment generation programmes and productive asset transfer through institutional credit and subsidy. Programmes of rural housing and area development, land reforms, drinking water and sanitation are specially designed to improve quality of life in rural areas.

During the current year (1997-98), Ministry's programmes for poverty alleviation and infrastructural development have been further modified to increase effectiveness and sustainability.

The Provisions of the Panchayats (Extension to the Scheduled Areas) Act, 1996 which came into operation on 24 December, 1996, extends to the tribal areas of eight States, namely, Andhra Pradesh, Bihar, Gujarat, Orissa and Rajasthan. This Act intends to enable tribal society to assume control over their own destiny to preserve and conserve their traditional rights over natural resources. All States except Bihar and Rajasthan have enacted State legislation in accordance with the provisions of the Act.

Implementation of these Constitutional provisions has been marked by the enactment of legislation by all the States in consonance with the provisions of the 73rd Constitution Amendment, Transfer of substantial funds has also been effected by the Central Government on the recommendations of the Tenth Finance Commission.

As a result of the elections of Panchayats in all these States, there are about 3.4 million elected representatives at all levels of Panchayats. Out of this an overwhelming majority are new entrants, particularly from the weaker sections of the society, i.e. Scheduled Castes, Scheduled Tribes and women.

The National Social Assistance Programme (NSAP) provides 100 per cent Central assistance to specific classes of beneficiaries uniformly throughout the country. The programme has three components - National Old Age Pension Scheme, National Family Benefit Scheme and National Maternity Benefit Scheme.

The focus of the Ministry through the existing programmes continued to be on provision of wage employment and self-employment, provision of safe drinking water and area development programmes.

The primary objective of Jawahar Rozgar Yojana (JRY) is generation of additional gainful employment for the unemployed and underemployed in rural areas. During 1997-98 the scheme has generated 3648.30 lakh mandays of employment.

The primary objective of the Employment Assurance Scheme (EAS) is to provide gainful employment during lean agricultural season to all able bodied adults in rural areas. The EAS is a demand driven scheme and provides a degree of assurance of 100 days of employment to the poor who seek and need employment. The scheme is operative in all rural blocks of the country from 1 April 1997.

Indira Awaas Yojana (IAY) which includes rural housing provides dwelling units free of cost of the weaker sections who are below poverty line in rural areas. Three per cent of the funds are earmarked for the benefit of persons with disabilities. During 1997-98 as on 31 March 1998, 6,41,325 houses have been constructed. The endeavour of the Ministry is to bring down the cost of constructon and to increase the acceptability of the houses under IAY.

The target group for the Integrated Rural Development Programme (IRDP) consists of small and marginal farmers, agricultural labourers and rural artisans whose annual family income is below Rs. 11,000 at 1991-92 prices. As a special safeguard for vulnerable groups, it is stipulated that atleast 50 per cent of the families should belong to SCs/STs, 40 per cent should be women and 3 per cent physically handicapped.

During 1997-98 total allocation is Rs. 1133.51 crores and the credit target is Rs. 2700 crore. Per family investment target is Rs. 17,500. The number of families covered is 16.02 lakhs.

The habitation level survey of availability of safe drinking water in rural areas undertaken in 1994 identified hardcore rural areas facing acute scarcity conditions as also areas where drinking water sources had water quality problems. A major initiative has been mounted under the Accelerated Rural Water Supply Programme (ARWSP) together with its counterpart State Sector Minimum Needs Programme (MNP) and under the Sub Mission Programme to tackle the situation. By the end of the Ninth Plan it is proposed to provide protected drinking water in adequate quantity to each and every rural habitation in the country.

Vigorous attempts are being made to invove the community in the operation and maintenance of rural water supply systems especially, handpumps, and in the upgradation of the environment of handpumps and public standposts. A massive human resource development programme has been initiated under which at least one volunteer in a cluster of villages is being trained as a self-employed mechanic to undertake the maintenance of handpumps. So far 83,300 habitations have been covered by safe drinking water.

Emphasis is also being laid on improving sanitation coverage in rural areas. Grass-root level training programmes are being organised for training of volunteers as masons to undertake construction of latrines and environmental sanitation works. Total sanitation, school sanitation, alternate delivery mechanism, demand driven approach and bankability of rural sanitary marts are given priority in implementing rural sanitation programme.

The programmes of the Ministry are aimed at the poorest of the poor and weaker sections — women, people from scheduled castes, scheduled tribes and physically handicapped persons. Similarly, special components are built in for women in most of the programmes. At least one-third of the total seats in Panchayats at all levels are reserved for women, including posts of Chairpersons. Forty per cent beneficiaries and 40 per cent trainees under IRDP and TRYSEM respectively are to be women. Under JRY 30 per cent employment opportunities are reserved for women. Under IAY priority is given to households headed by unmarried women and widows. Houses are allotted in the name of a woman or in joint names of husband and wife. Equal wages are to be made available to men and women. A specific sub-scheme under IRDP, namely, Development of Women and Children in Rural Areas (DWCRA) is being implemented for development of women through a group approach. Such safeguards for those who have been marginalised in the process of economic development will pave way to integrate them with mainstream economy.

To provide for closer linkages and to ensure effective coordination between PRIs and DRDAs, the organisational structure of DRDAs was revamped and they were placed under the control and directions of Zilla Parishads. Instructions were issued to State Governments to reconstitute the governing body of DRDAs under the Chairpersonship of Chairpersons of Zilla Parishads. Chairpersons of the various Standing Committees of ZPs and a 1/3rd chairpersons of Panchayat samitees (by rotation), as also representatives of local NGOs have been made members of the governing bodies. The technical wings of the DRDAs have also been augmented by inducting officers at appropriate levels to equip the DRDAs to handle the increased number of schemes and quantum of funds.

The monitoring mechanism has been geared up to improve its effectivness through involvement of elected representatives in various committees. Vigilance and monitoring committees have been set up at district and block levels for supervision of the programmes of the Ministry to ensure greater levels of transparency. The Committees include MPs, MLAs, elected members of PRIs and representatives of NGOs working in the area.

In the Golden Jubilee Year of independence, the Monitoring Division has introduced a high-tech review system by introducing the video-conference as an instrument to monitor the implementation of programmes of the Ministry.

The objective of the Integrated Wastelands Development Project Scheme (IWDP) is to start projects in the states aimed at integrated land management and wastelands development based on village/micro-watershed plans. The scheme also aims at rural employment besides enhancing the concept of people's participation in the Wastelands Development Programme. During the Eight Five Year Plan, 155 IWD Projects have been sanctioned for the development of 2.84 lakhs hectares of wastelands. For the Ninth Plan, an estimated financial outlay of Rs. 366.50 crores has been proposed for the development of 6.03 lakhs hectares of wastelands.

The Ninth Plan has been developed in the context of four important dimensions of State Policy — quality of life, generation of productive employment, regional balance and self-reliance. The focus of the plan is on "Growth with Social Justice and Equity".

With the multi-pronged approach adopted by the Ministry of Rural Areas and Employment through a wide range of programmes, identification of specific gaps and remedial measures thereto, and by improving the effectiveness of the delivery system, it is hoped that adequate productive employment will be generated to eradicate rural poverty which would lead to significantly better living conditions.

21

SMALL SCALE AND COTTAGE INDUSTRIES

(a) RBI Accepts 35 Recommendations of SSI Panel Report

The Reserve Bank of India (RBI) has accepted 35 of the 126 recommendations made by the S.L. Kapur committee on credit to Small Scale Industries (SSIs). The Central Bank has asked all commercial banks including RBIs to take appropriate action for implementation of the committee's recommendations. These include delegation of more powers to branch managers to grant ad-hoc limits, simplification of application forms, freedom to banks to decide their own norms for assessment of credit requirements and strengthening of the recovery mechanism. Other recommendations accepted include paying more attention to backward states, special programmes for training branch managers for appraising small projects and making the customer grievance machinery more transparent. RBI has asked banks to introduce tri-lingual loan application forms in Hindi, English and the local language and has also asked them to use the application forms prescribed for facilities up to Rs. 2 lakh, for facilities up to Rs. 10 lakh. Application forms prescribed for loan facilities up to Rs. 15 lakh may be used for facilities up to Rs. 50 lakh and that prescribed for limits of up to Rs. 1 crore, for loan facilities beyond Rs. 50 lakh and up to Rs. 2 crore and beyond.

RBI has indicated to banks that applications for amounts of up to Rs. 25,000 should be disposes of within a fortnight and those for amounts above Rs. 25,000 within 8-9 weeks. The central bank has advised banks to dispose of the applications in a time bound manner. RBI has asked banks to delegate powers to the branch managers to grant ad-hoc facilities to the extent of 20 per cent of the limits sanctioned ensuring that most of the credit proposals are decided at the branch level. Banks have also been asked, with the approval of their respective board of directors, to lay down clear guidelines for computing the working capital limits for various sub-sectors granted to SSI borrowers. RBI has also reiterated its earlier instructions that out of the total funds allocated by banks to the SSIs, at least 40 per cent should go to units with investment in plant and machinery up to Rs. 5 lakh and 20 per cent to units with investments in plant and machinery between Rs. 5 lakh and Rs. 25 lakh.

(b) SSI Investment Ceiling Reduced

In major decision on Feb. 17 the Cabinet has approved lowering the limit to qualify as a small scale unit to Rs. 1 crore from the existing limit of Rs. 3 crore. On the new investment ceiling for SSIs, Mahajan said that units which had moved Into the SSI sector as a result of the investment hand having been expanded will be denotified as small scale units. The investment limit to qualify as a tiny unit has been left unchanged at Rs. 25 lakh.

The government's decision to lower the qualification limit for SSIs comes as a surprise as the government had repeatedly said that it wants to extend the benefits of the SSI category to a larger number of units. Relatively small units had been complaining that they were coming under pressure from large units and multinational companies. As a result of the decision fewer companies will qualify in the SSI category which would leave a large number of companies in the cold.

(c) Reforms in the SSI Sector

Major initiatives were taken by the Department of Small Scale Industries and Agro and Rural Industries during 1997-98 to improve the competitive strength of small scale industries. As per the recommendation of the Expert Committee under the Chairmanship of Shri Abid Hussain and to off set the inflation, the investment limit on plant and machinery for SSI units was raised from Rs. 60 lakhs to Rs. 3 crores and for a tiny unit from Rs. 5 lakhs to Rs. 25 lakhs. In order to give a further boost to export from SSI sector, export obligation on large units manufacturing items reserved for SSI sector was reduced from 75 to 50 per cent.

Department has been reviewing the list of items reserved for small scale sector. The Expert Committee had suggested the abolition of the system of product reservation for the SSI sector. Another Committee of Officers had suggested selective dereservation of items to provide competitive stimulus to the industry. On careful consideration, it was decided that 15 items earlier reserved for exclusive manufacturing in the SSI sector may be dereserved, keeping in view the following factors:

- Technologically, it may not be feasible to manufacture certain items in SSI sector even after the enhanced limit;
- For better hygiene and to upgrade quality;
- To break monopoly and for promoting export;
- To reduce wastage and to improve packaging especially in our export front as this factor plays a major role; and
- Some items are not at all being manufactured in the SSI sector.

Several measures were taken for simplification of rules and procedures in order to achieve substantial deregulation. Disbanding of restricted list of small scale sector, simplification of registration procedures, decentralisation of decision making and liberalisation of Environment Laws are important policy initiatives taken in this regard. In order to relieve the small scale sector from shortage of working capital arising due to delayed payments to small scale and ancillary undertakings an Act on payment of interest has been enacted. Government also issued notification allowing 24 per cent equity participation by other industrial undertakings in small scale units. Government assisted scheme for technology support services was amended so as to provide Government grant on a matching basis to SSI associations for setting up technology-cum-training centres. Under this scheme, a training and design centre for hosiery promoted by Tirupur Exporters Association was commissioned. A CAD/CAM Centre sanctioned at Chennai at a cost of about Rs. 49 crores is being managed by the SSI associations.

A new centre for providing training and common facilities for software SSIs at a cost of Rs. 25 crores was cleared in principle for being set up at Delhi. A NSIC software technology park at Chennai was sanctioned.

(d) Performance of SSI Sector

The 1997-98 year witnessed continuous growth in the small-scale, cottage and Khadi industries sector. The number of small-scale units increased to gross 30 lakhs, the overall production in the small-scale sector was continuously maintaing a higher growth rate compared to the overall industrial growth. In 1996-97, the overall growth of production in SSI sector was 11.3 per cent (at 1990-91 prices) compared to an overall growth of 7 per cent for the industrial sector. In the current year also the production is expected to maintain the buoyancy recorded in the last few years. Similarly, the level of employment in this sector has also recorded a continuous increase. In 1996-97, the overall employment reached a level of 16 million persons. The overall employment in the small-scale sector has exceeded the targets set for the 8th Five Year Plan at 15 billion persons. The contribution of the SSI sector in exports has also been significant, and is maintaining the level of around 40 per cent of the total manufacturing sectors' exports.

(e) Initiatives to Increase Credit Support to SSI Sector

For ensuring better credit flow to the small scale sector, the Reserve Bank of India has taken decisions on many important recommendations of the Nayak Committee. With a view to providing fiscal support for industrialisation of backward districts, the five year tax holiday under Section 80 IA has been extended to new industrial undertakings located in other backward districts notified by the Central Government. Nearly 250 additional specialised bank branches were opened for catering to the credit needs of the SSI units exclusively. A Standing Committee for monitoring flow of bank credit to the SSI sector was set up.

A special scheme for providing credit from the banks for Village Industries was launched by channelising Government subsidy directly through the banks along with loan without involving any Government agencies. Government subsidy of Rs. 150 crores was released during September-November 1997. This is expected to have resulted in an institutional credit flow of Rs. 500 crores. Policy initiatives were taken for promoting growth of Micro Finance Institutions through NGOs. Policy Advisory Group headed by Mrs. E. Bhatt of SEWA has been constituted in the Department for advising the Government on a standing basis.

A special programme titled Trade Related Entrepreneurship Assistance and Development (TREAD) programme for assisting 1,00,000 women entirely through NGOs was launched with the SEWA project for assisting tribal women in the State of Gujarat in November, 1996. Since then, 31 projects for benefiting over 56,000 women have already been cleared by the Department.

(f) Infrastructure Support

To improve the infrastructure support to the SSI sector, Department has been implementing a plan scheme of Integrated Infrastructure Development for SSIs. Seventeen projects have so far been sanctioned at a total cost of Rs. 85 crores.

(g) Progress for Employment Generation and Support — KVIC and Coir Sectors

The Government of India constituted a High Power Committee under the Chairmanship of the Prime Minister for revitalising and improving Khadi and Village Industries sector. The important recommendations of the Committee have been approved as an action plan by the Government which include, generation of 2 million additional employment, special programme in the 71 seleced districts, intensive development of 125 blocks and infrastructure development.

Rural Employment Generation Programme (REGP) for generation of additional employment of 2 million persons at an estimated cost of Rs. 5600 crores through development of Khadi and Village Industries was accepted by the Government and an action plan was drawn up for implementation of the REGP. Additional employment for 5 lakh persons was generated by KVIC through setting up of viable Khadi and Village Industries units in rural areas. Plan outlay for KVIC was also substantially enhanced. Department considered the long pending problems of KVIC on Khadi rebate which were effectively resolved. Additional grant of Rs. 50 crores provided last year and committing additional Rs. 125 crores this year, for meeting KVIC's enhanced rebate liabilities.

For the development of the Coir sector which employs the weaker sections of society and creates wealth from the vegetable residue and waste, Integrated Coir Development Projects for Kerala, Tamil Nadu and Karnataka involving a total cost of over Rs. 60 crores has been sanctioned. Action Plan has also been formulated for the development of coir industry in the States of Tripura, Union Territories of Andaman & Nicobar Islands and Lakshadweep. Mahila Coir Yojana Scheme is already under implementation in Kerala, Tamil Nadu, Karnataka, Andhra Pradesh, Orissa and other coir producing States.

The Prime Minister's Rozgar Yojana, launched in October, 1993 with the objective to provide employment to unemployed youth by extending financial assistance to them in the field of industry, services and business made considerable progress during the current year. The scheme has envisaged setting up of about 7 lakh micro enterprises during the 8th Plan Period. As against this, the number of cases to whom loans have been sanctioned exceeded 8.2 lakhs. In 1996-97 alone loans were sanctioned to 2,89,000 persons as against the original target of 2,20,000 persons.

22

SOCIAL WELFARE

WELFARE OF THE SCHEDULED CASTES, SCHEDULED TRIBES, OTHER BACKWARD CLASSES, MINORITIES AND THE DISABLED

(A) Scheduled Castes

Introduction

There are 13.82 crores people belonging to the Scheduled Castes in the country. This constitutes 16.48 per cent of the country's total population. The States of Uttar Pradesh, West Bengal, Bihar, Tamil Nadu and Andhra Pradesh account for more than 50 per cent of the SC population, with Uttar Pradesh and West Bengal having more than 20 per cent of its population from the SCs.

Profile

Members of the Scheduled Castes mainly earn their livelihood through their own labour, either on land belonging to others or in occupations like scavenging, flaying and tanning of leather which reflect social and economic subjugation. More than three quarters of the SC workers are engaged in primary occupations, and the proportion of those engaged in the tertiary sector is nearly half the national average. Against the national average of 26 per cent, more than 50 per cent of the SC workers are agricultural wage, labourers. Despite the decline of untouchability practices, the caste system continues to confine—SC workers in occupations looked down upon by other communities. Though with the spread of urbanisation and governmental measures such as protective legislation and positive discrimination improvements have taken place in the occupational mobility and living standards of the SCs, the majority of them continue to be worse off than members of the other communities In the field of literacy, as against the National average of 52%, the literacy rate of SCs is around 37%. The situation is much more alarming amongst SC women where more than three quarters are illiterate. These disparities are further compounded by higher drop out rates in formal education. As a result of all these disavantages and disparities, the proportion of SCs below the poverty line is substantially higher than the National average. Amongst the SCs community itself, women are at an even greater disadvantage.

SCP Strategy

The vulnerability of the Scheduled Castes arising from these features severly constrains their access to facilities and programmes of ostensibly universal coverage. The concept of the Special Component Plan (SCP) was adopted from 1979-80 onwards in recognition of this fact so that there would be a focus on and enhancement of the flow of funds to the Scheduled Castes. The SCP has been an important element in the Government's strategy for their development and welfare.

National Commissions

The National Commission for Scheduled Castes and Scheduled Tribes was constituted under Article 378 of the Constitutin to provide for a high level independent body which will monitor the safeguards provided for SCs/STs and also review and report on issues concerning them. The Commission has wide powers and an extensive mandate and is required to be consulted on a major policy matters which effect SCs/STs. Like-wise, the National Commission for Safai Karamcharies focuses on the community of safai karamcharies within the SCs. Both the Commissions have presented their first annual reports.

Role of Welfare Ministry

The programmes and schemes of the Ministry of Social Justice and Empowerment are aimed at supporting and supplementing the efforts of the Union Ministries. State Governments/Union Territories and Voluntary Organisations by way of providing financial assistance in the form of grants etc. and to fill the critical gaps taking into account the situation of the SCs. There are schemes for educational development, economic development and social development [including protective measures under the Protection of Civil Rights Acts and SC/ST (Prevention of Atrocities) Act, and the policy of reservation in public employment and education]. The SCD Division of the Ministry administers these schemes which are implemented through State Governments/Union Territories as Centrally Sponsored Schemes. The Scheduled Tribe Component of some of these schemes are also dealt with in the SCD Division. An outlay of Rs. 2322.30 cr. had been approved for the 8th Plan and in the 9th Plan, Rs. 13774.69 cr. has been proposed.

Review

While the existing strategy and the schemes therein continue to be relevant with a satisfactory progress, a few deficiencies have been identified during the course of the 8th Plan and accordingly, some of the schemes have been revised in the 9th Plan. This has been done with an aim to enhance the impact of these schemes and make them more suitable to the needs of SCs in the changing times. During the terminal year of the 8th Plan i.e. 1996-97, the recommendations of the Dalit Manifesto and the report of the Working Group on Development and Welfare of SCs during the 9th Plan, submitted in May, 1996, have been taken into account while formulating the Action Plan for the 9th Plan. Both the above reports have emphasised upon setting apart a population-equivalent proportion of the plan funds and allocation of these funds as well as formulation and monitoring of the schemes through a separate institutional mechanism at the national, State and district levels. Recommendations have also been made for extensive coverage of SCs under irrigation schemes, expansion of residential schools facilities etc. Recommendations for Amendments to the Protection of Civil Rights Act and SC/ST (Prevention of Atrocities) Act and a statute on reservation have also been made. The Working Group has also recommended that the existing plan schemes of the SCD Division should be refined, strengthened and continued.

Educational Development

The Ministry's flagship scheme in the field of education is Post-Matric Scholarships for SCs/STs which has played a major role in the last 50 years in assisting SC/ST students ro pursue higher education. Around 20 lakhs students are provided Scholarships under this scheme each year. In the 8th Plan, changes such as enhancement of maintenance allowance, raising of income eligibility ceiling and relaxation of restrictions on the number of children in a family eligible for scholarship were effected. Further guidelines were also issued for timely disbursement of scholarships, keeping in mind the large number of institutions and students involved. The response to the associated scheme of Book Banks for SC/ST students has also been very satisfactory. The scheme of Pre-Matric Scholarships is primarily targetted at the children of those SCs engaged in unclean occupations such as scavenging. It was further liberalised in 1994 for wider coverage. The Scheme of National Overseas Scholarship for SCs/STs provides financial assistance to such students who wish to pursue higher studies in highly technical fields abroad. A large number of students have benefitted under this scheme and have undergone studies in well known universities in Europe, Australia and USA. The Scheme for upgradation of Merit of SC/ST students was transferred to the Ministry of Social Justice and Empowerment from the Department of Education, Ministry of Human Resource Development in 1993-94 and was reviewed in detail by all the state governments in 1996-97. Under the Scheme for Construction of Hostels for SC girls and boys, it was decided to take into account actual costs while computing the cental assistance. This scheme is very important as it helps to retain SC students in formal education by providing them with food and shelter. In June, 1996, a new central scheme for establishing free residential schools for SC girls below the poverty line was launched through the Zila Parishads in 48 districts where the SC female literacy rate was below to pursue.

Economic Development

Special Central Assistance is a powerful instrument to support SCP of States/ UTs. It is distributed among the States/UTs on the basis of population as well as SCP performance. The National Commission for SC/ST Finance and Development Corporation (NSFDC) and the State-level SCDCs to whom the centre provides equity, play a major role in the promotion of self-employment and income generating activities. In addition to the National Scheme for the Liberation and Rehabilitation of Scavegers wherein certain changes have been effected with regard to training norms, release of central assistance directly to the State Corporations, adoption of cluster approach etc., the National Safai Karamcharies Finance and Development Corporation (NSKFDC) was also established in 1996-97 with a financial provision of Rs. 2 crores. In the current years, Rs. 4.75 crores has been released to the NSKFDC and with the joining of a senior Joint Secretary level Office as Chairman-cum-Managing Director the Corporation is expected to be fully operational within the current financial year itself. Grant-in-aid continues to be provided to Voluntary Organsiations in order to help them to fulfil their vital role in providing vocational training and other services to the SCs. The Scheme of Coaching and Allied for SCs/STs provides comprehensive training and coaching for those candidates who are appearing for various recruitment examinations in the government sector.

Protective Measures

The Protection of Civil Rights Act and the SC and ST (Prevention of Atrocities) Act and Rules are important Central Statutes administered and enforced by the States, to whom financial support is provided under a Centrally Sponsored Scheme. The central assistance under the Scheme in 1996-97 at Rs. 15.50 cr. was higher than in previous years, reflecting greater emphasis on effective implementation and enhanced relief and rehabilitation norms laid down under the Rules framed in March, 1995 under the SC and ST (Prevention of Atrocities) Act.

Special Component Plan (SCP)

Scheduled Castes account for sizeable proportion of the country's population. They constitute 16.48 per cent of the total population of the country (1991 census). The State/UT wise distribution of the Scheduled Castes in the States/ UTs having significant population of the SCs is given below—

Table 22.1

SL. No.	State/UT	% of SC Population to the Total Population of the State/UT
1.	Andhra Pradesh	15.93
2.	Assam	7.40
3.	Bihar	14.55
4.	Goa	2.08
5.	Gujarat	7.41
6.	Haryana	19.75
7.	Himachal Pradesh	25.34
8.	Jammu & Kashmir	8.30
9.	Karnataka	16.38
10.	Kerala	9.92
11.	Madhya Pradesh	14.55
12.	Maharashtra	11.09
13.	Manipur	2.02
14.	Orissa	16.20
15.	Punjab	28.31
16.	Rajasthan	17.29
17.	Sikkim	5.93
18.	Tamil Nadu	19.18
19.	Tripura	16.36
20.	Uttar Pradesh	21.05
21.	West Bengal	23.62
22.	Chandigarh	16.51
23.	Delhi	19.05
24.	Pondicherry	16.25

It is observed from Table 22.1 that in the States of Himachal Pradesh, Punjab, Uttar Pradesh and West Bengal the scheduled castes constitute more than 20 per cent of the total population of the state. In the states/UT of Andhra Pradesh, Bihar, Haryana, Karnataka, Madhya Pradesh, Maharashtra, Orissa, Rajasthan, Tamil Nadu, Tripura, Chandigarh, Delhi and Pondicherry, the scheduled castes constitute 10 to 20 per cent of the total population of the State/UT. The scheduled castes constitute 2 to 10 per cent of total population in the states of Assam, Goa, Gujarat, Jammu & Kashmir, Kerala, Manipur, Sikkim.

The scheduled castes community suffered from and continues to suffer from below poverty line economic status, poor asset base, dependence on wage labour, subsistence farming, unclean occupations with attendant social and civil disabilities. The recognition of the fact in the late seventies that general development of the economy would not make a major impact on the condition of the SCs lead to search for an alternative development path for this group. It was realized that the strategy of development of the disadvantaged groups of the society would have to be based on comprehensive economic and human resource development efforts, so that this section of the population would acquire the ability to utilize its resource base more productively and reap the benefits of general economic development. With the objective of overall development of SCs to bring them above the poverty line and into the mainstream of national life with equal social and economic status with other sections of the population, the strategy of Special Component Plan was evolved in the year 1979.

Special Component Plan is designed to channelise the flow of outlays and benefits from the general sectors in the plans of States/UTs and the central Ministries, at least in proportion to their population both in physical and financial terms. It is not a scheme by itself. It is an umbrella under which all schemes implemented by State and Central Governments are dovetailed for addressing different needs of the Scheduled Castes.

Objectives

(1) Direct flow of benefits through family and individual oriented programmes aimed at economic development of the Scheduled Castes, covering the major occupational groups like agricultural labourers, small and marginal farmers, primary leather workers (flayers, tanners etc.), rural artisans, fishermen, sweepers and scavengers, urban unorganized labourers etc. The objective is to provide income generating assets and skill so as to enable the SC families to earn sustained income and cross the poverty line.

(2) Benefits to SCs of the services like provision of drinking water, health services, house sites and housing, drainage, link roads etc.; and programmes for extending facilities like education, vocational guidance etc.

At present 24 States/UTs having sizeable SC population are formulating Special Component Plan for the Scheduled Castes.

Flow of funds under SCP

Guidelines have been issued by the Government of India from time to time to the effect that earmarking of funds for SCP out of total state plan outlays should be atleast in proportion to the SC population in the total population of the respective states. Yet flow of benefits to SCs has not been to the desired level so far. The SC population of the country as per 1981 Census was 15.75 per cent of the total population of the country. It has increased to 16.48 per cent in the 1991 Census. The SCP outlay was however, only 7.61 per cent and 8.31 per cent of the total State Plan Outlay in the Sixth and Seventh Five Year Plan respectively. The SCP outlay as percentage of total state plan outlay has increased to 11.04 per cent in the 8th five year plan compared to 8.31 per cent in the Seventh Five Year Plan.

The details of total State Plan Outlays since Sixth Five Year Plan, given below clearly bring out this fact.

Table 22.2

Period	Total State Plan Outlay	SCP Outlay	% of SCP Outlay to State Plan Outlay	SCP Expen-diture	% of SCP Expenditure to SCP Allocation
6th Plan	47149.90	3614.66	7.67	2958.89	81.86
7th Plan	89413.89	7431.31	8.31	6916.92	93.08
8th Plan					
1992-93	31330.77	3099.65	9.89	2693.02	86.88
1993-94	32484.33	3656.15	11.25	3009.31	82.31
1994-95	37771.50	4154.38	11.00	3631.54	87.41
1995-96	47142.04	5503.15	11.67	4131.22	75.07
1996-97	54400.83	6007.00	11.04	4623.81	76.97
Total For The 8th Plan	203129.47	22420.33	11.03	18088.90	80.68

Statewise SCP outlay and expenditure during the period 1992-93 to 1996-97 (Eighth Five Year Plan).

The proposed outlays of the annual plan (1997-98) and the flow to SCP are as follows:

Table 22.3

(*Rs. in Crores*)

Sl.No.	State/UT	SC Population%	Annual Plan State Plan Outlay	1997-98 Flow to SCP	% of SCP to State Plan Outlay
1.	Andhra	15.93	3809.60	342.99	9.00
2.	Assam	7.40	1192.97	88.63	7.43
3.	Bihar	14.55	2200.00	354.79	16.13
4.	Goa	2.08	230.00	2.86	1.24
5.	Gujarat	7.41	4500.00	171.52	3.81
6.	Haryana	19.75	1576.04	202.65	12.86
7.	Himachal Pradesh	25.34	1008.00	122.58	12.16
8.	Jammu & Kashmir	8.30	1550.00	84.93	5.48
9.	Karnataka	16.38	4545.01	419.74	9.24
10.	Kerala	9.92	2855.00	95.58	3.35
11.	Madhya Pradesh	14.55	3656.00	326.27	8.92
12.	Maharashtra	11.09	8325.00	600.00	7.21

13. Manipur	2.02	410.00	4.13	1.01
14. Orissa	16.20	2810.00	282.04	10.11
15. Punjab	28.31	2100.01	210.00	10.00
16. Rajasthan	17.29	3500.00	528.19	15.09
17. Sikkim	5.93	200.00	4.22	1.92
18. Tamil Nadu	19.18	4052.60	752.23	18.56
19. Tripura	16.36	437.00	40.77	9.33
20. Uttar Pradesh	21.05	7080.00	1484.00	20.96
21. West Bengal	23.62	3922.87	300.38	7.66
22. Chandigarh	16.51	116.87	10.21	8.74
23. Delhi	19.05	2325.00	212.64	9.15
24. Pondicherry	16.25	218.00	35.47	16.17
Total		62639.44	6678.82	10.66

SCP expenditure in the agriculture and allied services, rural development, minor irrigation and village & small industries of direct relevance to SC families had been only 26.23 per cent, 27.56 per cent, 30.80 per cent and 33.32 per cent to total expenditure during 1991-92, 1992-93, 1993-94 and 1994-95 respectively.

Coverage

The details of SC families economically assisted to cross the poverty line, which was monitored under Point 11-A of Twenty-Point Programme, during the priod 1992-93 to 1996-97 are as under:

Table 22.4

Year	No. of SC Families Economically Assisted
1992-93	19,95,877
1993-94	23,23,722
1994-95	26,96,412
1995-96	24,82,075
1996-97	22,98,900
Total	117,96,986

The target for 1997-98 is to assist 24.80 lakhs families.

Of the families assisted 40 per cent families were covered under IRDP. The average investment per family/beneficiary had been Rs. 6418/I, Rs. 7134/1, Rs. 7830/I and Rs. 8704/I during 1990-91, 1991-92, 1992-93 and 1993-94 respectively. About 22 per cent of the assisted families were covered under the programmes of the State Scheduled Castes Development Corporations (SCDCs). The average investment under economic development schemes of SCDCs had been within the range of Rs. 5000/I to Rs. 8000/I during the period 90-91 to 93-94. Remaining 30 per cent of the families were covered under Animal Husbandry, Horticulture, Fisheries, Sericulture, Cottage Industries, Khadi & Village Industries etc.

Impact of Special Component Plans on SC Population

Significant improvement in the conditions of SC population is yet to take place. The inter-decennial trends in literacy rates and occupational trends (based on 1981 and 1991 Census) given below indicate that on major development indicators, the SCs have been unable to bridge the gap separating them from the general population. The Table 22.5 below indicates that in case of female literacy, this gap has widened during the period 1981-1991.

1. Inter-Decennial Literacy Level (literacy rate among SCs and the rest of the population)

Table 22.5

Year	Rest of the Poulation	SC Population
1981	41.22 (29.51)	21.39 (10.30)
1991	57.69 (44.82)	37.41 (23.76)

Note : Figures in brackets indicate literacy rate of female population.

2. The occupatinal profile reveals that dependence on agriculture based activities is still quite high. Deversification of occupation, particularly in respect of agricultural labourers, has taken place only marginally through the economic development porammes under the SCP of the State/UTs.

Table 22.6

Year	Cultivators	Agricultural Labourers	Non Agricultural Activities
1981	28.17	48.42	23.61
1991	25.44	49.06	25.50

3. The percentage of SC population below the poverty line during the last two decades is given below:

Table 22.7

Year	Percentage of SC Populatin Below The Poverty Line	
	Rural	Urban
1977-78	64.60	54.30
1983-84	53.10	40.40
1993-94	48.11	49.48

It may be seen that the percentage of SC population below the poverty line in the rural areas has come down from 64.60 per cent in 1977-78 to 48.11 per cent in 1993-94. The same in case of urban areas has show a dramatic fall from 54.3 per cent in 1977-78 to 40.40 per cent in 1983-84. But in the next decade this figure has gone up to 49.48 in 1993-94. This may be due to large scale migration of SC population from the rural to the urban areas.

Action Plan for Special Component Plan

In view of the situation described above even after the adoption of SCP strategy, the Ministry of Social Justice and Empowerment has consistently insisted upon that the State Governments need to give greater attention to proper formulation and implementation of SCP. States have been advised to:

(a) to allocate funds under SCP in proportion to SC population percentage in total population of the state;
(b) to open separate budget head for SCP inorder to prevent diversion, underutilization, and misutilization of funds earmarked for SCs;
(c) to make the department concerned with SC welfare and development as the nodal agency for formulation and implementation of SCP;
(d) to ensure that all the schemes under SCP are in accordance with specific needs and priorities of SC people;
(e) schemes in the core sectors like agriculture, dairy development, leather, weaving, textiles, handloom, etc. are formulated under SCP for the economic development of the SCs;
(f) to avoid notional allocation under SCP in sectors like power major Irrigation, Education and Health; and
(g) to strengthen Monitoring system to ensure proper and effective implementation of SCP.

Model of Special Component Plan Pattern

Constant monitoring of quantitiative aspect over the last three plan periods has lead to some improvements in financial allocations under SCP. It is observed from Table-22.3 that for the year 1997-98 the states/UTs of Assam, Bihar, Rajasthan, Tamil Nadu, Uttar Pradesh, Pondicherry have earmarked funds for SCP in proportion or nearly in proportion to SC population percentage in total population of the state. The Social Welfare Department of Uttar Pradesh has been designated as the nodal agency for formulation and sectoral allocation of funds for SCP. It is also responsible for monitoring the implementation of SCP. The Govt. of Uttar Pradesh have taken into account the above points while adopting the new model for formulation and implementation of SCP from 1996-97. The other states which have designated social welfare department/ department concerned for SC Welfare and Development as nodal agency for formulation and sectoral allocation of funds for SCP are Kerala, Maharashtra, Madhya Pradesh and Punjab.

Monitoring

Twenty four States/UTs formulate special component plan for the scheduled castes. Twelve states/UTs, namely Assam, Bihar, Goa, Gujarat, Madhya Pradesh, Maharashtra, Punjab, Rajasthan, Tripura, Tamil Nadu, Uttar Pradesh and Delhi have made their departments concerned with SC welfare and development as nodal department for formulation and implmentation of SCP. Andhra Pradesh and Pondicherry have made their departments concerned with SC welfare and development as nodal agency for monitoring the formulation and implementation of SCP by other concerned sectoral departments. The remaining states have been repeatedly requested to furnish information in this connection. Sixteen states/UTs, namely, Andhra Pradesh, Assam, Bihar, Goa, Gujarat, Haryana, Karnataka, Kerala, Madhya Pradesh, Rajasthan, Sikkim, Tripura, Maharashtra, Orissa, Himachal Pradesh and Uttar Pradesh have monitoring committees at State and District levels. The constant monitoring of SCP performance has lead to an increase in SCP allocations over the years.

Special Component Plan of Central Ministries

The strategy of special component plan at the central Govt. level involves participation of central government ministries/departments in formulating specific plans for the scheduled castes under Annual Plans of respective Ministries/ Departments. Many Central Ministries cater to the areas of vital importance to the SCs. The SCP at the Central Government level as a crucial role to play in the development of SCs. However, the performance of the Central Minsitries/ Departments has been observed to be poor. So far only 13 Ministries/Departments have formulated the special component plans. Even where special component plans have been formulated the percentage of SCP allocations has been far less than the SC population percentage of 16.48 per cent, despite clear guidelines on the subject that it should be at least in proportion to the percentage of SC population.

2. The Ministry of Social Justice and Empowerment has maintained close liasion with Central Ministries/Departments and impressed upon them the need to formulate and implement comprehensive Special Component Plan. The Ministries have also been requested to open separate Budget Head/Sub Head for Special Component Plan.

Special Central Assistance to Special Component Plan for the Scheduled Castes

The main objective of the Special Central Assistance to Special Component Plan for scheduled castes was that it would be used to give a thrust to the development programmes for scheduled castes with reference to their occupational pattern and the need for increasing the productivity of and income from their limited resources. It would help in bringing about occupational diversification in the labour surplus economy. Further the SCA was expected to fill the gaps which the various central and state development programmes are not in a position of fill any sector and this flexibility was an essential part of the scheme of SCA. It was realised that the programmes for which the SCA could be used by the state governments would vary from state to state and region to region within the same state depending on the local occupational patterns and the economic activities available. Even within the same state and region they would vary from time to time.

As an additive to the state's plan and programmes, the Special Central Assistance was expected to be an effective instrument in catalysing and strengthening the Special Component Plans as a whole in each state. The quantum of Special Central Assistance is related to the special component plans of the States/UTs, especially in concrete terms such as number of scheduled castes families that will cross the poverty line by the programmes and outlays in each sector, and the optimality of the state special component plan in comparison with the scheduled caste population in the state. The performance of the states in the implementation of the programmes for the scheduled castes is also taken into account.

As per the existing guidelines an amount upto 1 per cent of the total SCA released to a State/UT in a year can be utilised for staff for implementation, supervision, monitoring and evaluation.

Scheduled Castes Development Corporations

In March, 1979, the Centre initiated a Centrally sponsored scheme of assistance to State Governments for investing in the share capital of the Scheduled Castes Finance and Development Corporation (SCDCs) in the ratio of 49.51. At present, SCDCs are functioning in 24 States/UTs. This includes 9 SCDCs which are common to both SCs and STs. The State authorised and paid up share capital and Central share released during the last four years.

Functions of SCDCs

(i) Identification of eligible SC/ST families and motivating them to undertake economic development schemes.
(ii) Sponsoring the schemes to financial institutions for credit support.
(iii) Providing financial assistance in the form of margin money at low rate of interest and subsidy in order to reduce their repayment liability.
(iv) Providing necessary link tie up with other poverty alleviation programmes.

Implementation of Schemes

The SCDCs have been acting as guarantors and promoters and providing missing inputs by way of margin money loans and subsidy to the target group. They have a useful role in the mobilisation of finances for economic development of scheduled castes living below the poverty line. The SCDCs mainly take up employeemnt-oriented schemes in the following areas—

(i) Agriculture and allied
(ii) Minor Irrigation
(iii) Trade and Services
(iv) Transport
(v) Skill Development and
(vi) Self-Employment.

Performance

Project assistance from banks is arranged by SCDCs besides providing margin money assistance out of share capital assistance and subsidy out of Special Central Assistance (SCA) funds. The SCDCs are experiencing difficulties in arranging for bank finances. The share from banks is unduly delayed or highly inadequate. Besides, there are other structural, organisational and managerial factors which hamper the activities of the SCDCs. The beneficiaries covered so far under scheme are as under :

Table 22.8

Year	No. of beneficiaries (in lakhs)
1980-85	28.69
1985-90	29.22
1990-91	5.42
1991-92	4.52
1992-93	5.35
1993-94	5.32
1994-95	6.31
1995-96	4.20
1996-97	4.61

Budgetary Support

Table 22.9 : Plan outlay and expenditure details of Central share capital assistance to SCDCs

Year	Plan Outlay	Expenditure
1992-93	20.00	22.07
1993-94	22.00	29.34
1994-95	22.00	22.00
1995-96	30.00	31.00
1996-97	30.00	31.99
1997-98	45.00	45.00

Modifications in the Scheme

To enhance the viability of the scheme, certain modifications were effected with the approval of the Cabinet which included the following :

(i) The cost norms etc. may be left to the State Govts. and SCDCs.

(ii) The funds may be sent directly to the State SCDCs. Wherever necessary, the Ministry may route the funds through NSFDC.

(iii) The quantum and ceiling of subsidy may be the same as for the schemes under IRDP for beneficiaries below the poverty line.

(iv) There may be two nominees on the Board of Management of State SCDCs one from NSFDC and the other from Govt. of India. The nominee, as far as possible, should be professionals and need not be the officers of either the Central Govt. or the NSFDC.

National Scheduled Castes and Scheduled Tribes Finance and Development Corporation (NSFDC)

The National Scheduled Castes and Scheduled Tribes Finance and Development Coroporation (NSFDC) has established on 8th Feb., 1989 as a Govt. company not for profit under Section 25 of the Companies Act, 1956. The focus of NSFDC is on the special developmental and financing needs (loans only) of the SCs and STs over the above the credit available through priority sector lending of banks and other institutions. The NSFDC has an authorised share capital of Rs. 300 crores and its paid up capital stands at Rs. 300.00 crores.

Functions

NSFDC provides financial assistance at concessional rates for income generating activities and training in skill development to SCs and STs whose annual income is below double the poverty line criteria i.e. Rs. 22,000 per annum in rural areas and Rs. 23,700 p.a. in urban areas. The assistance is provided through the various States Scheduled Castes Development Corporations (SCDCs) and other State Channelising Agencies (SCAs) for implementing technically feasible and financially viable schemes/projects be sides providing grants for skill development programmes organised by SCAs and Non-Governmental Organisations (NGOs).

Centrally Sponsored Scheme of Post Matric Scholarshp to Studnets Belonging to SCs and STs

Objectives

The Scheme provides financial assistance to such students belonging to SCs and STs who pursue recognised post matriculation courses in recognised institutions, including correspondence courses, within the country.

Elements of Scholarship

The financial assistance includes provision of maintenance allowance, reimbursement of compulsory non-refundable fees, thesis typing/printing charges, study tour charges, book allowance for students pursuing correspondence courses and readers charges for the blind students.

Implementing agency and funding pattern

The Scheme is implemented by the respective State Governments and Union Territory Administrations which receive 100 per cent central assistance from Government of India over and above their respective Committed Liability, which is borne by them.

Centrally Sponsored Scheme of Prematric Scholarship to the Children of those Engaged in Unclean Occupations

Objectives

The Scheme financially assists the children of scavengers, sweepers having traditional link with scavenging, flayers and tanners, irrespective of their religion, to pursue education upto matriculation level.

Implementing agency and funding pattern

The Scheme is implemented by the State Governments and Union Territory Administrations. Central assistance is provided to the State Governments on 50:50 basis and 100 per cent to Union Territory Administrations over and above their Committed Liability.

Elements of Scholarship

The Scheme covers day scholars from class I to X with scholarship rates from Rs. 25 per month for classes I to V, Rs. 40 per month for classes VI to VIII and Rs. 50 per month for classes IX and X. The scheme also covers hostellers from classes III to X. The scholarship rates for hostellers in classes III to VIII are Rs. 200 per month and Rs. 250 per month for classes IX and X. The scholarship is provided for 10 months in a year. Besides scholarship, an adhoc grant of Rs. 500 per annum is also provided to day scholars as well as hostellers.

National Overseas Scholarships Scheme for SC, ST, etc. Students for Higher Studies Abroad

Objectives

The Scheme intends to provide financial assistance to meritorious students belonging to SC, ST, DNST, SC(C), LAL & TA categories, who have no means to fund themselves for higher studies aborad in courses for which adequate facilities are not available in India.

Brief Description

Under the Scheme Government meets the entire tuition fees, maintenance allowance of US $ 7700 p.a., $ 6600 p.a., 5940 p.a. for Post Doctoral, Ph.D/ Master's degree and Bachelor's degree respectively, contingency allowance of US $385 p.a. and air passage both ways. There are certain subject restrictions for Bachelor's and Master's degree. For Ph.D. and Post Doctoral courses there is no subject restriction. However, Medical Science, Agricultural and Allied subjects and subjects related to Indian studies are excluded. Maximum duration allowed for different courses are : 1½ years for Post Doctoral, 4 years for Ph.D, 3 years for Master's degree, 3½ years for Bachelor's degree. As for educational qualifications candidates are required to obtain 60 per cent 1st Class (50 per cent with Second Class for ST candidates) in the qualifying degree alongwith two years research teaching/working experience for Bachelor's and Master's and Ph.D degree and Five Years' research/teaching working experience with Ph.D for Post Doctoral degree. Age should be below 35 years and income not exceeding Rs. 5000/-p.m.

(B) Tribal Development

Tribal Sub-Plan (TSP)

Social economic development of Scheduled Tribes and their protection against exploitation has been on important agenda of the Ministry. Considerable progress in this has been made through the Tribal Sub-Plan strategy. The TSP strategy has been in operation since Fifth-five year plan with the twin objective of (i) bringing them on par with other section of the society and (ii) of protecting them from exploitation by various vested interest groups. A number of development schemes have been envolved over the year to bring the Scheduled Tribes up on the ladder of development. One the cornerstones of the strategy has been the attempt to ensure flow of funds for the Tribal Sub-Plan at lease equal to proportion of ST pouplation in each of the State/UTs.

2. Tribal Sub-Plan strategy is in operation is 18 states namely Andhra Pradesh, Assam, Bihar, Gujarat, Himachal Pradesh, Jammu & Kashmir, Karnataka, Kerala, Madhya Pradesh, Maharashtra, Manipur, Orissa, Rajasthan, Sikkim, Tamil Nadu, Tripura, Uttar Pradesh and West Bengal and two Union Territories namely Andaman and Nicobar Islands and Daman and Diu.

3. Many schemes/programmes and projects have been initiated for Tribal Development. Integrated Tribal Development Project (ITDP) have been setup in blocks or groups of block where the ST population is more than 50 per cent of the total population. Modified Area Development Approach (MADA) pockets have been formed in groups of village having population of 10,000 or more with 50 per cent or more Tribal Population 251 MADA pockets have been created, 79 clusters have also been formed in group of villages having population of 5,000 or more where STs constitute more than 50 per cent of the population, 75 Primitive Tribal Groups (PTGs) have been identified in 15 States/UTs on the basis of pre-agricultural level of technology and extremely low levels of literacy. The development of PTGs is undertaken through micro projects for these tribes.

Tribal Sub-Plan of Central Ministries

The Tribal Plan strategy seeks to ensure adequate flow of funds not only from the State Plan funds, institutional finances and central sector/centrally sponsored schemes of the Ministry of Welfare, but also from all the Central Ministries/ Departments. The Planning Commission and the Ministry of Welfare send letters to all the concerned Central Ministries/Departments every year on the need for quantification of funds from their annual plan accordance with the population percentage of the Scheduled Tribes in the country.

The policy formulation of the Planning Commission for the Ninth Plan and the guidelines of the Ministry of Welfare with regard to quantification of funds by Central Ministries has been given in detail in the Annual Report 1996-97 of the Ministry of Welfare.

The details of quantification of funds made by various Central Ministries during Eighth Plan period and 1997-98 is placed at Annexure XXI. As the deviationindex brings out, while there is generally an improvement is TSP flow in 1997-98 as compared to that of the Eighth Plan period. However, as against their total budgetary allocation, most of the Central Ministries had allocated much lower percentage of funds vis-a-vis the percentage of the Tribal Population (i.e. 8.08%). For Departments of Science & Technology and Deptt. of Electronics the Deviation Index is below 20 per cent.

Special Central Assistance (SCA) for Tribal Sub-Plan

The Special Central Assistance is given by the Ministry of Welfare to the Tribal Sub-Plan State Governments/UT Administrator to fill in the gaps in their financial outlays. The SCA is to be utilised in conjunction with the TSP flow with a view to meet the gaps which are not otherwise taken care of by the State Plan. It is basically meant for family-oriented income generating schemes in sectors of agriculture, horticulture, minor irrigation, soil-conservation, animal husbandry, forest, education, cooperatives, fisheries village and small industries and Minimum Needs Programme.

The criteria for allocation of Special Central Assistance have been fixed on the basis of certain norms of ITDP, MADA Pockets, Clusters, Primitive Tribal Groups and Dispersed Tribal Groups.

Table 22.10 : Allocation and expenditure for the years 1992-93 to 1997-98
(*Rs. in Lakhs*)

Year	Allocation	Amount Released
8th Plan (1992-93 to 1996-97)	1,25,000	1,47,985
1992-93	25,000	25,000
1993-94	29,500	29,485
1994-95	27,500	27,500
1995-96	33,000	33,000
1996-97	33,000	33,000
1997-98	33,000	32,916

Tribes Advisory Council (TAC)

An important mechanism for tribal develpment and welfare, is the Tribes Advisory Council under Para 4 of the Fifth Schedule to the Constitution. Eight States having Scheduled Areas, namely Andhra Pradesh, Bihar, Gujarat, Himachal Pradesh, Maharashtra, Madhya Pradesh, Orissa and Rajasthan and two Non-Scheduled Area States, namely Tamil Nadu and West Bengal have Constituted Tribes Advisory Councils.

2. The TAC consists of not more than 20 members of whom as many as 3/4 shall be the representatives of Scheduled Tribes in the Legislative Assembly of the States.

3. As per the guidelines issued by the Ministry of Welfare, the TAC should meet at least twice a year with a careful preparation of the agenda to make them effective. It is only then that TAC can become a meaningful and important forum representing tribal's interests. However, despite repeated requests by the Ministry, no State Government has reported about the TAC meetings held during 1996-97.

Girls Hostel for Scheduled Tribes

The scheme of girls hostel, which was started in the Third Plan, is useful instrument for spreading education among ST girls, whose literacy still stands at 18.19 per cent as per 1991 census against the general female literacy of 39.23 per cent. Under the scheme, Central Assistance is given to the States/UTs, for construction of new hostel buildings and/or extention of existing hostels. This is a Centrally Sponsored Scheme where the cost of construction of the hostel building is equally shared between the Centre and the State in the ratio of 50:50. In case of UTs, the Central Govt. bears the entire cost of the building.The cost of construction based on the State PWD schedule of rate or local CPWD schedule of rates, whichever is lower. Maintenance of the hostel is the responsibility of the concerned States/UTs. The number of seats in a hostel is limited generally to 100. The hostels are for ST girls in middle and high schools, colleges and universities.

2. For monitoring the progress of utilisation of funds and all the construction work, periodical report has been prescribed for the State Govt. to be furnished every six months.

3. Out of Rs. 1555.00 lakhs provided in the Annual Budgets during the Eight Plan Rs. 1507.50 lakhs has been released the States/UTs for construction of 273 hostels. State/UT-wise releases from 1992-93 to 1997-98.

Boys Hostel for Scheduled Tribes

This scheme was introduced in 1989-90 for construction of boys hostels. The norms followed are the same as those for the girls hostel.

2. For monitoring the progress of utilisation of funds and also the construction work periodical report has been prescribed for the State/UTs to be furnished every six months.

3. Out of Rs. 1572.00 lakhs provided in the annual budgets during the Eighth Plan, Rs. 1434.42 lakhs has been released to the State/UTs for construction of 291 hostels. State/UT-wise releases of funds from 1992-93 to 1997-98 is at Annexure-XXVII

Ashram School in Tribal Sub-Plan Area

The scheme of Ashram School, a Centrally Sponsored Scheme, was launched in 1990-91 with an objective to extend educational facilities like establishment residential schools for ST students in any environment conducive to learning. The funding for the scheme with the State is done on matching basis (50:50). While cent per cent assistance is given to UTs. The Central Assistance is mainly for construction of ashram school buildings, hostel and staff quarters. The expenditure on the maintenance, is met by the concerned State/UT. The scheme covers primary, secondary and senior secondary level of education.

2. For monitoring the progress of utilisation of funds and also the construction work, periodical report has been prescribed for the State Govts./UTs to be furnished every six months.

3. Out of Rs. 1300.00 lakhs provided in the annual budgets during the Eighth Plan, Rs. 1370.11 lakhs has been released to the State/UTs for construction of 266 schools.

(c) Welfare of the Other Backward Classes

Reservation for OBCs

The Supreme Court in its judgement in Indira Sawhney and others vs. Union of India and Others (Mandal Case), delivered on 16th November, 1992, upheld the reservation of 27 per cent of vacancies in civil posts and services under the Government of India in favour of Other Backward Classes (OBCs) subject to the exclusion of socially advanced persons/sections among them known as "Creamy Layer".

The Supreme Court had directed the Government of India to specify the socio-economic criteria for exclusion of the "Creamy Layer" from the OBCs. The Supreme Court had also directed the Government of India and each of the State Government/UTs Administrations to set up a permanent body for rcommending upon requests for inclusion and complaints of over-inclusion and under-inclusion in the lists of Other Backward Classes.

Notifying the List of OBCs

The common list of OBCs in respect of 14 States namely Andhra Pradesh,

Assam, Bihar, Goa, Gujarat, Haryana, Himachal Pradesh, Karnataka, Kerala, Madhya Pradesh, Maharashtra, Punjab, Tamil Nadu & Uttar Pradesh was published in the Gazette of India extraordinary Part-I, section 1 NO. 186, dated 13th September, 1993. The second common list of OBCs notified in the Gazette of India extraordinary Part-I Section 1 No. 163, dated 20th October, 1994 related to States of Orissa, Rajasthan, Tripura & West Bengal. On 25th May, 1995 vide Gazette of India extraordinary Part-I Section 1, No. 88, the common list of OBCs in respect of Jammu & Kashmir, Manipur, Sikkim and NCT of Delhi has also been notified. The Central Government has included/amended/modified the names of some castes/communities in the Central List of OBCs in respect of Andhra Pradesh, Kerala, Madhya Pradesh, Maharashtra, Orissa, Tamil Nadu, Tripura, Uttar Pradesh and West Bengal vide Gazette of India. Extraordinary Part-I Section 1 No. 60, dated 11th December, 1996 published in the gazette of India, Extraordinary dated 6th December, 1996. Besides, the common list of OBCs in respect of UT of Chandigarh and amendment to OBC list of Uttar Pradesh have been issued on 11.12.97 and 3.12.97 respectively.

National Commission for Backward Classes (NCBC)

The National Commission for Backward Classes (NCBC) Act, 1993 was enacted on the direction of the Supreme Court to set up as permanent body for entertaining, examining and recommending upon requests for inclusion and complaints of over-inclusion and under-inclusion in the Lists of Other Backward Classes of citizens. As per the provision of the Act, the advice tendered by such body shall ordinarily be binding upon the Government. The Commission was constituted on the 14th August 1993 for a period of three years. A second Commission has been constituted on 28th February, 1997.

National Backward Classes Finance and Development Corporation (NBCFDC)

National Backward Classes Finance and Development Corporation (NBCFDC) was set up by the Government of India under Ministry of Welfare on 13th January, 1992 as a company not for profit under Section 25 of the Company's Act with the objective of providing concessional finance to the members of backward classes living below double the poverty line for their socio-economic development by extending them loans for income generating schemes. The Corporation undertakes :

(a) to provide an additional channel of finance to backward classes for economically and financial viable schemes and projects; and
(b) Upgrade the technological and entrepreneurial skills of individuals or groups belonging to Backward Classes.

The authorised share capital of the Corporation was Rs. 200 crores and the same has now raised to Rs. 700 crores. The issued and paid-up capital of the corporation was Rs. 198.90 crores on 31.3.98.

The Corporation has so far sanctioned loans amounting to Rs. 539.46 crores of which Rs. 268.74 crores were disbursed as on 31.3.98.

Table 22.11 : The number of units covered, persons benfitted and the year-wise details of sanctions and dissbursements

Year	Amount (Rs. in crore)		No. of	No. of	Wage
	Sanctioned	Disbursed	Units	Benef.	Employees
1992-93	33.80	6.99	25821	31939	21302
1993-94	105.07	50.07	71855	76139	47840
1994-95	122.28	68.09	39018	40798	25099
1995-96	29.35	23.35	8084	7794	4300
1996-97	123.33	49.42	61706	72376	30925
1997-98	125.02	70.82	48127	48277	33730
Total	539.46	268.74	254611	277323	163196

(D) Welfare of the Minorities

1. *National Minorities Development and Finance Corporation*

Govt. has raised equity share towards National Minorities Development & Finance Corporation from 25 to 60 per cent.

2. *Pre-examination Coaching Scheme*

During 1997-98 Rs. 82.00 lakhs have been disbursed to 39 NGOs benefitting 1360 persons.

3. The scheme of "*Ex-gratia payment to Riots victims*" has been proposed.

4. Mrs. Veena Chhotray has been appointed as Managing Director, NMDFC.

5. *National Commission for Minorities*

The National Commission for Minorities have constituted a High Powered Study Committee for the socio-economic conditions of minorities in India. Former Hon'ble Minister for Welfare have attended the inaugural meeting of the said High Powered Study Committee on 30th July, 1997.

The National Commission for Minorities have sent their 4th Annual Report to the Ministry for examination and laying it on the floor of both the Houses of Parliament

The 12th Annual Report of the Minorities Commission for the period April, 1989 to March, 1990 Alongwith Action Taken Memorandum have been laid in both the Houses of parliament in August, 1997.

WAKF Administration

— The Corpus Fund of the Maulana Azad Education Foundation (MAEF), which was Rs. 30.01 crores as on 31.3.97, has been augmented by the Government of India to Rs. 70.01 crores with the release of another grant-in-aid of Rs. 40 crore in August, 1997. This would enable the Foundation to implement its objective of promoting education amongst the educationally backward sections of the society more effectively.

— During the financial year 1997-98, the Punjab Wakf Board, a composite Board for the States of Punjab, Haryana and Himachal Pradesh and the UT of Chandigarh, being administered by the Central Government in the Ministry of Welfare through an Administrator, achieved a record revenue collection of Rs. 8.75 crores. This would enable the Borad to widen the area of its welfare activities.

(E) Welfare of the Disabled

-Implementation of the Persons with Disabilities (Equal Opportunities, Protection of Rights and Full Participation) Act, 1995:

(a) A post of Chief Commissioner for Persons with Disabilities at Central level has been created.
(b) Central Coordination Committee was constituted on 21.2.97 and it met on 6.11.97. Central Executive Committee was constituted on 15.9.97 and it met on 14.1.98.
(c) Commissioner for Persons with Disabilities at State level have been appointed in 13 States.
(d) State Coordination Committees have been constituted in 16 States.
(e) Sate Coordination Committees have been constituted in 14 States.

— National Handicapped Finance and Development Corporation has been registered on 27.1.97 and has started functioning. Welfare Minister inaugurated the activities of the Corporation on 24.10.97.
— The National Fund for People with Disabilities was amended through a notification of 27th Oct. 1997. The Fund aims at creating services for the disabled for prevention and early detection, education, training, physical & economic rehabilitation. The last meeting of the Fund was held on 6.1.98 when funds were disbursed to NCOs for the first time.

DEVELOPMENT OF CHILDREN AND WOMEN

In addition to the normal schemes, the major new scheme that was launched in 1997 was the Balika Samriddhi Yojana (BSY). There were many initiatives taken for the development of women and children during the year. The major schemes are beiefly outlined below:

Balika Samriddhi Yojana (BSY)

The Scheme of Balika Samriddhi Yojana was launched on 2nd October, 1997 with the specific objective of changing female and community attitudes towards the girl child. The Scheme also encourages enrolment and retention of girl children in schools. Under the scheme, the mother of a girl child born on or after 15th August, 1997 in a family below the poverty line, in rural and urban areas, will be given a grant of Rs. 500. A scholarship will be given for education of the girl child when she attends school.

Integrated Child Development Services (ICDS)

The ICDS started in 1975-76 on an experimental basis in 33 blocks in the country is a major programme of the Department. It covers all the 5320 Community Development Blocks and 310 major urban slums in the country. At present, there are 5614 sanctioned ICDS projects. The ICDS benefits about 202.23 lakh children and 38.06 lakh mothers, in 4200 projects which are operational at present.

Adolescent Girl Scheme

The Adolescent Girl Scheme is a speical intervention for girls in the age-group of 11 to 18 years aimed at meeting their special needs in the areas of nutrition, health education and skill development. These special services were extended to 3.91 lakh adolescent girls through 507 selected ICDS blocks in the country.

World Bank assisted ICDS

The World Bank multi-state ICDS projects are extending certain additional services like income generation activities for women, interventions for adolescent girls, nutritional rehabilitation of the severely malnourished in the pre-dominantly tribal and backward areas in the States of Bihar (210 blocks), Madhya Pradesh (244 blocks), Orissa (191 blocks) and Andhra Pradesh (110 blocks).

Balsevika Training Programme

The Balsevika Training Programme is implemented through 25 Balsevika Institutes. The course of 11 months duration is conducted entirely through the Indian Council for Child Welfare, New Delhi. About 1250 Balsevika are trained annually.

Creches/Day Care Centres for Children

There are 12,470 creches providing day care services to the children of the age group of 0-5 years of migrant, casual, agricultural labourers and construction workers. The Scheme is being implemented by the Central Social Welfare Board, Bhartiya Adimjati Seva Sangha and Indian Council for Child Welfare. In addition there are 1805 creches set up under the National Creche Fund.

Early Childhood Education

Early Childhood Education (ECE) scheme is implemented as a strategy to reduce drop out rates and to improve the rate of retention of children in schools. The Scheme is run by voluntary organisations through 4365 ECE centres in nine educationally backward states of Andhra Pradesh, Assam, Bihar, Jammu and Kashmir, Madhya Pradesh, Orissa, Rajasthan, Uttar Pradesh and West Bengal.

Training of ICDS functionaries

The programme of training of ICDS functionaries at all levels such as Anganwadi Workers, Supervisors, and Child Development Project Officers, is being concurrently run through the National Institute of Public Cooperation and Child Development (NIPCCD) through its three regional centres, 18 middle level training centres and 300 Anganwadi Workers Training Centres. In addition, the Central Technical Committee on Health and Nutrition also gives training to medical and para-medical staff.

Hostels for Working Women

Since the inception of the scheme of Hostels for Working Women, 811 hostels have been sanctioned to provide accommodation to 56,974 working women, and day care facilities have been provided to 7,438 children in 284 hostels.

Support to Training and Employment Programme for Women (STEP)/NORAD

The STEP programme launched in 1987, seeks to provide updated sills and new knowledge to minor and assetless women in the traditional sectors such as agriculture, sericulture, handicrafts, fisheries, dairying, poultry, etc. for enhancing their productivity and income generation. During the year 1997-98, to projects were sanctioned to benefit 53,325 women.

Training-cum-Employment-cum-Production Centres (NORAD)

Assistance is being given by the Norwegian Agency for International Development (NORAD) for skill development and training, for self reliance through income generation for women through non-traditional trades. During the year under report, Rs. 14.46 lakh has been sanctioned to benefit 36,095 women through the projects.

Rashtriya Mahila Kosh (RMK)

The Rashtriya Mahila Kosh set up in March, 1993 as a National Instrument for extending credit to poor and needy women in the informal sectors, sanctioned credit worth Rs. 47.86 crore through 256 HGOs to benefit 2,50,312 women by 31.3.98.

Indira Mahila Yojana (IMY)

The Scheme of Indira Mahila Yojana is being complemented in 200 blocks on a pilot basis from August, 1995. The main strategy of the Scheme is to create an organisational base in all parts of the country for women to come together and to analyse and fulfill their needs through existing developmental programmes of the States and Central Government. More than 254 Indira Mahila Block Societies have been registered; over 28,000 small homogenous groups formed and 43 workshops have been held to train 1710 personnel so far.

National Commission for Women (NCW)

The National Commission for Women, a statutory body set up under the National Commission for Women Act, 1990 to safeguard the rights and interests of women, continued to pursue vigorously its mandated activities, namely review of legislations, intervention in specific individual complaints of atrocities and remedial action to safguard the interests of women where appropriate and feasible.

National Policy for Empowerment of Women

The National Policy for Empowerment of Women is being finalised. The Policy would prescribe strategies and action points to bridge the gap between the equal de-jure status and the unequal de-facto position of women in the country. It would seek to guide action at every level and in every sector by mainstreaming gender perspectives into all laws, policies, plans, programmes, regulations and budgetary allocation.

National Resource Centre for Women (NRCW)

The Department will shortly be setting up a National Resource Centre for Women (NRCW) with Danish assistance. This would be a nodal body to mainstream gender issues in policies and programmes for women by information dissemination, training, policy support, research and documentation.

National Plan of Action for the SAARC Decade of the Girl Child

The Government is implementing the National Plan of Action for the SAARC Decade of the Girl Child (1991-2000 AD) to assist equality of status of the girl child, laying dwn specific goals for survival, protection of development of the girl child while changing social attitudes and behavioural practices towards her.

Education Work for Prevention of Atrocities on Women

Financial support is provided to research and academic institutions and voluntary organisations to conduct legal literacy camps, para-legal workers training, to produce publicity material, to support seminars, workshops, campaigns and to provide studies on gender and violence.

23

STATE ENTERPRISES

(i) Performance of Public Enterprises

Department of Public Enterprises presents to the Parliament every year an overall view of the physical, financial and socio-economic performance of Central Public Sector Enterprises included in the Fourth Schedule of the Rules of Procedure and Conduct of Business in Lok Sabha. The survey does not cover the performance of departmentally run public undertakings and banking institutions.

The Estimates Committee, in their 73rd Report (1959-60) had recommended to the Government that in addition to the individual report of each enterprises laid on the Table of the House every year, a separate comprehensive report should be submitted to the Parliament indicating Government's total appraisal of the working of public enterprises. Accordingly, the first "Annual Report" was prepared in 1960-61 giving a composite picture of the working of these enterprises.

The Committee on Public Undertakings in their 46th Report (Fifth Lok Sabha) covered various aspects such as scope, coverage, classification of undertakings, content of report, time for presentation such other matters relating to Public Enterprises Survey and these recommendations have been taken into account while preparing the Annual Survey.

During the year 1997-98, Public Enterprises Survey 1996-97 is being prepared by DPE in bilingual for laying before both the Houses of Parliament. The data so collected from Central PSUs are analysed on the computer and presented in three separate volumes.

In Volume-I, a macro appraisal and analysis of the performance of public enterprises in terms of broad physical and financial parameter is presented.

In Volume-II, an analysis of the performance of these enterprises on different sectoral groups segregated further into individual enterprises is presented. It also contains a narrative description of their performance.

Volume-III of the Survey contains enterprise-wise analysis of data for three years consisting of summarised balance-sheet, summarised profit and loss account and important managment ratios.

In addition to preparation of Public Enterprises Survey every year, the Department also prepares CCEA Notes containing glimpses of information indicating trends about performance of the public sector enterprises.

The Department of Public Enterprises furnishes information to Committee on Public Undertakings as and when required by them on various issues relating to performance of public sector enterprises etc. and processes the report for consideration of the Cabinet.

Employees' Stock Option Scheme

With the objective of providing continuing involvement of employees in the performance of the enterprises, the identification with the company and to promote a mutuality of interests between the company and its employees, Govt. have introduced Employees Stock Option Scheme. The Scheme is applicable to all cases of disinvestment or fresh issue of equity by the enterprises and would be subject to the provisions of the Company Law and SEBI guidelines as applicable from time to time. Necessary guidelines for introduction of the Scheme in the PSEs have already been issued.

(ii) Reforms in Public Sector Enterprises

In the financial year 1997-98, a major initiative has been taken by the Government in granting substantially enhanced autonomy to 9 selected PSEs called NAVRATNAS. These enterprises are IOC, IPCL, ONGC, BPCL, HPCL, NTPC, SAIL, VSNL & BHEL. Later two more enterprises, namely, GAIL and MTNL were also extended enhanced autonomy of the Navratana enterprises. These enterprises, subject to certain guidelines would not enjoy full freedom to make capital expenditure, substantial powers for joint ventures, freedom to set up subsidiaries/offices abroad, to enter into technological and strategic alliances, to raise funds from the capital markets (international and domestic) and vastly enhanced operational and managerial autonomy. Their boards are being broad-based with the induction of non-official part time professional directors. These measures are intended to support them in their endeavour to become global players.

The Government have also granted enhanced financial, managerial and operational autonomy to other profit-making enterprises, called MINI-RATNAS. These enterprises should have earned profits continously for the last three years, have positive net-worth, do not seek budgetary support or guarantees from the Government and have not defaulted in the repayment of loans/interests to the Government. These enterprises can incur capital expenditure, enter into joint ventures, set up technological and strategic alliances, formulate schemes of human resources management, etc. subject to certain stipulations and guidelines. This is designed to make them more efficient and competitive.

A High Power Committee under a retired judge of the Supreme Court is going into the question of revising the compensation pakages for public sector executives. It is intended that PSUs should be able to attract and retain talented and efficient people and compete successfully both domestically and globally.

With a view to doing away with the plethora of guidelines issued over the last several decades, which may have outlived their relevance or utility, Government set up a Committee. Government have further examined the recommendations of the Committee and decided to delete 696 guidelines. This would give further freedom and autonomy to the Public Sector Enterprises.

(iii) Sickness in Public Sector Enterprises

The revival of sick public sector enterprises is the utmost concern of the Government and various steps have been taken from time to time for improvement in their performance to establish the commercial viability. the Sick Industrial Companies Act (SICA), 1985 was specifically amended in 1991 so as to include industrial public sector enterprises also under the purview of the BIFR.

As on 31.1.1998, 62 PSUs have been registered with the BIFR. The BIFR have appointed operating agencies in respect of such registered industrial PSUs for formulation of revival/rehabilitation scheme. A list of PSUs registered with the BIFR along with their status as on 31.1.1998.

So far, the BIFR have approved the revival package in respect of 21 PSUs, of which 2 PSUs, namely, Biecco Lawrie Ltd. and Mica Trading Corporation Ltd. has already been declared as no longer sick.

In regard to the remaining cases, the BIFR have recommended winding up in respect of 9 PSUs and notice has been issued in respect of another 4 PSUs for winding up. The employees of the Mining & Allied Machinery Corporation Ltd. have moved to the High Court for grant of stay against the final pronouncement of the Judgement of the BIFR and the High Court has granted Stay Order. Further, the position of the BIFR has been remanded by the Appellate Authority of Industrial Finance and Reconstruction (AAIFR) in case of UP Drugs and Pharamaceuticals Ltd.

In respect of 6 PSUs, draft scheme has been prepared by the operating agencies for consideration of the concerned authority. In case of another 3 PSUs, namely Nagaland Pulp & Paper Ltd., Bharat Immunologicals & Biologicals Ltd. and Manipur State Durgs & Pharmaceuticals Ltd., the BIFR have dismissed as non-maintainable. These companies have been asked to file relevant information under Secton 23 of SICA. There are 14 PSUs at the enquiry stage with the BIFR and in case of one PSU, namely, Bharat Coaking Coal Ltd. subsequent to its networth becoming positive, the case has been dropped.

(iv) Investment in Central PSUs

The Public Enterprises Survey 1996-97 tabled in Parliament has said investment in central public enterprises has increased by Rs. 15,522 crore to Rs. 1,93,121 crore in 1996-97 from Rs. 1,77,599 crore in 1995-96, an increase of 8.74 per cent. The survey points out that the number of employees decreased to 19.78 lakh in 1996-97 from 20.52 lakh in 1995-96. Gross sales have increased by Rs. 26,452 crore to Rs. 2,53,371 crore in 1996-97 from Rs. 2,26,919 crore in 1995-96. The growth rate recorded works out to 11.66 per cent in 1996-97 compared to the previous year.

Gross margin has increased to Rs. 44,501 crore in 1996-97 from Rs. 40,161 crore in 1995-96. The growth in gross margin works out to 10.8 per cent. Gross profit has increased to Rs. 30,574 crore in 1996-97 from Rs. 27,587 crore in 1995-96, thereby registering the growth of 10.8 per cent over the previous year. Increase in net profit by Rs. 684 crore from Rs. 9,574 crore in 1995-96 to Rs. 10,258 crore in 1996-97 an increase of 7.14 per cent. Gross internal resources generated by central public enterprises in 1996-97 of Rs. 25,533 crore is higher by Rs. 1,335 core compared to the previous year's figure of Rs. 24,198 crore registering a growth of 5.5 per cent. Export earnings of PSU has increased to Rs. 16,359 crore in 1996-97 from Rs. 16,269 crore in 1995-96.

Contribution to the exchequer in the form of corporate tax, excise duty customs and other duties and dividend has increased by Rs. 6,959 crore from Rs. 30,878 crore during 1995-96 to Rs. 37,447 crore in 1996-97, an increase of 21.27 per cent. And expenditure on social overheads has increased by Rs. 251 crore from Rs. 2,618 crore in 1995-96 to Rs. 2,689 crore in 1996-97. Value of inventories in terms of number of days of cost of production has been come down to 69 days in 1996-97 as against 70 days in 1995-96.

(v) Revamping of PSUs

Prime Minister Atal Behari Vajpayee has called for restructuring of public sector undertakings and according top priority to raising productivity in all sectors of the economy. "We just cannot afford to have huge national assets underperforming or worse still, becoming a drain on scarce budgetary resources. My Government is committed to PSU reforms that will safeguard both national and workers' interests," Mr. Vajpayee said in New Delhi on Oct. 14, giving away the Shram Awards for 1997. Calling for evolution of an alternative and communism, he come the shortcomings of both capitalism and communism, he conceded that so far "we have not succeeded in the effort." The Prime Minister pointed out that the challenge before the public and private sectors in the country was one of vastly and rapidly increasing productivity through better utilisation of human potential.

In the deeply-interlinked global economy that had currently come into existence, the only guarantee for survival and success was higher productivity, he said, stressing that the globalisation message "become more productive or perish" was valid for many of the public sector undertakings in the country. Regarding the swiftly-altering global scenario, Mr. Vajpayee said that capital was scarce and costly, particularly when viewed against the prevailing downswing in the national and international economies where market conditions had become very volatile. It was in this context that better utilisation of human resources and adoption of better technologies and work culture had become crucial, he said, stressing that productivity enhancement had to be accorded the highest priority in all sectors of the economy.

The Prime Minister also suggested the launch of a national work improvement campaign to create a new work culture in the country, with emphasis on team work and continuous learning in the workplace. In his welcome address, Union Labour Minister Satyanarayan Jatia said that efforts should be made to ensure that workmen acquired adequate skills to meet international challenges. Steel and Mines Minister Naveen Patnaik and Minister of State for Surface Transport Devendra Pradhan also attended the function. The top Shram Ratna award, carrying Rs. 2 lakh, was shared jointly by a team of workmen of the Bhilai Steel Plant, while the Shram Bhushan Award, carrying Rs. 1 lakh, went to four workmen of the Vindhyachal Superthermal Power Project of the NTPC and to an artisan of Bharat Heavy Electrical Ltd, Bhopal. Two women received the Shram Devi award jointly.

(vi) Disinvestment of PSUs

The government will go ahead with its disinvestment programme in key public sector undertakings at prevailing market prices and will not wait for the conditions to improve in the stock markets. "We are going ahead with out disinvestment programme. We have taken a decision in government that we will divest at the going market prices. Unlike in the past, we will not wait for the market to turn," Union Finance Minister Yashwant Sinha said. Mr. Sinha told reporters the government would not wait for the market to reach a certain imaginary level for starting disinvestment process. "This is a major departure in policy, therefore, we are confident we are going to disinvest and that the markets in India will improve," Mr. Sinha said. The governemnt had announced that it disinvest equity in four PSUs—Indian Oil Corporation, Container Corporation, Videsh Sanchar Nigam and Gas Authority of India—to mop up Rs. 5,000 crore during the year.

Recent reports had suggested that financial institutions had warned government that they might not get a good price for shares because of the lull in the stock markets worldwise. Mr. Sinha's assertion on going ahead with disinvestment programme comes at a time when Indian stock market is in the throes of selling pressure over Unit Trust of India's announcement that its largest scheme US-64 faced depreciation in its corpus. However, over the last couple of days, the markets have resumed their upward journey with the popular BSE-30 Sensex crossing the 3,000 point. When asked if Govt. would sell shares if the sensex was below 3,000 points. May be, it goes up or down for various reasons but we are going ahead with disinvestment programme," he said. He added that disinvestment would be both in domestic market as well as through GDRs.

The government on Jan. 13 approved sale of part of its equity in six cash-rich public sector companies including Indian Oil Corporation and Oil and Natural Gas Corporation through buyback or cross holding to meet the disinvestment target of Rs. 5,000 crore during 1998-99. Other public sector companies in which disinvestment has been cleared by the Cabinet are Gas Authority of India, Mahanagar Telephone Nigam, Videsh Sanchar Nigam and National Aluminium Co. an official spokesperson told reporters on Jan. 13. Sale of up to 12.5 per cent of government equity has been cleared in ONGC, up to 10 per cent equity sale in IOC and GAIL, up to five per cent sale in the two telecom gaints and part disvestment in NALCO.

Cabinet also decided to replace the group of ministers on disinvestment with a Cabinet committee under the Chairmanshp of Prime Minister Atal Behari Vajpayee to speed up the process. The Cabinet committee would comprise of Finance Minister Yashwant Sinha, Industry Minister Sikander Bakht and the Minister of the Administrative Ministry. Pricing of shares would be decided by the Cabinet committee on the recommendations of the core group of secretaries on disinvestment. ONGC, IOC and GAIL are expected to go for divestment through crorss holding of equity of each other, while Mahanager Telephone Nigam Ltd. and Videsh Sanchar Nigam Ltd. is likely to opt for buyback of shares. According to a proposal submitted by these oil companies, ONGC and IOC would buy 10 per cent stake from each other, while GAIL would pick up 2.5 per cent of ONGC, IOC and ONGC would take five per cent stake each in GAIL. Disinvestment in NALCO cold either be through buyback or cross holding. Board of directors of MTNL and VSNL have already approved buyback of shares ONGC and IOC which have free reserves of upwards of Rs. 30,000 crore have also proposed to buy out equity on the basis of an average market price of past 30 days.

- IOC to buy 10 per cent stake in ONGC for around Rs. 3,400 crore, while ONGC will spend Rs. 1,700 crore to purchase 10 per cent IOC stake. ONGC to buy another 10 per cent in GAIL for Rs. 700 crore.
- GAIL will pick up 10 per cent in ONGC later but at the moment will buy only 2.5 per cent as it has less each surplus.
- MTNL and VSNL will opt for share buy-back.
- Government to mop up over Rs. 6,000 crore from public sector oil companies alone

GAIL which has proposed to pick up 10 per cent equity in ONGC, is buying only 2.5 per cent as it has limited surplus. At present, government holds 96.58 per cent in GAIL, 91.14 per cent in IOC, 96 per cent in ONGC, 56.2 per cent in

MTNL, 65 per cent in VSNL and 87 per cent in NALCO. If the government goes ahead with the proposals in the current year, it is likely to mop up more than the targetted Rs. 5,000 crore.

(vii) 9 PSUs to Close Down

Government has identified nine Public Sector Undertakings (PSUs), which are terminally sick, to be shut down, the Rajya Sabha was informed on Nov. 30. Minister of State for Industry Sukbir Singh Badal said in a written reply that these nine PSUs under the Department of Heavy Industry have been recommended for closure by the Board for Industrial and Financial Reconstruction (BIFR) or the Disinvestment Commission at one stage or other. The nine PSUs are National Instruments, Rehabilitation Industries Corporation, Bharat Opthalmic Glass, Weighbird India, National Bicycle Corp. of India, Cycle Corp. of India, Mining & Allied Machinery Corp., Tannery & Footwear Corp. and Bharat Process & Mechanical Engineering the said. The government has decided to offer voluntary retirement scheme (VRS) benefits to employees of PSUs which are being closed down.

(viii) Plan to Retire 11,000 PSU Staff

The Industry Ministry has moved a Rs. 517 crore package for the Cabinet's consideration to retire about 11,000 workers from nine public sector undertakings (PSUs) identified to be closed down in 1998-99. Confirming the move Industry Minister Sikander Bakht said workers in companies, which are being would up are eligible for retrenchment benefits but the new package would give them the best possible benefits under an improvised Voluntary Retirement Scheme (VRS). "We are not interested in throwing out even a single worker on the road. We are going to be very generous with the workers," Mr. Bakht told PTI in an interview. The nine PSUs are National Bicycle Corportion (NBCIL), Cycle Corporation (CCIL), Bharat Process and Mechanised Engineering (BPME), Weighbird India (WIL), Mining and Allied Machinery Corporation (MAMC), Tannery and Footwear Company (TAFCO), Rehabilitation Industries Corporation (RIC), National Instruments (NIL) and Bharat Ophthalmic Glass (BOGL).

Mr. Bakht said though he did not expect workers to retaliate against the "extremely positive" package, which is expected to be cleared this month, there could be a "backlash from vested interests who are politically interested in keeping the issue going." Mr. Bakht declined to give details of funding of the package but said raising resources for the VRS would not be a problem. "There is going to be no difficulty in finding the money. As such we are already giving them money from the exchequer to pay their wages," he added. The new VRS package envisages a maximum of five years wages for a worker in these PSUs for 30 years of completed services, Industry Ministry sources said. At present the government gives a non-plan support of about Rs. 50 crore annually to pay wages and for working capital to these nine PSUs. Closure of nine PSUs is part of a five-pronged strategy for improving the performance of 48 PSUs under department of heavy industry (DHI).

(ix) Interim Relief to PSU Staff

The Government of India has decided to allow to empoloyees of public sector undertakings to the extent of 10 per cent of the existing basic pay as adjustable interim relief from Jan. 1, 1997, subject to a minimum of Rs. 280 per month. The interim relief from Jan. 1, 1997, subject to a minimum of Rs. 280 per month. The decision is based on the recommendations made by the Pay Revision Committee, set up by the Government for making recommendations on pay revision for the executives of Central PSUs following the Industrial dearness allowance (IDA) pattern, said an official release in New Delhi on Aug. 21. However, the decision will be subject to certain conditions, one of which states that these instructions are applicable to the employees of the Central PSUs following the IDA pattern.

The amounts paid as interim relief will be fully adjusted and subsumed in the final pay revision package. Moreover, no budgetary support will be provided to the PSUs for meeting the liabilities of this interim relief payment. The management of the public sector units, according to the release, would have the liberty to decide on the grant of interim relief to the officers and workers to the extent of 10 per cent of basic pay (subject to a minimum of Rs. 280 per month) taking into consideration the financial position of the enterprise and other implications of allowing such interim relief.

(x) More PSUs Up for Sale : FM

Finance Minister Yashwant Sinha on Dec. 30 said that the Government was fully confident to raise Rs. 5,000 crore from disinvestment of public sector enterprises for which more units would be put up for sale. The Finance Minister said that besides the targetted PSUs like the Indian Oil Corporation, Gas Authority of India, VSNL, and Concor, some other public sector units would be taken up for disinvestment during the current financial year. He said that while the Concor disinvestment process had mobilised only Rs. 225 crore, the balance of the targetted amount would be raised by further disinvestments. He, however, did not mention the names of the PSUs which might be considered for disinvestment. Asked whether the offloading of shares would be both in the international and domestic markets, Mr. Sinha said that a decision was yet to be arrived at regarding this.

Speaking at a function in Calcutta, the Finance Minister said that in spite of all pressures, the Government would try to maintain the fiscal deficit as targetted in the budget, which was 5.6 per cent of the GDP. Stating that controlling of fiscal deficit was the single most intractable problem in the management of public finances in the country, the Finance Minister favoured that Government borrowings from the market should be restricted. According to him, this would doubly help in controlling revenue expenditure as well as it would not crowd out private investments. On the revenue collection during the year, Mr. Sinha said that collection from indirect taxes was not within target, unlike direct taxes which were well on target. In this context, he also urged the states to control profigacy, which also help the Centre to contain revenue expenditure. Mr. Sinha said that the Government was determined to control expenditure, however unpopular step it might be.

24

TRANSPORT

CIVIL AVIATION

Air India (AI), Indian Airlines (IA) to Merge

The merger of Indian Airlines and Air-India has been act into motion with the joint board clearing the proposal of the creation of a holding company. Both IA and A-I will be 100 per cent subsidiaries of the holding company. The joint board on Dec. 7 totally approved the recommendations of their consultants. A F Ferguson & Co on the Indian Airlines-Air-India merger. "The proposal involves no expenditure on account of additional infrastructure and manpower. Also, the process is completely reversible if it fails to deliver the desired results," sources said. The consultants have also suggested a joint management group to support the holding company. This group will be an extra-statutory body set up by the top management of both airlines to implement the integration of specific activities.

The holding company will have a 'national' common balancesheet. It will have consolidated accounts and the individual airlines will also maintain their own balancesheets. "The consolidated account is a measure of combined performance and of shifting the foucs from individual to common bottomlines for greater synergy," the report said. To set the ball rolling, both the airlines will have to work for:

- Framing the memorandum and articles of association;
- Incorporation a new company;
- Transferring of shares of IA and A-I held by the government into the new entity;
- Amending the articles of association of both airlines.

Govt. Rejects Decision on IA, AI

The decision of the erstwhile joint board of Air India and Indian Airlines to set up a holding company for both airlines, will not be accepted by the Government. It will be sent back to the new boards for "reconsideration". In any case, the decision was subject to Government approval. The Government proposes to induct four functional directors each on the new, separate Air India and Indian Airlines board of directors, which are to be fully constituted. The joint board was dissolved last week and the Chairman was sacked. The functional directors representing the finance, engineering, commerical and personnel sectors could either be from the respective airlines or even from outside. In addition, there will be experts from aviation and finance sectors on the boards to expedite the Government's plan for disinvestment.

Sources said Mr. P.C. Sen, whose term was to end in Feburary next, showed undue haste in placing the proposal for setting up a holding company for a merged Air

India and Indian Airlines, without prior intimation to the Ministry and while disinvestment moves were on. What made matters worse was that the Minister for Civil Aviation, Mr. Ananth Kumar, learnt about it from next morning papers and moved to sack the board and its chairman. In his farewell speech in Airlines house last week, a dejected Mr. Sen said he would have liked to be associated with the airline in some manner or the other, either through the holding company or as a part-time chairman or even in some capacity in the Ministry of Civil Aviation. A 1967 batch, MP cadre officer, Mr. Sen holds the rank of additional secretary.

AI, IA Synergy Talks

The first step towards synergy between Air India and Indian Airlines was taken when the two agreed to make better utilisation of their space and accommodation besides engineering facilities. At a review meeting chaired by Minister of Civil Aviation Ananth Kumar on Jan. 7 it was decided that since Indian Airlines has land available at Goa, Rajkot and Vododra the two airlines will take immediate steps so that their respective requirements of space and accommodation are taken care of. Similarly, Indian Airlines has agreed to accommodate Air India within its existing premises at Ahmedabad, Bhopal, Pune, Cochin, Varanasi and Trivandrum. The meeting was attended by the managing directors of the two airlines. Secretary Civil Aviation. According to an official release both the airlines were further requested to identify more such locations where they can operate from common premises. Air India has agreed to offer 1,560 square feet area at Singapore to Indian Airlines. It was further agreed that at such stations where Air India and Indian Airlines are in rented accomodations, the possiblity of their moving into one common premises should be explored immediately.

It may be recalled that the Ministry of Civil Aviation had on Dec. 23 last constituted nine sub-committees to look into the entire package of synergy between the two airlines relating to information technology, ground transfer, scheduling of routes, fare rationalisation, engineering, space accommodation, appointment of common GSAs, advertising and marketing promotion activities and ground handling of flights. Today's meeting was a follow up on some of the recommendation made by the nine sub-committees.Thus as regard common technology, both the airlines have prepared a network integration plan and the directions of information technology of both the airlines are in the process of drawing up a detailed action plan to implement a common network in a time bound manner. This will invovle an initial outlay of Rs. 63 lakh, but will result in a recurring saving of Rs. 68 lakh.

Airlines to Remain Wholly Indian

Ruling out the possibility of allowing investment by foreign airlines in domestic airlines, the Union Minister of Civil-Aviation, Mr. Ananth Kumar, said no country in the world allowed such a practice. About Tata Airlines, Mr. Kumar said, the Foreign Investment Promotion Board (FIPB) would first take a decision on the matter and only then would the Ministry take a stand. Earlier, speaking at a seminar on "Building the subcontinent hub of the millennium in India", organised by the Confederation of Indian Industry (CII), Mr. Kumar stressed the importance of opening up of the country's civil aviation.

Mr. Kumar also emphasised the fact that there was need to create a separate infrastructure portfolio to put the country's transport systems in accelerated-growth mode and hence make them more viable. Saying that Delhi and Mumbai were ideal sub-regional hubs, Mr. Kumar added that attention should be focussed on developing regional as well as sub-regional hubs to strengthen the civil aviation system. Mr. Kumar stated that the government was also likely to decide on the ownership pattern and whether private participation would be allowed in sub-regional airports. According to the Civil Aviation Minister the issues in question were, democratisation of civil aviation that took into account the reach and viability of the system, anomalies in aviation turbine fuel, lease tax and operational costs that required rationalisation. Mr. Kumar said that he was persuading the Union Finance Ministry to take care of the automobiles so that margins for the investors, which are currently low, could improve. He also said that the decision upon involement in Indian Airlines was the first step towards opening of the sector and that public participation would be allowed in the company.

Airport Expansion Programme

The Airports Authority of India (AAI) is awaiting the Centre's clearance to start an ambitious expansion programme for the Delhi Airport at a cost of about Rs. 1,500 crore. The entire project report, including that on feasibility, has been submitted to the Government for approval. The AAI Chairman, Mr. Ranjan Chatterjee, told reporters in New Delhi on July 2 that the plan included creation of an additional international terminal to cater to about ten million passengers a year from the present capacity of 3.5 million and construction of a new domestic terminal near the internatinonal complex. Mr. Chatterjee, who took mediapersons around the new Indian Airlines alliance air departure terminal 1-a which was reconstructed after it was completely gutted on October 30 two years ago, said that this terminal had been constructed within a record span of eight months at a cost of Rs. 26 crore. This terminal, to be formally inaugurated tomorrow by the Union Home Minister Mr. L.K. Advani, and start operations from July 3, has been provided with hi-tech fire-fighting and security equipment, besides special facilities for the disabled and a child care centre.

A total of 34 check-in counters have been provided for in the terminal which include four fast-track express counters for passengers traveling with only a hand-baggage and two counters for the wait-listed ones. Mr. Chatterjee and other AAI officials said that this terminal could simultaneously handle about 1,500 passengers for five wide-bodied air-craft like A-300s during peak hours which was comparable with international standards. "This would enhance the capacity of handling domestic passengers from 4.7 million per annum to 7.2 million," he added.

Besides the VIP lounge, a separate lounge has been set up by AAI along with Indian airlines for Commercially Important Persons (CIPS). There is also a separate lounge for business-persons holding any recognised credit card, having facilities like phone, fax, photocopying and secretarial assistance.This counter would be manned by the Maurya group, which would also run restaurants in the new terminal. Referring to the lessons drawn from the earlier fire incident, they said the latest computerised intelligent fire-fighting equipment installed was a fire alarm, detection and fighting system with auto-sprinkling facilities. The airconditioned ducts have been fitted with smoke and flame arresters and the material used in construction were fire, they said.

100 per cent Foreign Equity in Airports: PM

Prime Minister Atal Behari Bajpayee on Jan. 1 said that the Government had decided to permit 100 per cent foreign equity participation for development of new airports in the country and evolve a new set of regulatory guidelines to expedite clearance of projects. Speaking after inaugurating the new international terminal building in Bangalore, Mr. Vajpayee said that the Government had decided to allow 100 per cent foreign equity participation for development of new airports of interntional standard wherever necessary. He added that the infrastructure task force committee, set up by the Government under External Affairs Minister Jaswant Singh, had made important recommendations in its reports, which included framing of regulatory norms for speedy clearance of airport projects. He further said that development of airports with international standard facilities was critical for the economic development of the country.

The infrastructure task force had made several important recommendations in its interim report, which included framing of regulatory norms for speedy clearance of new airport projects, Mr. Vajpayee added. At present, clearance had to be obtained by several agencies, resulting in delay in clearing the future proposals, he said. Apart from the upgradation of the existing international airports in the four metros of Delhi, Mumbai, Calcutta and Chennai, airports at Hyderabad, Ahemdabad, Amritsar and Guwahati would be corporatised in due course to provide class passenger amenities.

RAILWAY

Railway Budget Presented

Presenting his second Railway Budget in Parliament on Feb. 25, Mr. Nitish Kumar was unable to resist the pressures of populism given the unstable nature of the Central Government and the impending Assembly elections in several States. Mr. Kumar took the easy way out to mobilise extra resources by raising freight rates and tinkering with upper class passenger fares. He thus reversed the trend set in his maiden Budget of leaving freight fares untouched and cutting down the subsidy on passenger travel. The industry's expectation of relief in recessionary conditions was belied as Mr. Kumar proposed a uniform four per cent increased in freight rates though there were several minor concessions such as 25 per concession in freight traffic up to a distance of 50 km and lower rates for a couple of commodities. The exercise will bring the Railways Rs. 700 crore more during the next financial year.

On the passenger side, the heavily subsidised unreserved second class in long distance and suburban trains accounting for 90 per cent of passengers have been left untouched while increases have been made in all other classes including parcel and additional luggage. The revision will fetch the Railways Rs. 200 crore. From April 1, second classes sleeper fares will be 1.55 times, AC chair car will be three times, AC three-tier sleeper 4.5 times, first class 5.25 times, AC two-tier 7.2 times and AC first class a whopping 14.4 times that of second class ordinary fares. Fares of Rajdhani and Shatabdi trains have also been revised by 11 per cent to 16 per cent. According to Railway officials, the increase will vary from two per cent to 13 per cent—second class sleeper will be higher by eight per cent, first class and AC II by two per cent, AC III 13 per cent and AC I 10 per cent. For Rajdhani and Shatabdi the increased will be by an average of six per cent. Like his predecessors, Mr. Kumar chose not to heed the warnings signals emanating from frequent derailments due to saturated track capacity and announced the introduction of 14 new trains, increaesed the frequency of four and extended 11 trains. There will be four new DMU and EMU trains each on different sections. The coming year will also see preliminary surveys for 16 more new lines and gauge conversions of six more sections despite the backlog of projects worth over Rs. 35,000 crore. The more important task of doubling has been restricted to just the Yeshwantpur-Tamkur section and railway electrification will be effected on three sections in the north.

The coming year has been declared as the "Year of the Passenger" and the Railways propose to go "green" in a big way by planning afforestation of vacant land. The "Passenger Year" will be observed by making 30 Rajdhani and Shatabdi trains 'complaint-free' and clearing the four metros of touts. The Minister also appropriated several projects initiated by previous Railway Ministers which happen to be nearing completion during his tenure. These included a customer care institute in Delhi to impart training to customer-interface staff such as ticket checkers and booking clerks.

Railway Budget Highlights

Increase of 4 per cent uniformly on freight rate of all commodities.

Concession of 25 per cent in frieght rate for traffic up to 50 km. No increase in II-class fare of mail/express/ordinary trains and II-class season tickets.

With II-class ordinary fares of mail/express trains as base, fares for sleeper, first class and A-C accommodation have been raised as follows:

• Sleeper class	1.55 times
• A-C chair car	3 times
• A-C 3-tier sleeper	4.5 times
• I-class	5.25 times
• AC-2-tier sleeper	7.2 times
• AC I-class	14.4 times

Fares of Rajdhani/Shatabdi trains to be revised by making suitable adjustments
4 per cent increase to be applied on all parcel and luggage scales
14 new trains to be run
1999-2000 Annual Plan outlay proposed at Rs. 9,700 cr.

The continuing emphasis on computerisation will result in a 'national trains enquiry system' to provide information about any train from any location. Plans are also on to give passenger reservation terminals to travel agents. The MPs were also informed that unmanned level crossing could converted with fund from the MP local area development scheme. Learning no lessons from the fiasco suffered to the annual plan for 1998-99 which was revised downwards twice, the Railway Minister proposed an ambitious annual plan Rs. 9,700 crore for 1999-2000. The annual plan, is used to fund modernisation, replacement and new projects. The current year's annual plan was also in the same range and had to be finally reduced from Rs. 9,500 crore to Rs. 8,750 crore in two stages.

CCEA Clears 10 Railway Projects

The Cabinet Committee on Economic Affairs on Sept. 9 approved 10 railway projects involving a total expenditure of Rs. 4,700 crore for new lines of 1,343 km and 417 km of gauge conversion. Of these, one project is in the north-east and the construction on this line fro Diphu to Karong will meet the long-standing demands of Manipur for a rail line leading to their capital. The other lines include rail links to the pilgrims tourist resorts of Puttaparthi and Sabarimala and also the upgradation of the existing meter gauge links to broad gauge at the pilgrims centres of Sitamarhi and Rameshwaram. The new line from Chandigarh to Ludhiana will provide rail infrastructure to the industrial town of Mohali, link Chandigarh to Anandpur Sahib and also provide an alternative route between Ambana and Ludiana. The new lines in Bihar will link Giridh to Ranchi via Koderma, Hazaribagh and Barkhakhana.

Railway Freight Business Declines

The India Railways incurred a loss of Rs. 950 crore on freight business till November this year as the loading dropped by 19 million tonnes during the first eight months of the current fiscal. Due to the continued downturn in the economy, the railways could transport only 270 million tonnes of cargo as against the target of 289 million tonnes set for April-November this year, an official release said in New Delhi on Dec. 27. The shortfall was acute in the loading of coal, iron and steel and cement, which were going through a sluggish phase this year. Since the demand for cargo loading on the railways is a derived demand, any downturn in the economy will be reflected immediately in the freight business of railways. During April-November, the railways transported 129.30 mt. of coal, 24.06 mt. of raw materials, 6.97 mt of iron and steel, 7.79 mt of iron ore for export, 22.34 mt of cement, 16.90 mt of foodgrains, 17.98 mt of fertilisers, 21.35 mt of POL and 23.84 mt of other goods.

The railway budget for 1998-99 has fixed a freight loading target of 450 mt for the year, up 20 mt from the target of the previous year. However, the recession in the economy would see the railways finishing between 425 and 430 mt, and the loss on this account is expected to be more than Rs. 1,000 crore. One mt of cargo fatches Rs. 50 crore for the railways on an average. The railways had recently taken several measures to boost their freight traffic, including a new volume discount scheme for incremental loading of goods. The managers of zonal railways have also been given a tree hand to fix special station-to-station rates. Under the volume discount scheme, customers will be entitled to a 10 per cent discount for incremental loading of iron and steel, cement and iron ore over what they had offered during the first six months of the current fiscal. The Railway Board is also considering a 10 per cent cut in the Plan size to meet the financial crisis arising out of a steep slide in its freight business. The railway budget had fixed a Plan size of Rs. 9,500 crore.

PM Dedicates Konkan Railway

Prime Minster Atal Behari Vajpayee on May 1 appealed to all political parties to help evolve a consensus on key economic issues like infrastructure development. The Prime Minister made this fervent appeal while dedicating the 760 km. long Konan railway line to the nation at a function in Ratnagiri on April 30. The railway line connects Maharashtra, Goa, Karnataka and Kerala on the western sea coast, Mr. Vajpayee stressed the need for development of infrastructure, railways and power in the country without which, he said, the country would face major crisis. Underlining the need of keeping the key issues above politics, he said, "Had there been no frequent change in the government at the Centre in the last few years, the Konkan Railway Project would have been completed in just four years".

The Prime Minister complimented the Railway authorities for successful completion of the Konkan Railway Project, which, he said, proved to be the biggest and most difficult railway engineering project in South Asia. Mr. Vajpayee said, "The successful completion of Konkan Railway Project is a model for other States to follow". Mr. Vajpayee said consensus among political parties was necessary to keep democracy on the right track. In a democracy, there is no enmity but only difference of opinion. Politics will move on to the wrong track if enmity creeps in, he said. He assured changes in old methods of doing work and said the nation could not afford any delay now. He hoped that Konkan Railway would bring with it the message of prosperity and wished for many more such infrastructure projects in the country through people's participation on build, operate and transfer basis.

ROAD TRANSPORT

To keep pace with the economic development in the country and consequent surge in demand for transport services—both passenger and freight, various modes of transport have experienced substantial growth over the years. Road Transport, however, is the most dominant mode of transport both for movement of passengers and goods and is likely to continue to enjoy this status increasingly in the coming years. The users preference towards the road transport is on account of its inherent advantages viz. easy availability, adaptability to individual needs, door to door service, and reliability. At present, 80 per cent of passengers and over 60 per cent of freight is estimated to move by roads. It also acts as a feeder service to Railways, Ports and Air Traffic.

This Ministry is concerned with the formulation of broad policies relating to road transport, besides making arrangements for movement of vehicular traffic with the neighbouring countries. In its tasks for development of roads and road transport in the country, the Ministry is assisted by Transport Development Council. It is an apex advisory body on roads, road transport and inland water transport. Minister of Surface Transport is its Chairman; concerned Central Ministers namely Industry/Railways/Urban Development/Tourism/Rural Development/Planning Commission and Minister-in-charge of Roads/Road Transport, Inland Water Transport in States/UTs and Ltd. Governors/Administrators of UTs without legislature are its members.

Road Development

During the year 1998-99, it is expected that 300 kms. of National Highways will be widened from single lane to double, 40 kms. will be widened to four lane, 700 kms. of National Highways would be strengthened and 60 bridges are likely to be completed. Till December, 1998, 280 kms. has been widened from single lane to double, 10 kms. widened to four lane, 270 kms. of National Highways strengthened and 48 bridges have been completed (achievement is based on ongoing works completed after 31.3.98). Remaining works are at different stages of progress.

New Policy Initiatives

National Highways have been accorded the top most priority by the Government. Recently, the Hon'ble Prime Minister has announced six-laning of the North-South corridor connecting Kashmir to Kanyakumari and East-West corridor connecting Silchar to Saurashtra, in an aggregate length of 7000 kms. In this regard, a Task Force has been set up, which is headed by Dy.Chairman, Planning Commission and has Minister and Secretary (SFT) as Members, to monitor the project. The Task Force has finalised the alignment of these corridors and the Ministry proposes to commence construction works on atleast 20 locations out of which, work at one location at Bangalore has already commenced with the foundation stone for this project laid by the Hon'ble Prime Minister on 2nd January, 1999. The implementation of this programme has been handed over to the National Highways Authority of India.

National Highways Authority of India (NHAI) has already been entrusted with development of Golden Quadrilateral linking four main metros viz. Delhi, Calcutta, Chennai and Mumbai, which aggregates to a length of 5800 kms. NHAI has commissioned feasibility studies along these corridors, and projects will be identified after these studies are completed.

The Ministry has also embarked upon a strategy to plan and implement Expressways for rapid, unhindered and sale movement of fast moving vehicles leaving National Highways for normal traffic. The Ministry proposes to establish National Expressways Authority of India on the lines of National Highways Authority of India. The National Expressway Authority of India will be solely responsible to plan, design, develop and maintain the expressways in the country. A preliminary study for the construction of expressways has already been conducted by the Ministry. It is now proposed to conduct feasibility study followed by detailed project reports on a few of the expressways planned. In view of the severe resource constraints, it may be difficult to finance the construction of these expressways from general budgetary support. Efforts will be made to have the expressways implemented with private sector participation under Build Operate and Transfer (BOT) Scheme.

The Ministry of Surface Transport recently conducted an International Congress on Express Highways Development in India. The Congress was held at Vigyan Bhawan from 14 to 17 December, 1998. The foreign delegate participation was encouraging.

The Task Force has been coordinating all these development needs. It has been decided to integrate the North-South and East-West corridor with the existing plan for the Golden Quadrilateral. It has been decided to develop some of these stretches as expressways.

To encourage private sector participation, in continuation of facilitating meausres already taken, on December 28, 1998, a Model Concession Agreement has been released for major projects (costing more than Rs. 100 crore) to be undertaken under BOT Scheme. Further, foreign direct investment (FDI) up to 100 per cent have been allowed in the road sector (with total foreign equity up to Rs. 1500 crores) to attract foreign investors.

Besides speed and mobility of traffic on Highways, safety of users is another important aspect. An International Seminar on Highway Safety on 6th & 7th November, 1998 was held at Vigyan Bhawan, New Delhi, to disseminate knowledge on safety aspects/devices/methods etc.

World Bank Second National Highway Project

A loan Agreement was signed in Jun 1992 with World Bank for Second National Highway Project (LN. 3470/OR 2365-IN) comprising four laning of National Highway sections in the State of Haryana, Punjab, Maharashtra, Orissa, Madhya Pradesh and West Bengal. The total amount of the loan and credit is US $306 million. This project also includes reconstruction of damaged bridges on State Roads in Orissa. Works on all the six National Highway sub-project are in progress. The sub-project for reconstruction of damaged bridges in Orissa is also in progress.

Asian Development Bank — First Road Project Loan

Loan Agreement No. 918-IND was signed in December, 1998 with the Asian Development Bank (ADB) for a loan amount of US $ 198 million (revised to US $ 177 million), and is effective since April 1989 for financing road projects both in the Central and State Sectors covering the States of Andhra Pradesh, Haryana, Karnataka, Tamil Nadu and Uttar Pradesh. All the sub-projects under the loan have been completed. Loan has been closed with effect from 31st March, 1998.

SHIPPING

For the Shipping Sector, in the 9th Plan, an outlay of Rs. 5906 crores has been tentatively approved. During the first two years of the Plan i.e. the year 1997-98 and 1998-99, an outlay of Rs. 910.19 crores and Rs. 1177.61 crores respectively has been provided for the ongoing and new schemes.

It has been proposed to achieve a net growth in tonnage of 2 million GRT taking the total tonnage to 9 million GRT at the end of the 9th Plan by acquiring 3.7 million GRT (2 million on additional account and 1.7 million on replacement account) at an investment of Rs. 15000 crores during the 9th Plan period.

During the year, this Ministry has accepted 15 out of 26 recommendations accepted by the Empowered Committee constituted to examine the Report of the National Shipping Policy Committee. Necessary action on such recommendations has also been initiated.

Transchart (Chartering)

In general, the freight market has been weak and in a very bad shape throughout the year for dry bulk trades. Freight indices for handymax and large bulkers have dropped 20/34 per cent respectively since last December. The general view seems to be that the low levels will continue well in to the New Year 1999. The BFI (Baltic Freight Index) at the end of 1998 is at 752 points corresponding to its level of 1231 points at the end of 1997. This reflects the shipping market for dry bulk sector.

The tanker market when compared to the bulk cargo market though remained steady during the year in contrast to last year, showed weakness during the year.

During the year under review, Chartering Wing arranged shipment of approx. 218.82 lakh tonnes of Government cargoes (from January, 1998 to December, 1998). Out of this, 59.84 per cent was carried by Indian bottoms. The major items under dry/liquid cargoes for which shipping arrangements were finalised during the year included 74 lakh tonnes of coking coal, 97.21 lakh tonnes of Petroleum product, 21.82 lakh tonnes of Fertilizers/Fertilizers raw materials and

14.69 lakh tonnes of wheat. As a result of negotiations with member lines of IPBC Conference, rebate of tariff has been increased from present level of 15 and 17.5 per cent to 22.5 per cent for break bulk general liner cargoes and 35 per cent in respect of full container load (FCL). This is going to save a substantial amount in outgo of freight by importing PSUs.

Transchart successfully arranged charter of specialized vessel for XVIIIth Antarctica Expedition, an ambitious programme of Deptt. of Ocean Development.

Concerted efforts were made to provide shipping coverage at competitive freight rates as per the requirements of the indenting Departments.

Inland Water Transport

Activities related to development, management and regulation of Inland Water Transport (IWT) are being carried out by the Inland Waterways Authority of India (IWAI).

During the year, various developmental works have been executed for providing the necessary infrastructure for navigation and shipping in the three National Waterways. Many new initiatives have been taken to accelerate the pace of development of IWT in the country.

- National Waterways (NWs) viz; the Ganga (NW-1). Brahmaputra (NW-2) and West Coast Canal (NW-3) were maintained with improved navigational facilities.
- "M.V. Rajagopalachari" of IWAI continued promotional sailings in NW-1 (The Ganga) carrying various commodities between Allahabad and Calcutta.
- Movement of POI by HPCI between Kochi and Edapallikotta through NW-3 continued successfully during the year.
- Schemes for acquisition of two numbers hydraulic surface dredgers for NW-1 & NW-2 and two numbers new survey launches for NW-2 & NW-3 were santioned and construction commenced.
- Schemes for procurement of four numbers pontoons for providing floating terminal at Karagola & Ballia in NW-1 and Sadiya & Saikhowa in NW-2 were sanctioned and construction of pontoons commenced.
- Implementation of the schemes for providing 24 hrs. navigation facility on NW-1 & NW-2 has been commenced by placing orders for supply of lights and buoys.

Floating terminals at Haldia, Calcutta, Karagola, Bhagalpur, Monghyr in river Ganga (NW-1) and at Dhubri, Jogighopa, Pandu, Tezpur, Naemati in river Brahmaputra (NW-2) were maintained.

Work of construction of permanent terminal at Gaighat, Patna on NW-1 has been taken up through CPWD on deposit work basis. Action was initiated for setting up of another permanent terminal at G.R. Jetty, Calcutta on NW-1 for taking over land from Calcutta Port Trust. For permannent terminal at Pandu on NW-2, preliminary design and estimates are under preparation through CPWD. For NW-3, a scheme for construction of 11 Nos. permanent terminals was prepared and is under consideration.

Environmental clearance for proposed development of East Coast Canal in NW-3 was obtained from Ministry of Environment & Forests in February, 1998. Capital Dredging in this waterway has commenced after floating "Global Tenders"... Land acquisition also commenced for widening of narrow stretches and construction of terminals.

Techno-economic Feasibility Studies on the waterway stretches of Visakhapatnam-Polavaram canal system, extension of NW-3 from Kovalam to Kolachal, assessment of IWT tourism potential on NW-2, study on improvement of safety of life on river boats and a transport economic study for all the three National Waterways have been taken up in addition to ongoing studies and environmental impact assessment studies on identified waterways.

Scheme for installation of computer based Automatic Hydrographic Survey System at IWAI Head Office, Nodia and at field offices on NW-1 (Patna), NW-2 (Guwahati) & NW-3 (Kochi) has been sanctioned and is under implementation.

For NICNET connectivity among the offices of IWAI, procurement of computer hardware and software was completed at Noida, Calcutta, Patna, Bhagalpur, Guwahati and Kochi.

A conference cum Exhibition on IWT has held at Calcutta jointly by IWAI and the FICCI during November, 1998, where due publicity to the prospects and potential in India was disseminated among prospective IWT operators in the country. For training of IWT personnel, the work of construction of National Inland Navigation Institute at Patna was entrusted to CPWD.

The Regional Office (Sails) are responsible for the welfare of the sailing vessel industry in the respective regions. During the period under review, 477 fresh identity cards and 158 duplicate identity cards were issued and 1333 identity cards have been renewed.

National Welfare Board for Seafarers

As provided in Section 218 of M.S. Act. 1958, the Government of India Constituted a National Welfare Board for seafarers headed by the Union Minister of Surface Transport for advising the Government on the measures to be taken for promoting the welfare of seamen whether ashore or abroad.

Seamen's Provident Fund Organisation

The Seamen's Provident Fund Organisation has been set-up under the Seamen's Provident Fund Act, 1964 to provide institution of Provident Fund for Seamen w.e.f. 1st July, 1964.

National Shipping Board

The National Shipping Board is a permanent statutory body established in 1959 under Section 4 of the Merchant Shipping Act, 1958 to advise the Government of India on matters related to Shipping including the development thereof. The National Shipping Board has played an important role in the maritime development of the country. The Board has thus contributed immensely in the evolution of a sound and pragmatic National Maritime Policy over the years.

The Chairman and other members of the Board hold office for a period of two years. The Composition of the Board is as follows:

(a) Six Members elected by Parliament, four from the Lok Sabha from among its members and two from the Rajya Sabha from among its members;

(b) Such number of other members not exceeding sixteen as the Central Government may think fit to appoint on the Board to represent—

(i) The Central Government,

(ii) Shipowners,
(iii) Seamen, and
(iv) Such other interests as in the opinion of Central Government ought to be represented on the Board.

The Act provides that one of the members of the Board shall be nominated by the Central Government to be the Chairman of the Board.

In the current year, i.e. 1998, two meetings of the Board were held as per details below—

1) 98th meeting of the National Shipping Board held at Kandla on 17th April, 1998.
2) 99th Meeting of the National Shipping Board held at Cochin on 19th August, 1998.

National Shipping Policy Committee

A National Shipping Policy Committee under the Chairmanship of Director General of Shipping was constituted by Govt. The Committee in its report submitted in July, 1997, made 31 recommendations. The Empowered Committee subsequently constituted to examine the report, recommended acceptance of 26 recommendations and rejection of 5 recommendations. After detailed examination, Govt. have taken a decision to implement 15 recommendations with immediate effect.

The matter relating to acceptance of the remaining 11 recommendations is under active consideration by Government and final decision will be taken in due course.

Shipping Industry Beset with Problems

Even as the Indian shipping industry awaits the national shipping policy (NSP) based on the M.P. Pinto Committee recommendations, its current state clearly reflects the slowdown in the economy. The industry is going through a lean patch anyway following the elimination of the cost plus formula and the steep fall in the Baltic Freight Index (BFI). The Industry as well as the Ministry of Surface Transport will now seek to pursue the UN Liner Code and build up popular opinion among shippers to support domestic shipping with measures such as opting for full reservation of Liquefied Natural Gas (LNG) transportation for Indian shipping lines. The main thrust of the new NSP is expected to be on cargo support for domestic lines and the industry itself has urged Government and trade to support domestic shipowernes to ensure that the current market share is not lost to foreign shipping lines.

The new NSP has a three-pronged approach for the protection of domestic lines. The first is to make shipping more attractive to prospective investors with the help of novel tax concessions enabling shipping companies to pass on more profits to shareholers.This in turn is expected to attract more potential investors to the secondary market. The importance behind this move lies in the fact that by 2002, the country's freight bill will be over Rs. 55,000 crore, The second aspect of the new NSP relates to Sabotage Law which has been retained in the draft NSP to ensure more coastal cargo support to Indian lines. Under this law, only vessels carrying the Indian flag are allowed to play coastal servies. The third aspect of the new NSP rightly pinpoints the need to provide more manpower training facilities.

SCI to Acquire New Ships

The Shipping Corporation of India (SCI) has drawn up an amibitious plan for acquiring 17 vessels during 1998-99 at an estimated cost of around Rs. 1,800 crore. The company proposes to acquire around 44 vessels at a cost of round Rs. 5,600 crore during the Ninth Plan. The cost of acquisition for the current financial will be met through a combination of debt and equity in the ratio of 7:3. According to sources, the company has also made an application to the government for an external commercial borrowing (ECB) offer of around $120 million. Of the 17 vessels proposed to be acquired, 15 will be brand new ships. Seven of these will be used to transport crude. "The company is doing a great deal of introspection about its operations and exposure to various sectors in shipping", said a senior SCI official adding that loss-making units would be gradually weeded-out.

According to him, SCI has identified crude oil tankers, product tankers, LPG carrier, phosphoric acid/ammonia carriers and LNG carrier as high priority areas. The company already enjoy a major share in import of crude oil. Of the 70 per cent share held by Indian shipping companies. SCI alone holds 60 per cent of this portion which translates into an overall 42 per cent. "Global tenders for most vessels have already been placed and contracts with the shipyards will be signed soon", sources said, SCI has already floated global tenders for two Aframax (of 110,000 DWT) costing around $42 million each.

Ports

There are 11 Major Ports in the country viz., Calcutta (including Haldia), Paradip, Visakhapatnam, Chennai, Tuticorin on the East Coast and Cochin, New Mangalore, Mormugao, Jawaharlal Nehru, Mumbai and Kandla on the West Coast.

Cargo traffic handled at major ports

The major Ports handled a total traffic of 251.5 million tonnes during the financial year 1997-98 and 184.3 million tonnes up-to December '98 in the financial year 1998-99. The Port-wise details are given in Tables 24.1 and 24.2

Table 24.1 : Traffic handled at Major Ports

(in Million Tonnes)

Port	Target 1998-99 (April-Dec)	Actual 1998-99 (April-Dec)	1997-98 (April-Dec)
Calcutta	7.12	6.20	5.61
Haldia	15.36	14.45	14.54
Paradip	9.97	9.70	9.90
Visakhapatnam	27.07	26.89	27.08
Chennai	27.37	26.21	26.34
Tuticorin	7.65	7.47	7.50
Cochin	9.14	9.21	8.78
New Mangalore	11.17	10.62	11.23
Mormugao	13.13	12.03	13.66
J.L. Nehru	7.44	8.55	6.78
Mumbai	25.31	23.25	24.16
Kandla	29.34	29.70	28.74
All Major Ports	190.07	184.28	184.32

Table 24.2 : Cargo Handled at Major Ports

Commodity	Percentage to Total (April-December) 1998-99	1997-98
POL	41.9	41.0
Iron Ore	12.5	14.8
Fertiliser & Raw Materials	4.0	4.3
Coal	16.2	15.5
Others	25.4	24.4
Total	100.0	100.0

Selected Port Performance Indicators

The details of major performance indications of the Ports are given below:

Table 24.3

(in days)

Port	Average Pre-Berthing Detention (on Port A/c) (April to November)		Average Tum Round Time (April to November)	
	1998-99	1997-98	1998-99	1997-98
Calcutta	0.20	0.25	6.71	7.46
Haldia	0.44	1.06	4.33	6.03
Paradip	1.31	1.98	4.20	5.57
Visakhapatnam	0.91	1.74	5.92	6.13
Chennai	2.90	1.40	8.20	7.10
Tuticorin	1.05	1.33	4.85	5.01
Cochin	0.18	0.30	3.40	3.80
New Mangalore	0.47	0.71	4.17	4.41
Mormugao	0.43	0.53	5.26	6.01
J.L. Nehru	0.89	3.09	4.98	4.55
Mumbai	0.67	1.25	5.21	6.41
Kandla	1.77	3.82	4.83	7.45
All Major Ports	1.07	1.55	5.39	6.12

Finances in the Port Developments

The government has decided to invest Rs. 16,000 crore for development of major ports during the Ninth Plan. Talking to the mediapersons on May 20, Mr. Thambi Durai, Surface Transport Minister said that an amount of Rs. 2,000 crore would be made available by the Central Government, while Rs. 6,000 crore is expected to be raised by port trusts from their internal resources and borrowings. The balance Rs. 8,000 crore is targeted to be raised from private sector and captive users, he said. The Minister said the additional capacity in the major ports was proposed to be created by schemes to be funded by ports (35 mt), improvement of the capacities of existing assets (11 mt), schemes to be undertaken by the private sector (45 mt) and capacity to be created by the captive users (31 mt).

Mr. Thambi Durai said it was estimated that ports in the country would be required to handle about 424 million tonne by the end of the Ninth Plan. He said the major ports together had capacity aggregating to 215 million tonne at the end of the Eighth Plan. These ports were handling about 90 per cent of the total sea-borne trade traffic. According to the past trends, port traffic was constantly increasing and it was likely to continue in the future also. Mr. Durai said it was estimated that ports in the country would be required to handle about 424 million tonne by the end of Ninth Plan. He said the major ports together had capacity aggregating to 215 million tonne at the end of the Eighth Plan. These ports were handling about 90 per cent of the total sea-borne trade traffic. According to past trends port traffic is constantly increasing and is likely to continue in the future also.

Major Developments in Port Sector

Privatisation of Port Facilities : The Government has laid down guidelines for private sector participation in the port sector. Following areas have been identified—

(i) leasing out assets of the Port.
(ii) Construction and operation of container terminals, multipurpose cargo berths and specialised cargo berths, warehousing, storage facilities, tank farms, container freight stations, setting up of captive power plants, etc.
(iii) Leasing of equipment for cargo handling and leasing of floating rafts from the private sector.
(iv) Pilotage.
(v) Captive facilities for port based industries.

Government have also framed guidelines on joint venture formation in Major Port on 1st June, 1998.

25

DIVERSE ISSUES

ELECTION

Electoral Reforms

In the beginning of the year 1990, a Committee on Electoral Reforms headed by the then Minister of Law and Justice (late) Shri Dinesh Goswami was constituted to go into the entire gamut of electoral reform and to make recommendations with a view to purifying and strengthening the electoral process. The Committee submitted its report in May, 1990. On the basis of the recommendations of this Committee, the then Government introduced the following four Bills in Rajya Sabha in May, 1990:

(i) The Chief Election Commissioner and other Election Commissioners (Conditions of Service) Bill, 1990 (since converted into an Act of Parliament Act No. 11 of 1991). It provided for the conditions of service of the Chief Election Commissioners and matter connected therewith or incidental thereto.

(ii) The Constitution (70th Amendment) Bill, 1990—It sought to provide for mode of appointment of the Chief Election Commissioner and other Election Commissioners as also for an independent Secretariat to the Election Commission. The Bill was later on withdrawn.

(iii) The Constitution (71st Amendment) Bill, 1990—It sought to amend the Constitution to facilitate the delimitation of Parliamentary and Assembly constituencies on the basis of 1981 census without affecting the existing number of vacancies allocated to various States. The Bill was later on withdrawn.

(iv) The Representation of the People (Amendment) Bill, 1990—It sought to amend the Representation of the People Act, 1951 to incorporate certain proposals on electoral reforms. The Bill was later on withdrawn.

In 1993, the then Government introduced the Representation of the People (Amendment) Bill, 1993 with a view to strengthen the provisions of section 29A of the Representation of the People Act, 1951 by providing that political party bearing a religious name, etc. shall not be registered and for providing for deregistration of a political party if it no longer conforms to the principles of socialism, secularism and democracy etc. The Bill was later on withdrawn.

The Government in 1994, introduced the Representation of the People (Second Amendment) Bill, 1994 and to the Constitution (84th Amendment) Bill, 1994. These Bills while incorporating some of the provisions of the earlier (aforesaid) Bills (which were withdrawn) without any change, included some others with some modifications and also omitted certain provisions. These new Bills also contained some new provisions which were not contained in any of the earlier Bills. These two Bills, however, lapsed with the dissolution of the Tenth Lok Sabha.

The Government in 1996, on the basis of consensus reached amongst political parties on certain proposal on electoral reforms, introduced two Bills namely, the Constitution (80th Amendment) Bill, 1996 and the Representation of the People (Second Amendment) Bill, 1996, in Lok Sabha. The Representation of the People (Second Amendment) Bill, 1996 has since become an Act (Act No. 21 of 1996). The proposals on electoral reforms which have been give effect to by the said Act are listed at Appendix-XIII. The Constitution (80th Amendment) Bill, 1996, which sought to amend the Constitution to facilitate the delimitation of constituencies on the basis of 1991 census without affecting the existing number of vacancies allocated to various States has since lapsed on the dissolution of 11th Lok Sabha.

Discussions were, in the meantime, held with political parties on various additional proposals on electoral reforms (Appendix-XIV) in a series of meetings held on 29.8.96, 11.12.96, 17.12.96 and 29.7.97. In the last meeting held with political parties on 29.7.97, it was also decided that the Government may come forward with a Bill which itself can be debated by the political parties in Parliament. Government thereafter constituted a Group of Ministers under the Chairmanship of Home Minister to consider different pending proposals on electoral reforms and give its recommendations.

Salient Features of the Constitution (52nd Amendment) Act, 1985

The Tenth Schedule to the Constitution of India was incorporated by the Constitution (52nd Amendment) Act, 1985. It came into force w.e.f. 1.3.1985. The legislative intent behind the enactment was to curb and control the menace of crossing of the floor by the elected representatives of the people in legislatures. The broad outlines of the Anti-Defection law as contained in the 10th Schedule of the Constitution are summarised below:

(1) A member would be disqualified for being a member of the House concerned if (a) he voluntarily gives up his membership of his political party and (b) if he votes or abstains from voting contrary to any direction (whip) issued by his political party without obtaining prior permission of the party or his voting or abstention had not been condoned within 15 days from the date of his voting.

(2) The Speaker or Chairman is made the arbitrator in deciding the question of disqualification under the law. (The provision to oust Court's jurisdiction in the matter has been struck down by the Supreme Court).

(3) The Provision would apply to independent members also.

(4) A nominated member who is not a member of any political party on the date of his nomination would be escaping disqualification only if he joins a political party before the expiry of six months.

(5) The provisions would not apply to members if they constitute a group representing a faction arising out of split provided the said group consists of not less than 1/3rd of the total membership of the legislature party.

(6) The provisions of disqualification would also not apply to members if they become members of a party brought about by merger of his original party

and another party provided 2/3rd of the party agreed to such merger. This exemption would also apply to members who opted to function as a separate group not accepting the merger.

Under para (7) of the 10th Schedule there was a bar on jurisdiction of courts in respect of any matter connected with the disqualification of a member of a House. The Supreme Court, however, in the case of Kihota Hollohon vs. Zachilhu and others by a majority judgement have struck down said para as invalid. The implications of the judgement is that the decisions of the presiding officer can be scrutinised by the Courts.

Demand have been made, from time to time, for strengthening the Anti-defection Law on the ground that it has not been able to achieve the desired goal of checking defection. It has been criticised on the ground that it allows bulk defections while declaring individual defection as illegal. On the other hand, the law has also been criticised on the ground that it makes serious inroad into basic powers, privileges and immunities of members in regard to freedom of speech, freedom of action, which includes freedom of vote also.

Meeting of Panel on State Funding of Polls

A high-power committee set up by the Government has come out strongly in favour of state funding of elections and suggested creation of a corpus with matching contributions from the Centre and States totalling Rs. 1,200 crore annually. It, however, said that the funding should be in kind and not in cash and be confined only to the parties recognised as national or states parties by the Election Commission and to candidates fielded by such parties. State funding of elections is "fully justified—constitutionally, legally and also in the larger public interest," the committee, an offshoot of an all-party meeting on May 22 last year, said in its report presented to Union Home Minister L.K. Advani on Jan. 14. To begin with, the Central Government should contribute Rs. 600 crore annually, at the rate of Rs. 10 per elector, for the total electorate of about Rs. 60 crore, towards the corpus of the fund, the committee, headed by former Home Minister Indrajit Gupta, said. "The State governments, all taken together, may also contribute proportionately a matching amount of Rs. 600 crore annually, in accordance with the present financial arrangement beween the Centre and the states, whereby all capital expenses on election items are shared by them on 50:50 basis," the committee said.

Later, Mr. Advani said that it would not be difficult for the Government to enact a law on state funding of elections since the committee was unanimous in its report. Besides Mr. Gupta, members of the committee included Mr. Somnath Chatterjee, Mr. Manmohan Singh, Mr. Madhukar Sirpotdar, Mr. Vijaya Kumar Malhotra, Mr. R. Muthiah, Mr. Digivijay Singh and Mr. Ram Gopal Yadav. The committee came out with a series of "do's and dont's" to make the election process clean and transparent. It recommended that political parties should compulsorily submit their annual accounts regularly to the income tax authorities, showing all details of their receipts and expenditure.

No state funding should be provided to any party or its candidates if the party had failed to submit its annual return for the previous assessment year under the Income Tax Act. The political parties should also file a complete account of their election expenditure at every general election to the Election Commission of India. Such account should show the receipts and expenditure, both on the general party propaganda and on individual candidates. To bring transparency in party accounts, all donations received by parties above Rs. 10,000 should be accepted only by means of cheques/drafts and the names of such donors should be fully disclosed in their accounts.

HOUSING

(a) New Housing Policy

The Union Minister for Urban Affairs and Employment, Mr. Ram Jethmalani, on June 8 sought the State Governments, assitance in overcoming the opposition to the repeal of the Urban Land Ceiling Act. Recalling the petition submitted to the Prime Minister, Mr. A.B. Vajpayee, by a group of 64 MPs led by Ms. Shabana Azmi, against the repeal of the Act, he said he was intellectually and morally convinced the Act must go and was confident of convincing the MPs also on the futility of continuing with the Act. But, all the same, he wanted the State Governments to help by asking the MPs belonging to their States to support the move. Mr. Jethmalani also asked the States to get ready to take up follow-up action as and when Parliament repealed the Act. They must ratify it immediately. Though the Centre could not force them to do so, it has some "sanctions", which it could impose. The Centre could refuse it, if any State, which did not ratify the repeal, came to it for financial assistance. "Don't expect us to cooperate with you, if you do not cooperate with us", he said.

Observing that the Act, which was passed in 1976, had failed totally and there was an unanimous clamour that it must be repealed, he said, the Law Commission, on a reference by him, had also, in an informal well-reasoned note explaines why it should not be in the statute book. "Give me two years. If repeal also does not deliver the goods, the Act could after all, be brought back", he added. Mr. Jethmalani was inaugurating a two-day conference of State Housing Ministers convened by the Union Ministry for Urban Affairs and Employment to discuss a new national housing policy and a strategy for implementation of an action plan drafted by the Ministry for the construction of 20 lakh additional dwelling units over the above those built under the on-going housing programmes.

The Union Minister also clarified that the Budget proposal with regard to tax holiday for housing projects would not be available for all the projects, but be confined to those meant for economically weaker sections and the low income group. Mr. Babagouda Patil, Minister of State for Rural Development, urged HUDCO to double its lending in rural areas from the persent 15 per cent, particularly in the context of the rather minimal spread of and low availability of institutional housing finance in the rural sector.

(b) Infrastructure Status for Housing Sector

The major fiscal concessions granted by the BJP-led Government to the housing sector so far include infrastructure status, tax deductions on rental income, excise concessions on building materials, and customs concessions on various building equipment. In a review of the various measures taken by the Government during the past five months, the Urban Affairs Ministry on Aug. 25 noted that housing had been granted infrastructure status under Section 80A of the Income Tax Act. As a result, approved housing projects get 100 per cent deduction from profits for the first five years, and 30 per cent for the subsequent five years. In addition, deductions from taxable income like rental income have been increased from 20 per cent to 25 per cent under Section 24 of the Income Tax Act. Part of the interest repayment on loan taken for house building is deductable under the Income Tax Act in case of self-occupied houses, and the amount has been increased from Rs. 15,000 to Rs. 30,000 per annum.

Under Section 71 of the Income Tax Act, losses from house property have been permitted to be set off against other incomes in the same assessment year and the balance loss permitted to be carried forward for a maximum of eight subsequent years by adding Section 71B of the Income Tax Act. Added to this, land held as stock-in-trade has been exempted from assessment under wealth tax for a period of seven years instead of five years. Section 80GG of the Income Tax Act, in respect of reduction for rents paid out has been reintroduced, which would permit deduction up to Rs. 24,000 per year from taxable income.

(c) Housing Action Plan

The Government has drawn up an action plan for construction of 20 lakh additional houses every year as part of its new housing policy. As per the action plan, seven lakh houses will be constructed in urban areas and 13 lakh in rural areas, official sources said on Aug. 28. The sources said 4.56 lakh houses in the urban areas would be earmarked for Economically Weaker Sections and rest 2.44 lakh for Low Income Group. They said the total investment required for construction of new dwelling units in urban areas have been estimated at Rs. 4,000 crore. State-owned, Housing and Urban Development Corporation will finance one third of the target for urban areas while the rest will be financed through 25 other housing finance institutions. While institutional financing will be 70 per cent, the balance will be met partly as subsidy from central or state governments and partly as beneficiary contribution in cash, kind and labour, the sources added.

(d) Two Billion Houses for Weaker Sections

Union Urban Affairs and Employment Minister Ram Jethmalani on Oct. 18 said the Centre would construct two million houses throughout the country for economically weaker sections during the current financial eyar. Special emphasis would be given to development of the housing sector in the north-east where two million units would be set up with 1.25 lakh in rural areas, Mr. Jethmalani told newsmen at Raj Bhavan at Shillong. He expressed satisfaction over the 1000 hectare new township being set up by Meghalaya Urban Development Agency to house two lakh people. He said the financial assistance of Rs. 200 crore provided by HUDCO for the first phase of the work to be implemented during 1998-99 to 2001-2002 was given with provision of moderate interest and his department would closely monitor the progress. About the backwardness of the region, he said there was less representation in the industrial and other private sectors from the NE and asked the youth to join the national mainstream for the region's uplift.

He said a large number of training facilities would come upto help local youth to be at par with the rest of the country. Mr. V. Suresh, HUDCO Chairman and Managing Director said the corporation has decided to earmark ten per cent of its housing portfolio for the NE. The corporation, he said, has already allocated Rs. 146.30 crore this financial year for housing programmes in the region. Additional funds would be made available for city infrastructure and urban development programme of NE states based on specific demands and development needs, he said HUDCO had so far given Rs. 568.77 crore as assistance with project cost of Rs. 912.55 crore for construction of 1,15,640 houses, 24 urban infrastructure projects covering water supply, sewerages and solid waste management.

(e) Housing Sector's Funds Requirement

The Ninth Plan document has pegged the requirement of funds for the housing sector at Rs. 16,000 crore during the last four years of the plan period to give effect to the proposals under the Special Action Plan (SAP). The SAP has suggested construction of seven lakh additional dwelling units annually starting from the second year of the Ninth Plan. The Ninth Plan document which was likely to be approved by the National Development Council (NDC) later in the month, has estimated that Rs. 4,000 crore would be required annually for constructing seven lakh units. This comprises institutional finances of the order of Rs. 2,800 crore including equity support to be provided to HUDCO through the Budget, Rs. 1,200 crore as subsidy from the central/state governments and beneficiary contribution in cash, kind and labour. Assuming that physical output of formal sector institutions in the implementation of SAP would be commensurate with the investment requirement of 70 per cent, the target for formal sector financial institutions would be 4.9 dwelling units annually and the balance 2.1 lakh units would be provided by beneficiary contribution and subsidy.

The Ninth Plan points out that out of formal sector institutions, HUDCO is expected to build one-third of the total target namely 2.33 lakh dwelling units annually. However, since there is a likely delay in the implementation of the SAP as HUDCO is currently engaged with the task of providing roughly one lakh dwelling units annually through ongoing schemes, the additional target for HUDCO has been kept at a reduced level of 1.5 lakh dwelling units for 1998-99 instead of 2.33 lakh originally proposed. The shortfall in the current year (0.83 lakh dwelling units), the Plan panel suggests, may be undertaken by other formal sector institutions. During the remaining years of the Ninth Plan (1999-2002), HUDCO may take up one-third of the shortfall in 1998-99 over and above the original target of 2.33 lakh dwelling units.

The Ninth Plan has further suggested that as an incentive for taking up the additional targets in the formal sector through the various programmes, a corpus of approximately Rs. 100 crore be set up for leveraging additional resources for meeting the requirement of funds for housing the deprived sections of society. With regard to rural housing, the Plan panel has pegged the requirement of Rs. 8,790 crore from the central budget as DBS (domestic budgetary support). Under the SAP for rural housing, 13 lakh new houses are required to be set up annually in the rural areas in addition to the existing 12.3 lakh units per year. The total houses to be constructed annually would increase commensurately to 25.30 lakh.

(f) HUDCO to Give Loans to Individuals

The Union Minister for Urban Affairs and Employment, Mr. Ram Jethmalani, on Oct. 5 announced that the Government has decided to allow HUDCO to lend to individuals and also disclosed that it intended to soon come out with an ordinance to repeal the Urban Land Ceiling Act. The retail financing window of HUDCO, which would become operational from November, marks a significant step forward in overcoming the housing shortage in the country. It would help the agency to reach a wider section of the population. The HUDCO's board has recommended it about eight months ago. HUDCO's lending has so far been through bulk lending to the public sector institutions such as State-level housing boards, development authorities, local bodies, cooperative sector agencies, covering both primary and apex bodies, corporate employers, both in private and public sectors, the NGO sector and also through private sector and joint sector delivery modes.

The move to repeal the Urban Land Ceiling Act assumes importance as a Bill in this regard is presently under the consideration of the Parliamentary Standing Committee on Urban and Rural Development. The Government had introduced the Bill in Parliament during the Budget session, and was referred to the parliamentary panel for its detailed scrutiny following opposition from a group of 64 MPs led by Ms. Shabana Azmi. "I will see that an ordinance is issued in the next few days," Mr. Jethmalani declared. Inaugurating a two-day national seminar on safer cities on the occasion of World Habitat Day, Mr. Jethmalani also announced that the Ministry has evolved a new method of accountability, under which all kinds of informations would be freely available to the public on payment of a nominal fee. Irked by the corruption changes levelled against him by the Janata Party leader, Dr. Subrahmanian Swamy, the Minister said now onwards everybody will have access to any file or order on payment of a nominal fee. "They will ensure full transparency in the functioning of my Ministry," he said.

IRRIGATION

Water Resources Potential In India

Average run-off in the river system of the country has been assessed as 1869 Km^3. Of this, the utilisable portion is estimated as about 690 Km^3. In addition, there is a substantial replenishable ground water potential in the country estimated at 432 Km^3.

Rapid fall in the pre-capita availability of water is, however, becoming evident due to explosive population growth, large scale urbanisation and industrialisation in the country. From a fairly comfortable level of water availability per person in the early stages of development, a significant decline has been noticed in the share of water availability over the years.

The per capita has reduced from 5277 m^3 in the year 1955 to the present level in 1970m^3. The situation may aggravate in future due to the growing water scarcity in the river basins.

Irrigation Potential

At the beginning of the era of planning in India in 1951 the irrigation potential was 22 million hectare (m ha). The irrigation potential created up to the end of Seventh Plan was 76.52 m ha against the estimated ultimate potential of 113.5 m ha which has now been reassessed as 139.89 m ha. On a provisional estimation, it is expected that by the end of the Eighth Plan, it has increased to 89.6 m ha.

Major and Medium Irrigation

The ultimate irrigation potential of the country from Major and Medium Irrigation projects has been assessed at 58.5 m ha. This includes projects with a culturable command area of more than two thousand hectare. The potential created up to the end of the Sixth Plan (1980-85) was originally reported as 30.01 m ha. This was later on re-appraised at 27.70 m ha. The potential created up to the end of Seventh Plan (1985-90) was 29.92 m ha and upto the end of annual Plans 1990-92, it was 30.74 m ha.

A target of 5.09 m ha had been set for creation of additional potential during the Eighth Plan (1992-97) against which, according to a provisional estimate, the potential created is 2.22 m ha. Thus at the end of the Eighth Plan, the cumulative irrigation potential created from major and medium irrigation is anticipated to be 32.96 m ha.

Table 25.1: The Plan-wise progress of creation of irrigation potential through major and medium irrigation projects and the expenditure incurred

Period	Outlay/ expenditure (Rs. in crore)	Potential created (mha)	
		During	Cumulative
Pre-Plan Period		9.70	9.70
First Plan (1951-56)	376	2.50	12.20
Second Plan (1956-61)	380	2.13	14.33
Third Plan (1961-66)	576	2.24	16.57
Annual Plans (1966-69)	430	1.53	18.10
Fourth Plan (1969-74)	1242	2.60	20.70
Fifth Plan (1974-78)	2516	4.02	24.72
Annual Plans (1978-80)	2079	1.89	26.61
Sixth Plan (1980-85)	7369	1.09	**27.70
Seventh Plan (1985-90)	11107	2.22	29.92
Annual Plans (1990-92)	5459	0.82	30.74
Eighth Plan (1992-97)	21838	*2.22	*32.96
Annual Plan (1997-98)	8403 (Approved Outlay)	1.04 (Target)	

** Potential created from Pre-Plan period to end of Sixth Plan was re-appraised.
* Provisional

Note : Figures for 1998-99 have not been finalised by Planning Commission.

Major And Medium Projects

It is estimated that many major, medium and ERM projedcts will spill over in the Ninth Plan from the previous plans. This is given in the following Table 25.2,

Table 25.2

	Taken Up	Completed	Spill over into IX Plan
Major	362	200	162
Medium	1081	841	240
ERM	141	67	74

Provisonally, the aggregated present estimated cost of these schemes is Rs. 1,26,318.22 crore and the cost of the part spilled over is Rs. 79,317.45 crore.

Minor Irrigation

All ground water and surface water schemes having culturable command area (CCA) upto 2000 ha individually are classified as minor irrigation schemes. Ground water development is primarily done through individual and cooperative efforts of the farmers with the help of institutional finance and their own savings. Surface water minor irrigation schemes are generally funded from the public sector outlay.

The ultimate irrigation potential from minor irrigation schemes has been assessed as 81.43 m ha. Upto the end of the Seventh Plan, the potential created through the minor irrigation schemes was 46.60 m ha. During the Eighth Plan, additional irrigation potential of 6.25 (provisional) m ha has been created. Thus, at the end of Eighth Plan, provisionally the cumulative irrigation potential created through minor irrigation schemes is estimated to be 56.60 m ha.

LABOUR

(a) New Labour Commission

The government has decided to set up second national commission on labour to suggest changes in labour laws to bring them in tune with new economic scenario. An indepth and critical review of the labour situation had become necessary as domestic industrial climate and labour market had undergone radical changes and the laws appeared to be inadequate to meet the challenges thrown up by them. Labour Minister Satyanarayan Jatia said in New Delhi on Jan. 11. The commission comprising a chairman, two full time members and seven part-time members to represent government, industry and workers will have a tenure of 24 months from the date of constitution. The terms of reference of the commission will be to suggest rationalisation of existing laws relating to labour in the organised sector and also to suggests an umbrella legislation for ensuring a minimum protection to the workers in the unorganised sector.

Mr. Jatiya said the proposal for the second commission was first mooted in 1992 by the Indian Labour Conference adding that various central employers and the trade Union organisations had also written to the Labour Ministry suggesting setting up of such a commission. He said the commission would review labour legislations in both organised and unorganised sectors. In the unorganised sector, which employs about 320 million workers out of the total 350 million, working population, the main thrust would be to ensure a minimum level of protection to workers. Since the present laws like Minimum Wages Act 1948 and Payment of Wages Act etc. did not cover the total unorganised work force, the commission would try to suggest an umbrella legislation for the workers in the unorganised sector, the Minister said. As for the organised sector, the main focus of the commission would be to suggest rationalisation of the existing laws so as to make them more relevant and appropriate in the changing context of globalisation and opening up of the Indian economy, Mr. Jatiya said.

(b) Unemployment

The number of job seekers registered with employment exchanges all over the country was about 39.2 million in April, 1998 the Lok Sabha was told during question hour by Labour Minister S.N. Jatiya on July 28. The total placement of technically qualified during 1994 was 19.33 million and it was 6.78 million between January and June in 1995. The employment in the organised sector which was of the order of about 27.74 million on March 31, 1994 has gone up to approximately 28.24 million on March 31, 1997. Interestingly, Sikkim is the only state in the country where there is no employment exchange.

Of the unemployed, the number of job seekers—all of whom need not necessarily be unemployed belonging to the minority communities on the life register of the employment exhanges as on December 31, 1994, was of the order of five million. About 3,07,000 job seekers were sponsored during 1994 and about 18,300 placements were made. Mr. Jatiya said agencies registered under the Emigration Act 1983 are authorised to collect service charges ranging from Rs. 2,000 to Rs. 10,000 per person depending on the category of workers. But no service charges are allowed to be collected by the contractors registered under the Contract Labour (Abolition and Regulation) Act and Inter-State Migrant Workmen (Regulation of Employment and Conditions of Service) Act.

(c) Intensive Rural Employment Programme (IREP)

Union Finance Minister Yashwant Sinha on Nov. 10 cemmitted Rs. 1,000 crore for the Intensive Rural Employment Generation Programme (IREGP), to be utilised over the next five years for generation of additional 100,000 employment in select backward regions. The sop announced in Ranchi at a public function organised by the Khadi and Village Industries Commission (KVIC) is a follow-up meausre on the recommendation of a task force set up by Prime Minister Atal Behari Vajapyee in August to look for avenues of employment generation in rural areas. The KVIC will be the nodal agency to create, rejuvenate and integrate village industries for intensive employment in a more concerted way. Besides Chotanagpur and the Santhal Parganas region, for which a sum of Rs. 215 crore has been earmarked; the North-East region and 50 select pockets (called the Golden Jubilee Club) spread througout the country will top the IREGP agenda in the first phase.

In fact, the North-East will be the biggest beneficiary under the new measure as the largest chunk of funds totalling Rs. 300 crore will be spent on strengthening and promoting village industries in this region. The employment generation measures announced are in continuation of the IREGP, but with a clear difference that full package inputs will be insured in identified areas and sectors. Besides, location-specific programmes will be implemented through maximum possible participation of the concerned people and local institutions. Apart from planning and monitoring cells with work at regional/cluster levels, there will be every possible attempt to force collaborations and coordination with other relevant agencies.

POPULATION

UN Aid to Stabilise Population

The United Nations Population Fund announced a $ 100 million assistance towards India's population and development programme on July 10. The aid is the largest UNFPA country programme assistance in the world and covers a five-year-term (1997-2001). The aid is 30 per cent higher than the $70 million provided during 1991-96. The amount will be utilised for the Integrated Population and Development Projects covering 40 districts in six states, said the UNFPA representative in India, Dr. Wasim Zaman, on the eve of the World Population Day. The states include Rajasthan, Maharashtra, Gujarat, Orissa, Madhya Pradesh and Kerala. Dr. Zaman said 50 per cent of the UNFPA support in its Fifth Country Programme is for IPDS while remaining 50 per cent will be utilised for national projects such as strengthening logistic system for distribution of essential medicines and contracepatives and implementing the national policy for empowerment of women. The programmes has specifically earmarked $ 10 million or NGOs and voluntary groups.

Joint Secretary in the Department of Family Welfare Mr. K.S. Sugathan, who was also present said the aid will be utilised for integrating population issues within a wider human develoment context through research and institutional support. The UNFPA Fifth Country Programme covers the period roughly coinciding with government's Ninth Five Year Plan. The three major sub-programming of UNFPA's support as a part of overall programme are reproductive health—including family planning and sexual health, population development issues, advocacy for building support for population issues, education and women's empowerment.

SPORTS

Introduction

India has long tradition for sports and physical fitness. There are several references to excellence in Archery, Wrestling and other sports in the Ramayana, the Mahabharat and ancien' writings. After independence, importance of sports was formally recognized with holding of the 9th Asian Games in Delhi in 1982. A separate Department was created in 1982. The first National Sports Policy was announced in 1984. A Programme of Action for implementation of this Policy was laid before Parliament (in the monsoon session) in 1992.

During the year 1997-98, Mrs. Kunja Rani and Shri Leander Paes were awarded the prestigious Rajiv Gandhi Khel Ratna Awards for the years 1995-96 and 1996-97 respectively. Besides, Arjuna Awards for the year 1996 were presented to 18 outstanding sports persons at Rashtrapati Bhawan on 29th August 1997. Special Awards (Cash) were conferred on 63 sports persons/coaches at Vigyan Bhawan.

The revised draft new Sports Policy was discussed in different meetings/forums and views expressed were considered. The policy is under preparation.

The Sports Authority of India (SAI) which is a successor organization of the Special Organizing Committee (SOC) for the IX Asian Games held in Delhi in 1982 was set up in 1984 by the Government of India with the objective of maintaining and utilizing the stadia created/renovated for the 1982 Asian Games and to spot and nurture talented children under different sports promotion schemes to achieve excellence at national/international levels.

SAI through its Regional Centres located at Bangalore, Gandhinagar, Delhi, Chandigarh, Calcutta and Imphal and two sub-centres at Guwahati and Aurangabad are implementing various sports promotion schemes. The Regional Centres are equipped with sports science back-up and also provide conducive atmosphere and facilities for training of budding talent. Apart from these Regional Centres, SAI has got Academic Wings at NS NIS Patiala and LNCPE, Trivandurm. SAI also has a High Altitude Training Centre (HATC) at Shillaroo (HP). The Regional Training Sub Centre of SAI at Augrangabad is being transferred to the Maharashtra Government.

The Governing Body and the General Body in their meeting held in November, 1997 approved the restructuring of the Governing Body and the General Body taking into account the recommendations made by the Estimates Committee as well as the recommendations made by the Parliamentary Standing Committee on HRD (headed by Shri P. Upendra) and the Parliamentary Standing Committee on HRD (headed by Shri S.B. Chavan) on demand for grants for the year 1997-98.

To commemorate the 50th Anniversary of India's Independence, the 1st Independence Gold Cup Sub Junior Hockey tournament was held at National Stadium from 16th to 26th Spet., 1997. Orissa won this tournament by beating Punjab in the final. 13 terms out of 37 which played at the regional level qualified for the national level tournament.

A permanent Asian Games Flame was lit at the historic National Stadium - the venue of the 1st Asian Games 1951 - by Sheik Ahmed Al-fahad Alsabah, President of Olympic Council of Asia on 14th December, 1997. For all future summer and winter Asian Games, the flame would be lit at the National Stadium and travel to the venue of Games making Delhi the focal point of the Asian movement.

Sports Authority of India (SAI)

The different sports promotion schemes of SAI which were conceived and formulated during VII Five Year Plan for development and promotion of sports at grass root level in the country were reviewed at different fora from time to time. These schemes were last reviewed on 17th March, 97 by a sub-committee constituted by the Governing Body in its meeting held on 4th March, 97 and its recommendations which *inter alia* aims at consolidating the existing schemes in order to make them more cost effective and result oriented were duly considered and approved by the Governing Body in its subsequent meeting held on 29th July, 97. In pursuance to the decision taken by the Governing Body action is in hand in consultation with the concerned State Governments to revive the SAI schemes.

National Sports Talent Contest (NSTC) Scheme

The scheme aims at selecting the school children in the age group of 8-12 years through a battery of tests in Athletics, Badminton, Basketball, Football, Gymnastic, Hockey, Swimming, Table Tennis, Wrestling and Volleyball for their scientific training in the SAI Adopted Schools. At present 23 schools (including 8 day boarding) with 660 trainees are functioning through out the country.

Adoption of Akhadas for Promotion of Wrestling

In order to tap the rural youth who still continue to train in conventional Akhadas, there is a scheme of adoption of Akhadas. Under the scheme, boys under 14 years of age who have already shown prominence in wrestling while training in the Akhadas, are adopted by SAI and to meet their diet & school expenses, stipend is given to them. At present following 2 Akhadas in Maharashtra have been adopted under the scheme of NSTC:

(i) Krida Vikas Vyayam Mandal, Sangli - 10 Wretlers
(ii) Gokul Ustad Tamil, Pune - 11 Wrestlers

Army Boys Sports Company (ABSC) Scheme

The scheme which is an extension of NSTC Scheme provides for scouting of talented boys in the age group of 8-12 years for admitting them into the Regimental Centres of the Army for further training on scientific lines with due care to their regular education.

At present there are 16 ABSCs with 710 trainees.

TOURISM

(a) Establishment of Tourism Export Promotion Council

The tourism industry has set up a Tourism Export Promotion Council following the Government decision to accord "export house status" to tourism units and to enhance tourism's contribution to country's foreign exchange. The new body is the first umbrella organisation which brings together various segments of the industry. It will function as an institutional mechanism to secure export benefits for the industry, a Hotel Association of India release said. It will act as a nodal agency for promoting Indian tourism product, services, facilities, projects, management and technical consultancy. It will help create a niche for Indian tourism industry in the global market.

The Council will be headed by Mr. S.S.H. Rehman, Managing-Director, ITC Hotels as its President, Mr. L.P. Gupta, Chairman, UP Hotels, was elected vice-president and Mr. Pradip Madhavji, Chairman, Thomas Cook, and Mr. Ravi Bhoothalingam, Chairman, Tourism Committee of Confedertaion of Indian Industries, were elected Treasurer and Honorary Sectretary respectively. The broad activities of the Council shall be to plan, promote, support, protect and increase the growth, efficiency, image and standards of export-oriented activities of hotels, travel agencies, airlines, railways, surface transportation, tour operators, tourism-related finance or any other such activities related to tourism.

(b) Implementing Tourism Policy

The Ministry of Tourism has drawn up an action plan to implement the national tourism policy. Under the programme, it has identified 50 cities initially to be developed as sustainable tourist destinations. The state governments and the union territories have been asked to lay aside Rs. 1 crore each for the development of infrastructural facilities and a matching grant of Rs. 1 crore will be given by the central Government every year. During the first year, Jammu, Anandpur Sahib, Agra, Amritsar and Kanyakumari will be among the select cities earmarked for this grant, said Minister for Tourism and Parliamentary Affairs, Madan Lal Khurana in New Delhi on Jan. 20 while addressing a seminar on 'National Tourism Policy' organised by the Federation Indian Chamber of Commerce and Industry (FICCI). He said several states including Kerala, Rajasthan and Uttar Pradesh have given their consent.

On the new tourism policy, Mr. Khurana said it was taking time due to the need for coordination among various ministries like civil aviation, railways, human resources and environment adding that the policy should be in tune with the economic liberalisation policies of the government. It would focus on integrated developments of North-East, Himalayan region, Jammu and Kashmir and the islands of Andaman and Nicobar and Lakshadweep, he said. Mr. Khurana said that for speedy implementation and synergisation of tourism development activities the department of tourism has already been elevated to a ministerial level and a group of ministers and standing committee have been constituted.

To advise the government on tourism development, a separate national tourism promotion council with representatives from the state governments and industry has been set up. To promote, build and manage tourism infrastructural facilities, the Ministry has decided also to involve the private sector. The private parties will be allowed to take up projects ensuring preservation and protection of tourist destinations, Mr. Khurana said.

(c) ITDC Expansion Plan

The India Tourism Development Corporation Ltd, which runs its flagship venture, the Ashok Group of Hotels, is contemplating a Rs. 800-crore expansion, with plans to set up hotels in the states of Punjab, Maharashtra, Karnataka and Andhra Pradesh. Sources close to the group told *The Asian Age* that, at Chandigarh and Anantpur Sahib of Punjab, it plans to build two three-star hotels at a total investment of Rs. 200 crore. The 100-room hotel, planned in Chandigarh will be targeted mostly at business travellers. The property at Anantpur Sahib will be a 51:49 joint venture between the Ashok Group and the Punjab Tourism Development Corporation. Mumbai is likely to get an ITDC managed, Rs. 200 crore five star hotel, added the sources. Although, few projects have been cleared, other proposals are still at discussion level, said the sources.

Commenting on the recent recommendations for privatisation made by the disinvestment commission, the sources said that the centre is likely to shed 74 per cent of its shares in ITDC with the aim of bringing in greater private participation from both, the foreign and domestic sectors. Once the government off loads its majority shares, the group can be taken over by any existing hotel chains like ITC, hinted the sources. The sources felt that privatisation could be the real turning point in the history of ITDC where it can position its undertakings better in order to compete with the bigger players in the industry. Privatisation is further expected to bring in greater efficiency and aggressiveness. ITDC currently runs 33 hotels, a series of duty free shops and resorts across the country. The company had posted a turnover of Rs. 313.40 crore during the fiscal 1997-98, as against the previous year's turnover of Rs. 315.73 crore. During the period, its operating profit declined from Rs. 86.10 crore to Rs. 60.97 crore and the net profit after tax declined from Rs. 55.80 crore to Rs. 43.30 crore, compared to the previous year. As a fall out of the South-East Asian economic crisis, 1997 witnessed considerable slowdown in the growth of tourism world-wide, the company said.

YOUTH PROGRAMMES

Introduction

Youth in all ages, has beenin the vanguard of progress and social change. Thirst for freedom, impatience for a quicker pace of progress and a passion for innovation, coupled with idealism and creative fervour, saw the youth in the forefront of the freedom struggle on our land. "Youth" represent the hope and future of a country. They constitute a vibrant resource of our society. They have a vital role to play with regard to the fostering and strengthening of social consciousness against communalism and social evils. The immense resources of youth, if galvanised, can work as a major force of socio-economic change. To channelise their energy into constructive work, this Department is implementing several programmes to inculcate the values of secularism and national integration, training and upgradation of their skills to open up economic opportunities for them, and to develop leadership qualities in them.

National Youth Policy

Current National Youth Policy

The Current National Youth Policy was evolved and tabled in the Parliament in November-December, 1988. The main objective of the current Youth Policy are to instill in the youth respect for the principles and values enshirned in our Constitution; to promote among the youth an awareness of our historical heritage; to help develop in them the qualities of discipline, self-reliance, justice and fair play; and to provide the youth with maximum access to education in addition to developing their personality. It also aims at making the youth conscious of international issues and involve them in promoting world peace and a just international economic order.

New National Youth Policy

A need was however, felt for a new National Youth Policy geared not only to the fast changing socio-economic scenario in the country but also to address the future concerns of the youth. The Department accordingly drafted a new National Youth Policy which was circulated to all State Governments, Central Ministries/ Department universities, Youth Wings of Political Parties and Youth NGOs for their comments. The comments received have been compiled. A meeting on the draft New National Youth Policy was held by the Minister of State for Youth Affairs & Sports with the NGOs concerned with youth development. The Draft Youth Policy was also discussed in the National Convention on Youth Policy during the National Youth Festival held at Chennai in January, 1998.

The Salient Features of the Draft New Youth Policy

The draft new National Youth Policy recognises that youth development is a multi sectorial concept and calls for an integrated approach. It also stresses that the youth should be given more access to the process of decison making and implementation.

Some important objectives of the Policy are to provide the youth with proper educational and employment opportunities; to give access to all relevant information; create adequate sports and other recreational facilities; to create among the youth awareness about Indian history, culture and heritage and to inculcate a scientific temper in them.

The Policy endeavours to provide basic rights to youth relating to education, training, employment, health services, etc. and at the same time, it enumerates their obligations towards the society. In the area of Youth Empowerment, the Policy proposes the creation of a three-tier Youth Council at the District, State and National levels with well defined roles and objectives

The Policy recognises the key sectors of concern for yough, such as Education, Training and Employment, Health and accords high priority to certain categories of youth such as, youth with disabilities, rural youth, unemployed youth and street children etc. Besides Education, Employment, and Health, the Policy also focuses on Adolescent Health, AIDS and Sexually Transmitted Diseases, Nutrition, Environment, Sports, Recereation and Leisure, Arts and Culture, Gender Justice, Science and Technology, Civics and Citizenship.

The final draft of New National Youth Policy is under preparation.

Committee on National Youth Programmes

Government of India as constituted a Committee on National Youth Programmes (CONYP) as per the guidelines of National Youth Policy. The Committee replaces a earlier National Youth Council. It has 50 members with Prime Minister as its Chairman. The functions of the committee are to:

(i) suggest policy measures and programmes for youth;
(ii) advise Government on implementation of the "Plan of Action" of the National Youth Policy;
(iii) review the coordination between various Departments of the Central/State Governments and voluntary organisations/other agencies involved therein; and
(iv) provide feedback on implementation of the national yough programmes.

The first meeting of CONYP was held on 22.8.94 in Parliament House, New Delhi under the chairmanship of the then Prime Minister. The PM had said that the first meeting was explanatory in nature and a day long meeting of the Committee could be convened later, so that the members could discuss in detail the issues related to the youth programmes. He had stressed the need for having more coordination in implementation of various youth programmes and emphasised the role of the Committee in achieving this coordination. The suggestion of the members of the Committee for induction of representatives of important Ministries/Departments of Govt. of India for achieving better coordination was accepted.

The second meeting of CONYP was held in Bhopal on 13.1.95 and was chaired by the then MOS (YA&S). It was decided that the topic for the next meeting would be "AIDS & Grugs abuse". MOS (YA&S) had observed that it would be great contribution for CONYP if it can draw up a National Perspective Plan for youth which should include all aspects relating to youth and help the Department in proper utilisation of funds provided under various schemes. Now 7 more members have been added to the Committee raising the total number to 57.

National Service Scheme

National Service Scheme, popularly known as NSS, was launched in Gandhiji's Birth Centenary Year 1969, in 37 universities involving 40,000 students with primary focus on the development of personality of students through community service. Today, NSS has over 13.75 lakh student volunteers on the roll spread over 174 universities/ + 2 system. From its inception, more than 1.52 crore students from the Universities, Colleges and Institutions of higher learning have benefited from NSS activities, as NSS volunteers. Due to its overwhelming popularity and demand, the scheme was extended to the students of +2 level in selected institutions.

The National Service Scheme has two types of programmes, viz. "Regular Activities" and "Special Camping Programme" undertaken by its volunteers. Under 'Regular Activities', students are expected to work as volunteers for a continuous period of two years, rendering community service for minimum of 120 hours per annum. The activities include improvement of campuses, tree plantation, constructive work in adopted villages and slums, work in welfare institution, blood donation, adult and non-formal education, health, nutrition, family welfare, AIDS awareness campaigns, etc. Under "Special Camping Programme", a camp of 10 days' duration is conducted every year in the adopted areas on a specific theme like "Youth Against Famine", "Youth Against Dirt & Disease", "Youth for Afforstation and Tree Plantation", "Youth for Rural Reconstruction", "Youth for Development", Youth for Mass Literacy", "Youth for Social Harmony", etc. The theme for 1996-97 and 1997-98 were "Youth for Sustainable Development" and "Wasteland Development and Watershed Management".

The expenditure on programmes of NSS is shared between the Centre and the State Governments in the ratio 7:5, except in the case of Jammu & Kashmir and Union Territories without Legislature, where the entire expenditure is met by the Central Government. The Central Government also meets the entire expenditure on administration, training, research, monitoring, evaluation and publications pertaining to the Scheme and the administrative expenses of NSS State Liaison Cells set up in the concerned Departments of State Governments. The existing pattern of expenditure on NSS regular Activities and Special Camping Programme is Rs. 120 and Rs. 200 per volunteer respectively.

For the implementation of NSS Programme throughout the country, the following organisational structure is in operation. At the national level, Department of Youth Affairs & Sports in the Ministry of Human Resource Development, decides the policy and programme guidelines for this scheme. Under the Department, a subordinate organisation "National Service Scheme" is operating with 15 Regional Centres and one Programme Adviser's Cell, located at Ahmedabad, Bangalore, Bhopal, Bhubaneshwar, Calcutta, Chandigarh, Guwahati, Hyderabad, Jaipur, Lucknow, Chennai, Patna, Pune, Trivandrum and New Delhi. In the Department, there is a Programme Adviser to advise the Government of India on matters pertaining to the NSS Programme development. At the State level, the State Advisory Committees under the Chairmanship of the Minister of Education/ Youth Services and State Liaison Cells are functioning. The State NSS Cells are expected to coordinate with the Central Liaison Cells are functioning. The State NSS Cells are expected to coordinate with the Central Government, NSS Regional Centres, Universities, Colleges/Institutions of higher learning and Schools in matters of timely release of grants and proper implementation of the programme. At the University level there are University NSS Advisory Committees under the chairmanship of the Vice-chancellors and the University NSS Cell is headed by a Programme Coordinator. There is an NSS Programme Officer at the grassroots (college/school) level who mobilises students for implementation of all NSS Programmes. One Programme Officer is incharge of one NSS Unit consisting of 100 students.

For providing training, research and evaluation of the scheme and to motivate the equip the Programme Officers with requisite skills, 4 Training Orientation and Research Centres (TORCs) and 14 Training and Orientation Centres (TOCs) have been set up. The Department meets the entire expenditure on maintenance of these TORCs and TOCs. Each TORC/TOC organises 5 orientation expenditure on maintenance of these TORCs and TOCs. Each TORC/TOC organises 5 orientation training courses and 3 refresher courses of 10 and 5 days' duration respectively for the NSS Programme Officers, apart from work of research, evaluation and publications on NSS. In each training course, around 35 Programme Officers participate. Five focal areas have been identified for NSS work i.e., (i) National Integration and Social Harmony, (ii) Literacy (iii) Gender Justice, (iv) Villge Adoption and (v) Life Style Education. An AIDS awareness programme for students called "University Talk AIDs" has been introduced. Indira Gandhi NSS Awards were introduced in 1994 to provide incentive to NSS functionaries and volunteers. A number of other programmes, i.e. revision of NSS Manual, training manual for NSS functionaries, exhibition on NSS, material development for NSS Programme, production of films on NSS etc. have been conducted to improve the NSS programme. One NSS theme song has also been prepared.

For 1997-98, the target was to enroll 13.75 lakh student volunteers which was fully achieved. 6764 special camps on "Youth for Sustainable Development" and "Wasteland and Watershed Management" were conducted. Besides, 6764 villages were adopted for literacy and other development activities. Under AIDS Awareness Programme, 600 teachers and 60,000 peer educators were trained, and 30 lakh students were sensitised towards HIV/AIDS. There is need to reorganize NSS as third dimension of education. A number of universities have already integrated NSS into the curriculum. There is tremendous scope for further increse in the number of NSS volunteers in the country but, due to resource crunch, it has not been found possible to do so.

Nehru Yuva Kendra Sangathan

Nehru Yuva Kendra Sangathan (NYKS) is an autonomous organization under the Department. It is the largest grass-root level organization in the Asia-Pacific region, catering to the needs of more than 8 million non-student rural youth in the age group of 15-35 years enrolled through 1.82 lakh village based Youth Clubs covering education, training, employment promotion, income generation, self-employment, enterprise creation, etc. In addition, activities for the overall development of the rural communities such as health and family welfare, preservation and enrichment of eco-system, adult literacy, peoples' empowerment; eradication of social evils and supersititions, AIDS and drug abuse etc. are organised with emphasis on values, vision and voluntary action. The basic idea is to bring rural youth into the mainstream of national development as active participants, responsible and productive citizens of modern technological India. Consequently, NYKS has emerged as a mass movement. At present, about 500

Nehru Yuva Kendras are working all across the country.

Responsiveness to the Needs

In order to fulfill the needs and aspirations of non-student rural youth (the target group), various programmes and activities were organized through the network of trained cadre of youth coordinators, national service volunteers, youth leaders and social workers throughout the country. The schemes of different developmental agencies and departments were coordinated so that the benefit of their developmental programmes could reach the needy.

INDEX

81r Bhatt Books Distributers

11/2/2012

R